RISKY WRITING

Risky Writing

Self-Disclosure and Self-Transformation in the Classroom

JEFFREY BERMAN

University of Massachusetts Press
AMHERST

Copyright © 2001 by University of Massachusetts Press
All rights reserved
Printed in the United States of America
LC 2001005765
ISBN 1-55849-337-9 (cloth); 1-55849-338-7 (paper)
Designed by Jack Harrison
Set in Electra with Avant Garde display type
Printed and bound by the Maple-Vail Book Manufacturing Group

Library of Congress Cataloging-in-Publication Data

Berman, Jeffrey, 1945–
    Risky writing : self-disclosure and self-transformation in the classroom / Jeffrey Berman.
        p. cm.
Includes bibliographical references and index.
    ISBN 1-55849-337-9 (lib. cloth : alk. paper) — ISBN 1-55849-338-7 (paper : alk. paper)
    1. English language—Rhetoric—Study and teaching—Psychological aspects.
2. Creative writing (Higher education)—Psychological aspects.
3. Self-actualization (Psychology) 4. Risk-taking (Psychology) 5. Self-disclosure.
I. Title.
PE1404 .B465 2001
808'.042'0711—dc21
                    2001005765

British Library Cataloguing in Publication data are available.

To my expository writing students, past, present, and future:
Gladly would they learn and gladly teach

CONTENTS

ACKNOWLEDGMENTS

I could not have written *Risky Writing* without the help and enthusiastic support of my expository writing (English 300) students, to whom I gratefully dedicate this book and acknowledge my greatest debt. Those students who have given me permission to use their writings and to acknowledge their names here include Forrest Addor, Emil Alper, Nancy Augello, Pam Bates, Simone Belgrave, Marianne Belotseyenko, Meredyth Bennett, Keith Bresciani, Clarisse Butler, Teresa Caputa, Robert Charlebois, Lorraine Cummings, Susan Daigneault, Erin Davies, Kim De Barbieri, Danielle Delaney, Jeff Dishaw, Aimee Domenico, Marlene Febus, Kristen Finne, Luke Gaul, Laura Genovesi, Ramon Guerrero, Shauna Halper, Eric Henderson, Christopher Holt, Ezekiel Honig, Megan Jackson, Anne Jung, Nicol Kaiser, Kathy Kaleta, Meredith Keilty, Izaak Kent, Radislav Kizhnernan, Kelly Kunath, Andrea La Fata, Maryrose Laguiro, Erin Lawlor, Gina Manes, Steven Markovits, Anna McMahon, Kezban Mehmet, Stephanie Mindell, Denise Mitchell, Gary Morse, Lisa Mullany, Brian Nava, Tricia O'Brien, Marlo Osterweil, Christopher Patino, Consuelo Pinales, David Podrid, Natasha Reeves, Careen Reid, Mimli Roychoudhury, Teresa Russell, Melissa Ruttanai, Keri Scherer, Tami Schwartz, Jessica Shea, Melissa Smith, Tara Southwell, Katie Sparkes, Amy Stadelmaier, Barbara Stubblebine, Elizabeth Swinton, Sara-Maiz Thomas, Richard Tommer, Christy Torres, Stephanie Unger, Michelle Vincent, Michael Weinberg, Lisa Wong, and Frederick Wood. Many other students gave me permission to use their writings but did not want their names acknowledged here. Nearly all the students in the five sections of expository writing on which this book is based consented cheerfully to being "research subjects." They shared their writings with their classmates and teacher, explored how they felt while writing personal essays, and in both signed and anonymous evaluations discussed the benefits and risks of personal writing.

I am deeply grateful to Linda Martin for her contribution to this book. A former student who is now a professional writer, Linda unobtrusively sat in on one of my sections of expository writing for an entire semester, spoke with several students both inside and outside of class, and kept a journal of her impressions of the course. In the afterword, "Confronting and Exploiting the 'Cringe Factor,'" she offers her own perspective on what was happening in the classroom.

I am also grateful to the colleagues and friends who read the manuscript carefully and made helpful suggestions for revisions. I single out three of my colleagues at the University at Albany whose comments were particularly valuable: Randall Craig, interim chair of the English Department; Stephen North, also in the English Department; and Jerome Eckstein, professor emeritus of Judaic

Studies. Generous with their praise and even more generous with their criticism, they expressed the skepticism and reservations that many readers will have about the wisdom of encouraging students to write about personal conflicts. It is a scholarly convention for authors to acknowledge that they alone are responsible for the mistakes in their books, but this is particularly true here. Other colleagues and friends who read the entire manuscript and offered helpful criticisms are Marshall Alcorn of George Washington University; Mark Bracher of Kent State University; Jerome Bump of the University of Texas; Gustavo Guerra of Olivet College; Ira Marks and Susannah Marks; Dan Ross of Columbus College; and Iliana Semmler of the University at Albany. Anne Jung has contributed importantly to this book in so many ways—as a student, astute reader, and trusted friend. Special thanks to Mary Ellen Elkins, who responded eloquently to the query I posted on Norman Holland's listserv PSYART, agreed to read the entire manuscript, and made supportive comments and suggestions for revision. I am grateful to the many other professors and graduate students who responded to my PSYART query and who allowed me access to their e-mails for this book. Thanks also to Edith Cook, whose doctoral dissertation at Middle Tennessee State University allowed me to evaluate my work from another point of view. I am grateful to Jean Wyatt of Occidental University, who allowed me to quote from her response to an abridged version of chapter 4 that I presented at the Sixth Annual Conference of the Association for the Psychoanalysis of Culture and Society at Santa Barbara in November 2000.

A University at Albany Faculty Research Grant-in-Aid offered timely financial assistance. I appreciate the help I received from the staff of the University Human Research Institutional Review Board, with whom I have worked closely.

I am once again grateful to the staff of the University of Massachusetts Press, which also published the first two volumes of this trilogy, *Diaries to an English Professor* (1994) and *Surviving Literary Suicide* (1999). I will always be indebted to Clark Dougan, senior editor, whose enthusiasm, wise counsel, and support have been so important to me. Special thanks to Anne R. Gibbons for her expert copyediting.

Part of chapter 4 appeared as "Sexual Self-Disclosures in an Expository Writing Course" in the fall 2001 issue of *JPCS: Journal for the Psychoanalysis of Culture and Society*. Chapter 5 appeared under the title "Unmasking Shame in an Expository Writing Course" in *Scenes of Shame*, edited by Joseph Adamson and Hilary Clark, published by the State University of New York Press in 1999. Part of chapter 7 appeared under the title "Teaching Students at Risk" in *PSYART: A Hyperlink Journal for the Psychological Study of the Arts*, February 2001.

Finally, I thank my wife, Barbara, my daughters, Arielle and Jillian, and my new son-in-law, David Albert. To love and be loved by one's family is a great blessing; to love one's work is another blessing; to love one's family *and* work is, for me, the greatest blessing of all.

J. B.

RISKY WRITING

Introduction

I feel nervous and anxious as I write this essay. My palms are clammy, my mouth dry, and I feel as if I might be sick to my stomach. Recalling this incident sickens me. I feel as if this has just happened to me all over again. DIANE

The above passage, excerpted from an essay on child sexual abuse, illustrates risky writing. Diane confronts for the first time a traumatic experience she has never revealed to anyone. Writing about the event fills her with dread—her entire body seems to relive the event. Past and present begin to blur; she seems both in and out of control. Why would a student choose to write about such a painful subject—literally, to make herself sick—and then read her essay aloud to a group of strangers in a college expository writing course?

Diane's decision to write about a dangerous subject raises crucial questions about classroom self-disclosure. These questions have provoked controversy but surprisingly little scholarly inquiry. Will writing help her to come to terms with a distressing childhood experience or retraumatize her? If writing about certain topics is hazardous, might reading about these topics also prove dangerous, overwhelming the reader with sadness? Should students be allowed to write on risky topics, and if so, how should teachers respond? Might teachers themselves become at risk, unprepared for the emotional, legal, ethical, and pedagogical consequences of their students' self-disclosures? Are there ways to minimize the risks and maximize the benefits of personal writing?

All types of writing may be risky—a book review, a letter to the editor, a dissertation, a personnel report, a job application, a recommendation, a satire, a diary entry, a love letter. Risky writing tends to be personal writing, but not all personal writing is risky. Consider, for example, the following essay written by a returning student in a third-year expository writing course. The assignment was to write about a favorite interest, hobby, activity, or sport. I have not edited her language.

Seeing a loaf of bread or pan of rolls on the counter that I have made gives me a feeling of accomplishment. I feel smug. There are not many concrete

1

signs of achievement in the business of motherhood and housekeeping. The laundry mushrooms, the floors are replete with muddy footprints, and the cupboards are perpetually bare. A loaf of homemade bread can be the exception to this futileness. If I am not home for dinner but I have provided a loaf of bread that I made with my own hands, I feel less guilty. When I can provide bread that I have mixed, kneaded, and baked, I feel proud. Baking bread is about more than providing the staff of life. It represents the precious commodity of time. In our world where few have extra time to bake, presenting a loaf of homemade bread represents real caring. It stands for commitment. This is one way that I show my family that they are important to me. When they come home and see the bread on the counter and smell the aroma, they know that I made an extra effort to provide for them. There is never any homemade bread left over. This is how I know baking bread is worth my while.

I first learned to bake bread with my maternal Grandmother. Everything about her was special, even her name. I called her Geanie. She first taught me to bake bread on the holiday week the summer I was ten years old. An entire day was devoted to making bread. She patiently and painstakingly took me through every step. This was a most special day. When the bread was finished baking, she took a picture of the loaf of bread I had made as if it were an important work of art. It was beautiful. She was so very proud of everything that I did. She evoked a sense of self-worth and pride in me. At the end of that baking day, my heart was bursting with pride. At that moment, I felt that there was nothing I could not do.

To this day, baking bread is therapeutic. When I am feeling stressed or restless I find myself making bread almost in an unconscious way. I begin to mix up a batch of dough out of instinct. Before I know it, my thoughts are more organized and I am calm. The smell of yeast transports me. Mixing the dough with my hands empowers me. Kneading the dough is an outlet for my frustrations. When the dough is pliable and soft and the kneading is complete, the dough and I rest. I cover the dough with a damp cloth and place it in a protected spot to rise. At this point, the dough is fragile, like a newborn baby. Mindful of the perils of a draft, I place the dough on an electric heating pad and let it rest. I check it every so often. I put my hands on the bowl to feel the warmth. It is sometimes difficult to wait an hour to see if the dough is rising. A plea runs through my mind at this point. I ask the yeast god to please let my bread dough rise. I do not wish to start the entire task over again.

Folding back the towel, I inspect the dough. When the dough has doubled in size I move on to the next phase. This time the kneading is more loving and gentle. The dough is shaped and molded to fit my needs. It is again covered and placed in a warm spot to rise. When the dough has reached satisfactory size for baking, I place it in the warm oven. Opening the door of the oven I feel the warm heat radiating from within. I am comforted by this heat. The house is soon permeated with the aroma of bread. I am never far from the oven while the bread is baking. I check it every so often to be sure the temperature is never too hot. I begin to feel confident that this will be a successful baking when I see the loaf firming and browning through the oven door. I am happy.

Baking bread it not a difficult task. There is an endless variety of results that can be achieved with baking bread. You could spend a life time trying to attain different consistencies and crusts. There are many variables with baking bread. What makes baking bread so rewarding is that it is very basic. It does not require any fancy technology. The ingredients do not vary greatly or waiver. Bread has a history; it is consistent and dependable. No expert has ever warned us of the danger of having bread in our diets. Bread is just bread.

The best part of baking bread is to see the spirits lifted of the children who come in the door and find the bread. When they fight over the last piece or are scrounging in the bread drawer for leftovers, the task has been worthwhile. Homemade bread confirms for my family that I have their best interest at heart. I don't have to find the words to tell them how I feel. I bake and the bread speaks for me. Because many people do not make the time to bake bread, it has become something quite special. To me, baking bread is a labor of love and part of my routine. It gives the baker a purpose. It is a way for a person to express an artistic side of himself without the risk of criticism. Criticism does not enter into bread baking for even the inferior loaf is widely acclaimed and far better than store bought bread. Baking bread should be prescribed by doctors. Our world would be a better place if we just had more homemade bread.

Far from being a risky paper topic, the wholesomeness of the subject is matched by the student's quiet self-confidence. Baking bread is an act of creativity, and the reader shares in her pleasure. She convinces us that baking bread is vital to her existence, and while she never disparages those of us who have been raised on bleached flour euphemistically labeled "Wonder Bread," we realize we have been missing one of the joys of life.

We also see how the writer's pride and self-esteem are invested in baking bread. She recognizes this and ironically pokes fun at herself in the second sentence when she acknowledges feeling "smug." Yet there is nothing complacent about her: one feels an undercurrent of tension throughout the essay, beginning with the opening paragraph's description of the drudgery associated with parenting: "The laundry mushrooms, the floors are replete with muddy footprints, and the cupboards are perpetually bare." Anxiety pervades the essay, but it is magically dissipated by the rising bread. The resolution at the end would be less persuasive without this underlying tension.

It is not difficult to comment on this essay. Apart from a typo ("Baking bread it not a difficult task") and the use of "waiver" instead of "waver" in the fifth paragraph, the essay is technically strong, well organized, compressed, and filled with effective imagery. Like any good writer, the student knows that showing is better than telling, and she allows us to visualize a process we may never have seen before. Baking bread becomes a metaphor for "family values" that cannot be reduced to a shallow or cynical political cliché. Additionally, the artistry of baking bread parallels the essay's craft. The writing is sensuous, expertly formed, neither over- nor underdone. She uses evocative language: the image of instinctual kneading, along with the rising and swelling of the dough, culminates in an act of creativity comparable to the birth of a child. She informs us in the final paragraph that baking a loaf of bread symbolizes love for her family: "I don't have to find the words to tell them how I feel. I bake and the bread speaks for me." Nevertheless, she *does* find the words in this delightful essay.

Now consider an essay the same student wrote two weeks later in response to a very different assignment:

When I read the chapter in Dr. Berman's book Diaries to an English Professor, *entitled "Sexual Disclosures" several weeks ago, I never dreamed I would disclose an incident of a sexual nature. In this chapter, Dr. Berman presents an introduction to the subject of sexual disclosures and then provides diary entries from his students on various topics related to this subject. What was so painful to read in these essays was the raw emotion which was experienced by the students. Whether the incidents were single in nature or repeated over a period of time did not seem to matter. They were all very revealing and telling about the experiences so many of us share as humans. The entries have distinct similarities. Guilt, shame, secrecy and feelings of victimization were expressed by every contributor.*

I imagined that I would read this chapter and that would be the end of thinking about this subject. If only this were true. Exploring this subject caused a reaction in my subconsciousness; my memories. I began to remem-

ber an incident which I had shrugged off as minor many years ago. One of the reasons this personal writing course has affected me in such a profound manner is that I have been forced to think about many occurrences that I have pushed out of my immediate thought process. During this semester, many negative feelings, repressed memories, and even anger have surfaced. At times, I have been overwhelmed. Perhaps at some point this will be a very positive experience. Being honest with one's self is one of the most painful and difficult states to achieve. I have to believe that after I finish this essay, I will be all right. Surely this will work out the same way as the other essays have. The only real risk I am taking in disclosing such a memory is feeling foolish in front of my classmates. At my age, this is not the worst experience in the world.

When I was a child, my family frequently visited my Grandmother in her rural home. These weekend trips were always greatly anticipated. We would start out on a Friday night after my Father left work. The two hour car ride was very nerve wracking for me because I suffered from car sickness. I feared that I would lose control and become sick in the car and then my Father would be angry with me. I remember spending the entire trip concentrating so hard on not becoming ill. The ride seemed to go on forever. The highlight of the trip would be feeling the car slow down and making the abrupt turn into the driveway. We were always greeted with open arms and warmed by the smell of dinner simmering on the stove. I felt safe and secure as we all ate together. I slept in the same double bed with my Grandmother and would fall asleep comforted by her presence. By the time I awoke the next morning, she had been up for hours brewing coffee and baking cinnamon buns.

I realize now as an adult and a mother, how challenging it must have been to keep the three small children occupied on such weekend visits. There were no television stations in the country and no neighborhood children available for play. It was the notion of keeping us occupied that began the visitations to Mr. Anzio's house. Across from my Grandmother's house was a large building which once housed a corner store. It had been closed for years but a single gas pump remained in operation. The owner's daughter lived in one part of the house and the original owner, Mr. Anzio, now an elderly man, lived in the rear of the store. He had a separate entrance to his part of the house on the side of the building. Along with the gas pump remained a soda machine. My Grandmother would treat to a soda during our visits. My brothers and I would venture across the road and stand at that machine for an eternity choosing between Grape Nehi and orange soda. The soda machine dispensed ten ounce glass soda bottles with skinny necks. The soda always tasted better from that machine. Flipping the top off the soda bottle with an opener built in the front of the machine was also part of the wonderful tradition. I can still remember how sweet and good that grape soda tasted. It was also part of our adventure to stop in and say hello to Mr. Anzio. He was in his eighties and suffered from arthritis. He didn't get out of his house very often. Once in a great while we would find him weeding his asparagus patch. He would be bent over supporting himself with a cane and I recall the noises he used to make. He had a thick accent and spoke broken English. He groaned a great deal. His gravely voice used to talk about the "old country." His eyes often filled with tears as he would talk to us about his memories. He was clearly thrilled to have company and we were always encouraged to visit him. He had been my Grandmother's neighbor for over forty years. Whenever we would visit he would hobble over to his stove and insist on preparing special fried potatoes. The smell of stale olive oil hung heavily in the air of his small, dark apartment. As an adult, I now recognize urine as another prevalent odor. Mr. Anzio was never clean shaven and he smelled sour. As a child, I did not think too much of this. He soon became a person I trusted. He became part of our routine of visiting my Grandmother. My parents encouraged me to visit and he always went out of his way to provide a treat for us. Many times he would send us on our way and would telephone my Grandmother's house when the potatoes were ready. My brothers and I would take turns returning to pick up the fried potatoes. I can still see the mountain of tin pie plates he had in his pantry. He used them for exactly such purposes. The potatoes were the best I had ever had. My family never cooked with olive oil. They were warm, salty, crispy, and oozing with oil. They would disappear in minutes. My parents always enjoyed the potatoes with us. I realize now that this was another signal from them that this was an acceptable ritual for us as children. By visiting Mr. Anzio, we were giving him purpose. He had someone to cook for, someone to treat. His daughter raved to my Grandmother about the pleasure he experienced from our visits. The company always lifted his spirits. Visiting an elderly shut-in did not seem like a huge sacrifice to me as a child. I always enjoyed the potatoes.

One time I ventured to Mr. Anzio's house by myself and this is when my trouble began. I imagine I was around ten or eleven years old, at this time, although I could not swear to this fact. My younger brothers were engaged in other play and suggested that I go and bring home the fried potatoes. Little did I know how that innocent gesture would affect me so greatly. Mr. Anzio was indeed excited to see me. As he began to prepare the potatoes, I noticed a striking change in his appearance. One side of his jaw, neck and flesh under his chin had vanished. His voice was even more raspy than usual. I could hardly understand his utterances. I later learned that he had had a *portion of his neck and throat removed along with a cancerous tumor. His appearance frightened me. I had never seen anyone who experienced such radical surgery. I remember feeling uncomfortable but thought it was because of his disfigurement. He tried several times to tell me to get a pie pan out of the pantry but I had trouble understanding him. His voice came out in grunts like an animal. I finally realized what he wanted me to do. I went to the pantry and began to open a cupboard to find the pie pan he wanted. When I stood up and turned around, he was standing right in front of me, blocking my exit from the pantry. The pantry suddenly became very small and closed in around me. I became very scared. I remember my heart starting to pound and the feeling of panic that came over me was like a cold chill. To this day I recall exactly how I felt. I get the same feeling as I recount this on paper. He was so close to me that I could smell his horrible breath. His face was covered with white stubble and the incision in his neck loomed toward me. It was grotesque. In a quick and sudden movement he reached over and grabbed one of my nipples between his thumb and finger. His huge hands pinched me several times. He hurt me. He smiled and when I looked in his eyes, I saw his pleasure. His mouth came forward to kiss me. He murmured words to the effect that my "tittys would be beautiful soon" and laughed. I remember I pushed his hand away and squeezed by his body and through the doorway of the pantry. As I ducked down to escape past his body, I saw how filthy his clothes were. It was only when I was very close to him that I recognized the dirt and grease on his baggy clothing. I kept going. I felt as if I was going to throw up. I ran out of the house, down his front steps and back to the safety of my Grandmother's yard. I remember being too scared to turn back and see if he was following me. I was crying by the time I reached the house. I remember feeling that something too terrible to even talk about had just happened. When I went inside my Grandmother's house, my brothers demanded to know where the fried potatoes were. I don't recall what I told them. At some point, they went over to retrieve the potatoes. I did not ever eat his fried potatoes again. The mere thought of them made me sick.*

My visits to my Grandmother's house were never quite the same after that incident. I made excuses after that point and never did visit Mr. Anzio's house alone. The few times I did go to say hello, only at the insistence of my Mother, I was so scared that I only stayed a few minutes and left. The man terrorized me.

To most people, this would not seem to be a traumatic event. An old man touched a young girl's breast which hadn't even begun to develop. What harm could there be in that? I am here to say that this single incident has affected my entire life. At that moment, I began to feel ashamed. I burned with embarrassment. It was a shock that I even knew the implications of being touched in a sexually explicit way. I felt dirty. I knew enough to feel awful. I was withholding a secret from my parents and my Grandmother. I did not want to tell anyone about what had happened to me. At the same time, I was disappointed that my Father did not go over to Mr. Anzio's house and do something drastic to him. Then I became worried about what my Father's reaction would have been. Maybe he would have gone out of control and hurt Mr. Anzio. Before this, I have never told another person about this incident. I find it difficult to admit to myself that it happened.

I have never connected this incident to my feelings about my sexuality as an adult. Maybe there is no correlation between this shame I endured as a child and the fact that I have never enjoyed having my breasts fondled by any of my lovers. In fact, I have always had a very negative reaction to this stimulus. This causes great puzzlement for the men I have been intimate with in my life. It is through their reactions that I have begun to realize that my negative responses are not quite normal. Instead of feeling pleasure and warmth with this form of intimacy, I become nervous and agitated. I am very offended by the word "tit." I have always accepted this reaction in myself. While I would like to have a more positive response, I have never known what to do to change. It was only after I read about other people's disclosures that I began to think about the relevance of this incident in my life. Upon exploration, it seems that this incident has influenced my life in a negative way. I slowly came to the realization that I am a thirty-nine year old woman who is unsure about many aspects of my sexuality.

When I was a teenager, Mr. Anzio died. I remember feeling a huge sense of relief when I heard that he was dead. Good riddance, I thought to myself. I felt guilty that I was glad that he died. I thought that my memory of him and what he did to me would die along with him. If this were true, my life might be a little more pleasurable.

He was everything the characterization of a "dirty old man" brings to mind. Luckily for me, he was quite feeble. The likelihood of serious harm was slight. I realize this as an adult. I did not know this at age ten. What is so significant to me is that he took advantage of a situation and of a child. As an adult, I can think of no act that is more despicable. I loathe him and the putrefied smell of his body. Realizing how close I came to being molested by this man enrages me. I am angry at my parents for encouraging me to visit Mr. Anzio; for trusting him. I am angry that they failed to protect me. Mr. Anzio betrayed the trust of a child. I am angry with myself for never saying a word. Perhaps this makes me as guilty as he was. While I know this is not a rational thought, it is an emotional reality for me.

Now that I have disclosed and admitted this to myself and to my reading audience, I wonder how I will come to terms with it. Perhaps this is the first step toward getting beyond this incident; remembering every vivid detail. I feel nervous and anxious as I write this essay. My palms are clammy, my mouth dry, and I feel as if I might be sick to my stomach. Recalling this incident sickens me. I feel as if this has just happened to me all over again.

I must find a way to let go of the shame and guilt that should belong to Mr. Anzio. I did nothing wrong. I need to find an outlet for my anger. I need to reconcile my feelings and memories and put this into perspective. I need to find a way to return this to my distant memory. I need to heal.

Ultimately, reading about the sexual disclosures of other students and revealing my own has sensitized me. While my experience was not as dramatic as some of the stories presented in the book, it left an indelible mark on me at a vulnerable age. I am more fortunate than some people who have been molested or abused. I feel as if I am one of the lucky ones because I have become informed. I have a chance to get beyond these memories.

I owe a good deal of credit to my classmate Roberta. Because she read her sensitive essay aloud to the class, I found the strength to write this. I have nothing but compassion for Roberta. I admire her for what I saw as a triumph over her memories. I would be willing to guess that she found the act of revealing her private thoughts to be empowering. I can only hope that I too might achieve some of the same results.

We are startled upon realizing that Diane wrote both the breadmaking and sexual abuse essays. The two papers could not be more different, the first with its proud vision of home and hearth, the second with its almost unspeakable horror and indignation. The first composition evokes love, joy, and serenity, while the second elicits shame, confusion, and anger. It is almost as if the writer were depicting parallel universes. Ironically, both essays describe events that occurred when Diane was about ten years old—the age when she was first taught by her grandmother to bake bread and when she was molested by a trusted friend of her family.

Diane's second essay suggests that risky writing arises from an unsettling or destabilizing subject. Risky writing threatens nothing less than the writer's identity and self-respect. Shame is the key emotion in risky writing: the writer experiences shame even when he or she has done nothing wrong. The fear of being shamed encourages silence, which not only makes self-disclosure impossible but also freezes the shame permanently. Risky writing releases negative, unruly feelings, including fear and anger, which may literally sicken the writer, as in Diane's case.

What are the risks of personal writing? There are dangers for the students, classmates, teachers, and even college administrators. Students may feel pressured to disclose personal experiences; even if they are willing to disclose an experience, such as drug or alcohol addiction, they may later regret the disclosure because of a teacher's or classmate's criticism. Students may fear that a self-disclosure will later come back to haunt them. In addition, students who write about traumatic experiences may find themselves retraumatized by the process of writing. There are risks for classmates too. Risky self-disclosures may produce anxiety or depression in the reader who witnesses suffering. The fear or anger in an essay may be contagious, infecting susceptible readers. Teachers who encourage personal writing may find themselves emotionally or legally unprepared for their students' self-disclosures, fearful that controversial pedagogical assignments or methods will render them vulnerable to criticism from their departmental chairpersons, who themselves may fear phone calls from irate parents complaining about their children's inappropriate self-disclosures. All these risks are real and should never be underestimated or ignored.

But there are also risks in *not* writing about certain subjects, including the possibility that students will not have the opportunity to write about the most important issues in their lives. As Marian MacCurdy points out: "If we shy away from offering our students the opportunity to tell their truths, we may be preventing them from learning what control they can have over their own lives" ("From Trauma to Writing" 197). Many of the fears of writing are symptomatic of fears of emotion. Can students be truly educated if they do not have the opportunity to develop what Daniel Goleman calls "emotional intelligence" or what Jerome Bump calls "emotional literacy"? The inability to talk or write about sexual victimization, for example, may perpetuate the victimization, particularly since conflicted emotional issues are rarely resolved through silence. Knowledge may not always lead to power, but in general, talking or writing about a problem is better than not talking or writing about it. Students who take risks in personal writing may find themselves achieving educational and therapeutic breakthroughs that might not have otherwise occurred.

Aesthetics and Therapeutics

One can sense, for example, the power in Diane's writing, the attention to aesthetics, the craft of writing. Despite the striking differences between her breadmaking and sexual abuse essays, both are well written, suggesting that risky writing can be artistically forceful. Indeed, though the second essay is twice as long as the first, it contains only one grammatical error, the use of a semicolon instead of a colon. Overwhelmed by the traumatic nature of sexual abuse, she nevertheless remains firmly in control of every element of her composition: grammar, diction, tone, organization, and point of view. She begins her story, as do many storytellers, by evoking suspense, in this case, wondering whether she will be able to narrate the long-repressed experience and, if so, survive the ordeal of expression. She uses specific details and images to evoke a distant past: the grape Nehi and orange soda in ten-ounce glass bottles dispensed by a machine; the crispy fried potatoes, oozing with olive oil; and Mr. Anzio's dark, sinister apartment. She recalls not only a wealth of concrete details that she observed at the time but also impressions whose significance she understood only in retrospect.

Diane's essay captures a central feature of autobiography: the contrast between one's present and past self. Jerome Bruner has described in *Acts of Meaning* (1990) one of the most curious aspects of autobiography: "It is an account given by a narrator in the here and now about a protagonist bearing his name who existed in the there and then, the story terminating in the present when the protagonist fuses with the narrator" (121). We see this in Diane's depiction of her changed attitude toward Mr. Anzio, whose altered appearance—the terrifying disfigurement of his neck, throat, and jaw—signifies his metamorphosis from a kindly old man into a child molester.

Little escapes Diane's attention as she recounts her feelings and responses nearly thirty years earlier. She uses active verbs, varies the length of her sentences, and conjures up the sounds and smells of his house. She describes how her experience with Mr. Anzio has affected her feelings about sexuality and her relationships with men. She plays many roles in the essay: she is a storyteller, constructing a powerful narrative; a psychologist, probing her feelings and seeking relief and healing; and a witness, alerting others to a lurking evil. Anne Hunsaker Hawkins's observation about authors of books describing personal experiences of illness applies equally well to many authors engaged in risky writing: "the need to *tell* others so often becomes the wish to *help* others" (25). Arthur Frank makes a similar comment about the ways in which "wounded storytellers" can heal their readers. "As wounded, people may be cared for, but as storytellers, they care for others. The ill, and all those who suffer, can also be healers. Their injuries become the source of the potency of their stories. Through their stories, the ill create empathic bonds between themselves and their listeners" (xii). Diane ends her essay by paying tribute to a classmate whose essay on a similar subject encouraged her to tell her own story, one that readers are not likely to forget.

How does a teacher comment on an essay like Diane's? Risky writing poses challenges to the teacher, who must avoid making students feel ashamed of their self-disclosures. To begin with, teachers must reject the temptation to play a role for which they are not trained. Notice that Diane does not regard her reader as a psychologist from whom she seeks advice or counseling. Nor does she regard the reader as a caretaker. She states that she must "find a way to let go of the shame and guilt that should belong to Mr. Anzio," but she does not ask anyone to help her unburden herself. Nor does she wish her reader to be a "critic," invalidating her experience: "I am here to say that this single incident has affected my entire life." She accepts the risks and responsibilities of searching for her own solutions. She cannot predict how the self-disclosure will affect her life or whether it will help her come to terms with the past. She does not use the word "therapeutic" to characterize the essay, as she did to describe baking bread in the earlier essay. Nor is she certain she made the correct decision to disclose a shameful secret; the most she can say is "[p]erhaps at some point this will be a very positive experience." She ends her essay by returning to what the Russian critic Mikhail Bakhtin calls the "inconclusive present." It appears, though, that writing about molestation has allowed her to express the heretofore unexpressed and thus to construct a meaning that will provide aesthetic satisfaction and psychological relief.

Diane's essay reveals a fusion of aesthetics and therapeutics: the wish to write clearly and powerfully about a subject that is vital to her personal growth. Both the artistic and therapeutic impulses are equally important for her, and neither is subordinated to the other. Nor does she privilege the intellectual over the emotional, the mind over the heart: she searches for the widest possible integration of thought and feeling. She chooses a topic that has the greatest relevance to her *entire* life as student, wife, and mother. In confronting shame, she seeks an empowerment that yields educational and psychological benefits.

Risky Writing is the final volume of a trilogy examining the impact of writing and reading about traumatic subjects. *Diaries to an English Professor* (1994) explores the ways in which undergraduate students use psychoanalytic diaries to probe conflicted issues in their lives. *Surviving Literary Suicide* (1999) investigates how graduate students respond to "suicidal literature"—novels and poems that portray and sometimes glorify self-inflicted death. *Risky Writing* describes the ways in which teachers can encourage college students to write safely on a wide range of subjects often deemed "too personal" for the classroom: grieving the loss of a beloved relative or friend, falling into depression, coping with the breakup of one's family, confronting sexual abuse, depicting a drug or alcohol problem, encountering racial prejudice. These subjects arouse shame and are enshrouded in fear, secrecy, and silence. Nearly everyone has difficulty talking or writing about shame, especially college students who are emerging from adolescence and find themselves at institutions that rarely promote self-disclosure.

When I began writing *Diaries to an English Professor,* I did not know that I would continue with two more related volumes. But as my undergraduate students discovered the educational and psychological benefits of psychoanalytic diary writing, in which they probed connections between literary texts and their own lives, I began to wonder whether graduate students could also use reader-response diaries to explore their feelings about a subject that haunts twentieth-century literature and that remains the second-leading cause of death among young people. The personal writing component in my graduate seminar on literary suicide turned out to be for many students the most valuable part of the course, allowing them to discuss feelings they had seldom revealed to anyone. While writing *Surviving Literary Suicide,* I began to wonder whether undergraduate students in an upper-level expository writing course would be able and willing to write formal essays (as opposed to diaries) on a variety of personal topics and share their writings with their teacher and classmates. My major research interest in *Diaries to an English Professor, Surviving Literary Suicide,* and *Risky Writing* has been teaching, requiring me to understand as precisely as possible how classroom experiences affect students.

Using a Case Study Approach

Throughout this book I use a case study approach to explore the educational, psychological, and pedagogical implications of self-disclosure. Only by looking closely at students' essays can we begin to understand how risky writing affects writing skills, psychological well-being, and educational growth. These questions have been asked in a variety of ways, but only a few studies, such as Marilyn Sternglass's *Time to Know Them* (1997), have looked closely at actual student writings—and no study has investigated "risky writing." We live in a highly theoretical age, but I believe that theory needs to arise from and explain empirical facts. Freud often quoted a statement by his early mentor Jean-Martin Charcot: "La théorie c'est bon; mais ca n'empeche pas d'exister" [theory is good, but it doesn't prevent things from existing] ("Extracts from Freud's Footnotes" 1:139). Professional journals abound with articles written by teachers who offer their conclusions about what happens in a composition classroom, but unless they actually ask their students for their own responses—including both signed and unsigned evaluations—they cannot know how students feel and think about their writing.

Conducting Human Research

Academic scholars who are engaged in human research must abide by the rules of their university's Institutional Review Board (IRB), which oversees all research. The IRB ensures that human subjects receive adequate information, participate voluntarily in the investigator's research, have their confidentiality protected, and are aware of the potential risks. Working closely with the IRB, I distribute to my writing students the following handout on the first day of the semester.

> **English 300:** *A Research Project on the Benefits and Risks of Personal Writing and Self-Disclosure in an Expository Writing Course*
>
> For twenty years I have encouraged students in my literature-and-psychoanalysis courses to write personal diaries, which they have allowed me to read to the class, but until a few years ago I had not encouraged students in an expository writing course to be self-disclosing. There are both benefits and risks involved in classroom self-disclosure, and I am interested in determining whether the experiment will be a success or a failure from your point of view and mine. It is for this reason that I intend to ask you at the end of the semester to fill out an anonymous questionnaire evaluating the course's emphasis on personal writing and self-disclosure.
>
> I am also interested in writing a book on self-disclosure in the classroom. I propose to explore my students' writings, their responses to *Diaries to an English Professor*, the classroom dynamics, and their feelings and thoughts about the course. I would also offer my own reactions to the class. An important part of my research would be selections from my students' writings. I have received permission from the University at Albany Institutional Review Board, which must approve all requests for human research.
>
> Here's how I envision the project. All of your writings (40 pages, typed, double spaced), most of which I will have already read, are due on the last day of the semester. At the beginning of that class, I will ask each of you to show me the folder containing all your writings. Once I see that you have submitted 40 pages, you will have passed the course. (Like most writing courses in the English Department, English 300 is pass/fail.)
>
> At that point, you can decide whether to give me permission to use one or more of your writings for my book. If you do give me permission, you could photocopy some or all of your writings and allow me to keep the photocopies. Or you could give me the folder containing your writings, tell me which

essays I can use, and I will photocopy them and return them to you. I will ask you to make whatever changes you wish in your writings to preserve your anonymity. If you give me permission to use your writings, I will ask you to fill out a permission slip.

If I use any of your writings, I will not, of course, refer to you by name. (You can choose your own pseudonym.) In addition—and this step is most important—before I submit my book for publication, I will send each of you a copy of that section of the book containing your writings. In this way, you will know exactly how I intend to use your writing. *If, after reading the section of my book containing your writing, you feel uncomfortable, you can then withdraw permission, and I will delete your writing from the book.*

There is an important difference between *Diaries to an English Professor* and my proposed book, *Risky Writing*. In the former the students wrote anonymous diaries; none of the diarists in the book knew other diarists' identities. By contrast, most of you will probably sign your essays with your own names. Thus, although I will be able to prevent readers of the book from knowing your identities, I may not be able to prevent the members of the class from knowing each other's identities. But since you will know in advance how I intend to use your writings, you will be able to withdraw permission if you believe your confidentiality is compromised.

The IRB did not require me to show my students *how* I planned to use their writings in my research, but I wanted to do so for their and my own protection. Not only did the students own their writings, but they were in the best position to judge whether I represented their words accurately and maintained their confidentiality. As Paul Anderson and Gesa Kirsch have argued in separate publications, scholars engaged in human research must try to avoid distorting, misappropriating, or decontextualizing their subjects' words.

Risky Writing is based on five different sections of Expository Writing that I taught from 1995 to 1999. Of the 115 students who took the course, all but 4 have given me permission to use their writings for this book. No student has withdrawn permission after seeing how I have used his or her writings. I have included the writings of dozens of named students, such as Diane, and many other unnamed ones, whose writings help us to understand readers' responses. Most of my students were younger than Diane and represented a cross-section of those who attend a relatively large northeastern public university. Most were junior or senior English majors or minors. Some were drawn to my section of expository writing because they heard about it from a friend, but most were enrolled because they needed a three-credit writing course that was scheduled at a convenient time. While the total number of my students is relatively small, their experiences offer insights into personal writing.

I have not changed any of the writings that appear in this book except to disguise the authors' identities. These disguises include changing students' names, birthdays, addresses, and other identifying information. Most students have chosen their own pseudonyms, as I requested them to do; others have relied on me to name them. Although the percentage of Asian American, African American, and Latino students has been increasing at my university, the number of minority students taking upper-level writing courses is still relatively small, and accordingly, unless a student insisted upon a particular pseudonym, I have avoided names that are exclusively associated with a particular ethnic or racial group.

It is a truism that every investigation changes the object under study. Lynne Layton has pointed out that even when psychoanalysts scrupulously inform their patients how their identity will be disguised in a case study and receive permission for publication, the analytic relationship is changed. So, too, may the teacher-student relationship be changed by the former's use of the latter's writings for scholarly publication. Although ethical considerations compelled me to inform students at the beginning of the semester that I was interested in using their writings, their essays do not appear unusually self-conscious, as if indicating they were "writing for publication." I doubt that my students would have written differently had I waited until the end of the semester to inform them of my wish to use their writings for this book. I encourage my students throughout the semester to record how they feel while engaged in risky writing, and their increased self-reflexivity constitutes an important part of this book.

The quality of the writing varies from student to student. Some began as good writers, others as poor writers. Nearly all improved in their writing by the end of the semester, though some improved more than others. I encouraged revision, but since the students turned in an essay nearly every week, they did not have time to revise a paper once it was submitted. None of the essays in this book has been revised for publication. Indeed, I have reproduced their essays word for word, including grammatical, spelling, and typographical errors. I always circle or underline technical faults when I come across them in a student essay, but I have resisted making any silent editorial changes. Teachers of writing will not be surprised by the multitude of basic grammatical mistakes that appear in many of the quoted essays. Other readers, however, who may be unaccustomed to the realities of teaching at the turn of the century, will be surprised and perhaps distressed. Scarcely a day goes by when my colleagues or I do not complain about the tedium of reading and correcting poorly written essays.

Yet I would remind my readers that publishing scholars have many people who read, evaluate, copyedit, and proofread their articles and books. Scholarly writing goes through a long process of examination, beginning with the colleagues to whom authors show their manuscripts; to the external readers, who are chosen by the publisher to report on the quality of the manuscripts; to the copy editors, who smooth the language and catch grammatical and typographical mistakes. Despite this lengthy process of quality control, awkward, jargon-ridden, and not infrequently grammatically incorrect sentences find their way into print. I mention this because my purpose in quoting students' essays exactly as they were submitted (without, admittedly, reproducing the coffee stains that sometimes appear on the pages) is not to bemoan the general decline in college writing but to demonstrate both the form and content of risky writing.

Chapter 1, "Risky Writing: Theoretical and Practical Implications," explores the issues of shame that underlie self-disclosure and the pedagogical strategies necessary to minimize risk. I discuss, in particular, academic opposition to personal writing, the ways to respond to personal writing (including the importance of empathy and other befriending skills), the similarities and differences between the "talking cure" and the "writing cure," and the role of the audience in the self-disclosing classroom. Chapters 2 through 6 look at five different sections of English 300 that I taught between 1995 and 1999 at the University at Albany, each chapter focusing on a different class. Chapter 2, "Seeing Ourselves through the Eyes of Others," describes a series of writing assignments in which students became their classmates' biographers. The chapter reveals how personal writing can escape from the narcissistic self-absorption about which its critics complain. Chapter 3, "The Dark Side of Diversity," demonstrates the classroom conditions necessary for students to write truthfully about an explosive topic: racial fear and prejudice. Chapter 4, "Sexual Disclosures Revisited," investigates the pervasive nature of sexual abuse, a subject that many of our students know all too well. Students' self-disclosures can aid not only those who have been sexually victimized but also those who have had no experience with molestation, incest, or date rape. Chapter 5, "Unmasking Shame," centers around a single student, Nick, whose revelation of a terrible secret proved to be a turning point in his life. Chapter 6, "Writing under the Influence," highlights one of the most serious problems affecting American college students, binge drinking, a subject that proved sobering for them to write on. Chapter 7, "Pedagogy of Risk," summarizes the results of a detailed questionnaire given to each student evaluating the benefits and risks of self-disclosing writing; I also discuss the risks associated with reading serious literature, a subject that has been largely ignored by educators. In the afterword, Linda Martin explores how students respond to the "cringe factor." The appendix contains classroom material that may be helpful to teachers who encourage self-disclosing writing.

The title of this book underscores the perils of self-disclosure. No student dropped the course after the first week. Nor did anyone, to my knowledge, complain about the course to my departmental chair or dean. Quite the opposite: students were nearly unanimously enthusiastic in their signed and anonymous course evaluations. There were always many more new students trying to get into the course the following semester than I could possibly accept. Nevertheless, three-quarters of the students who took the course found one or more writing assignments painful. They did not regret writing on painful topics, but the course was more challenging than they had expected. Consequently, one should never minimize the dangers of personal writing. Teachers are not physicians and are therefore not bound by the Hippocratic oath, but those who encourage self-disclosure must take special precautions to avoid harming their students.

I rely extensively upon student evaluations in judging the success of a course, but self-reported studies are susceptible to many biases. Students' idealization of a professor may subtly influence their judgment. They may unconsciously wish to please their professors, telling them what they think their professors wish to hear. The possibility that students' writings will be published in their professor's book and used in future classes is an affirming experience, one that may exaggerate students' evaluation of the course. Awareness of their professor's enthusiasm for self-disclosure may also influence their evaluation and judgment. Students do not usually believe that their work is of great interest to a teacher, and when they discover that it is, they are surprised and gratified. All these factors limit the reliability of student testimonies.

Nevertheless, student evaluations are indispensable for judging the success of a course. Such evaluations are not the only measure of a course's success, but they are a starting point. I have long believed that students are remarkably candid in their evaluations of a course's strengths and weaknesses. These evaluations are especially important in allowing students to express their feelings about a course.

My own objectivity is also limited. I enjoy teaching all my courses, but since most of my recent research has focused on writing rather than literature courses, I have devoted more time to the former than to the latter. This investment has been both personal and professional. If large numbers—or even small numbers, for that matter—of students had found themselves harmed as a result of taking my expository writing course, then I would have stopped teaching it. Nor would I recommend personal writing to other teachers. Have I simply been lucky that none of my students has regretted taking a personal writing course? Will the conclusions reached in this book be replicated by other teachers? Can writing about one's problems be a transformative experience, as my subtitle suggests? These are important questions for future research.

Many of the writings in this book focus on traumatic subjects, and readers may wonder whether college students' lives are as traumatic as these selections imply. "The chances in this culture of being exposed to trauma appear considerable," Anna Salter reports. Research indicates that over the course of a lifetime, "the probabilities were high of being victimized by fire (11%), by robbery (25%), by a car wreck sufficient to injure someone (23%), and by having a loved one die from suicide, homicide, or accident (30%). Overall, the chances of suffering some sort of trauma were 69%, a figure that has been corroborated by other studies of lifetime trauma" (204). Although these statistics apply to an adult's entire life, not just the first twenty years, college students often write about traumatic experiences affecting their families and friends. According to a 1994 poll conducted by *USA Today*, "almost one-half of young adults had witnessed an act of violence in the last year, and nearly a fourth were crime victims" (qtd. in MacCurdy, "From Trauma to Writing" 192). Kirby Farrell's 1998 book *Post-Traumatic Culture* chronicles literature's preoccupation with these dark events. What is perhaps most disturbing about the topics my students write about is that they are no longer considered out of the ordinary. I am always impressed, however, by the courage and strength students convey in their writings, especially when they write on traumatic topics.

Throughout the book students describe their experiences with self-disclosure *in their own words*. In addition, I offer my own perspective, including my role in the process of self-disclosure. I comment on my responses to wrenching essays and the impact of my self-disclosures on the class. It is easier to describe the factual details of my life—a professor in his mid-fifties, married with two grown daughters, who has been privileged to teach college students for the past thirty years—than to analyze in depth my motivation for encouraging undergraduates to engage in personal writing. Although risky writing may imply risky teaching, I do not view myself as a risk-taker. Nor do I believe that only a small number of teachers will be able to respond successfully to the challenges arising from a personal writing course. I remain committed to this form of writing because I believe it can be valuable for students in a variety of ways. Like many teachers, I feel most empowered when I can help empower my students. This empowerment involves, in part, a respect for students and a willingness to teach and be taught by them. Empowerment also involves, to modify a concept derived from the British psychoanalyst D. W. Winnicott, the idea of being "good enough": that is, being closely attuned to another person's growth and development and allowing that person to tolerate frustration. Good-enough teachers are able to acknowledge their own limitations and help students acknowledge theirs.

The writings that appear in the following pages reveal, I believe, a fascinating glimpse into students' lives. I have tried to avoid a "true-confessions-of-college-life" approach, one that offers a melodramatic or sensationalistic view. Instead, I have selected essays in which students seek to gain a larger understanding of themselves and the world. I find myself drawn to these writings because they demonstrate students' efforts to confront and master aspects of their lives seldom disclosed in more traditional writing courses. Students who engage painful subjects write from the point of view of a survivor rather than a victim; their writing is not confessional but transformational. Readers may find themselves transformed in the process, bearing witness to another's pain and later testifying to the healing power of language. Students who write on risky subjects want to be understood; they do their best to find the right words and, in the process, usually experience both aesthetic and therapeutic satisfaction. Writing about risky subjects enables students to venture into previously uncharted territory. Even those students who considered themselves low self-disclosers and who, as Buckler, Franklin, and Young have observed, would ordinarily react negatively to personal writing, benefited from the experience of opening up in the classroom. Shame can silence a writer forever, but it can also awaken a writer's creativity and inspire moving and insightful essays. This is the central paradox of risky writing, one that we pursue in the following chapters.

CHAPTER 1

Risky Writing
THEORETICAL AND PRACTICAL IMPLICATIONS

Shame is central to risky writing, and teachers who encourage their students to write about personal subjects must be able to understand and respond to this darkest of emotions. Curiously, shame has been neglected not only by literature and writing teachers but also by many therapists. Leon Wurmser, perhaps the leading psychoanalytic theorist of shame, has offered a vivid definition that captures its complexity:

> [T]he word shame really covers three concepts: Shame is first the *fear* of disgrace, it is the *anxiety* about the danger that we might be looked at with contempt for having dishonored ourselves. Second, it is the feeling when one is looked at with such scorn. It is, in other words, the *affect of contempt* directed against the self—by others or by one's own conscience. Contempt says: "You should disappear as such a being as you have shown yourself to be— failing, weak, flawed, and dirty. Get out of my sight: Disappear!" One feels ashamed for *being exposed*. . . . Third, shame is also almost the antithesis of the second one, as in: "Don't you know any shame?" It is an overall *character trait* preventing any such disgraceful exposure, an attitude of respect toward others and toward oneself, a stance of reverence—the highest form of such reverence being called by Goethe (1829) "die Ehrfurcht vor sich selbst," reverence for oneself. This third form of shame is discretion, is tact, is sexual modesty. It is respect and a sense of awe—a refusal "to touch, lick and finger everything, a nobility of taste and tact of reverence," as Nietzsche calls it in *Beyond Good and Evil.* . . . In short, we can discern *three forms of shame: shame anxiety, shame affect as a complex reaction pattern, and shame as preventive attitude.* (67–68; emphasis in original)

Wurmser's definition allows us to understand the peculiar ambivalence implicit in risky writing—the wish to reveal and conceal experiences that awaken so much revulsion. As Donald Nathanson suggests: "The very word shame is derived from an Indo-European root (*skam* or *skem*) which means 'to hide,' and from which also derive our words *skin* and *hide*, the latter in both of its meanings: the hide which covers us naturally, and that within which we seek cover" (8). Shame usually involves the "unspeakable," which, as William Cohen observes, "condenses two meanings: something *inca-*

pable of being articulated as well as something *prohibited* from articulation" (3; emphasis in original). Joseph Adamson and Hilary Clark remark in the introduction to *Scenes of Shame* (1999) that "[a]mong the negative emotions, shame is the emotion that functions most to discourage the expression of other affects, including itself" (16). Even as one part of the self yearns to disclose shameful feelings, another part of the self remains paralyzed, precisely because of the third meaning of shame, discretion, which shrinks from the disclosure of anything perceived to be undignified or unseemly.

Psychiatrists point out that men and women react differently to shame: men tend to become angry whereas women tend to become depressed. Culture also shapes the subjects that are perceived as shameful. Sandra Lee Bartky maintains in "The Pedagogy of Shame" that women are typically more shame-prone than men, a phenomenon she attributes to patriarchal society (226). She also observes that many female students are often apologetic about their work and use self-denigrating language in the classroom even when their essays and exams are stronger than male students' work. I believe these gender differences exist, yet the shame experience appears universal. "The phenomenological experience of the person having shame," notes psychiatrist Michael Lewis, "is that of a wish to hide, disappear, or die. Shame is a highly negative and painful state that also results in the disruption of ongoing behavior, confusion in thought, and an inability to speak. The physical action accompanying shame includes a shrinking of the body, as though to disappear from the eye of the self or the other" (75).

Self-disclosure and shame thus exist in a reciprocal relationship: the more one self-discloses, the greater the threat of shame. The concept of self-disclosure, remarks Gordon Chelune, "has its roots in the existential and phenomenological philosophy of Husserl, Heidegger, Sartre, Buber, and Merleau-Ponty. To *disclose* means to show, to make known, or to reveal" (19). Exposing one's most private feelings, desires, and fears to other people always involves the threat of rejection, misunderstanding, or ridicule. Self-disclosure, then, by its very nature is risky, particularly for those whose identities or selves may be precarious to begin with.

Nowhere is our ambivalence toward shameful self-disclosure better seen than in the popularity of television talk shows hosted by celebrities such as Geraldo Rivera and Oprah Winfrey. These programs broadcast to millions of viewers aspects of dysfunctional lives that people seldom speak about in private. Andrew Morrison has stated in *The Culture of Shame* (1996) the ways in which the mass media have popularized and often sensationalized human tragedy: "Frequent examples of spouse abuse, drug addictions, and other compulsive behaviors dominate these shows, where participants are eager to explain their various humiliations and to attain some degree of acceptance and relief. The immense popularity of these shows, and the broad demand from viewers to experience and participate in tales of degradations and self-abasement, document the prevalence of the shame culture in contemporary American society" (196).

The problem with many talk shows is that too often they exploit rather than explore human suffering. Driven by the need to maintain large audiences, they sensationalize domestic violence and do little if anything to solve the injustices they purport to redress. Even Oprah Winfrey, one of the most compassionate television celebrities, has acknowledged this dilemma, conceding in an interview with the *Sunday Times* of London that daytime TV has become a "vulgarity circus" in its lurid portrayal of family problems. Announcing her intention to leave her talk show after the expiration of her contract, she observes, in a reference to her rival Jerry Springer: "Unless you are going to kill people on the air, and not just hit them on the head with chairs . . . there comes a point when you have oversaturated yourself" (qtd. in *Albany Times-Union*, 10 February 1999).

Academic Opposition to Personal Writing

Many of the criticisms of talk shows have also been applied to the self-disclosing essay, which detractors view as perpetuating the same excesses. The opposition to personal writing, however, has a longer and more complex history. Since its introduction into American composition classrooms in the late nineteenth century, notes Richard Murphy, the personal writing assignment has been subject to criticism. The controversies over personal writing have long reflected larger educational, social, and political differences. Robert Connors indicates in his brief history of personal writing in composition courses that proponents dominated in the 1960s, when the progressive education movement was popular. Beginning in the mid-1970s, however, opponents of personal writing began a strong neoclassical countermovement under the banner of a "back-to-basics" approach.

The proliferation of memoirs in the last decade has increased the criticism of personal writing in the classroom. Political conservatives such as Gertrude Himmelfarb have linked the growing popularity of memoir writing in university courses to exhibitionistic talk shows, concluding that autobiography is not a proper academic study. "Now it is the universities that are displaying the same self-absorption, self-indulgence, and self-revelation—all decked out in the latest theory proclaiming the personal mode a higher form of scholarship than the impersonal 'footnote voice'" (qtd. in *New York Times,* 18 June 1997). Roger Rosenblatt, the author of a memoir on his experience at Harvard in the 1960s, agrees with Himmelfarb's criticism: "I don't think anyone ought to teach memoir writing to undergraduates, because they don't have enough to remember" (qtd. in *New York Times,* 18 June 1997).

Political leftists have also been highly critical of personal writing, which is often called "expressionist" writing. As Carolyn Ericksen Hill remarks in *Writing from the Margins* (1990), expressionist writing, identified with James Britton, Don Murray, and Peter Elbow, "carries with it a negative value judgment nowadays for some people in composition studies: expressive writing as opposed to the more serious expository. To express oneself has been associated with pressing something out from an inside (often, an emotion-full subject presumably needing to release pressure), as opposed to indicating to others something 'objective' which is already outside oneself" (109). Many of the most visible opponents of personal writing are staunch foes of capitalism and believe that writing teachers should train their students to critique and "resist" society. Foremost among these highly ideological composition theorists is James Berlin, who has attacked "expressionistic" rhetoric for its political naïveté and "cultivation of the self" (*Rhetoric and Reality* 73). Berlin argues that this type of writing can never succeed in changing or criticizing society: "In the name of empowering the individual, however, its naivety about economic, social, and political arrangements can lead to the marginalizing of the individuals who would resist a dehumanizing society, rendering them ineffective through their isolation. This rhetoric also is easily co-opted by the agencies of corporate capitalism, appropriated and distorted in the service of the mystifications of bourgeois individualism" ("Rhetoric and Ideology in the Writing Class" 493).

One can agree with Berlin that writing always has an ideological component without concluding, as he does, that personal writing is at best politically ineffective and at worst reactionary. Nor must we accept the dichotomy he creates between emotional ("expressionistic") and intellectual (what he calls "social-epistemic") rhetoric. As Peter Elbow observes, "Personal expressive writing happens to be one among many registers or discourses we can use for academic duty. Because personal writing invites feeling does not mean that it leaves out thinking; and because it invites attention to the self does not mean that it leaves out other people and the social connection" ("Forward" 10).

Since the 1960s the writing classroom has become socially and politically charged, with teachers advancing their own ideological agendas. Students sometimes find themselves caught in the middle, not knowing which ideology to espouse or resist. Marshall Alcorn has noted that students sometimes perceive teachers' ideological analyses of student writing as an act of political terrorism: "they are being assassinated, as subjects, by a discourse that purports to be educational" ("Changing the Discourse" 337). Teresa Ebert has emerged as one of the most strident of these critics. In arguing for a "materialist Red Feminism that insists on a transformative emancipatory politics," she implies that all approaches to writing and reading that are not doctrinally Marxist are an "accomplice of capitalism" (796). From Ebert's highly ideological perspective, "nurturing pedagogies" hopelessly participate in and reproduce unequal and unjust social relations. Other Marxist educators, such as Alan France, voice a similar suspicion of personal writing: expressivist writing instruction performs its ideological work by "masking the contradiction between individual self-fashioning and the hegemonic power-relations of capitalist social organization" (600). And Patricia Bizzell, an advocate of "critical pedagogy," which she defines (following Henry Giroux) as one of the "Marxist-influenced theories of education" that seeks to "delegitimate forms of pedagogy that imitate and generate unjust social power relations" (55), darkly hints that while she prefers persuasion over coercion, teachers must sometimes use their authority in the classroom "to the task of moving students in the direction of . . . left-oriented political goals" (57). Thomas Newkirk has stated that the danger of substituting one form of coercion over another is even greater "in a pedagogy that has the stated goal of moving students toward politically preferable positions" (90). In the introduction to *Taking Stock* (1994), Lad Tobin suggests that "[t]he leftist or cultural critique of the writing process movement starts from a different point than the back-to-basics one, but ends up, ironically, in many of the same places—with an attack on the writing process movement's radical support for student writing and student freedom" (Tobin and Newkirk 6).

Apart from believing that autobiography is a narcissistic or easily co-opted genre, many academics are uneasy when their students disclose personal problems. The title of Lucia Perillo's article in the *Chronicle of Higher Education*—"When the Classroom Becomes a Confessional"—implies that some subjects are best left for priests or therapists. Perillo cites the example of a poem written by an older female student describing her sexual molestation by an uncle several years earlier. The class was stunned by the poem and, with lowered eyes, waited silently for the teacher to respond:

In this instance, after praising the poem—for there was much to praise in it, most strikingly an incantatory rhyme scheme that linked the experience to childhood forms of speech, like nursery rhyme—I launched my standard patter about structure and shape and specificity of image. A minute into my comments, however, I realized that a black cloud had descended on the class. A young female student cut me off and stood up to deliver an impassioned speech about the courage the writer had demonstrated and how she ought to be applauded for sharing her experience.

After she sat down, the class looked my way accusingly, no doubt wondering why I wasn't the one who'd said these things. I tried blustering a bit about the difference between poetry's therapeutic and aesthetic uses, but before I could even make the terms of that distinction clear, I realized that no one was listening. Not to applaud the act of confession flew in the face of everything my students had learned from popular culture. Trailing off into inaudibility, I had the feeling that we had all somehow astral-traveled to Oprah Winfrey's studio. And I was the bad guest, the expert who'd been brought in for the audience members to attack. (A56)

One can sympathize with all the participants in this unsettling classroom drama. The vulnerable writer risked humiliation by standing in front of the class and reading a poem that was presumably wrenching to write and no less painful to share with her teacher and classmates. The angry female student felt compelled to defend a beleaguered classmate, perhaps offending the teacher in the process. And the anxious teacher believed she had only two choices, neither of which was satisfactory, namely, "to appear heartless on the one hand or to overstep . . . professional boundaries on the other." In short, risky writing had suddenly created a risky classroom situation, and no one seemed to know what to do.

Perillo concedes that personal grief is often the impetus behind poetry. Nevertheless, she implies that whenever she has attempted to explain what various critics have said about confessionalism as a literary movement, her undergraduates have been confused (or worse, bored), largely because they value a poem's therapeutics over its aesthetics. Indeed, she believes that the "interjection of aesthetic value judgments is often seen as trivializing the horror of the experience." She also maintains that since "wounds come easily" in the undergraduate classroom, a teacher's constructive comment on a poem about molestation will be experienced by the poet as a textual molestation, thus replicating the violation the poet has depicted (A57).

Must risky writing inevitably result in revictimization of the writer, traumatization of the classmates, and demonization of the teacher? As we have seen with Diane's essay, aesthetics and therapeutics can coexist. Is there a way to create a classroom situation in which writers are free to disclose dangerous subjects without wounding themselves or others? Given the fact, as Perillo notes, that writing and literature teachers are not trained to be therapists, can they find ways to encourage their students to write about suffering and survival while simultaneously helping them improve the quality of their poetry and prose?

Before returning to these questions, I raise another objection to personal writing, one articulated by its most influential and outspoken opponent, David Bartholomae. In "Writing with Teachers: A Conversation with Peter Elbow," Bartholomae argues that "academic writing is the real work of the academy" and dismisses personal writing as "sentimental realism (the true story of what I think, feel, know and see)" (69). He rejects personal writing for both moral and educational reasons: "I don't think I need to teach sentimental realism, even though I know my students could be better at it than they are. I don't think I need to because I don't think I should. I find it a corrupt, if extraordinarily tempting genre. I don't want my students to celebrate what would then become the natural and inevitable details of their lives. I think the composition course should be part of the general critique of traditional humanism" (71).

Bartholomae repudiates not only his students' "nonacademic" writings but also a long and honored tradition of personal writing that includes Saint Augustine, Jean-Jacques Rousseau, John Stuart Mill, Benjamin Franklin, Henry David Thoreau, Frederick Douglass, Henry Adams, and James Baldwin. Contrary to what Bartholomae implies, personal writing can be among the most intellectually rigorous genres, demanding self-discipline and self-criticism. Additionally, he creates a false opposition between personal writing, on the one hand, which he equates with narcissism and solipsism, and academic writing, on the other hand, which he associates with the search for truth. By defining personal writing as the "true story," he uses tabloid language to imply that there is something lurid about such self-disclosures. He also contends that personal writing always involves the same deterministic story: "There is a student in my class writing an essay on her family, on her parents' divorce. We've all read this essay. We've read it because the student cannot invent a way of talking about family, sex roles, separation. Her essay is determined by a variety of forces: the genre of the personal essay as it has shaped this student and this moment; attitudes about the family and divorce; the figures of 'Father' and 'Mother' and 'Child' and so on" (66–67).

Bartholomae claims here that all students who write about their parents' divorces express the same tired story, one that has been culturally determined and repeated ad nauseam. His denial of human agency is striking. Writers are given no credit for their own uniqueness and are denied the ability to imagine solutions to psychic conflicts. Nowhere does Bartholomae suggest that personal writing may lead to self-discovery and self-empowerment. He also devalues reading, for if everyone writes the same "master narrative of family life" (67), in which all fathers, mothers, and children are identical, then why should anyone read that story? Bartholomae sounds patronizing even when he begrudgingly permits teachers to allow this type of writing: "Of course we can help the student to work on this essay by letting her believe it is hers" (67).

Honesty and Truth

Much of the controversy surrounding personal writing centers around questions of honesty and truth. In *Fragments of Rationality* (1992), Lester Faigley objects to the claim that autobiographical writing is more "truthful" than nonautobiographical writing (120–21). Although an overwhelming majority of my students report in anonymous questionnaires at the end of the semester that they have been honest in their writings, one cannot "prove" this. Moreover, honesty and truth are two different issues. One can write honestly but not truthfully (the writer may sincerely believe in a delusion) and truthfully but not honestly (the writer may unintentionally express the truth in telling a lie). As I suggest in *Diaries to an English Professor*, "even when people believe they are scrupulously telling the truth, they are still selectively remembering and forgetting experiences, editing biography and history to make them conform to their own self-perceptions" (28). Elements of both self-discovery and self-creation inhere in all autobiographical writing. In the words of the nineteenth-century biographer (and father of Virginia Woolf) Leslie Stephen, an autobiography is valuable "in proportion to the amount of misrepresentation it contains. . . . [I]t is always curious to see how a man contrives to present a false testimonial to himself" (qtd. in Fleishman 8). More recently, Leigh Gilmore has argued that autobiographical writing is inevitably "duplicitous" because it can never adequately re-present the writer's life. Unlike Gilmore, I believe that the gap between a writer's self-representation and life can be narrowed. I rarely question the honesty and truthfulness of my students' writings: my role is not to be a lie-detector but to help them write better, an approach that has the support of the research on self-disclosure, which suggests that there is a "likelihood of candor" when people wish to self-disclose (Rawlins). I don't claim that risky writing is more authentic than other types of writing, but I believe that it reveals students' efforts to tell the truth as they see it, including *shameful* truths that are hidden from view. In *Telling Writing* (1980), Ken Macrorie offers excellent advice to teachers who are interested in creating a climate that encourages truthtelling: "Tell students: 'No one speaks truth always. We all lie, consciously and unconsciously. I ask you to try for truths. I am going to try. You will be astonished by the difference that is made by a constant effort to raise the level of truth in this room'" (283).

Autobiography and Identity

At its best, autobiographical writing offers the most vigorous inquiry into the origins, ambiguities, and mysteries of identity. Although postmodernists have called into question the unity of the "self" and speak instead of "subjectivity," Margaret Byrd Boegeman's observation about the value of autobiography in freshman composition courses is worth recalling: "The examination of the self leads not to narcissism, as some would fear, but to a sense of growth attendant upon analysis, which is the basic paradigm of autobiography" (668). Autobiography is, as Jay Parini has remarked, the "essential American genre, a form of writing closely allied to our national self-consciousness" (A40). The problem with personal writing is that despite its new popularity it has not undergone the same scrutiny afforded other types of writing. Nor has risky writing received much attention despite its efforts to cast light on shameful secrets.

Minimizing the Risks of Personal Writing

Empathizing

Teachers who encourage students to write about shameful secrets must adopt specific pedagogical strategies, lest the classroom become a dangerous place. An empathic classroom is essential for risky writing. Empathy is a central concept in psychology and counseling, but it is less well known in literature and writing, despite the fact that the term originally derives from late nineteenth-century German aesthetics. According to art critic Edgar Wind, Robert Vischsler first used the term *Einfühlung* in 1873 to imply a "feeling into" an object of beauty (150). Theodor Lipps elaborated on the concept in 1903, and E. Titchener then translated the word in 1909 as empathy, after the Greek word *empatheia*, which means "in suffering or passion" (Wispe 21). Titchener viewed empathy as synonymous with imaginative identification, observing in his 1915 book *Beginner's Psychology*: "We have a natural tendency to feel ourselves into what we perceive or imagine. As we read about the forest, we may, as it were, become the explorer; we feel for ourselves the gloom, the silence, the humidity, the oppression, the sense of lurking danger; everything is strange, but it is to us that strange experience has come" (qtd. in Wispe 22).

Carl Rogers placed empathy at the center of his client-based psychotherapy, regarding it as a process of entering into another person's point of view and suspending judgment: "It involves being sensitive . . . to the changing felt meanings which flow in this other person. . . . It means temporarily living in his/her life, moving about in it delicately without making judgments, sensing meanings of which he/she is scarcely aware" (4). Freud mentioned empathy only briefly, observing in a footnote to *Group Psychology and the Analysis of the Ego* (1955) that a "path leads from identification by way of imitation to empathy, that is, to the comprehension of the mechanism by means of which we are enabled to take up any attitude at all towards another mental life" (8:110n. 2). Empathy is related to but not identical with identification. "What separates empathy from identification is its recognition of the otherness of two persons, of their difference and distinctness as something to be maintained rather than annulled" (Vetlesen 204).

The leading psychoanalytic proponent of empathy is the Viennese-born Heinz Kohut, who founded a new movement, self-psychology, based on the empathic-introspective stance. "Empathy is the mode by which one gathers psychological data about other people and . . . imagines their inner experience even though it is not open to direct observation" ("Forms and Transformation of Narcissism" 262). Kohut viewed empathy as serving three functions: first, it is an indispensable tool of observation, the mode by which one person understands the feelings and thoughts of another person; second, it constitutes a powerful bond between people, counteracting human destructiveness; and finally, it is an invaluable psychological nutriment that sustains life.

The concept of "feeling oneself into the other" has long been familiar in mystical theology, as Karl Morrison has shown in *"I Am You": The Hermeneutics of Empathy in Western Literature, Theology, and Art* (1988). Martin Buber, the most famous theological proponent of empathy, felt that it was the way toward mysticism. "Empathy means . . . to glide with one's own feeling into the dynamic structure of an object . . . or even of an animal or a man, and as it were to trace it from within, understanding the formation and motoriality of the object with the perceptions of one's own muscles; it means to 'transpose' oneself over there and in there" (97).

Theorists disagree whether empathy is significantly different from sympathy. Empathy is generally viewed as a more active process—a feeling *into* another person's point of view rather than simply a feeling *with* the other person. This distinction, however, is often blurred, especially in literary criticism. Walter Jackson Bate states in *From Classic to Romantic* (1961) that it is "one of the common tenets of English romantic criticism that the imagination is capable, through an effort of sympathetic intuition, of identifying itself with its object; and, by means of this identification, the sympathetic imagination grasps, through a kind of direct experience and feeling, the distinctive nature, identity, or 'truth' of the object of its contemplation" (132). The concept of sympathy, Bate adds, had a broad moral appreciation in British romantic thought. The influential American social psychologist George Mead defined sympathy as a feeling with another person that becomes a feeling into the other. "We feel with him and we are able so to feel ourselves into the other because we have, by our own attitude, aroused in ourselves the attitude of the person whom we are assisting" (299). Mead believed that sympathy arises from the same capacity to "take the role of the other person with whom one is socially implicated," which he noted is commonly called "putting yourself in his place" (366). I pursue Mead's idea in chapter 2 when I discuss how students write their classmates' biographies.

Empathy has an important prosocial function. "[T]he other's distress must be alleviated if one's own distress is to end" (Hoffman 54). Moreover, empathy helps to decrease aggression and other antisocial behavior. Nancy Eisenberg and Paul Miller conclude in their empirical study of the relationship between empathy and behavior that "[f]or adults, a variety of measures of empathy have been found that, in general, relate positively to indices of prosocial behavior" (310).

Empathy has significant educational benefits. Studies indicate that teacher empathy relates strongly and positively to student achievement (Goldstein and Michaels 148). Teacher empathy has other benefits for students, including better school attendance, more positive self-esteem, and fewer disciplinary problems. High-empathy teachers, as opposed to teachers rated low in classroom expressions of empathy, "use significantly more praise and encouragement, use less criticism, more frequently accept student expressions of feeling, elicit more student-initiated talk, have fewer instances of silence or confusion, and smile more at their students" (Goldstein and Michaels 150).

Psychologists have developed psychoeducational skills training programs to improve interpersonal relationships. Bernard Guerney's relationship enhancement therapy centers around the "empathic responder mode," which he explains to his clients in the following way: "In the empathic responder mode, the attitude that you adopt is the most important thing. You must strive to put yourself in a receptive frame of mind. Your attitude must be: Nobody can help seeing things the way they see them, and nobody can help feeling the way they feel" (qtd. in Goldstein and Michaels 215). I don't agree with all of Guerney's assumptions—for example, he explicitly rules out asking one's partner questions such as "What makes you think that?" Nor do I believe, as he does, that we can *completely* understand or merge with another person's viewpoint. Perfect empathy does not exist: we remain grounded in our own point of view even as we attempt to fuse with another. He also curiously rejects "specific" communication, whereas I would argue that communication should be as detailed and precise as possible.

Avoiding "Critique" in the Self-Disclosing Classroom

Many of the empathic techniques used by Guerney and other psychologists can be adapted to the writing classroom. Since risky subjects involve shame, secrecy, and stigmatization, I believe it is best to adopt an empathic approach. I do not critique personal essays in the same way that I critique fictional stories or scholarly arguments. Neither critique nor contestation is conducive to self-disclosure; indeed, both impede self-disclosure since the admission of vulnerability weakens one in an argument or battle. Students will not self-disclose when they know that their words will be critiqued, contested, or challenged. Writing about a topic such as sexual abuse or depression is demanding enough without subjecting a student to a teacher's or classmate's critical analysis. It is difficult to imagine anything more painful than being told that one's feelings are not valid or, worse, self-pitying, melodramatic, hysterical, or excessive. Such criticism will silence most students and put an end, perhaps permanently, to all attempts to write about emotionally charged topics.

Critique has a long tradition in philosophy and is associated with ideological exposure and unmasking. The implication is that the critic knows more than his or her subject and thus lays bare something that was concealed, consciously or not. Psychoanalysis makes the same assumption: the analyst knows more than the analysand. As useful as these critical approaches are, they are not appropriate for a personal writing class. The writer, not the teacher, must be willing to disclose risky subjects without external pressure. One must unmask one's own shame—it cannot and should not be done by another.

As a rule, I am reluctant to tell authors of highly personal essays anything about their lives that they do not already know. This restraint is in marked contrast to my discussions of literature, in which I analyze—and, no doubt, overanalyze—fictional characters. Real students, unlike fictional characters, can be harmed by a teacher's or classmate's critique or interpretation of a personal essay, particularly if there is no narrative distance between the author and the "I" of the essay. Authors of highly self-disclosing essays may be distressed or even devastated if they hear that their essays reveal "excessive grief"over the breakup of a relationship or contain "disguised homosexual imagery" or "white middle-class guilt." Highly personal essays require readers to renounce their claims of omniscience and instead to embrace active empathy.

Empathy is crucial for another reason. In our desire to critique, we often do not listen attentively: we hear only what we want to hear and then rush to judgment. The abundance of talk shows and "instant analyses" discourages most people from active listening. Our wish to be "right" means that we must prove someone "wrong." As Deborah Tannen observes, we live in an "argument culture" where everything is contested and often litigated. "In the argument culture, criticism, attack, or opposition are the predominant if not the only ways of responding to people or ideas. I use the phrase 'culture of critique' to capture this aspect. 'Critique' in this sense is not a general term for analysis or interpretation but rather a synonym for criticism" (7). Tannen also suggests that the argument culture gives rise to "slash-and-burn thinking":

> Approaching situations like warriors in battle leads to the assumption that intellectual inquiry, too, is a game of attack, counterattack, and self-defense. In this spirit, critical thinking is synonymous with criticizing. In many classrooms, students are encouraged to read someone's life work, then rip it to shreds. Though criticism is one form of critical thinking—and an essential one—so are integrating ideas from disparate fields and examining the context out of which ideas grew. Opposition does not lead to the whole truth when we ask only "What's wrong with this?" and never "What can we use from this in building a new theory, a new understanding?" (19)

The fundamental principle in my writing classes is that everyone is entitled to his or her feelings. Once the teacher and students agree to this principle, the classroom becomes a safer place to explore affective issues that are generally excluded from academic discussions. Self-disclosure occurs in the classroom when students know they will not be criticized for their value judgments and emotions. Empathy does not imply agreement but rather the desire to understand: to enter into another's person's point of view without losing sight of the difference between self and other. As Peter Elbow advises in *Writing without Teachers* (1973), "Never quarrel with someone else's reaction. If someone reports something that seems crazy, listen to him openly. Try to have his experience. Maybe what you see is truly there and he's blind. But maybe what he sees is there too. Even if it contradicts what you see" (94).

Perhaps because of the empathic class atmosphere that I try to create, I have never received the kind of "unsolicited oppositional discourse" about which Richard Miller complains in his essay "Fault Lines in the Contact Zone" (390). Students are less likely to write racist, homophobic, misogynistic, or anti-Semitic essays when they are encouraged to anticipate how their classmates might feel. If I did receive such an essay, I would have a conference with the writer to discuss the offensive nature of hate speech. While it is possible, as Miller speculates, that "transgressive" writings might "simply curl up and go underground for the duration of the course" (396), it is more likely that the authors' anger level will be defused when they realize the wounding nature of their words.

I don't wish to idealize empathy or suggest that it is a panacea. Society may one day suffer from an excess of empathy, though that time will not occur in the foreseeable future. Empathy may be a liability in the law school or criminal justice classroom, where students are trained to be adversarial, but not in a personal writing classroom. The writing teacher is neither a lawyer, seeking to discredit a hostile witness's testimony, nor a prosecutor, trying to determine whether a crime has been committed. Nor is it the writing teacher's purpose to challenge the "truth claims" of his or her students. Rather, the writing teacher's task is to help students express themselves on a wide range of subjects, some of which may be risky. I don't believe teachers need to be unusually empathic in order to encourage self-disclosing writing, but they must be willing to acknowledge empathic lapses when they occur, as they inevitably will.

There are, admittedly, limitations to an empathic approach to personal writing. Since it is easier to identify with victims than with victimizers, students may be less willing to write about their darker, aggressive side. Yet, students are astonishingly open in acknowledging past actions that they now deeply regret. I encourage students to write about their stories from their own points of view, but I do not require them to hear counterstories—other versions of the truth that might qualify or contradict their own perceptions or interpretations. These counterstories are important, if only to serve as feedback, but they might prove disabling or silencing in a personal writing class. My primary aim is to help students write about their life experiences and reflect upon their significance, without the fear of being contradicted.

Empathy is not easily learned, but teachers and students can train themselves to become more empathic. Empathy training is as valuable to a teacher as it is to a therapist. Some people dismiss empathy as a sentimental or anachronistic humanistic notion, inimical to rigorous thought and political change. The cultural anthropologist Clifford Geertz has argued, for instance, that insofar as no one can truly place himself or herself into the position of the other, empathy is "ethnocentric sentimentalism" (119), deceiving Westerners into believing they can understand other cultures. Yet as Nancy Chodorow suggests in *The Power of Feelings* (1999), the assertion that trained observers cannot use empathy to understand another person's point of view forces Geertz to the conclusion that "the native's inner life does not exist, for the anthropologist or perhaps for the native either" (148). Postmodernist psychoanalysts have criticized empathy for running counter to the analyst's spontaneity and authenticity. As Judith Guss Teicholz observes, however, empathy need not be a threat either to the patient's or analyst's autonomy (130). Postmodernist educators are similarly dubious of empathy, concluding that it is simply a recycling of the subject positions of "us" and "them." Many of these criticisms strike me as unreasonable in their assumption that anything that is imperfect is valueless.

I realize that my rejection of critique in a self-disclosing classroom is precisely the danger about which Bartholomae warns. It is not that I fail to take student writings seriously or that I maintain their writings are above or beyond criticism. Rather, I believe that risky writing requires a different pedagogical approach, particularly when there is narrowed distance between author and text. Critique plays a central role in the literature classroom, where fictional characters are routinely analyzed, dissected, and "unmasked," but the same approach is dangerous in the personal writing classroom, where human characters remain all too vulnerable. William Wordsworth may not have been thinking about higher education when he observed in his poem "The Tables Turned" that "[w]e murder to dissect" (107), but every teacher and student has experienced critical analysis that deteriorates into a postmortem. (Of the long list of epithets Vladimir and Estragon hurl at each other in Samuel Becket's tragicomic play *Waiting for Godot* [1954], the most damaging is the word "Crritic" [48].) Teachers must be more careful when responding to a student's personal essay than to a canonical text. Dead authors cannot be harmed by critics labeling their works "sentimental" or "melodramatic"; by contrast, most students *will* be harmed—and silenced—if their personal writings are criticized in these ways.

If critique is too risky for personal writing, what is the teacher's appropriate response? I believe the writing teacher has three roles: to inspire his or her students to do their best work, to help them improve their writing skills, and to raise questions for further writing. First, I regard a teacher as an advocate, encouraging students to confront challenging topics. It takes courage and strength to discuss those issues in which a writer's identity and self-esteem are invested. A teacher's warmth, genuineness, responsiveness, and acceptance are especially important when a student is writing about a growth-enhancing subject. A moving sentence will elicit a comment like "this is powerful"; a painful realization will prompt a comment like "this must have been difficult for you to acknowledge." I try to avoid formulaic or boilerplate comments because I want my students to know that I am reading their essays closely and that I am being affected intellectually and emotionally by their writings. The importance of positive reinforcement has long been known; nevertheless, studies of teacher interactions at elementary, secondary, and postsecondary levels indicate that praise constitutes less than 10 percent of instructor feedback (Sadker and Sadker 180). Composition scholars such as Janet Emig and Donnalee Rubin have argued persuasively for the importance of a teacher's nurturing comments on student writing.

Second, I focus on technical aspects of writing: diction, grammar, syntax, punctuation, tone, and organization. I usually ask the same questions about every essay discussed in class: what are the strongest and weakest sentences? I then choose one of the latter and ask for a revision. It may seem counterintuitive to believe that students will not react negatively to such technical criticisms, but they have little difficulty accepting grammatical or stylistic revisions if they are offered gently and constructively. I don't claim that students welcome technical criticism, but they rarely feel emotionally threatened when told that a sentence contains a comma splice, a dangling modifier, or a colloquialism. These are *safe* comments because the writer's emotions are not invalidated.

Technical discussions of writing provide another kind of safety, helping students to realize that language can not only *convey* crisis but also *contain* it. This process of containment is essential for emotionally charged writings, for by focusing on the mechanics of an essay, the writer is able to defuse its explosive content. Joseph Conrad was well aware of the psychological significance of this process; as the Marlow of *Chance* observes shrewdly, "to be busy with material affairs is the best preservative against reflection, fears, doubts—all these things which stand in the way of achievement. I suppose a fellow proposing to cut his throat would experience a sort of relief while occupied in stropping his razor carefully" (340). A discussion of an essay's "surface truths"—its diction, grammar, syntax, punctuation, tone, and organization—can help both the writer and reader come to terms with its "deeper truths." Technical discussions thus enable students to sharpen their writing skills and to work through the conflicts about which they write.

I spend at least a third of each class on writing drills. I distribute a sheet containing one poorly written sentence from each student's preceding essay, divide the class into groups of three, and give each group three sentences to revise. We then reconvene, and each group offers revisions of its sentences. These exercises not only sharpen the students' writing skills but also create a bond among classmates. Students combine into new groups each week. Group work encourages collaborative learning, which Kenneth Bruffee and others have shown to be so important, and also establishes a relaxed, friendly atmosphere.

I also discuss the rhetorical elements of writing, including figurative language, point of view, irony, and ambiguity. Questions for discussion might include whether an essay's central conflicts are clearly depicted and whether these conflicts are resolved at the end. Other topics for discussion are voice, description, dialogue, setting, and characterization—all those elements that help a writer show and not merely tell. I encourage students to explore points of view other than their own; for example, if they are writing about a conflict with a parent, they might imagine how their parent would respond in a letter. Imagining other characters expands the writer's self-understanding, creating valuable narrative distance and authorial control. Students generally enjoy writing about other people, whether they be friends, classmates, or slightly different versions of themselves. One assignment I give asks students to write a classmate's biography; another assignment invites them to change an element of their identity for a day— their race, class, gender, sexual preference, or religion. Such assignments are not only interesting to write and discuss but also help students to see how they can change their lives by changing their point of view in an essay or story.

Third, I try to raise questions for the writer to think about for a revision. These might involve going into more depth, citing further examples, acknowledging ambivalence, or exploring other points of view. Some of these questions include, as Lee Odell recommends, the basic meaning-making strategies that reflect research in cognitive psychology and studies in interpersonal interaction, such as creating/acknowledging dissonance and varying one's perspective (230). Since it is dangerous to force students to disclose personal information they are not ready to reveal, I limit my questions if I believe that writers have chosen a risky topic.

For example, I would not hesitate to ask Diane on her first essay to describe the different types of bread she bakes and whether they might reflect different moods or tastes. If she were developing her essay, I might ask her to sketch briefly the history of bread and when it began to be mass-produced. Has she taught her children to bake bread? What are the gender implications of bread baking? Do her roles as bread baker and college student complement or conflict with each other? It is not likely these questions would be threatening. By contrast, I would be reluctant to raise questions about Diane's second essay. How does she know that she has accurately recalled the details of her encounter with Mr. Anzio? Is she aware of the research on recovered memories? Did her experience with Mr. Anzio undercut her trust in men? How did this experience affect the way she has brought up her own children? These are questions she might not be ready to pursue.

In addition to inspiring students to do their best work, helping them improve their writing skills, and raising questions for further writing, teachers can be good listeners. As psychoanalyst Alice Miller suggests: "Learning is a result of listening, which in turn leads to even better listening and attentiveness to the other person" (101). Teachers can bear witness to a student's honest efforts to grapple with precarious issues, and they can lend silent support to the process of self-discovery.

Observing Professional Boundaries

Personal writing requires an empathic environment, but other protocols are necessary to minimize the risks of personal writing. It is essential for teachers to preserve professional boundaries and avoid, as Freud notes in *The Ego and the Id* (1961), playing the role of "prophet, saviour and redeemer" (19:50n). Observing boundaries implies a recognition of one's limitations and the rejection of omnipotence and omniscience. The observation made by psychoanalysts John Maltsberger and Dan Buie applies to teachers no less than to clinicians: "As experienced therapists know, the three most common narcissistic snares are the aspirations to heal all, know all, and love all. Since such gifts are no more accessible to the contemporary psychotherapist than they were to Freud, unless such trends are worked out in the physician, he will be subject to a sense of Faustian helplessness and discouragement and tempted to solve his dilemma by resort to magical and destructive action" (275–76).

Nearly all colleges and universities have ethical codes forbidding faculty members from having sexual relationships with their students, as John Braxton and Alan Bayer indicate in *Faculty Misconduct in Collegiate Teach-*

ing (1999). Despite these codes of conduct, teachers who encourage personal learning may transgress professional boundaries, to the detriment of their students and themselves. The most recent example of this is Jane Gallop, whose 1997 book *Feminist Accused of Sexual Harassment* advocates consensual sexual relations between teachers and students. Her book focuses on a sexual harassment suit, widely reported in the media, brought against her by two of her female graduate students. The affirmative-action officer conducted a thorough investigation and determined that while there was no truth to the students' claim that Gallop pressured them to have sex, she did violate the university's consensual-relations policy—a policy that conflicts with what she calls the "erotics of pedagogy." In Gallop's view, the teacher can help her students experience authentic learning by dissolving the boundary between the sexual and the intellectual. "At its most intense—and, I would argue, its most productive—the pedagogical relation between teacher and student is, in fact, a 'consensual amorous relation.' And if schools decide to prohibit not only sex but 'amorous relations' between teacher and student, the 'consensual amorous relation' that will be banned from our campuses might just be teaching itself" (57). She then invokes the psychoanalytic theory of transference to intimate that the student's anger toward her was a projection of the student's anger toward her own parents:

> In my formal response to the student's complaint, I used the psychoanalytic notion of "transference" to explain her relation to me. In psychoanalytic theory, transference is the human tendency to put people in the position our parents once held for us. It is a nearly universal response to people whose opinions of us have great authority, in particular doctors *and teachers*. Since our feelings about our parents include an especially powerful form of love, transference is undoubtedly an "amorous relation." But transference is also an inevitable part of any relationship we have to a teacher who really makes a difference. (56; emphasis in original)

I have an interest in Gallop's work because, like her, I believe that both feminism and psychoanalysis can play valuable roles in the classroom—can indeed help students transform their lives, as feminism has done for her, and as psychoanalysis has done for me. I also believe, with Gallop, that personal teaching can be intensely rewarding and challenging for teachers and students alike. Like Gallop, I encourage students to choose writing assignments that will allow them to analyze their feelings about a wide range of topics. As a teacher, I try to arouse my students—but not in the way Gallop urges.

Sexuality is always present in the classroom, as Gallop, Ann Murphy, and Ann Pellegrini have pointed out. Both teaching and therapy awaken powerful desires and fantasies that are shaped by transference and countertransference issues. Gallop discusses the student's transference relationship but conveniently ignores her own countertransference—the analyst's or teacher's projective tendencies. There is a crucial difference between working through these desires and acting them out: between talking or writing about them in the classroom or analyst's office, and playing them out in bed. Consensual sexual relations between teachers and students, or between therapists and patients, always involve an inequality of power and often lead to an abuse of power. Consensual sexual relations also lead to conflicts of interest (though Gallop has also tried to place a positive spin on this; see her essay "Resisting Reasonableness"). There may be students or patients who are not always disadvantaged by this relationship—and who may be occasionally advantaged by it, as Gallop claims was the case with her and some of her students—but in general such relations are a prescription for disaster.

Only by preserving boundaries can analysts and teachers enable their patients and students, respectively, to engage in self-discovery and self-empowerment. Only by preserving boundaries can analysts and teachers maintain their integrity and preserve their patients' and students' trust. Although on one level the transgression of boundaries may result in a certain kind of knowledge—forbidden knowledge, the dark knowledge that Oedipus knew too well and that led to his blindness—on another level the preservation of boundaries results in knowledge of a more humanistic kind, in which analysts and patients, teachers and students, engage in a dialogic relationship that withstands the test of time.

Choosing Not to Write on a Topic

Apart from maintaining professional boundaries, I give students the option not to write on any topic they regard as too personal. They must not be coerced or subtly pressured into self-disclosure. For example, I told Diane and her classmates that they did not have to write about sexual abuse: they could choose a different topic. It's helpful to give students a list of alternative topics that they can use whenever an assigned topic proves too personal. If they do decide to write on the assigned topic, they can choose the degree of self-disclosure. Many of Diane's classmates wrote nonpersonal essays on child abuse, including crimes against children in novels like Dickens's *Great Expectations*.

Grading Pass/Fail

Most of the writing courses in my department are graded pass/fail, which minimizes the possibility that students will feel that they must be self-disclosing in order to receive a good grade. Teachers should never grade a student essay on the degree of its self-disclosure. I would suggest to teachers whose writing courses are letter graded that they give their students the option of pass/fail when writing a personal essay. Freedom from a letter grade encourages students to be more candid and forthright than they might otherwise be, thus making possible voluntary self-disclosure.

Allowing Anonymity

Students have the option of anonymity when it is their turn to have an essay read in class. I run my writing courses as workshops in which students are expected about once every three weeks to bring in enough copies of their essays for everyone in the class. If they choose to remain anonymous to their classmates, then I read aloud their essay. (I do not pass out copies of an anonymous essay unless the author requests me to do so.) In this way, authors can share their writings with classmates without having their identity known. Authors of anonymous essays not only choose whether to have their essays read aloud but also whether to permit class discussion of their writings. Although students use the anonymity option sparingly, the knowledge that it is available is reassuring to them. I always write comments on my own copy of anonymous essays, which I discreetly return to the writers, so that they can benefit from my responses.

Prescreening Essays

Whenever possible, I try to prescreen essays to make sure that they are appropriate to read aloud. I am reluctant to have students read aloud essays indicating that they are in a present crisis. Such essays may be too difficult for a writer to read (even if he or she wants to) or too distressing for classmates to hear. Teachers may wish to alert students in advance to an essay that may be especially disturbing so they can leave the room if they wish to. If a student writes about a parent's death, for instance, a classmate who has suffered a recent loss may not be emotionally prepared to hear the essay or participate in a discussion. I don't always have the opportunity to prescreen essays, however, particularly in courses that meet once a week, in which students submit essays that are read on the same day. Prescreening essays is helpful but not essential for personal writing classes. Teachers may feel more in control when they know in advance the content of the essays to be discussed in class.

Protecting Self-Disclosures

I tell my students at the beginning of the semester that they must use discretion when self-disclosing, particularly since their self-disclosures will be read or heard by their classmates. Writers should not disclose more than they want to. The use of discretion is essential to self-disclosure, as Sissela Bok suggests:

> At is best, discretion is the intuitive ability to discern what is and is not intrusive and injurious, and to use this discernment in responding to the conflicts everyone experiences as insider and outsider. It is an acquired capacity to navigate in and between the worlds of personal and shared experience, coping with the moral questions about what is fair or unfair, truthful or deceptive, helpful or harmful. Inconceivable without an awareness of the boundaries surrounding people, discretion requires a sense for when to hold back in order not to bruise, and for when to reach out. The word "tact" conveys the physical sense of touching that these boundaries evoke. (41)

Self-disclosers have an implicit understanding with their audiences, who become in effect confidants. As Sandra Petronio suggests, recipients of self-disclosures enter into a contract of responsibility to be co-owners of this knowledge. Teachers must do everything they can to make sure that students' self-disclosures are treated with care, dignity, and respect. Although teachers cannot enforce this contract of responsibility—a classmate may discuss a highly personal essay with someone who is not a member of the class—they can remind students that discretion implies a respect for people's secrets, even when those secrets are made public in a classroom.

Balancing Risky and Nonrisky Assignments

I offer my students a balance between risky and nonrisky assignments. Students could not write every week on topics as intense as sexual abuse. Nor could the class read emotionally wrenching essays every week without feeling overwhelmed by grief or distress. There are many more essays on subjects like breadmaking than on sexual abuse. These nonrisky essays predominate in nearly every class, providing a comfortable, often humorous atmosphere. Most students tend to write on only a few risky themes during the semester, always by their own choice.

Having Conferences

I have at least two conferences with my writing students during the semester. We talk about the development of their writing skills, the appropriateness of the paper topics, their reaction to class discussions and to my written comments on their essays, and suggestions for future paper topics. The conferences allow me to track my students' progress in the course and respond proactively to potential problems. Students will sometimes ask me during a conference whether I think they should read a particular essay aloud. They may wish to share an essay with classmates but fear that it is not "good enough" or "too personal," meaning that they are worried about their classmates' responses. For example, Diane came to my office before class to express her ambivalence over reading her molestation essay aloud. I told her that I was almost certain that her classmates would respond positively, as they did. Conferences are particularly important in personal writing courses because they demonstrate a teacher's concern and availability. Even a small detail such as giving out one's home telephone number can be significant.

Making Appropriate Referrals

Teachers who suspect that a student may be at risk have a legal and ethical obligation to make an appropriate referral to the university counseling center or to the campus police if the student seems likely to harm him- or herself or another person. Dan Morgan observes, in an article entitled "Ethical Issues Raised by Students' Personal Writing," that in his experience, "hardly any students have ever welcomed referrals to counseling — or agreed to them" (323). Many of my students write about having been in therapy, and while teachers need to be cautious in making referrals, I believe students are more open-minded about counseling than Morgan implies. Occasionally a student will ask me for the name of a psychologist or counselor, and I always comply with the request. I also ask students if they would like me to suggest resources that are available to them, such as helpful pamphlets on drug and alcohol addiction, depression, suicide, eating disorders, and AIDS. Pamphlets on these and other subjects are readily available at the counseling center. Students with a shaky support system often find the university counseling center a valuable resource. Although being in therapy or counseling is still regarded as a stigma, most of my students who write about this experience view it as highly worthwhile, as do I.

Perhaps once a semester a student in a writing or literature course will turn in an essay or diary that is cause for concern. It is not always clear whether students are describing urgent problems or even whether they are writing about themselves. Consider, for example, the following reader-response diary, entitled "Confessions of a Mad Woman," that a student submitted in a literature course in which we were discussing Sylvia Plath's novel *The Bell Jar*:

> *Frustrated at my inabilities, I am becoming increasingly human. Sometimes I don't like what I see. Everything made more sense when it was all just kept a smile. They force my life to be complicated and they wonder how people kill themselves. My best intentions never amounted to much, but I never expected any more then I ever got.*
>
> *A vertigo grips me all at once. My soul, my head, my heart—I am bound by my own lack of ambition. I can count what I have to be grateful for on one hand now and sometimes I think this may be the happiest I have ever been.*
>
> *There is nothing like drowning in ones own fear. My ability to survive has drained away—I am, left to die another day. I won't let them drag me in— stronger. I will never topple over the edge—stronger. I am forever now what I will never be and they, still what they have always been.*
>
> *The colors of my life have all stopped fading. The black, the white, the gray are dissipating. The lines that I had once drawn around me are now embedded in my past and self-inflicted confusion lies to waste.*

Is the student writing about Esther Greenwood's depression or her own? If the latter, is she describing a past or present crisis? Unable to answer these questions, I wrote the following comment on her diary: "I think you succeed in capturing the kind of fear and depression that we can see in *The Bell Jar*. If these are *your* fears, then perhaps you should visit me during my office hours so that we can talk about your diary. If these are not your own fears, then you are good at re-creating Esther's point of view." The student did not show up during my office hours, but I was still concerned, and so I telephoned her. She thanked me for calling and told me that she was describing *both* the novel and a past depression, one that she was able to overcome with the help of medication. She later sent me a note in which she said that she could not have written the entry had she not experienced certain feelings in the past. "Esther and I are put together in this diary." Neither she nor I felt uncomfortable with our telephone call, and she later asked me to read an essay she had written a year earlier for another course in which she described the descent and gradual lifting of her own bell jar.

College teachers seldom receive the basic training that is necessary to make referrals to the university counseling center. For this reason, it may be helpful to reproduce the following information, which comes from the University at Albany Counseling Center:

How to Make a Referral

When you decide a student might benefit from counseling services:

- Express concern/interest in the student's well-being
- Be specific regarding the behavior patterns that concern you
- Except in emergencies, leave open the option for the student to accept or reject your referral
- If the student is reluctant, accept the reaction so that the student feels free to reject the referral without rejecting you
- Unless there is clear urgency, go slowly

Avoiding Legal Problems

In an article entitled "Legal Rights and Responsibilities in the Writing Classroom," Frederic Gale warns that "writing teachers may respond to students' writing in ways that are sensible, responsible and ethical in their own minds and in the minds of their colleagues and still subject themselves and even their schools to civil or criminal liability" (21). Gale, an English professor and former attorney, singles out two areas of law that vitally affect writing teachers in particular: the obligation to intervene or not intervene in the life of another, and the right to privacy. In both areas, a teacher's moral or ethical impulse may come into conflict with a complex legal question. For example, although teachers are required to contact authorities in the case of students who disclose that they intend to harm themselves or others, other situations are more complex, such as whether to intervene if students disclose that they committed or intend to commit a crime. "[T]he obligation to prevent injury or death by reporting presumed facts in a student's paper to authorities may be limited by the prohibitions on invasions of privacy" (25). Moreover, a teacher may be unsure whether a student's self-disclosure is real or fictional. To complicate matters, even the Good Samaritan rule, which generally protects those who intervene to do good, has exceptions.

Many of the privacy issues Gale cites are easy for teachers to avoid, such as by not requiring students to write on a topic that is too personal, not forcing them to read personal essays aloud, not discussing students' personal essays with colleagues, and not publishing students' writing without receiving their permission. Other situations, while extreme, are more difficult to avoid. For instance, Gale believes that a student's right to privacy may be violated if he or she gives the teacher oral but not written consent to read an essay aloud. "It seems pretty clear to me that telling or even asking a student to read a paper aloud in class can be considered a publication that meets the test for slow death by litigation. Most students would not dream of withdrawing their oral consent to read to the class, but it only takes one recantation and litigious parents to produce a memorable result, hence my insistence on written consent" (32). In light of Gale's alarming examples of real or potential lawsuits, along with his warning about conservative parent and religious organizations that scrutinize textbooks and writing assignments for what they perceive to be invasions of privacy, how can writing teachers encourage self-disclosures without consulting a lawyer about every paper topic?

There are no easy answers to this question, and Gale himself concedes that he raises more problems than he can resolve. His conclusion—that teachers need to familiarize themselves with their schools' legal guidelines for dealing with intervention and privacy issues—is helpful but not entirely reassuring, since sometimes there are no clear-cut protocols. My own experience suggests that it is unlikely that teachers will find themselves in a legal quagmire. To begin with, I have never had a student disclose that he or she committed or intended to commit a serious crime such as murder, rape, burglary, or theft. I have had students reveal in personal essays that they have engaged in past illegal behavior, such as shoplifting or taking drugs, which may have led to problems with the law, but the students generally neither condoned these activities nor suggested that they were continuing. An exception, as we see in chapter 6, "Writing under the Influence," is underage drinking, but the students knew about my disapproval of this widespread college problem. As a general rule, college students do not disclose more than they want to. I have not found it necessary to warn students, as Dan Morgan does, that they should avoid submitting essays about past or present illegal activities. Whether they are writing for their classmates or for their teacher alone, students remain aware of their audience and use discretion. Most of my students are juniors or seniors and thus adults; those who write about being victims of sexual crimes seek neither legal advice nor psychological counsel from me. Nor have I had to consult the counseling center more than a couple of times in the past twenty years about students who seemed clinically depressed. In the case of "Julie," whom I wrote about in *Surviving Literary Suicide,* I was assured by her psychiatrist at the university health center that it was appropriate to allow her to take my graduate course on literary suicide. Teachers who encourage rather than require personal writing can avoid most if not all the nightmarish legal scenarios that Gale cites. In addition, the university's Institutional Review Board provides teachers and researchers with expert legal guidance on how to secure students' permission to publish their writings. Teachers can add a second level of protection by showing students exactly how their writing will be used.

There is no guarantee, however, that teachers who follow these protocols and who work hard to establish a safe, empathic classroom will avoid legal problems. To an extent, risky writing implies risky teaching, if only because of the volatile emotions that are released through personal writing. As Gale himself acknowledges: "Powerful writing, as all writing teachers know, often comes out of personal experience, especially in the case of high school and first-year college students" (32). Even if a teacher secures a student's written permission before asking him or her to read an essay aloud—something I have never thought necessary to do—that student may remain conflicted about disclosing a painful or shameful subject. Since teachers who view themselves as "encouraging" self-disclosure may be perceived by their students as subtly (or not-so-subtly) coercive, it is essential for teachers and students to develop mutual trust and understanding. Risky writing awakens intense ambivalence within student authors, as well as within their classmates and teacher, and this ambivalence may create unforeseen and undesirable legal and psychological consequences. Teachers who promote self-disclosing writing must be attentive to these risks without being unduly intimidated by them.

It may not be possible for teachers to set into place all the above protocols, but I believe they contribute to a safe classroom for personal writing. These protocols or "safeguards" reduce the possibility that students will be harmed. Most of the published accounts of students becoming at risk as a result of a personal essay reveal that many of these protocols were not established—either a teacher pressured a student into self-disclosure, responded unempathically, violated professional boundaries, or failed to make an appropriate referral. (See, for example, the article entitled "A Professor's Personal Teaching Style Wins Him Praise and Costs Him His Job" appearing in the *Chronicle of Higher Education* [14 November 1997] about a professor who allegedly coerced his students into writing essays about their lives and then made sexually tinged comments.) I would never teach a personal writing course without these protocols in place, nor would I want my children to take a personal writing course without the teacher taking adequate precautions. Otherwise, the risk of harm is too great. As I suggest in *Surviving Literary Suicide*, reading and writing are powerful activities, able to transform us, for good or ill, into different people. As Franz Kafka remarked to a friend,

> I think we ought to read only the kind of books that wound and stab us. If the book we're reading doesn't wake us up with a blow on the head, what are we reading it for? So that it will make us happy, as you write? Good Lord, we would be happy precisely if we had no books, and the kind of books that

make us happy are the kind we could write ourselves if we had to. But we need the books that affect us like a disaster, that grieve us deeply, like the death of someone we love more than ourselves, like being banished into forests far from everyone, like a suicide. A book must be the axe for the frozen sea inside us. (16)

More so than other types of expression, personal writing can be the ax for the frozen sea inside us, enabling us to get in touch with feelings and thoughts long hidden from view, but it is an instrument that must be wielded carefully, lest we injure ourselves or others.

A Therapeutic Model of Teaching

My model of teaching approaches a therapeutic one in affirming self-esteem and personal growth. Lest I be misunderstood, I am careful not to psychoanalyze my students or their writings. I am not trained to offer clinical interpretations, and if I did, my students would surely perceive them as inappropriate and intrusive. Teachers are not hired to engage in psychotherapy or dispense medication; therapists do not grade their patients or require them to master bodies of knowledge. Nevertheless, without conflating the teacher's and therapist's roles, I believe that a pedagogical model of classroom self-disclosure has many elements in common with therapeutic models. Lad Tobin, one of the few educators who has acknowledged these commonalities, suggests in *Writing Relationships* (1993) that "most writing teachers know that therapeutic models can help explain and explore the teacher-student relationship, but because they find this comparison threatening they publicly deny it" (29). Teacher-student and therapist-patient relationships both involve relational situations in which affective and cognitive issues are discussed from a variety of theoretical perspectives. Empathy, warmth, and genuineness are among the most important qualities for effective teachers and therapists. Teachers and therapists both seek to empower their students and patients, respectively, and the act of empowerment requires a safe and protective setting. Investigations of point of view, plot, character, symbolism, language, irony, and ambiguity are central to both writing teachers and therapists.

In his classic study *Persuasion and Healing*, first published in 1961, Jerome Frank argues that all psychotherapies share at least four effective features:

1. "An emotionally charged, confiding relationship with a helping person (often with the participation of a group)"
2. "A healing setting"

3. "A rationale, conceptual scheme, or myth that provides a plausible explanation for the patient's symptoms and prescribes a ritual or procedure resolving them," and
4. "A ritual or procedure that requires the active participation of both patient and therapist and that is believed by both to be the means of restoring the patient's health" (Frank and Frank 40–43)

All these features may be seen, in one form or another, in the self-disclosing classroom. Teachers help students write about emotionally charged subjects in a safe classroom setting, construct their own interpretations, and seek both aesthetic and psychological resolution.

The Writing Cure

Writers have long been aware of the therapeutic benefits of self-expression. As I suggest in *Surviving Literary Suicide* (1999), even writers who eventually took their own lives extolled the writing cure. Virginia Woolf affirmed repeatedly the therapeutic nature of writing. "Melancholy diminishes as I write," she declares in a 1920 diary entry (*Diary* 2:72). Although no Freudian, at times she sounded like one, especially when she admits in "A Sketch of the Past" that the invisible presence of her deceased mother haunted her into her forties. Woolf maintained that she ceased to be obsessed by her mother only upon writing *To the Lighthouse* (1927): "I suppose that I did for myself what psycho-analysts do for their patients. I expressed some very long felt and deeply felt emotion. And in expressing it I explained it and then laid it to rest" (*Moments of Being* 81).

Like Woolf, Ernest Hemingway had no use for psychoanalysis, but he, too, affirmed the parallels between the talking cure and the writing cure. When asked if he had an analyst, he replied: "Sure I have. Portable Corona number three. That's been my analyst" (Hotchner 152). Hemingway sometimes expressed this vision of writing through his autobiographical projections. Robert Jordan tells himself in *For Whom the Bell Tolls* (1940) that he will write a "true book" about his war experiences when he returns to the United States from Spain. He expects that writing will help him make sense of the absurdity of war and, though he is reluctant to mention it, come to terms with the most traumatic event of his life: his father's suicide. "But my guess is you will get rid of all that by writing about it, he said. Once you write it down it is all gone" (165). Hemingway later reiterated Jordan's affirmation of writing as rescue. "There's a paragraph in *For Whom the Bell Tolls* that . . . well . . . took me twenty years to face . . . [my father's] suicide and put it down and catharsize it" (Hotchner 115).

Sylvia Plath's most affirmative statement about writing as therapy appears in a 1958 journal entry: "Fury jams the gullet and spreads poison, but, as soon as I start to write, dissipates, flows out into the figure of the letters: writing as therapy?" (*Journals* 255). Plath's view of art as a purgation of toxic emotions is strikingly similar to Woolf's and Hemingway's. "If I could once see how to write a story, a novel, to get something over," she records in a 1959 entry, "I would not despair. If writing is not an outlet, what is?" (*Journals* 290).

Anne Sexton was convinced of the therapeutic nature of writing, and there are at least half a dozen statements in her correspondence affirming the relationship between poetry and healing. "Poetry has saved my life and I respect it beyond both or any of us," she wrote to fellow poet W. D. Snodgrass in 1958 (42). She repeated this theme one year later to her former creative writing professor, John Holmes: "[P]oetry has saved my life; has given me a life and if I had not wandered in off the street and found you and your class . . . I would indeed be lost" (59). Sexton believed writing was therapeutic because it heightened self-understanding and allowed her to master, if only temporarily, anxieties that might otherwise be overwhelming.

William Styron has also commented on the extent to which his writings may be viewed, psychobiographically, as an effort to work through potentially disabling conflicts. Speaking through his autobiographical narrator Stingo in *Sophie's Choice* (1979), Styron observes: "my writing had kept serious emotional distress safely at bay, in the sense that the novel I was working on [Styron's first novel, *Lie Down in Darkness*] served as a cathartic instrument through which I was able to discharge on paper many of my more vexing tensions and miseries" (438).

While some critics have argued that Woolf, Hemingway, Plath, and Sexton were victimized by the creative process, they themselves believed, with justification, that their writing held in check their suicidal feelings and prolonged their lives. Writing is not a perfect therapy, but it fosters self-understanding and self-control, thus combating feelings of helplessness.

Health Benefits of Self-Disclosure

New research affirms the many health benefits of self-disclosure. James Pennebaker's book *Opening Up: The Healing Power of Expressing Emotions* (1997) provides striking confirmation of the therapeutic value of talking and writing. Pennebaker has demonstrated in careful empirical studies of hundreds of college students that talking or writing about trauma dramatically improves one's physical and mental health. Pennebaker notes that self-disclosure produces dramatic physiological changes: "When disclosing deeply personal experiences, there are immediate changes in brainwave patterns, skin conductance levels, and overt behavioral correlates of the letting-go experience. After confessions, significant drops in blood pressure and heart rate, as well as improvements in immune function, occur. In the weeks and months afterward, people's physical and psychological health improved" (56). Moreover, high self-disclosers experience greater health benefits than low self-disclosers. "People who wrote about their deepest thoughts and feelings surrounding traumatic experiences evidenced heightened immune function compared with those who wrote about superficial topics" (37). Pennebaker conjectures that writing about trauma reduces the biological stress associated with inhibition, encourages an understanding of the traumatic event, and enlarges one's perspective. "By talking or writing about previously inhibited experiences, individuals translate the event into language. Once it is language-based, people can better understand the experience and ultimately put it behind them" (10). Pennebaker regards such writing as "preventive maintenance" (197).

Pennebaker's thesis has been confirmed and extended by a study appearing in a 1999 issue of *JAMA* (*Journal of the American Medical Association*). In an article entitled "Effects of Writing about Stressful Experiences on Symptom Reduction in Patients with Asthma or Rheumatoid Arthritis," Joshua Smyth, Arthur Stone, Adam Hurewitz, and Alan Kaell scientifically demonstrate for the first time that writing about stressful experiences can help those who are suffering from clinical illnesses. (Pennebaker's studies, by contrast, have been limited to physically healthy people.) Using rigorous scientific procedures for enlisting and measuring physical illness, Smyth and his collaborators chose more than a hundred patients suffering from two common diseases. They divided the patients into two groups, both of which were asked to write for twenty minutes on three consecutive days each week for a period of four months. Patients in the experimental group were asked to write about the most stressful experiences in their lives, while those in the control group were asked to describe their plans for the day. All the writings were anonymous, and neither the participants nor the researchers discussed the content of the writings.

The results were dramatic. Four months after treatment, asthma patients in the experimental group showed improvements in lung function, while control group patients showed no change. Similarly, rheumatoid arthritis patients in the experimental group showed improvements in overall disease activity, while control group patients did not. Approximately 47 percent of the experimental patients showed clinically relevant improvement, while only 24 percent of the control group patients showed improvement. Even the researchers seem astonished by the results of their study. "Although it may be difficult at times to believe that a brief writing exercise can meaningfully affect health, this study replicates in a chronically ill sample what a burgeoning literature indicates in healthy individuals" (1308).

The researchers raise many questions about which they are reluctant to speculate. How long will the improvements shown by patients in the experimental group last? Will writing therapy help those suffering from other illnesses? Most important of all, *why* does writing therapy work? They cautiously offer two explanations. First, the psychophysiological changes experienced by the experimental group patients, such as elevated heart rate and blood pressure, may strengthen the writers' immune systems. Second, "participants' cognitive and memory representation of past traumas may be altered by this writing exercise, perhaps facilitating improvements in coping with stressful events" (1308). The researchers might have quoted D. H. Lawrence here to support their theory: "One sheds one[']s sicknesses in books, repeats and presents again one[']s emotions, to be master of them" (90).

Neither Pennebaker's students nor Smyth's patients shared their writings with anyone—and therein lies a crucial difference between clinical and classroom self-disclosures. Pennebaker's students wrote only for themselves and later destroyed their writings without showing them to anyone:

> In many cases, it is wise to keep what you have written to yourself. You might even destroy it when you're finished (although many people find this hard to do). Planning to show your writing to someone can affect your mind-set while writing. For example, if you would secretly like your lover to read your deepest thoughts and feelings, you will orient your writing to your lover rather than to yourself. From a health perspective, you will be better off making yourself the audience. In that way, you don't have to rationalize or justify yourself to suit the perspective of another person. (41)

There is a gain and a loss in destroying one's writings without showing them to others. One gains safety and anonymity but loses the opportunity to express one's experiences to others. Nor is there any sharing of points of view or realization that most of the fears we think are uniquely our own are part of the human condition.

Self-Disclosure in the Classroom

Self-disclosure has a reciprocal effect, encouraging others to disclose themselves. Diane's decision to write her essay on molestation was influenced by an essay on physical abuse that her classmate Roberta read aloud two weeks earlier. Reading essays aloud creates a dialogic relationship that facilitates an active sharing of experiences. Reading an essay aloud is often the most valuable part of self-disclosure: the writer acknowledges a painful experience and allows classmates to bear witness. Students discover, to their surprise, that many of their classmates have survived traumatic experiences.

In the past decade, literary scholars from a variety of critical perspectives have advocated self-disclosure in the classroom. Daniel Rancour-Laferriere's edited volume *Self-Analysis in Literary Study* (1994) investigates how psychoanalytic self-analysis enables readers to gain a deeper understanding of literature and themselves. Insofar as every interpretation reveals something about the interpreter, an understanding of the latter always casts light on the former. The contributors to Rancour-Laferriere's volume explore a wide range of subjects and reach a similar conclusion—in the editor's words, "self-analysis can be a boon to other-analysis, including psychoanalysis of literature" (29).

David Bleich admits in "Collaboration and the Pedagogy of Disclosure" that "modes of self-disclosure are what many students have longed for since I have been in school but were taught to confine to ultra-private, often unsharable social locations apart from school" (48). Bleich distinguishes between confession and disclosure: the former, apart from its religious implications, takes place "in either completely private or completely public contexts," whereas the latter refers "to telling things in more intermediate contexts like groups, subgroups, classrooms, and lecture halls" (47–48). Bleich argues in *Know and Tell* (1998) that disclosure "desentimentalizes writing groups, teaches the discipline of interacting with others, and adds collective achievement to what can be learned in school" (127).

Many of bell hooks's books are highly self-disclosing. In *Remembered Rapture* (1999), she makes a useful distinction between "confession as an act of displacement and confession as the beginning stage in a process of self-transformation" (6). Hooks states in "Engaged Pedagogy" that teachers cannot expect their students to be self-disclosing without being self-disclosing themselves: "Professors who expect students to share confessional narratives but who are themselves unwilling to share are exercising power in a manner that could be coercive. In my classrooms, I do not expect students to take any risks that I would not take, to share in any way that I would not share. When professors bring narratives of their experiences into classroom discussions it eliminates the possibility that we can function as all-knowing, silent interrogators" (237).

In *A Life in School* (1996) Jane Tompkins calls for a "more holistic approach to learning, a disciplinary training for people who teach in college that takes into account the fact that we are educators of whole human beings" (218). Although her 1990 essay "Pedagogy of the Distressed" has been criticized for its self-referentiality, Tompkins, along with Nancy Miller, believes that teachers and students must overcome the fear of exposure instilled in them by many years of schooling if they are to confront honestly the real issues of education. Other composition scholars, such as Mike Rose in *Lives on the Boundary* (1990), have noted that students invariably write about personal experiences. Several of the literary critics who contributed statements to the October 1996 issue of *PMLA*, which asked readers to comment on the role of the personal in academic scholarship, responded positively to the "inevitability of the personal," including Norman Holland, Claudia Tate, Joseph Boone, and Sharon Holland.

While neither Rancour-Laferriere, Bleich, nor Tompkins advocates the use of self-disclosure for risky topics, as I do, other teachers are doing this, with good results. Marian MacCurdy, a writing professor at Ithaca College, creates open-ended assignments that allow her students to write on difficult topics and share them with their teacher and classmates. Her experience is that nearly all students choose to write about painful topics regardless of whether their teachers ask them to or not. MacCurdy affirms the many similarities between the therapeutic process and the writing process without ignoring essential differences. She helps her students to connect with their emotions by finding the concrete images that hold in place painful memories. The healing process can begin once these images are expressed. "The personal essay carries us into a universe of shared experience and shared humanity. And when the essay moves into sensitive areas, we are reminded that trauma is an integral part of human experience. We cannot proclaim our humanity without acknowledging our capacity for suffering and the results of that suffering" ("From Image to Narrative" 101). Many of the essays in *Writing and Healing: Toward an Informed Practice* (2000), edited by Charles Anderson and Marian MacCurdy, demonstrate the diverse ways in which college teachers encourage their students to write about traumatic subjects. In *Writing as a Way of Healing* (1999), Louise DeSalvo describes many of the benefits of writing about illness: "Through writing, we can maintain control over our lives; create a work of art that will live on after our death; express our feelings (especially anger, grief, rage, jealousy of those who are well); keep disabling fear at bay; fight the idea that our illness has robbed our life of its meaning; resolve unresolved issues in our lives; share with others what we have learned about illness and, perhaps, what we've learned about effective treatment" (202).

In *The Writing Cure* (1999) Mark Bracher demonstrates how a psychoanalytic perspective can offer valuable insights into the writing process. He is the first literary critic to develop a comprehensive psychoanalytic writing pedagogy based on a Lacanian model. Bracher argues that most writing problems are caused not mainly by deficiencies in knowledge or cognition but rather by inner psychological problems involving, in Lacanian terms, conflicts among Real, Imaginary, and Symbolic components of identity. Psychoanalysis can enable a teacher to help students overcome interpsychic conflicts and thus become more effective writers. While acknowledging that he has not yet tested his psychoanalytic writing paradigm, Bracher offers many intriguing insights in *The Writing Cure*, including the hope that a "truly psychoanalytic pedagogy would allow students to confront the contingency of their identity and the ineluctability of their unconscious desires and gratifications at their own pace, taking care that the student's level of anxiety never became overwhelming" (6).

Marshall Alcorn also advocates the use of psychoanalytic pedagogy in writing courses. Alcorn's book *Changing the Subject in English Class* calls for an "ethics of identity" that will allow students to appreciate the complexity of human subjectivity. "Rather than supporting a theory of composition that purports to teach the correct ideology, I want to advocate a theory of democratic participation that allows events and expression about human experience to circulate in discourse communities with the least amount of pathological distortion." Alcorn notes a central paradox of teaching: conflict is essential to human growth, yet too much conflict in the classroom will cause students to become defensive and withdraw. Both Bracher and Alcorn realize that "oppositional pedagogies" often create unproductive tensions, transforming the classroom into a battlefield.

The Audience

The audience plays a key role in the self-disclosing classroom, either heightening or diminishing a writer's feelings of embarrassment or shame. It is the teacher's challenge to create an empathic environment in which the writer can trust his or her audience. In a less obvious way, the audience must trust the writer's discretion over the appropriateness of a classroom self-disclosure. Diane noted, in her response to reading an early draft of this book, that she feared her essay on molestation might be too painful for her classmates to hear:

I did fear when I wrote the essay. Among other fears, I was afraid of the affect this writing would have on others. I did not want to instill or inflict pain or discomfort on anyone. Retrospectively, I recognize that it was my feelings of responsibility toward my readers that tempered my writing. There is a fear in disclosure which can only be overcome by instilling feelings of trust. All of this emotional tumult is part of what makes risky writing such a curious phenomenon. Each of the elements must be in place—trust in the audience, non-judgmental guidance from the professor, protection of identity if necessary—for the writing to occur.

The audience performs many functions in the self-disclosing classroom, ranging from attentive listening to support and validation. In psychoanalytic terms, the audience becomes a "holding environment" in which the writer's toxic self-disclosures can be safely neutralized. But more than simply serving as a container, the audience offers writers the recognition for which they are searching. The relationship between writer and audience is part of a larger intersubjective bond between self and other that psychoanalytic theorists such as Jessica Benjamin have proposed: "the need for *mutual* recognition, the necessity of recognizing as well as being recognized by the other—this is what so many theories of the self have missed. The idea of mutual recognition is crucial to the intersubjective view; it implies that we actually have a need to recognize the other as a separate person who is like us yet distinct" (23; emphasis in original).

To judge from the anonymous evaluations at the end of the semester, students do not feel like voyeurs or "rubbernecks" when hearing their classmates' writings. Rather, they remain empathic—largely because they are confronting what Deborah Britzman calls "difficult knowledge," that is, knowledge about our vulnerability, which always arouses intense resistance. Sometimes the audience experiences empathic distress when hearing about the writer's suffering. This is one of the hazards of listening. Psychoanalyst Dori Laub has observed that bearing witness to a traumatic story can itself be traumatic. "By extension, the listener to trauma comes to be a participant and a co-owner of the traumatic event: through his very listening, he comes to partially experience trauma in himself" (57).

Teachers cannot predict when a student will experience empathic distress in response to hearing a classmate's essay. Sometimes empathic distress takes the form of a student becoming misty-eyed during the reading of an essay. Other times empathic distress results in the absence of any verbal reaction: students may not know what to say. Sometimes silence is the most appropriate response. Students generally follow the teacher's lead in responding to an emotional essay. If the teacher responds sensitively and appropriately, so will the class.

Teachers who encourage their students to engage in risky writing should have some familiarity with fields that may seem far removed from rhetoric and composition, including clinical psychology and trauma theory. This does not mean teachers must have clinical training, but it does mean they should be sensitive to their students' classroom responses. Although interdisciplinary work is now encouraged, unlike thirty years ago, when young literary scholars were trained not to pursue "extraliterary approaches," many literature and writing teachers harbor a deep suspicion of psychotherapy, believing, as Nabokov's Humbert observes mordantly in *Lolita*, that the difference between "the rapist" and "therapist" is a matter of spacing (147). Even psychoanalytic literary critics feel anxious about inviting their students to write on personal topics, fearing that the classroom will become a site for inappropriate self-disclosures. My own classroom experience suggests, however, that students neither regard their teachers as therapists nor make inappropriate demands if professional boundaries are established early in the semester.

Befriending Skills

Colleagues from other universities have remarked, in response to hearing sections of this book presented at psychoanalytic conferences, that they would never permit their students to engage in personal writing. Like most academics, they believe that self-disclosure has no place in a university course. Some feel that the personal is subsumed by the theoretical, which they feel should be the only proper focus of any academic course; others assert that their students are already too self-absorbed and need to know more about the world; still others concede that even if personal knowledge is important, they lack the clinical training to encourage their students to write safely about their lives.

I find it ironic that while literary scholars have wide and deep knowledge of many fields that touch upon psychoanalysis, including philosophy, linguistics, and political theory, they seem to draw the line at clinical psychology or counseling, which they maintain is off-limits to them. If teachers can master complex and often arcane theory, why cannot they understand the basic befriending skills that are so important in the classroom? These befriending skills include, as Scott Poland observes, remaining compassionate and humble; sharing a person's pain; listening instead of offering advice; and providing acceptance, empathy, and caring (170). Marilyn Valentino has offered sensitive guidelines to help teachers respond to essays about traumatic personal experiences; she writes in the margins of these essays reflective statements like "This must have been horrible for you," "That must have been upsetting," or "You seem upset. Is there someone you can talk to about this? Would you like to speak to a counselor?" (281). Valentino also points out that it is often sufficient for a teacher simply to ask the following question in response to a student essay describing an unresolved personal crisis: "What would you like me to do?" In many cases the student's response is equally simple: "nothing—just listen."

As I argue in *Diaries to an English Professor*, teachers can be caring without becoming caregivers. Teachers are often in the position to recognize when students are at risk and make appropriate referrals to the university counseling service. Wendy Bishop has suggested that writing program teachers and administrators should be provided with the basics of counseling to support their work. In "Teaching Emotional Literacy," Jerome Bump discuses the Group Participation Guidelines that he gives to his writing students, guidelines that affirm mutual support and nonjudgmental listening and sharing. Other scholars, such as Alice Brand, Louise DeSalvo, Arthur Frank, Judith Harris, Anne Hunsaker Hawkins, Ira Progoff, Tristine Rainer, and Jacqueline Rinaldi, have written about textual healing. Befriending skills are almost never discussed in literature-and-psychology classes, and they are certainly not intellectually "cutting edge" or "high-tech." Nevertheless, they are more necessary now than ever before.

Writing and Personal Growth

To understand what it is like to be a member of a personal writing course, in which emotional development accompanies intellectual development, we must rely on the students' own words, beginning with Diane's evaluation of the course.

If you are not a participant in Dr. Berman's expository writing course, then it would be almost impossible to understand what this course is all about. This is a case of showing is better than telling, as we are told right from the start. This is a course about improving writing skills. This is a course which involves concentrated listening. This is a course which will sensitize the most crusty individual. Self- disclosure is a large part of this course. You must be prepared to involve yourself in deep thinking about your life. This is an experience I relate to going to the dentist. While you are formulating the essay in your mind, it can be as painful as a tooth abscessing. Your thoughts swirl around in your head and cause great discomfort. Reading an essay aloud in class and disclosing some very personal experiences to strangers is as uncomfortable as being in the dentist's chair. After the reading is over, a huge sigh of relief is heard around the room. This is the same feeling which occurs when the dentist turns off his drill and removes the protective paper from your chest. Suddenly, the pain has ceased. The anxiety and anticipation have built to a climax and then resolved. This course is not as simple as it sounds. I found myself thinking about writing even when the assignment was not due immediately. I found personal writing becoming a habit for me through the semester. I found it comforting to put some ideas on paper. I developed confidence in my skills. I grew as a person.

No professor at the college level has ever been concerned with personal writing before. Somewhere around fifth or sixth grade, we all stopped writing personal essays. Personal writing was, before this course, a distant grade school memory. It seems at times as if this is a purposeful effort on the part of grade school teachers. Suddenly it was not important what we were thinking as students, only what we could find in the way of research. In a way, this course was a flash back to the early grades of elementary school where the teacher was very interested in developing our thoughts. It was a time of more individual thinking, more original thoughts being recognized and considered. This course reminded me of the philosophy of individuality that I thrived under in my early school years.

In order to take this course, one must be prepared to be uncomfortable at times. Many of the essays that I wrote and listened to were painfully honest. It was painful to write an essay and it is painful to experience another person's trauma and tragedies. By the nature of this class, we became connected to one another. We have witnessed thoughts and emotions that were not shared with many people before. We became an inner circle. When I met a classmate from Expository Writing on campus, we would greet each other in a knowing way. A sense of mutual confidence was established by this course. While the thoughts and ideas shared in this class were important and relevant to the participants, they would not mean very much to an outsider. It would be impossible to recount the emotion that we heard as the voice of a classmate wavered as the essay was read. At times, I was riveted to my seat listening to very revealing essays.

This class was very important for a number of reasons. It forced me to share, to reflect, and to listen. Focusing on another person's ideas for a dedicated period of time is a lost art. We are a generation of people who flip from one idea to another and rarely focus on thoughts for long periods of time. Spending three hours a week dedicated to listening to classmates words was engrossing. This course is not for everyone. I would recommend it only to students who are willing to be part of a process. For this course to be effective, a student must be willing to let go of the conventionality of a classroom. This is a class of imagination and free thought. This is a class free of criticism, except for an occasional grammatical reminder. The pressure is purely self-induced. The amount of personal growth is also a matter of choice.

Going to the dentist can be an unpleasant experience. There are aspects of personal writing that can be unpleasant as well. It can be uncomfortable to think about unfavorable occurrences. Like the dental visit, it is necessary to talk and write about our favorite experiences. This allows us to put our ideas into perspective. One of the ultimate rewards of this course is one of pleasure. It is pleasurable to have a person trust you enough to share intimate thoughts. It is refreshing to experience honesty. We laughed, cried and were able to empathize with one another. This is a rare but desirable opportunity. As an added bonus of this course, writing skills were honed. By the end of the course we could not help but be improved as writers.

Painful Self-Disclosures

If personal writing resembles a visit to the dentist's office, then a certain degree of discomfort, even pain, seems inevitable. Resistance to self-disclosure is intense and should never be underestimated. As Erik Erikson points out in *Gandhi's Truth* (1969), the "term resistance was . . . adopted by Freud not as a moral opprobrium but as part of the physicalistic vocabulary of his time: some 'resistance' is in the nature of all response to inquiry" (65). Resistance is especially intense in inquiry that unmasks shame. The protocols I have outlined can minimize but not eliminate the inherent risks of personal writing. In some ways, writing is *more* painful than going to the dentist. A dentist can give a patient Novocain or nitrous oxide before extracting a tooth or filling a cavity. The teacher can offer no such anesthetic. Artists are notorious for relying on alcohol—the liquid muse—to overcome writer's block, but self-medication is generally destructive to their art. Writing is a lonely, introspective, and often torturous process, and students engaged in self-disclosure may confront fears that are more terrifying than those encountered in the dentist's chair.

Roberta: "All of the Feelings I Had Bottled Up for Two Years Were Unleashed in a Fury"

Reading an essay aloud adds another element of risk because the writer exposes these ghosts to the audience. Students have the option to remain anonymous and have me read their essays to the class; those who choose to read an essay aloud may find themselves unexpectedly at risk. This is what happened to Diane's classmate Roberta. Like Diane, she was a returning student, highly motivated and articulate, but midway through reading aloud an essay about an abusive relationship that had ended several years earlier, Roberta's voice began to falter, and everyone could see that she was becoming overwhelmed with emotion.

What's Love Got to Do with It?
We had been dating a few weeks. I was fourteen, he was seventeen. He told me he loved me. I laughed. We broke up two weeks later.

I never meant to be unkind. It was ridiculous to think that he could be in love after such a short time. We barely knew each other. Perhaps he loved me, but I doubted it.

Love is a difficult concept to define, because its meaning is different to everyone. An individual's definition is also subject to change. Time and experience contribute to love's dynamic status.

When I was a teenager, I was in love with the idea of love. I held an ideological view of what it was supposed to be. In my naivete, I believed that romance equaled love.

As a freshman in high school, I had a crush on a senior. He was an enigma to me, and that fueled my interest. He was athletic, moody, and played bass guitar in a band. His dream was to become an airline pilot. I was smitten. I did not let him know how I felt. He would never be interested in me. I was just a kid.

He graduated and went to college. I entered my sophomore year of high school. Like all crushes, this too, cooled. I enjoyed school, dating, and extracurricular activities. I had forgotten him, until a chance meeting brought us together. Summoning my courage, I told him of the crush I had on him the prior year. My heart was pounding. To my surprise and delight, he asked me out. I said yes. I would later regret doing so.

I was sixteen, he was nineteen. I knew my parents would never approve of the age difference, so I told them he was eighteen, and a senior. I felt terrible about lying, but considered it necessary.

The fights began almost immediately. I was uncomfortable with confrontation and attempted to diffuse difficult situations through compliance. This was a pattern I had already established in my life, so it was easily transferred to my romantic relationship. I needed to be the perfect daughter, student, and girlfriend. I could not disappoint others. If I had to compromise to keep the peace, I would do so. Compromise implies that both parties yield to come to an agreement. Unfortunately, I was the only one expected to bend.

This was one of many warning signs that I chose to ignore. He was older and more worldly than I, therefore, he knew what was best. I believed this. My lack of experience and trusting nature led to his total manipulation of me.

It started subtly. He "suggested" where we went, what we did, what time we left. My ideas were rejected as stupid or boring. This pattern continued slowly, but steadily, until it began to cover all areas of my life. He dictated my behavior even when I was not with him. I began to lose my identity.

He told me he loved me. I told him I loved him too, even though I didn't. It was expected of me. He pressured me to have sex with him. People in love were supposed to be intimate. I was scared. I wasn't ready, but complied. He was my first. It was awful.

I lived under a microscope of scrutiny. Every aspect of my life was controlled from the clothes I wore, what I ate, phone calls I made, music listened to, television programs watched, and people I spoke with. He picked me up from school everyday. I had less than five minutes from the end of my last class to go to my locker and get to his car. If I took too much time, a fight ensued. He constantly accused me of cheating on him, and tried to make me jealous by leaving phone numbers of other women in plain view in his dresser. All of my time was devoted to him. I became isolated from my friends and family. There were comments, but I ignored them. Friends and family raised concerns that I was withdrawn and unhappy. I denied it. I never felt so lonely in my life.

I could not understand how our relationship had anything to do with love. My ego was battered, and my self-esteem was non-existent. Love was power and I felt powerless. Any retaliatory attempt I made escalated into violence. I was afraid and ashamed. I hid my misery as well as I could. I carried eye drops in my purse to conceal from my parents that I had been crying. Every night when he took me home, I sat outside until I was composed enough to face my parents. I cried every day for two years.

He hit me. It started as an occasional slap on the face, but at times, he used his fists. It was my fault for making him lose control. I fought back, but it only made confrontations worse. One day, during a fight, he shoved me into a wall and I fell. I hit my head so hard I saw stars. From that moment, I decided that I would never let anyone do that to me again. (To give levity to an otherwise terrible situation, one could say I had some sense knocked into me.) As he tried to comfort me, I yelled. I told him to get out. I hated him. He left, but came back the next day. I accepted it.

Roberta began hyperventilating as she recalled the violence of the relationship. It became obvious that she was having difficulty, and when I asked her if she wanted me to read the rest of her essay, she exclaimed, "No! I can finish this!" She regained her composure after a few seconds and completed the essay in an assertive voice.

It took me another week to harness all the rage I was feeling. I summoned the courage to leave him forever. I was home alone, and he entered through our sliding glass door, just as he had done a thousand times. When I saw him, I screamed. All of the feelings I had bottled up for two years were unleashed in a fury. The only words I could form were "GET OUT!" I screamed these over and over, while he stood in the doorway with his mouth agape. My knees buckled. I fell to the floor, but did not stop screaming until he turned and left the house. It was cathartic. I was emotionally spent, but felt as if the weight of the world had been lifted from me, and I was free. I was eighteen years old.

I felt empowered. I was strong. I realized that I had been in an abusive relationship which had been operating under the guise of love. My instincts were not wrong. I had never been in love.

Rather than see myself as a victim, I relished my new life. I decided to view the experience as character building. This was one of the first steps I took toward independence. I did not need to be in a relationship to feel complete. I was responsible for my happiness.

I spent the next five years on my own. While there were occasions when I felt it would be nice to be in a relationship, I was not ready for a commitment. Occasional dates were satisfying enough. When I was twenty-three, I began dating seriously again. While the man I was involved with was kind and loving, I did not love him. Our relationship was comfortable, but dull. We had little in common. I think each of us liked the stability a relationship offered.

Suddenly, my life changed forever. While doing seasonal sales work, I met William. He made me laugh. We became friends. After a month, he confessed his feelings for me. I resisted. I was already in a relationship. I told him I only liked him as a friend, but it was a lie. He knew it, too. William was respectful, but persistent. Couldn't I see that we belonged together? Our meeting was fate. We belonged together. It was destiny.

I laughed at this, yet every night when I went home, I thought of him. I was torn between my stable existence and wanting to be with William. The longer I tried to deny how I felt, the more I yearned to be with him. I cried over my predicament. I didn't want to hurt anyone. My desire to be with William was so strong that when I was away from him, I physically ached. I had heard of heartaches from love, but had never experienced feelings re-

sembling this before. I had never been in so much pain before, yet had never been so joyful. I was in love. I broke the news to my boyfriend. He was hurt and confused. He suspected infidelity. Admittedly, I betrayed him in my heart, but was never physically unfaithful. I hoped I was making the right choice. I followed my heart.

That was more than five years ago. William and I have built a life together. Our relationship is based on commitment, understanding, and respect. We enjoy each other's company, and surprise each other with romantic gestures. When we found each other, we found love.

Roberta's essay contains some of the shame issues seen in Diane's, including fear and powerlessness in the presence of a man whose actions stripped her of her dignity. Like Diane, she experienced this humiliation as a form of silencing, and she tried to convey to her audience the rage and self-loathing she felt at the time. It was precisely during the moment when she described the violence against her that Roberta found herself unable to proceed with the narration. This was the moment of her greatest vulnerability, when her shame was overwhelming. The memory of that experience was still traumatic more than a decade later. But the story changed from one of victimization to self-empowerment once she was able to get past the passage where she left her abusive boyfriend, and she had no trouble reading the second half of the essay.

Opponents of personal writing warn that students may unwittingly open a Pandora's box when disclosing certain subjects. This may sometimes happen, but my own classroom experience suggests that it is more common for students to unleash the power of personal writing. Roberta herself uses language that evokes a creative explosion of emotion. The most forceful part of her essay occurs when she refers to her ability to "harness all the rage" she was feeling at the time: "All of the feelings I had bottled up for two years were unleashed in a fury." Roberta's creativity is released, paradoxically, when she acknowledges her moment of greatest shame. The short sentences that she uses earlier in the essay suddenly expand, as if to contain and hold in check violent emotions. Analyzing the ambiguities of love, infatuation, and idealization, she is not afraid to tell the reader how, after extricating herself from one unsatisfactory relationship, she later found herself in another, from which she was once again able to escape.

Roberta's essay was the last one read that evening, and since it produced so much empathic distress among her classmates, we ended class without much discussion. I would not have asked Roberta to read the essay had I known how disturbing it would be for her and her classmates. As noted, I try to prescreen essays to make sure they are not too intense for classroom discussions, but she had turned hers in at the beginning of class, and I felt it would be appropriate to read. Roberta agreed to read the essay, though I later realized that she was surprised by my request. I would not have asked her to read the essay aloud had she been describing an ongoing abusive relationship—such situations are generally too unsettling for the writer and the audience. The abusive relationship had ended several years ago, however, and the essay reflects clarity and control, suggesting that Roberta could safely write and talk about it. Yet one can never predict when a "safe" essay will become risky for the writer or reader.

After class ended, I did not know whether Roberta regretted sharing the experience with her classmates. She recounted in the essay that years earlier she had "lived under a microscope of scrutiny." In disclosing that time in her life, she was once again subjecting herself to scrutiny, this time from her teacher and classmates. She described her abusive boyfriend as a manipulator. Had I, too, manipulated her into doing something against her better judgment? Would her essay on victimization inadvertently lead to revictimization? Nor was I reassured by the Post-it note she attached to her next essay: "Based on the difficulty I experienced reading my essay last week, I have chosen anonymity for this one. I am uncomfortable with the thought of even hearing this read aloud, but, of course, if you want me to read it to the class, I'm sure I'll be okay." The following week Roberta turned in a detailed response essay in which she described how she felt about her previous self-disclosure to the class.

I don't know why I chose to write about my past abusive relationship. The assignment we were given was "Falling In and Out of Love." My experience did not involve love. It's strange that when I thought about what I was going to write, that relationship came to mind. It was not love, but as a naive girl of sixteen, I was told that was what it was. It happened twelve years ago and I believed I rarely thought of it. This was not the case. It is still a part of me, and it will always be. The emotions I experienced writing about this subject were similar to what I felt when writing the paper about my mom. I was moody, depressed, and distracted. I was also short-tempered and I hadn't yet written a word. While thinking about what I would disclose in my essay, I had to relive the events of those two years of my life. That was terrible. I decided that although I felt vulnerable and uncomfortable, I would be as honest as possible. It was time to explore how I felt after all of these years.

I felt empowered after leaving the relationship. I see myself as strong and secure with whom I am. When I sat down to write the essay, I became a scared teenage girl again, and I didn't like it. I had to harness my feelings in order to tell my story. This was hard for me to do, because as I wrote, the experiences came to life on the page. They were real. I think part of me always wanted to deny what happened. I have always felt guilty for allowing myself to get into that situation to begin with. I knew I shouldn't blame myself, but I realized that I do. I told myself after I was out of the relationship that I was not angry at what happened. I chose to go on with my life. I realized when writing the essay that I have unresolved anger that I have never allowed myself to feel or express. I needed to vent my emotions.

I have only told my story to a few people in my life, but not in detail. I had never written it down before. I think by doing so, I was finally able to face the feelings I have been carrying with me for all of these years: shame, anger, and guilt. It felt good to put the words on paper. I felt safe knowing I could share my feelings with someone. Once again, I felt empowered. It reminded me of a passage in the Willa Cather short story, "Paul's Case." In Paul's life there had been "the shadowed corner, the dark place into which he dared not look, but from which something seemed always to be watching him . . ." (76). When he finally faced his fear, he was relieved. "It was bad enough, what he saw there, but somehow not as bad as his long fear of it had been" (83). When I read the story, I identified with Paul. I, too, did not want to face certain events in my past, but decided it was necessary. When I did, I felt better, as Paul did. "He had a curious sense of relief, as though he had at last thrown down the gauntlet to the thing in the corner" (76). Yes.

When I handed in the paper, I did not expect to read it aloud. I hesitated briefly when you asked me to read it to the class. I knew you had only skimmed it. I was scared, but said yes. I had the strength to live through it, so I knew I could read it. My worry was burdening my classmates with my depressing tale. No one wants to hear the woes of another. We have enough problems of our own without having to shoulder someone else's. I decided that since it was so far in the past, it would be okay to read.

When you chose others to read before me, I could barely concentrate on what was being said. My heart was pounding so hard I thought it would beat out of my chest. I was nervous; I couldn't sit still. My face felt flushed, and I wanted you to call on me so I could get my turn over with. In spite of my nerves, I never thought of not reading the paper aloud. I did not realize that I would have so much difficulty saying the words aloud.

When it was my turn, I was terrified. I looked down at my hands and they were shaking. I didn't know why I was so scared. Perhaps I didn't want to admit that this had happened to me. I took a deep breath and started to read. I felt as if I could do it. I spoke slowly and purposefully. My voice started to quiver. I was not handling my nerves well. When I started to explain some of the events that took place in the relationship, I had to stop for a moment. I couldn't breathe. My heart was pounding fast and hard. The noise it made in my ears was deafening. I tried to take deep breaths to better control my shaking voice, but nothing was working. I could not look up from my paper. I focused all of my energy on containing my emotions. When I had a particularly long pause, you asked me if I wanted to have you finish reading it for me. This was such a kind gesture, but I could not consider accepting the offer. I lived this experience and it was up to me to own it. As I explained events at the end of the relationship, I was angry. The words "GET OUT" resonated in my mind. I wanted to scream them aloud, just as I had done twelve years earlier. As I neared the end of my essay, I was more in control, but could not slow my heartbeat or stop my hands from shaking.

When I finished, I felt relieved. The room was silent. I looked only at you when I handed the paper back. You ended class. My face felt so hot. A few women came up to me to see if I was alright. I was. It took me twenty minutes to drive home. My heart raced the whole time. The memories flooded my mind, and could not be suppressed. I took deep breaths to slow my body down, but it did not work. When I got home, my boyfriend's smile greeted me. He was making dinner for us, and he wanted me to sit in the kitchen with him and keep him company. I couldn't. I had to be by myself for awhile. I explained what had happened in class, how I struggled reading my paper. He understood and asked me if he could do anything. I said no.

It took another half an hour for me to completely calm down. My heart rate returned to normal, but I still felt uncomfortable. The feelings I had buried so long ago were back and I hadn't expected them to be so powerful. The momentary vulnerability I experienced while reading the paper was worth it. I had faced the thing in the dark corner and thrown down the gauntlet, and it felt good.

Neither Roberta nor Diane had disclosed these shameful experiences before. Writing compelled them to relive the details of their traumatic experiences and uncover the depth of their unresolved anger. In addition, writing enabled them to find the words to describe harrowing experiences and construct coherent meanings that would initiate healing. Reading their essays aloud momentarily brought back all the terrors. Both described in strikingly similar words the ways in which the symptoms of risky writing are inscribed on the body: flushed face, pounding heart, quivering voice, shaking hands. Both wondered about the outcome of their self-disclosures. I, too, wondered. Even as Roberta described how she had "thrown down the gauntlet," as does Willa Cather's troubled protagonist, I couldn't help but silently observe, "Yes, but Paul throws himself onto a rushing train at the end of the story."

What if Roberta had gotten into a car accident after class? I often think about this question. She tells us that her heart was racing the entire trip home and that memories of the distant abuse flooded her mind. Was she experiencing symptoms of posttraumatic stress disorder? Did the writing—or reading—of the essay endanger her health? I had spoken to her briefly after class and she assured me that she was okay, but what if she wasn't? If she had injured herself or others on the ride home, would I have been partly responsible—not necessarily in a legal sense (although Frederic Gale might argue to the contrary here) but in a more ambiguous psychological sense?

Roberta's story has a happier ending than does "Paul's Case," but this does not resolve the question of a teacher's responsibility to his or her students. I suggested earlier that teachers must maintain professional boundaries, yet at the same time I must acknowledge that reading an essay like Roberta's creates a bond that may not exist in a more traditional writing classroom. This connection is deepened when teachers and students share personal information with each other that exposes vulnerability. A student's story about sexual violence may place his or her teacher or classmates in a painful situation. "The intimacy of the reading experience," Laura Tanner suggests, "often allows us to come close to characters and experiences that we might otherwise never encounter; by the same token, however, it can force our intimacy by subtly pushing us into imaginative landscapes of violation from which it is difficult to extricate ourselves" (ix). I was worried about Roberta's well-being, as were her classmates; one cannot fail to be moved when hearing a story about abuse. Nevertheless, I trusted that Roberta was all right and that she would make it home safely. And she trusted that her classmates would be able to understand and appreciate her essay without becoming unduly burdened. Neither Roberta's anxiety nor my own implied a breakdown in boundaries, trust, or control.

Transformative Experiences

Literature teachers often talk about reading and writing as potentially transformative experiences, but we must be careful not to misuse the word, since we cannot know whether another person is truly being transformed. Moreover, genuine transformations must endure the test of time, and I do not have long-term data on any of my writing students. Nevertheless, many of the writings that appear in this book, including Diane's and Roberta's, may be viewed as "transformative tales," which Richard Haswell defines in the following way: "In gist, the transformative tale relates how an initial state of internal instability is shocked into a kind of self-reflection that learns a new knowledge or skill by unlearning and revising old knowledge or skill" (131). Transformative tales tend to focus on risky topics that have been repressed for a long time and evoke intense resistance when expressed. Although transformative tales often involve pain or shame, they also affirm insight, agency, and change, the possibility of overcoming past traumas or mistakes and forging a new life. These stories recall the ancient Socratic injunction, Know thyself. Phrased in terms of contemporary cognitive theory, transformative stories reveal how the construction of a new interpretation enables the writer to remake the self. The writer's search for the right words to describe a risky story thus involves nothing less than the search for wholeness. This search requires teachers and students to be sensitive to language, the instrument for change and development. As James Baumlin, George Jensen, and Lance Massey observe in an article on the ethics of growth, a "more sophisticated approach to autobiography . . . would reveal the simultaneous presence of two rhetorics. One, a rhetoric of identity, seeks out the stable, knowable characteristics of the self; the second, a rhetoric of transformation, discovers those moments in time, typically crises and 'conversion experiences,' when the self is changed and *identity thus remade*. Identity ranges across a continuum of transformations" (206; emphasis in original).

To judge from her own words, Roberta's essay helped her to discover and vent the unresolved anger arising from a traumatic experience. The essay has both aesthetic and therapeutic value: it is well written, specific, and compelling, supporting bell hooks's observation in *Remembered Rapture* that "one can have a complete imaginative engagement with writing as craft and still experience it in a manner that is therapeutic; one urge does not diminish the other" (14). Reading the essay aloud turned out to be the riskiest part of the process, but despite Roberta's fear that the essay would prove onerous to her classmates, several observed in their final evaluation that it was one of the most memorable writings of the semester. Witness this comment from a male student:

There were many interesting moments from the class this semester. The one memory which I will never forget was when one student read aloud her experience of being in an abusive relationship. She began her essay telling everyone how the relationship started. She was a teenager and she started a relationship with a person whom she had a crush on. The essay started with what appeared as a positive relationship. Like her relationship, the story became more hurtful. As she was speaking I noticed that her voice was start-ing to crack, her face became red, and tears swelled in her eyes. I wanted to get up from my seat, walk over to her, and put my hand on her shoulder. I did not because I knew that I was not the only one in the class who wanted to help her. The entire class was conveying their support to her, by being atten-tive and listening. There were no gestures just a silent understanding. She paused to let her heart slow down and catch her breath. Dr. Berman asked if she would like him to finish her essay for her, and she refused. At this point in her essay where she became strong and left her boyfriend, so did her voice. As she spoke of a new love, she smiled again. The class had to end. Leaving the room I felt proud of my class. Rarely are students here polite or sympa-thetic. There were other stories told that night which dealt with similar sub-ject matters. All of the other essays were just as serious and they proved how strong people can be when they have to. This situation will never occur in a class taught in a lecture center, or where your behavior influences your grade. It could only happen in a room where every person wants to be more human.

How, one might ask, is this experience—indeed, the entire course—different from a talk show? To begin with, students read their essays qui-etly, without any rhetorical flourishes. Their voices may reflect the emo-tional content of their writings, but the dramatic moments do not deteriorate into melodrama. One might expect students to write sensationalistically, but this rarely happens. Most students know what to reveal and what to conceal, and they remain sensitive to their audience, not wishing to bur-den classmates with more than they can endure. I don't sense competition among students to write the most shocking essay but rather a growing will-ingness to disclose something important about themselves, something they wish to share with classmates. A self-disclosure is an offering or a gift that allows insight into the writer's life. The most intense self-disclosures gen-erally occur near the end of the semester, when students realize that the course is ending. They may become visibly distressed while reading an essay aloud, and occasionally my own eyes water. Yet one need not feel ashamed of these moments: tears are as appropriate as smiles.

Unlike talk show viewers, students do not respond to a classmate's essay with thunderous applause or Clintonesque cries of "I feel your pain." In-stead, they remain silent for a few seconds and then offer affirming com-ments, at first tentatively and then more boldly. Students may be shocked by an essay on molestation or physical abuse, but they are always respectful and attentive. It is true that students will occasionally respond to the completion of an essay with lowered eyes and wait for the teacher to begin, as Lucia Perillo reports, but I don't feel the necessity, as she does, to "patter about structure and shape and specificity of image." Since I write extensive comments on an essay before I return it to the student, it is not always necessary to discuss it in class. Some risky essays may elicit little classroom discussion, but they have a powerful impact on an audience, heightening the reader's empathic imagination. The silence produced by certain essays is not unlike John Keats's Negative Capability: "that is when man is capable of being in uncertainties, Mysteries, doubts, without any irritable reaching after fact & reason" (261).

It is time to look at some of the risky subjects that students describe in their expository writing class. These topics emerged from rather unusual biographical assignments and produced both Keatsian and non-Keatsian uncertainties, mysteries, and doubts in the students and their teacher.

CHAPTER 2

Seeing Ourselves through the Eyes of Others

In Thornton Wilder's Our Town, *Emily Webb was given the chance to see her life from an outsider's point of view. Through our biography assignments, we were afforded the same opportunity.*

How do college students write about themselves? What events do they identify as the most significant in their lives? Which topics are the most painful for them to write about, eliciting anguish, guilt, and shame? To what extent are they willing to share personal aspects of themselves with classmates, in the process narrowing the distance between self and other? Can a painful or shameful subject awaken a writer's creativity?

These are some of the questions I explore in this chapter. I focus on three biographical assignments that I gave to my expository writing students at the beginning of the semester. The assignments were unusual in that they encouraged students not only to write about their lives but also to share their experiences with classmates, who would become their biographers. I asked the students to "take the role of another person," in George Mead's words, and to understand and empathize with their classmates' lives.

The Assignments

Assignment 1

Draw up a chronology of ten important events in your life, ranging from birth to the present. For each event, write one or two paragraphs on its significance. Such events may include your first day in school, the birth or death of a relative, your first love experience, a particular success or failure, a serious illness, a memorable college experience, an event that shaped your career plans, etc. Provide enough factual material for the details of your life to be known to another person, and enough psychological material to make your autobiography interesting. The autobiographical events should focus on the past but also suggest the kind of person you are now and how you might be in the future.

Assignment 2

After you have drawn up this autobiographical chronology, exchange it with a classmate. Your classmate will read your chronology, interview you for additional material, and get to know the salient details of your life. You will do the same with your classmate, interviewing him or her for additional information. Your classmate will go home and write a biography of you, using your material as a basis for the biography. Just as your classmate is writing a biography of you, so will you be writing a biography of him or her.

Please start working on your autobiographical chronology immediately. It is due next week; at that time, I will pair you with a classmate whom you will be interviewing. He or she in turn will interview you during the same class. The completed biography of your classmate is due in two weeks. Please bring twenty-five copies of your biography with you on that date. Your classmate will bring twenty-five copies of his or her biography of you. All of us will be reading and discussing these biographies for two or three weeks. The biographies should be at least two single-spaced pages long.

Since you will be writing about a classmate's life, it is especially important to be sensitive and accurate. It might be a good idea to telephone your classmate after you have written a first draft of your essay so that you can receive his or her reactions to it.

Assignment 3

I will assign you a new partner with whom to work. Choose one biographical event that you find intriguing in your classmate's essay, interview him or her in class about the details of this event, and then develop it into a new essay. Your classmate will do the same with you.

A few suggestions for Assignment 3:
- Make sure your classmate is willing to elaborate on the biographical event that you wish to write about. Be sure to handle sensitive material sensitively.
- Don't assume that your reader will be familiar with your classmate's biographical essay. Describe the event in detail: showing is better than telling. Try to capture your classmate's feelings during this moment in his or her life.
- It might be interesting for the two of you to choose a similar event to write about, such as leaving home for the first time, falling in or out of love, losing a relative, going away to college, etc. If you do write about similar events, you might want to discuss (toward the end of your essay) the extent to which your classmate's experience of this event resembles your own.
- If you need more time to interview your classmate, try to find another day this week that is convenient for both of you.
- This assignment should be written in the form of an essay rather than an interview. The essay is due in three weeks. You need make only two copies of assignment 3, one for your classmate and the other for me.

Each student was thus paired with two classmates and collaborated with them in the writing of two different biographies. The first assignment, the autobiographical paragraphs, would be the basis for the second and third assignments, but only the second assignment would be read by the entire class. The three assignments emphasized collaborative learning and multiple perspectives: each student would be both a biographer and biographee.

Since one of the purposes of the biographical assignments was to encourage the students to get to know each other, they did not have the option to remain anonymous. They could remain anonymous, I told them, in their later essays, in which I alone would know their identities. The students retained the right to determine the degree of self-disclosure of their autobiographical paragraphs: they could simply omit any experience that was too personal.

Before handing out the first two biographical assignments, which I modified from Scholes and Comley's *The Practice of Writing* (1981), I stressed the importance of empathy. The students had two good reasons to remain empathic: as biographers, they did not want to hurt their classmates' feelings, and as biographees, they did not want their own feelings to be hurt.

What Did Students Write About?

Death, love, and birth were the three most common subjects students wrote about in their autobiographical paragraphs. Nineteen of the twenty-four students acknowledged the death (in decreasing order of frequency) of a grandparent, friend, parent, or sibling. Fifteen wrote about love or friendship. Twelve referred to a birth, either their own, which they recorded without much commentary, or that of a sibling or cousin. Next came writing about a hobby or sport (twelve), describing their parents' separation or divorce (eight), going to college (eight), graduating from high school or college (seven), being sexually assaulted (six), arriving in the United States for the first time (four), going to camp (four), and attending the first day of kindergarten or elementary school (four).

I did not ask the students to determine how many of their ten autobiographical events seemed a risky subject on which to write. To judge from their descriptions of each event, the risky topics included academic dismissal, the breakup of a relationship, parental separation or divorce, sexual assault, depression, and death. The number of risky subjects each student wrote on differed widely. Six students wrote on one risky topic, five students on two, six students on three, three students on four, two students on five, one student on six, and one student on seven.

I focus on four students—Kevin, Alexandra, Colleen, and James. They did not know each other before the course began, but since they sat near each other during the beginning of the semester, they wrote one or both of their biographical essays on students in this group. (The pairings were not perfectly symmetrical because Colleen and James had one of their biographical essays written by students outside of this group.) Each wrote about at least one emotionally charged event in the autobiographical paragraphs and returned to this or a related event in a later essay, in the process elaborating on what was written earlier.

Their essays dramatize the dynamics of risky writing: the writer discloses, often hesitatingly, a painful or shameful event and then returns to it weeks or months later, offering additional details. We can witness students overcoming resistance as they confront traumatic events for the first time. The biographers play a crucial role in their subjects' writings, for they not only tell their classmates' stories publicly for the first time but also lay the groundwork for later essays.

The quality of the four students' writing skills differs considerably: some of the essays are relatively well written while others are filled with grammatical, spelling, and typographical errors. Kevin, Alexandra, Colleen, and James were neither the strongest nor the weakest writers in the class. Although some of them had endured shocking experiences, no one could tell from looking at them that their biographies were unusual. Their lives were touched by tragedy, but they did not regard their lives as tragic. Seeing themselves not as victims but as survivors, they didn't believe their stories are depressing, nor do I.

Kevin: "At the Time of the Divorce I Didn't Have So Much Respect"

Kevin wrote about three topics that caused him great pain: the death of his baby sister when he was six, the divorce of his parents a decade later, and the death of his grandmother shortly thereafter.

Death of my sister: *I had to be around 6 years old (my brother was around 4) or so when my sister died. At the time I think I had just accepted her as a family member and so it was pretty shocking to hear that she had passed away. I actually remember the night fairly clearly. My family was visiting my aunt and uncle (where my only living grandmother presided as well) for dinner one night and my sister was put to bed on my grandmother's bed. The next thing I remember, a flurry of activity was under way — an ambulance arrived and my brother and I were left staying on a side of the house not sure what to think. I was too young at the time to really have a full grasp on the events that were taking place as I can remember the funeral as a time where I watched everyone and didn't quite know what they were crying for.*

As it turns out, my sister passed away that very night in my grandmother's bed (or soon after). She was a S.I.D.S. (Sudden Infant Death Syndrome) baby and so there was nothing that could have been done. It was her time to leave this world yet none of us could grasp that reality, and rightfully so.

In 3rd grade I remember my first response to her death. I was sitting in a group and we were sharing things that happened in our lives and I started relating her story. I don't remember why I picked that story but that was the day when I realized that I had had a sister and that she was gone. Needless to say I started bawling my eyes out! It sticks out to me because for a long time after I thought I was extremely embarrassed over crying in class like that but now I am happy I did so.

Divorce of My Parents: The next logical follow-up would be to tell about my parent's divorce. I believe it happened when I was about 16 years old (my brother would be around 14). Some of the events that may have caused it are the death of my sister (never having recovered from the loss), my father's habit of golfing and drinking on Friday nights (something he has done for as long as I've known—he isn't a violent man though), and the fact that in life they were heading separate ways. I do not know any more then this nor do I really want to. It was their choice and I truly respect it.

At the time of the divorce I didn't have so much respect. The times leading up to the divorce and the short time where they presided in the same house while going through the divorce were really painful for me and my brother. I remember doing a lot of stupid things such as smashing doors and breaking glasses on the kitchen floor to take out my aggression. I don't remember my brother doing as much violent outward stuff but I think that hurt him more because he bottled it up inside.

The divorce procedure had my brother and I having to choose where we would live. Actually I remember I had the right to choose, but my brother being only 14 didn't have a choice, though I would have stayed with him and fought for him. We chose to stay with whoever would get the house. At that point I didn't really want to relocate anywhere so this was the best possible move.

For awhile it didn't seem like either parent would back out and move out but then my grandmother (my mom's mother) died and her house on the next road up became available (the houses are connected through the woods). My mom made a bold decision and undoubtedly a painful decision and moved into that house, letting my father win the rights to the house my brother and I wanted to stay in.

I regret not having spent more time after the divorce with her as I know she went through a lot of pain trying to get her life together and having her sons living somewhere else didn't help. I know that was a time when my brother and I might have felt like she abandoned us. We were still angry with her for being the catalyst for the divorce, as Dad seemed to be happy and content to have the marriage continue on. I think many of the memories and such have faded away and my relationship with my mother has improved greatly. She is in a way my mentor, my guiding light through college as I try to find something occupation-wise that I can live with.

Death of Grandmother: I wanted to include this as it ties into the previous entry a little but also as I remember this grandmother as someone I used to go talk to all the time and visit continuously. She smoked (yuck) and because of this her lungs were in terrible shape, most likely a reason leading to her untimely death. I remember crying at the funeral in remembrance of her, remembering how she wanted me to drive her around town because she could no longer drive herself. I regretted for awhile after her passing not ever having the chance to take her shopping or out to visit her friends. In a way she was one of my friends when I was younger and extremely introverted.

Kevin writes clearly about each of these painful events, though he has neither the time nor space to develop any of them. Contrasting his older and younger selves, he implies that the former is better able to understand these events than the latter. He acknowledges actions that he later regrets, and one senses that the three losses he describes are in the distant past— they have shaped his life, but he has come to terms with them. He refers to "doing a lot of stupid things" during his parents' divorce, but he doesn't elaborate on his feelings at that time.

Kevin's first biographer, Alexandra, used many of the concrete details he had given her and frames them to emphasize the theme of loss. She elaborates on the pain of divorce for parent and child alike, noting that "children have serious amounts of aggression that they either repress or act upon." She has a keen understanding of the difficulties created by divorce. "We all want our family to stay together happily ever after, but the realization that your family is not is rather tough. Teenagers have a normal tendency to hate the world anyway . . . and aggressive action is the outcome many times, even from typically good kids."

Kevin's second biographer, Colleen, focuses on his "hellish" pain, a word she uses three times, and her essay contains a dramatic power that is absent from Alexandra's account. Attuned to suffering, Colleen seems to know from experience that people often act unwisely during crises. She begins her essay by using the second-person pronoun, and once she lures the reader into the story, she enters into her classmate's inner life. "Sixteen is a hard enough age to handle; emotions, hormones, decisions about your future, *the prom*. Life is complicated, so you feel, so news that your parents are going to get divorced doesn't make life any easier. In fact, it can actually make you feel like you're in hell. For Kevin, hell was about to break loose in his family." She uses the present tense to describe one of Kevin's acts of aggression following news of his parents' divorce. "One night in particular, Kevin vividly remembers that his parents had done something to make him very upset. Anger, aggression, frustration, and confusion come together at once as Kevin smashes a glass onto the floor. This happens on a few occasions, along with the occasional door smashing, as Kevin needed to vent his anger. He felt so resentful towards his parents for breaking up the family." Colleen is careful to avoid blaming anyone for the conflicts in Kevin's family, and she ends her essay hopefully, affirming her subject's bright future.

Alexandra: "This Was the Longest Day in My Life"

Three of Alexandra's autobiographical paragraphs focused on painful events: her parents' separation and divorce when she was sixteen followed by her grandfather's illness and death:

April 1993: *Within a two week span, my parents split up, and my sister, mom, and I move to a new community. The neighborhood is nothing what we are used to. My sister and I are absolutely miserable there. I start my first job, working at Subway, the same day that I started my new school. The job lasts two weeks until I quit. I purposely graduated a semester early, just so that I can get out of school quicker.*

May 1993: *I went to visit my grandparents, my grandfather was not feeling well. I made a few phone calls, to find out what was wrong. He went to the hospital the next day, he needed to have his kidney removed as soon as possible. They had found a tumor on it. Everything went well, he was feeling better. As time progressed, he looked healthier than he had in years.*

September 18, 1997: *My grandfather passes away. He had been in and out of hospitals for the past three months. He had been on chemo for a year (the cancer had come back after 2 years, and was now everywhere). My housemate gets the message from my sister while I was in class. She meets me at the bus stop on campus because we were supposed to go to the mall. She tells me right then and there. I break out in tears in front of 200 SUNY students. I get on the bus, wearing a friends sunglasses, and go to my house.*

I pack while my 3 housemates call a cab, call the bus, and make me a sandwich. I feel numb, and I don't know how I make it out to my grandmothers house. This was the longest day in my life.

Unlike Kevin, Alexandra does not describe her feelings about her parents' divorce, focusing instead on her grandfather's illness and death. Perhaps it was easier for her to write about Kevin's parents' divorce than her own. Her autobiographical paragraphs are brief and largely factual.

Alexandra's first biographer, Kevin, expanded on the reasons for her parents' divorce and revealed a detail that she had omitted from her autobiographical paragraphs. "She is hesitant to admit that her father is a recovered alcoholic. The alcohol drove her away from her father when she was 15. One day she entered her house and found her father passed out drunk. She was so upset that she packed up her things and went to her grandmother's house. She angrily refused to go home until the next day, but even then she would not speak to her father." Kevin is quick to point out that Alexandra's father eventually stopped drinking and that the two of them have improved their relationship.

Alexandra's second biographer, James, explored in detail the devastation arising from her grandfather's death. James begins his essay by suggesting that the way we confront death reveals something important about the way we confront our lives. "Death is an obstacle that every man, woman, or child must face at some point in their lives. People deal with the reality of death in a variety of ways. Some people cry, others shut themselves off from the rest of the world, while others pretend not to let it bother them. The manner in which we deal with this pain, the loss of a loved one, is one of the defining characteristics of our humanity. In essence, the way we handle our emotions plays a role in establishing ourselves against everybody else."

Colleen: "There Was One Event That I Will Never Forget"

Colleen was familiar with tragedy: seven of her autobiographical events described painful losses, including the tragic death of a high school boyfriend.

While living in another state, still at fifteen, there was one event that I will never forget about, less than a year after my grandmother's death. School was going pretty good and I was making a lot of new friends. I started to really like one guy in particular who was in my English and drama class. I told a few friends over a period of a few weeks, but of course the whole school found out. It got back to him. He confronted me one day after drama class and asked me for my phone number. We spoke a couple of times over the phone and I was so happy. I couldn't believe he liked me too. We set up a date for the following Friday. That Wednesday I was sick and stayed home from school. He called me to see how I was doing and told me he couldn't wait for Friday night. Later on that evening he stopped by to say hi. We talked for a little while on the porch before my mom came home from work. It was a chilly December night and he gave me his sweater to put on. He kissed me goodbye and hugged me tight. The next day I was still sick and stayed home again. My friend called me up in the afternoon and told me that Sam had died late last night. He was crossing the street late at night to go to a friend's house and was hit by a drunk driver. I dropped the phone and cried. A knock came at my door. Three of my friends were standing at the door crying. He was only fifteen years old.

Colleen offered few concrete details in her autobiographical paragraphs about her boyfriend's death, perhaps because these details were too distressing to reveal. Nor did her first biographer, from another group, elaborate on this incident. But her second biographer, Kevin, imagined how she must have felt grieving her boyfriend's death. Kevin notes that she remembers crying over the graphic descriptions of the death. Although he may have sensed that the inclusion of these details in his biographical essay might be too upsetting to her, he offers enough specific details to convey the tragedy to the reader, including a reference to the death car, which "emerged out of the darkness with no lights on." Kevin also tells us that Colleen dressed as the "Grim Reaper" during Halloween, a detail that captures her preoccupation with death. Kevin does not dwell on morbidity or sadness, however, and his final sentence memorializes the young man whose spirit remains alive to Colleen.

James: "It Was the Hardest Thing I Ever Had to Go through in My Life"

Three of James's autobiographical paragraphs were devoted to his father, Thomas, whom he mentions immediately after recording the details of his birth twenty-two years ago:

My memory skips a few years after that until I was about five. Myself and my two parents lived in a tiny apartment in Staten Island. My father and myself had grown a very close bond by then. I was his first born and for a while his only son. I developed a hero like image of my father when I saw him save a man's life. An elderly lady came banging on our door screaming that her son had died. I was told to stay put, but I could not resist. I sneaked into her apartment and watched my father give him CPR. I remember the paramedics saying that he saved the boy's life.

The bond with my father continued to grow when we moved out of that apartment. My parents bought a house in Staten Island and the move was very fun for me. The house needed a lot of work. My father used to let me help him. I was probably getting into his way, but it made me feel like I was really helping with the house. For a while I can truly say that my father was my best friend.

Twenty years old, summer of my second year at Albany, my father passes on. Well you can imagine how I would have felt, but I didn't have time. My mother was a mess, almost like she was in a coma. She cried for three days straight. I had to take care of all the arrangements. It was better this way, it kept me busy. It was the hardest thing I ever had to go through in my life. My friends and family were there for me, but those are feelings only you can deal with. The whole experience taught me how to be a man.

James asks us to "imagine" how he felt when his father died but offers no clues. He acknowledges, however, his mother's devastation. One senses, perhaps, that he doesn't wish to share these feelings with the reader—"those are feelings only you can deal with."

James's first biographer, from another group, tries to imagine what it must feel like suddenly to lose a parent but provides few additional details about the death. We learn neither the cause of his father's death nor its impact on his life. Answers to these questions emerge from James's second biographer, Alexandra, who describes Thomas's long history of hospitalization for manic depression and the "family secret" that prevented his children from knowing about the illness. She recounts a fateful argument that occurred between father and son when he was a sophomore in college. "One of the biggest regrets that James has in his life was the fight that him and his father had when James was home on Christmas break. James's best friend had come by to pick James up to go watch a football game. Thomas started to have a panic attack, saying that he wanted to go to the hospital. It had been previously agreed by the family and the doctor he was going to try and work on this at home. Every time that he had been to the hospital, he would leave after two days or a week. On this day, Thomas threatened to kill himself if James left the house. James handed him the knife and dared him to do it; Thomas did not. His father still wanted to go to the hospital. James grabbed him, threw him down to the ground, told him that he was not going there, and then left. He saw the look on his father's face, and knew that he had made a big mistake. It was too late now to change it." After informing us in a brief sentence that Thomas eventually shot himself in the head, Alexandra describes the "scary relief" James felt. "It had been two and a half years of fighting, and tension, and Thomas had not gotten any better. In a sense, he was glad that the whole thing was over. This is not to say that he wanted something like this to happen, he just felt relief."

Student Biographers

The autobiographical paragraphs reveal the students' willingness to write about events that are seldom discussed in a university classroom. For the most part, the writers are not afraid to disclose experiences associated with intense pain or shame. Thus Kevin acknowledges "doing a lot of stupid things" in response to his parents' divorce; Alexandra recalls breaking out in tears upon learning of her grandfather's death and feeling numb afterward; Colleen remembers crying when she learned her friend was killed by a drunk driver; and James recollects his father's death as the "hardest thing I ever had to go through in my life." The autobiographers could do little more in one or two paragraphs than to record some of the details of these events and convey their feelings at the time, but the first assignment succeeded in giving their classmates material for the biographical essays that followed.

The biographers remained remarkably sympathetic and insightful. Kevin is careful to balance the death of Alexandra's grandfather with the impending births of her nieces. James begins his second biographical essay on Alexandra by noting that the manner in which we deal with the loss of a loved one "is one of the defining characteristics of our humanity." Alexandra observes that the "scary relief" James experienced after his father's suicide is "common and reasonable." Despite grammatical errors and occasional colloquialisms and clichés, their language remains for the most part interesting and lively. The biographers avoid reducing their classmates to clinical case studies or to sentimentalized victims. The essays are serious in tone but not without humor. Alexandra's statement that "[t]eenagers have a normal tendency to hate the world" aptly characterizes the stormy period Kevin experienced after his family's breakup. No one would claim that the biographers are Tolstoyean in their vision of human nature, but they succeed in conveying the novelist's observation in *Anna Karenina* that while happy families are all alike, every unhappy family is unhappy in its own way.

Though I had not discussed endings, the biographers concluded on a note of genuine affirmation. Alexandra ends her sketch of Kevin by remarking that his relationship with his mother has now improved. Colleen concludes her paper on Kevin by indicating that although life still holds "challenges" (she does not use the more negative word "problems"), his future is bright. Kevin closes his biography of Alexandra with a reference to her "striving to find happiness in her career and putting the problems of the past behind her." James completes his account of Colleen's life by conceding that while she and her family still have difficulties with her grandfather's "passing," his life and death have contributed to the person she has become—a conclusion that is no less true of James's relationship with his father. Kevin finishes his essay on Colleen with an eloquent tribute to her friend: "But even recently her thoughts wander back to that handsome man who had her heart for a time, a memory of a brief love that will last a lifetime." Despite the advice that Alexandra gives James in her concluding paragraph—"Life sucks"—she is able to craft a final sentence (albeit with a comma splice) that ends with a positive image: "It is always so much easier to look at the bad things that happened, we tend to overlook what once made us smile." The hopeful endings of the biographies confirm a finding reported by Thomas Newkirk. "In a survey reported by David Levine, President of Teachers College, Columbia, students were generally pessimistic about the country's social institutions—the media, government, corporations, even the American family. Yet a robust majority, nine out of every ten respondents, were optimistic about their personal futures" (38).

Kevin, Alexandra, Colleen, and James all wrote their second biographical essays on a risky topic—either divorce or death. They could have written on lighter topics but chose not to do so. Indeed, they selected painful events in their partners' lives, events to which the biographers could relate on a certain level. Not only did they write about sensitive issues, but they also developed them to an extent that their classmates probably never would have anticipated on the first day of the semester.

Evaluating the Biographical Assignments

The biographical assignments occurred during the first three weeks of the semester, and I was curious about the students' reactions to them. Consequently, I asked them to discuss in the next assignment how they felt (1) writing about their classmates' lives, (2) writing and hearing about their own lives, and (3) reading about their classmates' lives.

Kevin

Kevin found the experience of writing about his classmates moving: "it was impressive to learn so much about another person when in most cases one doesn't learn a thing about anyone in their class." Despite the many differences he felt with his two biographical subjects, he experienced important similarities, identifying with Alexandra's closeness to her sister and with Colleen's feelings about divorce. It was difficult for him to write about Colleen's biography: "I didn't have much surprise or shock when I decided to write about the tragic death of her boyfriend. It had already been introduced to me [by Alexandra]. What shocked me was the actual death and the way she related the gory details as counselors had told them to her. It was a horrific event that I wouldn't wish anyone to go through."

Kevin felt apprehensive when he heard his own biography read aloud, fearing the loss of privacy and control. "It was a little frightening at first, as if I was revealed, and it wasn't even by me! Someone else had my life in their hands and then would write it as they saw it and declare it to the class." And yet he found the assignments interesting, remarking that "it allowed us to get to know our classmates and to share others things we would otherwise keep inside." He felt that the assignments confirmed that he was not alone in experiencing conflicts: "others have shared the same experiences as me." He believed that his two classmates did a "pretty good job" in writing about his life, though he was disappointed that his first biographer did not go into more depth. "I think that Alexandra could have used more of the biographical information I had provided instead of turning my life into a statistic." He felt that his second biographer went into much more detail and therefore captured more of his story. "[Colleen] seemed to have used everything I gave her about me, plus somethings that I had only mentioned in passing."

Reading about his classmates' lives showed Kevin "how diverse each member in the class was in regards to family structure." He felt that the biographical assignments "brought out the inner person of the physical being that sits before us in class" and demonstrated that everyone was "quite human." He concluded that the essays were "a self-exploration and learning experience for all." Though he was initially wary of this self-exploration, he now felt that he would like to explore in a future essay the extent to which his parents' divorce has influenced his relationship with women. "The only thing is that this would be quite a personal thing for me and something I would not like to share with the class."

Alexandra

For Alexandra, the main value of writing about her classmates' lives was the discovery that she was not the only person with problems. She noted that death, divorce, and a father's alcoholism were problems in Kevin's life (her first biographical subject) and her own. She had little in common with her second biographical subject, James, except for their reactions to a beloved relative's death. "James's father had passed away. My grandfather was like a father figure to me. I could not stand my father for a long time, and I used to wish that my grandpa was my dad." Alexandra stated that when she decided to write about James's father's death, she did not know how he died, since the first biographer omitted this information. The news of the suicide, which she learned about through a telephone call with James, was shattering to her, but she felt compelled to write about it. "I feel like nothing could shock me. I am the person that many of my friends come to if they need someone to listen to them. I am also rather calm, and have learned to expect the unexpected. However, it was the way in which James's father died that surprised me. Upon reading the biography that his other partner had written, I noticed that he did not disclose the way in which his father died. When we agreed that death was going to be our topics, I came across a great shock. His father had committed suicide after being manic-depressive for many years. I did not know how to approach this material. Honestly, how can a person make this material sound softer? I learned that the only way to write about it, was to just come straight out and say what needed to be said." Hearing how James's father had died allowed Alexandra to release many of the feelings she had tried to suppress concerning her grandfather's death. "When I hung up the phone after relating the story of my grandfather, I ran to the kitchen sobbing. My best friend was there, and she was holding me like a baby for about five minutes. I felt relieved. I had pushed my true feelings aside for the past year, and I found myself saying aloud what I had not been able to since he passed away. In all honesty, I was glad that I spoke about this particular subject. I have since been attempting to work out the feelings that I have conveniently hidden away from the rest of the world."

Colleen

Colleen began her evaluative essay by admitting that "it is always hard to discuss any personal occurrence, good or bad, in your life to perfect strangers." She feared that self-disclosure would heighten her vulnerability, since other people might become judgmental. Yet she also believed that people can sympathize if they recognize commonalities with others, as she and

Kevin were able to do because of their parents' divorces. She was uneasy about hearing her biography read aloud. "After thinking about it for a while, though, I felt happy remembering the good memories of my past. When I remembered those I lost, I realized that those memories are the only photographs inside my head that I have left and the less I think about them, the easier they fade away." She felt that her biographers succeeded in describing the aspects of her life that she had shared with them and welcomed the opportunity to write about her past. "I feel comfortable with the events that have happened in my life, and I have no problem discussing any of them in further detail in later essays."

James

James believed that the biographical assignments encouraged students to "discuss traumatic events in their lives" and to "teach other students to empathize with certain issues." He was struck by how many of his classmates wrote about a loved one's death. He was not surprised that some of the biographical essays dealt with sensitive issues such as rape and suicide. "I have been through enough in my own life to realize that these things do happen." Writing about these tragedies required special sensitivity. "You have to do justice to the story you are trying to tell. That means not leaving out important details and staying strictly to what you were told."

James admitted that he did not know how he felt when he heard his biography read aloud. "I wasn't embarrassed. It was just the first time I heard my life read out aloud. I soon realized that I had nothing to feel odd about." Although he did not reveal in his autobiographical paragraphs how his father died, he did disclose this information to his two biographers. "I relayed all the information, I was completely honest, and it would have been a lie to myself to hold anything back." He did not comment on his first biographer's decision to omit the details of his father's death; instead, he praised both his biographers, particularly Alexandra, "who did a very good job handling a sensitive subject."

James conceded that the biographical assignments put him at risk: "risk to what other people may think of me. However this is not by any means a negative thing or did I get any negative feelings from it. The events of my life shape who I am today. I am not embarrassed by them or afraid to speak of them." He felt that while he did not learn anything about himself as a result of disclosing details of his life to classmates, "what I did get out of it was a way to say things out loud in a very different environment." The assignments were "in a peculiar way therapeutic." James thought that in a future essay he might return to the subject of his father's suicide. "I know that I have come to deal with this tragedy and maybe in the position to help other people. It is not an easy thing to live with. I believe that I have come to understand all the events surrounding it and his explanations and mistakes."

Kevin's, Alexandra's, Colleen's, and James's classmates all felt that the biographical assignments helped the semester to begin on a constructive note. They inferred from my opening discussion of empathy that they needed to be as compassionate as possible when describing their class-mates' lives. There is some evidence to suggest that students began to view themselves differently as a result of the biographical essays. "What I learned about myself as a result of this assignment," observed one woman, "was that I do have the ability to see the best in people after all. So often I feel very critical of others and yet when I wrote my partner's biography, I was able to create a positive and complimentary sketch of her as a person. This was a surprise."

Few students felt that it was difficult to write the autobiographical para-graphs, but most were anxious when their lives were read in class. This is where, in my view, the greatest risk arises in personal writing: the threat of public disapproval or humiliation. Four students indicated that their anxiety was so intense during the reading of their biographies that they experienced a flushed or burning face, palpitating heart, sweaty palms, or butterflies in the stomach—the same symptoms of distress that Diane and Roberta reported in their essays. The students used different strategies to cope with their anxiety. Some chose not to read the biographical essays written about them when copies were distributed in class. Others tried not to listen when the essays were read aloud. A few students were absent dur-ing the class in which their essays were read aloud, and I didn't know whether they were ill or had decided to use one of their two permissible "cuts" to avoid an anxiety-provoking situation. One person telephoned me with the request not to have her biography read in class; she regretted disclosing so much personal material to her biographer and feared she would be embarrassed in front of her classmates. She thought that her biographer had written a sensitive essay but nevertheless felt extremely uncomfortable about sharing it with her classmates. Students seldom re-gret a self-disclosure during the biographical assignments, but I always defer to their wish not to read an essay aloud.

Some students remarked that they could not immediately recognize their own biographies, not because they were inaccurate but because they were hearing about their lives from another perspective. More often than not, this defamiliarization had a positive effect, as one person observed. "It was odd reading about myself in class. It almost felt as though I was reading someone else's story. I found myself looking at my life from a new perspective. As a result of the biographical assignments, I learned that I am a strong, intelligent, and independent young woman. I have goals and dreams for my future."

With few exceptions, the students believed that their classmates wrote largely accurate and sympathetic biographical essays. Those who were disappointed felt, as Kevin did, that their partner either oversimplified their life or omitted important information without which their life could not be understood. One person stated that his biographer's exclusion of embarrassing material created the impression that he was a "pretty nice guy," which he felt was not entirely true. A second concluded regretfully that "it is impossible to write an accurate biography in a few pages"—an observation with which authors of thousand-page biographies would also agree. A third objected to her biographer's efforts to narrate her biography in the first person. "I felt that he was putting words into my mouth, which in fact was exactly what he was doing." And a fourth admitted ruefully that he was caught off guard when he heard his essay read aloud. "Hearing my own biography in class was embarrassing. I was late for the class and the next biography read was the one written about me. I do not believe that I will ever be late for class again."

To judge from the evaluative essays, students felt safe during class discussions of their essays. They did not feel that their classmates criticized their lives or said anything to make them feel uncomfortable. No one felt shamed by a class comment. Class discussions were limited to what readers found interesting and effective about their classmates' essays. The writers experienced their classmates' revision of their sentences as nonthreatening. The knowledge that one can write about the most wrenching subject without being judged or critiqued helped to overcome the resistance to self-disclosure.

The biographical assignments broke down many of the students' stereotypes of their classmates, one of which involved the belief that others' lives are trouble-free. "When reading biographical essays by classmates, I found my stereotypes were being contradicted. I found myself assigning everyone a straight and narrow life. No curves or detours were added to anyone's life. It should have come as no surprise to me when I heard my classmates' stories, because in reality, life isn't straight or narrow."

"Personal Intelligences"

The biographical assignments helped students explore the two types of "personal intelligences" Harvard educator Howard Gardiner discusses in *Frames of Mind* (1993). Contrasting Freud's and William James's different notions of the self, Gardiner writes:

> Freud was interested in the self as located in the individual and, as a clinician, was preoccupied with an individual's own knowledge of himself; given this bias, a person's interest in other individuals was justified chiefly as a better means of gaining further understanding of one's own problems, wishes, and anxieties and, ultimately, of achieving one's goals. In contrast, James's interest, and, even more so, the interests of the American social psychologist : who succeeded him, fell much more on the individual's relationship to the outside community. Not only did one's knowledge of self come largely from an ever-increasing appreciation of how others thought about the individual; but the purpose of self-knowledge was less to promote one's personal agenda, more to ensure the smooth functioning of the wider community. (238–39)

Both forms of personal intelligences, knowledge of one's self and knowledge of others, may be seen in the biographical assignments. The essays reveal expanding knowledge of both biographers and biographees. Students shift perspectives, examine increasingly complex material, acknowledge ambiguity and ambivalence, dispel stereotypes, and enlarge their points of view. They gaze both inward and outward, gaining understanding of themselves and others.

Later Essays

In the rest of this chapter, I return to Kevin, Alexandra, Colleen, and James and discuss how they used later essays to explore risky topics. I include one essay by each—an essay that goes significantly beyond the biographical assignments' disclosures. The later essays allow me to pursue a question that is central to any personal writing course: does self-disclosure lead to good writing?

Two of the later assignments involved responses to *Diaries to an English Professor*. Kevin and Alexandra wrote their essays on the chapter called "Sins of the Fathers," a study of how college students write about being children of divorced families; Colleen wrote her essay on both "Sexual Disclosures" and "Suicide Survivors," and James wrote his essay on "Suicide Survivors." Kevin and Alexandra wrote their essays during the middle of the semester; Colleen and James wrote theirs at the end of the semester.

Kevin

"Sins of the Fathers" is not always the situation in a family. In my case my mother was the one I saw splinter my "stable" family. She, being unhappy with her situation broke away from it in the divorce proceedings. It was a hard thing for her to see my father, who she had married as a mate for life, go a different path in life then she herself wanted to follow. My parent's divorce did allow me to align myself with the stories of the individuals in the book, but I didn't share resentment for my father. In fact, at the time I began to hate my mother for destroying the strong family structure I thought we had. It took quite awhile to forgive her for her choices, but I have since recovered and understand the nature of their divorce. My father, on the other hand, has not yet completely recovered and lives a life away from relationships, only to retain comfort in his two sons, his family and the land around him.

I very aggressively displayed my displeasure with the divorce as it took place. I violently broke many things such as doors and glassware to desperately try to get the parent's attention diverted from their heated arguments. I even remember taking my four-wheeler on a crazed spree through our back woods as fast as I could (without a helmet) trying to show them how unhappy they had made me. These immature outbreaks took place when they argued before the divorce, and even continued with my mother after the divorce had taken place! I remember a day maybe a year after the divorce when I went to visit her and she was upset about a glass sculpture she thought I had broken. I was so furious at being accused that I turned everything else she said into an indication she didn't love me anymore. I lost control and amongst other things I screamed that she was a "whore," that she didn't love me, that she was such a "dumb fuck" that I didn't want to be her son anymore. I very successfully discharged almost every pent-up emotion I had in me that afternoon and stormed out of the house. My grand finale consisted of backing my car onto her nicely pruned lawn and letting the tires tear it apart as I screamed obscenities at her. It was such an event that took place that I think her new "boyfriend" was scared of me for a long time afterward. I completely regretted the outburst as soon as I drove home to my father's house. I began to cry and try to comprehend what I had just done. The emotions kept flowing when I got home and I broke down again in front of my father as I told him what had happened. He was very supportive and listened without trying to anger me more. This was only one example of the fury I felt towards my mother as a part of my resentment.

I remember that my brother shared my views, but he kept much more of the anger within himself. He tried to make my mothers' life hell without *letting her know of his intentions. Our outbreaks of such powerful emotions were previously unknown to us. Neither of our parents was abusive towards us, except for the younger years of spankings for times when we misbehaved, but even that was quickly outgrown. In fact, our father fit the category discussed in* Diaries to an English Professor. *As Ron stated "I often wonder if my father is able to express emotion at all." This is very true of my father as well. He is a kind man and can be emotional if he chooses, but mostly I never witness any of it. During the divorce the most emotion I witnessed was when he learned that my mother didn't want to spend her life with him anymore. He became extremely depressed and for a time he would only go to work and watch television (and nothing else). When the divorce proceedings were heading toward a close he expressed that he couldn't bear to live without his sons. This display of affection was the most he had ever shown us, and I was very touched by it.*

This chapter did not awaken strong emotions. I did find myself agreeing with certain aspects of the accounts given, but nothing more. It is interesting to see how the experience [of divorce] differed between males and females. I can't say that I lost self esteem over the divorce or that I was drastically altered, but I do know it did change certain things within me.

When the parent's finally divorced my brother and I were left living with my father, as it was agreed that he and I would stay with the house. I felt it was the only tangible decision I could have made that wouldn't have devastated one parent or the other. As an outcome of the divorce, both parents agreed that my brother and I would have to see a psychiatrist to deal with our emotions. I remember vividly talking with one for a single visit and never returning. My mother suggested another psychiatrist who she had been consulting with and I decided to give it a try. The experience left me bewildered and worse off because the psychiatrist told me during the last session with her that I had many problems. She told me that I should continue seeing her! I thought nothing that drastic was wrong, and especially nothing she mentioned. In fact, I just thought that she said what she said to extract extra money out of my family. I stopped going. It was quite a statement to be told by a shrink that you are in need of serious help. To this day I haven't spoken with a psychiatrist again and don't plan to anytime soon. I survive with the help of the close friends I have gathered around me, who I treat as my many hands during times when I feel troubled.

I would have to agree with the psychiatrist to some extent. I have been affected by the divorce. Two of the strongest areas in which I believe I have biases are in dating and marriage. My relationships always start out strong and fade away around 3–4 months later. Some have told me it is because I have not found the right person but sometimes I wonder. I am never confident enough to even discuss marriage. It seems like a dream to me. Perhaps I am dissuaded as I consider my parent's divorce just another example of a bleak commentary of marriages in general? Maybe it is the bond with my father, who has never moved on to date anyone, and doesn't even seem to have an interest. Or could it be my mother, whom I had resented and who moved on to a man who is about 15 years her senior and a worse alcoholic than my father ever could be. Granted alcoholism was only a stepping stone in the divorce it was something that remained in my memory. It was quite a double standard for me to witness her leave my father who sometimes came drunk on a Friday and start something with a man who gets so drunk as to drool milk at the dinner table.

Maybe I am being too harsh. Let me paint a better picture of this individual. The man my mother has been with is a salesman who fits the story of surmise in Death of a Salesman. *He is very friendly and talkative, but many times no one can understand what he is discussing. I get the feeling that he is heading down a path of self-destruction and my mother is the hopeless savior trying to hold him back. It is sad to see, as he is a genuine gentleman who would help anyone, but like everyone else he has his flaws. It is strange to say but sometimes when I have to be around both of them, I feel almost like the father taking care of them.*

My mother thinks so highly of me and helps me with my life choices, but we are also like friends. I can casually discuss her friend and his problems with her. In fact she and I have become close in other ways and discuss just about anything. I think part of this was due to the fact that I gave up resenting her for the divorce. I allowed myself to see that she didn't do anything to harm me but rather heal myself. It was an important stepping stone in reviving our mother-son relationship. Even my brother has forgiven her, and we have recovered nearly completely from the ordeal that once split us apart. We have grown into a new family, not necessarily what we once were but something we can all now happily live with. I only wish the individuals in the shared diary entries had such luck in getting back a family member that they had lost. I suppose in most of the cases I read the father was someone who didn't want to change at all and became selfish to his own cause and not those of his children. It was sad to read how many of them would never again consider their father as their own, at least not in the way I have regained my love and understanding for both my parents.

My only regret is that parent's have to make the choices that they do around the children. I can say I was lucky, but divorce is such a painful thing for so many children and sometimes could be avoided much earlier through better communication. It used to be thought that people stayed together for children. The current trend doesn't protect the child from such harm. In our ever-evolving society the individual has been stressed as important. Yet many times the younger, more vulnerable child is forgotten in the moment of decision. It is forgotten that they are people too.

Kevin stated in his autobiographical paragraphs that many of the memories of his parents' divorce have "faded away," but if so, they emerge vividly in this essay, which he read to the class. The essay contains several technical problems. The writer still has difficulty with the apostrophe, confuses "then" with "than," and uses colloquialisms ("give it a try") and other imprecise words such as "things." Occasionally the diction needs improvement: he refers to *Death of a Salesman* as a "story of surmise" when he probably means "demise," which itself is not the best word. Despite these errors, Kevin's essay is insightful and engaging. He uses specific details that are absent from his biographers' essays, and the reader can now visualize the ways in which he acted out his rage in high school. Kevin makes no attempt to soften or rationalize the violence—he writes with unflinching honesty about this confusing period of his life. Indeed, he captures the feelings of explosive anger and irrationality he experienced then. His most shameful disclosure—the words he screams at his mother—forms the most vivid sentence in the essay. Nor is he afraid to qualify past judgments. He now acknowledges, for example, that the psychiatrist whom he reluctantly visited a few years earlier may have been right to suggest that the breakup of his parents' marriage was causing serious problems for him.

Additionally, Kevin wonders whether he has been harsh in his characterization of his mother's companion, whom he compares with Willy Loman. He himself is no Biff Loman: the reader does not sense that he will sabotage his life to spite a parent. Self-analysis allows him to explore other points of view, including those of his mother, father, brother, and his mother's companion, and there is nothing solipsistic about his autobiographical writing. He ends the essay by moving beyond his own situation and reflecting on the vulnerable child, who may have neither the inner resources nor the loving parents to survive the family's breakup.

Alexandra

I find myself numb to the reactions of the students in "Sins of the Fathers." I have heard many stories, and seen many cases of divorce. I always find it unfair how a child is made to choose a parent, or how a child is dragged through custody battles. I feel that I have always had a semi-realistic ap-

proach to divorce. Sometimes, it just needs to be done. I know that my parents were always fighting. I realized at an early age that they were not happy together, and their unhappiness affected my sister and I. Their intentions were good; they wanted a two parent household for their kids. I felt that I would have been better off if I saw my parents separately. When they are together, I feel like a referee.

Many people thought I was strange as a child. I wanted my parents to get divorced. It was not that I did not love either parent, I just knew that it would be better if they were not together. My father is an alcoholic, and this caused many fights within my household. Although he is recovered now, there are too many years of resentment between my parents. I know that my father was devastated when we finally left him when I was 15. However, it caused him to become a better person because he had hit a point not long after where he realized that in order for his children to respect him, he needed to change his life.

The relationship that me and my father shared has much to do with the way that I am today. I am like the diarist Mara in a sense. Although her father was non-existent, mine may as well have been. He would disappear occasionally, sometimes for hours; other times for weeks. I am definite that my mother was aware of his whereabouts, but she never told us the truth. I have my suspicions. I remember the summer that I was 11, he disappeared. He went to California, and left my mother in debt. I remember coming home to an eviction notice posted on the door to my apartment. It was scary. I learned not to trust him, and this distrust spread to a general distrust of all men.

Mara states that "Whenever I meet someone that I am interested in, I get very nervous and lose all sense of composure. I don't like to let my true feelings show, and I'd rather admire them from afar. I think that the reason for this is the fact that I can't deal with rejection from another man." As soon as this was read, I recalled an anecdote that my mother occasionally reminds me of. My father was always breaking a promise. There were times when he would say he would buy me something, or just show up somewhere, and he would not follow through. When I was about 9, there was another broken promise. My mother told me that I turned to her and said "Why does he always break my poor little heart?" As a child, I felt that I had done something to deserve this. I was constantly feeling rejected by him. Even though we lived with my father, it was always as if he was an absent figure in our lives. He just slept there. As we got older, and understood that he had a problem, my sister and I showed him absolutely no respect. He would show up at home later and later every night because he knew how my sister and I felt about him. I actually hit him once across his face. I told my friends how happy I was that his glasses flew off his face, and how the blow caused his glasses to scratch him and make the bridge of his nose start to bleed. I didn't care about his feelings anymore. I felt that he had ruined my life.

The problems that Mara has in dealing with men are similar to my own in the sense that I do not know how to deal with them on a serious level. I never expect anything from men. What I mean by that is, I feel that they won't be around long, so why bother getting serious? I usually have someone that I am dealing with, but it rarely progresses too far. I have a tendency to shut men out of my life. My family is composed of very strong women. We all possess one common characteristic: sarcasm. Basically smart ass is the best term to describe this. My mother and my aunt are bad, but my sister and I are probably worse. We use this a test. If someone stays around and can handle us, then this sarcasm disappears. It is usually geared at someone that I really like. I started seeing someone recently, and I think that he is probably the only male that can match me when I put this trait to use. We actually begin to make each other laugh. It is really scary how alike we think sometimes. Unfortunately, I find myself pushing him away. I find myself going too far, and this leads to arguing. I doubt everything he says to me. If he tells me I'm pretty, I make a comment that suggests that he's lying because he wants something else from me. At least I realize what I am doing. Actually, at least I am talking to him. I used to be much worse. I used to not talk to men without stuttering. I would prefer to "admire them from afar." The strangeness of it all is that now that my father has a more positive role in my life, I find myself to be more trusting of men. Unfortunately, not too much more trusting, but I am getting there.

My relationship with my mother was always strong. Like Mara, "Most people don't understand the relationship that me and my mother have. I can speak to her on any subject, and she will truly listen to me. She may be the only real friend that I have to confide in" (p. 47). I am going home on the weekend of November 7th, and my mother is taking me out for my birthday. I turned 21 two weeks ago, and it has been a long running joke that my mom was going to take me out and get me drunk. Most people do not understand this. Me and my mom are friends. She is a mother when she needs to be. I have always been a good kid, and have never given her any serious problems. I can talk to her about anything, and she knows that she can trust me.

I respect my mother for everything that she has been through with my father. You never knew what he would be like when he was drunk. I saw him hit her once. I was about six years old, and me, my mom, and my sister had come home from the park. I remember my father yelling at her. Next thing I *remember, my sister and I were kneeling over her screaming, "Mommy, Mommy." We thought that she was dead. My father had knocked her unconscious. I remember this as if it was yesterday. I can not understand how my mother dealt with him for so long. I always tell myself if a man hits me, he will find himself in a hospital.*

I also have a very strong relationship with my sister. We basically went through everything together. We used to crawl in each others bed's when the yelling was too loud. Sometimes it would get so bad, that we would miss school the next day because we did not fall asleep until 3 a.m. All I ever wanted was peace. My sister can give me that. We would defend each other if my father was yelling at either one of. I'd jump in if he was about to start on her. I remember that she pulled a knife out on him once when he was about to hit me for telling him to "shut the fuck up." I know that I should not have said that to him. He had called my mother a name. I was 12 at the time. My sister was only 10. I know that this relationship does not seem normal, but it just made my sister and I realize that we would be there for each other at all times. To this day, I would do anything for her. Although my sister and I focus on positive subjects now, we have discussed the craziness of our childhood. We both respect our father much more since the divorce. We actually like him now.

I have learned how to deal with the way my childhood is. I have been to Alateen meetings a few times. They are specifically geared towards children of alcoholics. It made me learn that a person can love someone, but not like them. Everything seems to be working out much better after the divorce. My father now holds a steady job. My mother now has her own business. We all live in the same town. My parents still argue, but it has become more playful now. They have put the past behind them to some extent. I take walks with my father when I am home. We get ice cream and talk for hours. I actually look forward to spending time with him. I will be home this following weekend, and I can not wait to see him! I feel that after all these years, he is finally there for me. He is trying really hard to make up for past wrongs, and I am giving him a chance. It is as if we are learning about each other. It is like I met him for the first time.

If I had written this a few years ago, I would have felt bitter, and angry. I now except this as part of my life. I have become a much stronger person, and this reflects on the fact that I have forgiven both of my parents. My father for not being there for me the way I needed him to be, and my mother for waiting so long to divorce him. I have begun to understand that there is a reason for everything. These experiences have only helped to shape me in to the person that I am still becoming.

Alexandra devoted only one sentence in her autobiographical paragraphs to her parents' divorce, but she wrote perceptively about the subject in her biographical essay on Kevin. Her observation that children of divorced parents "have serious amounts of aggression that they either repress or act upon" is strikingly demonstrated in her own essay on "Sins of the Fathers." In his biographical essay, Kevin noted that Alexandra is "hesitant to admit that her father is a recovered alcoholic," but she now recounts in abundant detail how his drinking problem destroyed his marriage. I doubt Alexandra would have written about this nightmarish period in her life without the option of anonymity; she would have felt too ashamed to risk the disapproval of her classmates. Anonymity allowed her to feel safe enough to write her story and disclose those experiences that have shaped her life.

Part of the strength of Alexandra's essay lies in its ability to juxtapose past and present feelings toward her family. She reveals feeling guilty that she was somehow responsible for her parents' marital difficulties and captures the confusion that so many children feel about this situation. Like Kevin, she acknowledges actions toward a parent that she now regrets. She evokes both the "craziness" of her childhood and the relative stability of her present life.

Alexandra's essay reveals a few grammatical errors, but it is more polished than her earlier writings. She correctly uses the apostrophe, which she had avoided entirely in her biographical essay on Kevin, and she begins to experiment—though not always correctly—with the colon and semicolon. She has also reduced the number of comma splices. She still confuses the nominal and objective forms of the first person singular pronoun: she begins a sentence with the "relationship that me and my father share." Her failure to distinguish between "I" and "me" may be seen in her misquotation of Mara's observation in *Diaries to an English Professor* that "Most people don't understand the relationship my mother and I have." In the last paragraph, Alexandra uses "except" instead of "accept"—a common grammatical error that may indicate in the context of the sentence a Freudian slip. Yet despite her technical mistakes, Alexandra's essay is an improvement over her earlier writings, and the maturity of her prose style may reflect personal growth.

Colleen

As I read the two chapters, "Suicide Survivors" and "Sexual Disclosures" in the book Diaries to an English Professor, *I knew that writing this paper would be hard. I read the chapter, "Hunger Artists," as well but I did not relate to it as I did the other two chapters. However, I was saddened and compelled by the student's accounts of their problems with eating disorders. Fortunately, I have never known anyone with the problem or dealt with the problem personally.*

At first I didn't know which chapter to write about. I have dealt with suicide and sexual abuse in my life and have had friends that have dealt with both also. They have had a strong impact on my life. After thinking for a while, I decided to incorporate both into this paper. I will talk about these two subjects, but I will not go into too many details, as it is difficult to write about and personal.

When I was a young girl my family and I used to take vacations to either Maine or California every summer. We would alternate the two because my mom's side of the family had relatives in California and my dad's side of the family has relatives in Maine. I have wonderful memories of these vacations up until the very last time I went to California. This particular time I went alone with just my brother and cousin. My parents did not come with us. We were staying with my cousin's grandmother and other relatives. There was a man who worked at the home (it was a huge house) to help with gardening, cooking and cleaning. I was left home many times to help cook and clean because I was the only girl among my brother, my male cousin and their friends. They would go out behind the house and hike up the mountains. Sometimes they would be gone all day. We were scheduled to stay in the house for the entire summer: three months. I never felt uncomfortable around anyone. Even the stranger staying in the house doing his work. It was like one big family.

One day, about 2 weeks after we arrived, everyone was out. No one was home except the worker and me. I was busy in my room playing when he came in and asked me to help him with something in his room. I said "sure" and we went into his room. He closed the door and locked it. I asked him why he was doing that, because no one was home, and he said "sshh, it's a secret." I thought it was strange but I didn't expect what was to happen next. He picked me up and placed me on his bed. He then took all his clothes off. He told me that what we were doing was a secret and that I shouldn't tell anyone or else my mommy and daddy would die. I didn't understand what he meant. Why would my mom and dad die? Why did he have to take his clothes off? Then he came and sat on the bed with me. He took my clothes off. I got off the bed, tried to get out and screamed. He ran over, put his hand over my mouth and told me not to scream or resist or I'd never see my mom or dad again. He told me I was a bad girl and if I wanted to be good again, then I would have to play with him. He never raped me, but he made me perform oral sex on him and he touched my body everywhere. This went on for the entire summer I was there. I have managed to block out most of the occurrences when he locked me in his room. But that was not the only place he would do it. He would make me come into the shower with him and one particular time he took me outside. In the backyard they had a little farm with animals. Over by where the cows were, was a little ditch in the ground with a metal rod that water poured from. We would sometimes wash pigs and other animals over there. One day, again when no one was home, he took me out there. He made me kneel in the hole and perform oral sex on him. I can still smell the mixture of the smell from his penis and the smell of the animal's manure. It still makes me nauseous today. Every time he made me perform oral sex on him I would run into the bathroom, throw up and wash my mouth out with soap. Once I threw up on him in the middle of performing and he beat me. He would beat me up enough so that I was in pain, but not enough to leave big bruises. I was ten years old.

Most people didn't understand why I tried to kill myself when I was nineteen. My life had taken a bad turn and I felt that I didn't want to be here anymore. I felt as if I was a failure and everything I did was wrong. A few months before I tried to kill myself I was sexually assaulted on campus. I was almost raped while being held with a knife to my throat. I was beaten up a little and had everything on me stolen. I also felt like everyone important to me was dying. Death was always a big part of my life and I felt that maybe it was the right choice for me. All of my grandparents died within three years of each other. My uncle, who I was very close to, died of lung cancer. I never thought I'd find love for many reasons but mostly because someone that I cared for very much died the night before our first date. After that I thought it just wasn't meant for me to find anyone. These and many other things lead me to suicide. I had given up on myself and I felt completely empty inside. I had many friends and family but I felt more alone than anyone else in the world. So, I decided that it was time for me to go away and not be a burden to everyone anymore. I swallowed three half-full bottles of pills in my medicine cabinet. I was found by my best friend, who just happened to come by to say hello, and was rushed to the hospital. There, they pumped my stomach. This was the worst experience in my life. I had swallowed somewhere between 75 and 80 pills. They had to stick a thick long tube down my throat, slowly. Of course you are awake during this horrific ordeal. Five people had to hold me down while they slide this tube into my mouth, down my esophagus and into my stomach. Then they stuck a strange looking article into the tube and pumped out the toxins. Then they poured charcoal into my stomach and pulled the tube out of my mouth. I was throwing up as they took out the tube. Then they handcuffed me to the bed because anyone who tries to

kill himself or herself is considered a threat to himself/herself. The police-
man staying with me, though, was very sweet and told me I didn't need to
keep them on. He said "I wasn't crazy at all and that he couldn't understand
why such a beautiful young girl as myself would try to do something so silly
when so many people hadn't gotten the chance to meet me yet." He made me
feel so much better and stayed with me the whole time. There is much more
to that story, such as when my family found out and arrived, but it is just too
personal and too painful.

   While I was reading Diaries to an English Professor *I immediately began*
to relate to these two chapters. I never realized how many people have gone
through similar occurrences in their life as well. I always thought I was alone
and no one else could possibly understand what I was going through. I never
talked to anyone about what I felt inside. Only recently have I opened up to
extremely close friends and relatives. I know that is one of the major reasons
that I tried to commit suicide. I kept everything inside until one day I just
exploded. I couldn't control my life and I felt like I was going crazy. I am very
lucky to be able to sit here and talk about it now. I feel that in some warped
way I have gotten another chance at life, even though I was the one trying to
take my life. I don't regret what I did, I only feel that it was a horrifying
experience that has made me stronger and that I will never repeat. No one's
life gets that bad where you feel you have to end it. Suicide is not the answer
to any problem. No matter what has happened to me, there is always some-
one else who has it much worse.

   In the last three and a half years, my life has changed drastically and I
have finally put the past behind me. My life is better than it's ever been and
I know I have become a stronger person from the tragic ordeals I have faced
in my life. I once thought that life could only get worse, but I see now that it
can only get better, if you make it better. It is hard to let go of my past for it
still haunts me to this day. I know I will never forget the memories I have.
But I also know that none of them were my fault and I finally stopped blam-
ing myself. I now have something to live for again and that is life.

   Since Colleen did not list a suicide attempt in her ten autobiographical
events, we can assume she did not wish to disclose this detail to a group of
strangers at the beginning of the semester. It was apparently easier for her
to state that she had been sexually assaulted on campus than to admit that
she tried to end her life. Kevin writes in his biographical essay that there
was a "black time in her life" when she began to brood on death, "[n]ot
her own, of course," but her loved ones' deaths. Colleen remained silent
about her suicide attempt until her last essay, which she read aloud on the
final class of the semester.

Colleen's essay is written with restraint, control, and quiet dignity. The writing is nearly flawless. No less remarkable was her willingness to read her essay aloud, a sign of her trust in the class. She is able to transmute traumatic experiences into evocative language, and her essay, like those of Kevin, Alexandra, and James, affirms human agency: she controls her words rather than being controlled by them. One can see how writing leads to healing: expression is the opposite of keeping "everything inside," which in Colleen's case resulted in a suicide attempt. Rather than romanticizing suicide, she captures its horrifying consequences. I have never read a more detailed or moving account of the process of having one's stomach pumped after a drug overdose. The contrast between the impersonality of the hospital and the compassionate response of the policeman is striking. The reader can understand why Colleen wished to end her life and what she has learned from this ordeal.

James

I preface James's essay with two letters he wrote during the middle of the semester. The first was to his father, and the second was his father's imagined response. This dual letter writing was not an assignment I had given to James's class (though I have used it in other expository writing courses) but one that he decided to write on his own—with powerful results.

Dear Dad,

It has now been a little over a year since you took your life in Whispering Pines cemetery. Let's start by saying that I am no longer angry or feel hatred for the mistake you made. Can't say the same for mom and my brother. It was always you and me verse them, just like pictionary. However my problem is that even though I am not angry, I am just as confused. I don't think I will ever be able to comprehend your desire to leave your family behind. I realize that things at work were unbearable and money was tight, but we needed you. I know I acted like I didn't but believe me I did. What you didn't understand was that I didn't need a father any more. I was twenty years old. There was nothing that you had left to teach me that I had to find out for myself. You taught me all you could, all I was willing to learn from you. What I am saying is that I didn't need a father anymore, what I needed was a friend. Someone who would give me thoughtful advice, listen to my problems, and love me unconditionally. I needed you to listen to me when I bitched about my girlfriend, my wife, my kids. Then there is that issue. You are going to miss my wedding, my brother's wedding or his first girlfriend for that matter, most importantly your grandchildren. Wasn't all that impor-

tant to you? Who is going to dance with mom at my wedding. I could go on forever with things you will miss out on. For all the pain you may have been going through last year, look at all the pleasure you have given up.

Please believe me when I tell you that I am not angry with you anymore. Anger is a difficult thing to hold on to for a year. Mom is doing a good job though. To be perfectly honest I am hurt. You made a conscious decision to abandon your family when your chips were down. You were selfish in thinking only of your pain and not ours: before, during, and after your death. I will never be able to understand why you did what you did.

Dear Son,

I don't even know where to begin, what to say, how to make things right again. When you were growing up I remember always saying, "Sometimes sorry are not enough." I never knew you felt that way about me. In the last four years you and I grew so distant and cold towards each other, I just never realized. I know that doesn't make it right by you, mom, or your brother but I realize that I royally fucked up. It was just that with my illness I was only consumed with my problems. I could just focus on the negative aspects and could not see any hope or happiness in my life. This included me. Then, because of all the medicine I was taking, when I wasn't dwelling on the negatives I was sleeping. Son, we all make mistakes and in the past I was hard on you to teach not to make the same mistake twice and to stand up for your mistakes. Well the irony is that you can't be hard on me and I can't stand up for what I have done. For that I am truly sorry, regardless of what it means or does for yourself, mom, and your brother. I love you, you were my number one son.

There is something else, James. You have become the man of the house. You have to watch out for your mother and brother, especially your brother. Do not do to him what I have done to the two of you. Be there for him, teach him all he needs to know about girls, sex, and any other crap he is going to get himself involved in. I know you are strong and have grown into a man that I am proud of. Please do not make the same mistakes I have, be considerate of others, and make all your decisions carefully.

"All things are made eternal, and I endure eternally. Abandon all hope those who enter here." This is a quote from Dante's Inferno. It is supposed to be part of the quote above the gates to hell. It implies eternal torture and anguish. I believe that this sentiment can easily be applied to those affected by suicide, both the suicide victim and those he or she leaves behind. Which is not to say that the people left behind are not victims. I feel that for one

single person to want to take their own life they must have some seriously difficult issues. They must feel like there is no way out or back from the dark roads they endeavored upon. They chose of their own free will and accord to end their lives and neglect to see all the wonderful circumstances life may yet still hold for them. Truly it is their darkest hour.

Although I have no factual evidence on which to base this, but I firmly believe that more people are affected by suicide today then in any other point in history. There are many more dilemmas that have arose as a result of modern man. Drug abuse, divorce rates, depression, and work related stress have all been increased due to today's society. Nobody is safe from the horror of suicide, including myself.

I have just sat down to write this paper. I seem to have some difficulty in deciding exactly where to start. My story is long, intricate, and unlike a fairy tell doesn't have a happy make believe ending. To relieve the tension in the class I will start with the end first. I know there have been times within the class when I have felt some what uncomfortable about hearing certain things about your lives. I apologize if you do not feel the same way and I seem presumptuous for making the assumption that you would be uncomfortable. No turning back now.

On August 18, 1997 between the hours of four and five o'clock my father sat in the bathroom of Whispering Pines cemetery, just after visiting his own father's grave, stood a rifle on it's but end, lowered his mouth to the gun, and pulled the trigger. My hands are shaking. I'm still not turning back. I have brought you to the end of my story. Personally I am relieved that the hardest part of this essay is over. Let me now take you back to the beginning.

In what seems like a long time ago in a galaxy far, far, away, for all you Star Wars fans, I was five years old. Myself, my father, and my mother lived in a tiny apartment in Staten Island. I guess you can say I lived a lonely existence. There was not one other child my own age in the building. The only friend I had was my father. He was my mentor, my hero, my best friend. In my eyes Thomas could do no wrong. On weekends or sometimes even after he would get home from work, he would take me to the movies. This was a tradition that lasted for many years. I think we both enjoyed the fantasy world that a major motion picture could provide. I remember him teaching me how to play chess. We would listen to the Beatles White Album together, Rocky Raccoon was always my favorite. I could provide you with hundreds of examples about the close relationship my father and I shared. However that is only part of what this essay is about. Just take my word that for many years my father was my best and only friend.

Let us press fast forward on the VCR remote, don't want you to get up, *and move to June 12, 1984. My brother was born sometime in the middle of the night. We had moved out of the apartment by then and into a residential house, still in Staten Island. Moving and fixing the house was another bonding experience for my father and me. He let me help him, when I was obviously in the way. He made me feel important. By that time I had made some friends in my new neighborhood but dad was still number one. He had begun training me for baseball. We played catch for hours. I remember him making me watch Mel Stotlymyre's tape on instructional pitching before every game. I hated that damn tape. There came a point when I was able to quote it word for word. My father still could do no wrong.*

This may seem like cheating and if your even half interested in this essay then you may not like this, but we are taking a huge leap in time. We have arrived in my first year in SUNY Albany, half way through the first semester. The ten previous years where essentially normal. I grew up, I made many friends, even a girlfriend or two. My father and I grew apart. We had two terribly similar tempers. My puberty brought out the best in the two of us. He was still my mentor and my hero, I still loved him, but we stopped spending so much time together. I know this was a part of growing up, yet it is still sad when one thinks about it.

I was sitting on my bed, studying for one useless anthropology test, my apologies to any anthropology majors, my phone rings. It was my mother. I could tell she was upset. She told me that my father was in the hospital for the same reason he was when I was younger. I was told, I was about six, that my father had suffered a heart attack. He was gone for a month and I was to young to see him. She explains to me that she lied to me when I was younger because what she was about to tell me I couldn't have understood. My father was a manic depressant. I wasn't mad at my mother, I understood why she didn't tell, I wouldn't have understood. I told her I was coming home this weekend. She said your father may not want to see you. I came home anyway. I thought my father needed me.

Walking into a mental ward of a hospital is not an easy thing. You are surrounded by gates, you need to be let in, and some of the people there really look as if they lost their mind. That may sound mean but it is an apt description. My father was sitting at a table with two of my uncles. We chatted for a while and then they left us so we could be alone. He explained to me that there was a new boss in his company that he could not work with. He lost the respect of his peers and was on the verge of being fired. He told me money was tight, he had no relationship with his younger son, I had grown distant from him, and his wife and the whole world thought he was a failure. With the exception of having no relationship with my brother, this was either untrue or grossly exaggerated. My father never put the time into his relationship with my brother like he did with me. My brother knew this and now it seems he hates him for it. My father also said I might have to come home from school to save money and get a job to help the family. That statement, in fact the whole conversation I had with my father that night, in essence ensured the fact that my father and I would never have the same relationship again. You see my father was a "blamer." He blamed everybody else for his problems. I was selfish, my mother wasn't supportive enough, my brother hates him. This were all things we heard frequently in my house. Instead of attempting to work with his new boss he avoided him. He began a three year stretch of excuses, blames, and lies.

The next three years were for all intents and purposes, hell. My father lived in and out of the hospital. Seven trips in two and a half years. When he wasn't in the hospital he was in work, in body anyway. His mind was not there. Over this time my perfect idea of my father was shattered. I learned that he had become depressed two times before this. Both times over his job. My family fought. Many members of my family blamed my grandmother for not getting Thomas help as a child. My grandmother though her son could do no wrong and it was our fault for not understanding him. My aunt, my father's sister, told me many things about his childhood. He was a very nervous child, and he could not complete his military service in the National Guard. I am not sure of the details, but my grandmother paid a certain amount of money, and my father received an honorable discharge. Of course I always believed my father was GI Joe. Another piece of the glass came shattering to the ground.

I withdrew from my family. I took shelter in Albany. I hated coming home. I would call home at night, when I knew my father was sleeping. The medicine he was on made sure that the majority of the time away from work was spent in bed asleep, anyway. I felt terrible for my brother and mother. Having to deal with him on an every day basis. He started crying in front of them. I saw him cry many times. No son wants to see their father cry. It breaks many of the ideals that boys believe about their father. I was ashamed. By this point my brother had no father. This was his defense mechanism about the issue. I don't blame him, I have no right to.

The situation worsened. The summer of 1997 was a terrible summer for all members in my family. Then came a day I will never forget, the biggest mistake of my life was made on that day. It was a Sunday morning. My father was having a panic attack. He asked to be taken to the hospital. It was agreed by his doctor and my mother, that my father would not go back to the hospital. He only uses it to escape. I would not drive him. He pleaded with *me, threatened to kill himself. I dared him to. I called his bluff. He knew that my friend was coming over to pick me up so we could go play football. A tradition in my neighborhood on Sunday mornings. He said he would ask my friend to take him. I commanded that he didn't. My friend walked in the door, he never knocks. My father ran at him screaming to take him. I walked over, adrenaline running through my veins like a waterfall. I picked my father up and threw him on the ground. He crumbled to a ball. I yelled something. He turned around and I saw the look of fear and confusion in his eyes. What have I done? I left to play football, he was still alive when I returned.*

The situation never improved. We have arrived back at that fated night in the beginning of this essay. It is now 6 o'clock and I am playing poker at a friends house. I am up a lot of money, fairly ironic. My friend's father walks in the door and tells me I need to come home, it is very important. I already know. I arrive at my door, I see my mother, and she tells me something I will never forget. The police told me your father expired, what does that mean? I never cried. I took a deep breath. My aunt and uncle were on their way over. My mother was hysterical. For the next three days my uncle, aunt, and myself handled all the arrangements. I needed to keep busy. The days seemed like one long continuous day. Everybody was very helpful. We were not alone for two weeks, even after the funeral. It as in many ways a relief. The torment and uncertainty in my family was over. Now we could move on. It wasn't the ending we wanted, but it was and ending just the same.

Now to the present. My father has been dead for a little over a year. I miss him immensely. I would give anything to have him back, but I can't. I learned a lot from this experience. I learned that my father was a man. He fell off the pedestal I held him on, because he was a man. A man succeeds and a man fails. Ultimately his failures are what killed him and his death was a failure in and of itself. That is something that he had to deal with. The family he left behind is his legacy of success. In the end I took more from my father then I gave to him. He taught me the world and in his death he taught me how to be a man. I will always love him and in time I will forgive him for his mistake. Time heals all wounds.

I was shocked by James's essay, which he turned in a few days before the last class of the semester. Over the years I have received scores of diaries and essays about attempted or completed suicides, but I have never received a more disturbing essay than this. My horror arose not over the news of his father's death—Alexandra had written about this in her biographical essay, and James himself wrote two letters about this subject—

but over the memories the essay evoked in me. Reading James's essay, I found myself transported back into time, thirty years earlier, when my best friend telephoned me with the news that he was in the process of committing suicide. In *Diaries to an English Professor* I describe my feelings of helplessness, confusion, anger, guilt, and grief over his death.

James had read my story and told me, in a conference a few weeks before the end of the semester, that he was planning to write about his father's suicide and intended to read the essay aloud. Even as I told him to "do a good job" on the essay so that he could "do justice to the subject," I wondered whether he would have the emotional control to read it to his classmates, most of whom did not know about the suicide. I also wondered how his classmates would react upon hearing the essay—Alexandra described in her evaluative essay on the biographical assignments how she had broken down in tears upon hearing the news. Would James's classmates be able to hear the essay without being traumatized?

I was also worried about myself. The essay was so wrenching that I could not read it without choking back tears. The story haunted me, not only because of its associations with a nightmarish period in my own life but also because I didn't know whether I would be able to remain in control when James read it aloud. I feared that if anyone in the class—James, his twenty-three classmates, or I—broke down during his reading of the essay, the result might trigger a chain reaction.

Three days before class, I telephoned James and asked him whether he really wanted to read the essay aloud. The question surprised him, but he expressed confidence in his ability to read it. I was still apprehensive, though, and asked him whether he thought I should warn his classmates that the essay might be disturbing and that anyone who wished to leave could do so. He said he wasn't sure a warning was a good idea.

James stopped into my office a few minutes before class and told me that he was ready. If he felt anxious, he didn't show it. I was nervous enough for both of us. In fact, I had never felt so apprehensive about having an essay read aloud. I had saved his essay for last—I could hardly imagine a more unsettling paper. Ironically, Colleen's essay, which I had not read in advance, was so distressing that many of us felt emotionally spent by the time it was James's turn. I warned James's classmates that his essay might prove disturbing to hear and that they could leave before he started reading. None did.

James began reading the essay in a voice that seemed louder and faster than usual. His tone seemed to falter slightly toward the end, when he described throwing his father onto the ground, but he executed the reading like an athlete performing at a competition. I use the simile deliberately, for no sooner did he finish reading the essay than he triumphantly raised his arms high above his head and began waving them, like a football player scoring the winning touchdown. I don't think his classmates knew how to react to this display—the contrast between the somber tone of the essay and his exultant smile afterward must have startled them.

I breathed a sigh of relief when James was finished with his reading, and I spoke about the essay in the remaining minutes of class. When a paper is as intense as his, we sometimes have little or no class discussion: simply hearing it is enough, and I wait until I reread it after class before making written comments. But in this case, I did speak about the essay for a few minutes, pointing out that while it is filled with sentence fragments, comma splices, and typographical and spelling errors—so many errors, indeed, that one doubts that the author revised or even proofread the essay before printing it up—the writing is forceful. I told the students what I had told James in my office, namely, that while the essay might deserve only a C in terms of its technical skills, I thought it was a more powerful piece of prose than anything I have ever written.

James uses several aesthetic devices to narrate the story, with extraordinary results. He begins with the quote from the *Inferno*, warning the reader to approach with caution, and then reveals in the second paragraph that no one, including himself, is safe from the horror of the story he intends to narrate. In the third paragraph, he addresses the class in the second person, establishing a close connection with the reader, as if he were Coleridge's Ancient Mariner seizing upon a reluctant Wedding Guest. Noting that his hands are shaking, he announces in the fourth paragraph the gruesome details of his father's death. Having intentionally violated traditional rules of storytelling, which require the climax to occur not in the beginning but at the end of a story, James then proceeds with his tale. The story builds to a second and more wrenching climax, the horrifying confrontation between father and son.

One of the difficulties in writing about a subject like suicide is that it is agonizing to acknowledge the conflicting emotions the event produces, particularly relief, which most suicide survivors do not wish to admit, since it produces so much guilt. Alexandra's willingness to write about these feelings concerning her grandfather's death may have encouraged James to elaborate in his last essay. Now, for the first time, he discloses his complex feelings for his father and, in the final paragraph, eulogizes his fallen hero in a way that rivals, to recall Kevin's literary allusion, the ending of *Death of a Salesman*.

Reading and Empathic Distress

The empathic distress I experienced while reading James's essay was unlike that described by Nathaniel West in his darkly satirical 1946 novella *Miss Lonelyhearts*. The story's eponymous protagonist is a newspaper reporter who is assigned to answer the increasingly desperate letters he receives from readers seeking his advice and help. The letter writers include a sixteen-year-old girl born without a nose, a boy writing about his "deaf and dumb" sister who has just been raped, and a wife battered by her husband. The letters are filled with unending, unmitigated misery. Turning to art, sex, and religion to find answers to the enigma of suffering, Miss Lonelyhearts finds his idealism dissolving into cynicism, sympathy turning into explosive rage, and eventually he is overwhelmed by grief and destroyed. The story can be read as a cautionary tale of the perils of reading and witnessing. Miss Lonelyhearts perishes because of his inability to maintain cautious optimism amid despair and because he is victimized by messianic fantasies that transform his life into a living hell.

I have never felt like Miss Lonelyhearts while reading a student's self-disclosing essay. Unlike the letter writers in West's tragicomic novella, James seeks neither advice nor help from his readers—only compassionate understanding. We cannot help but admire the strength and courage he demonstrates in his story. He begins with a Dantesque warning to abandon hope, but he himself never loses faith, not even when he describes horrific events that are rarely described in college classrooms. The essay moves from the father's death to the family's recovery, a resolution that is fully earned. James's moving eulogy is an act of love and reparation—an essay that I will never forget.

A Letter to James

Part of the drama of an essay like James's is its unpredictable impact upon the audience, in this case, his classmates and teacher. I had spent more time than usual discussing his essay, and consequently, few of his classmates were able to offer their reactions to it. I suspect that they might have been too stunned to speak even if I had remained silent. Did the essay affect them as deeply as it affected me? I didn't know. I had asked the students in their final assignment to evaluate the course and indicate the most memorable essays of the semester, but since the assignment was turned in at the last class, no one had yet read James's essay. A few days after the last class, however, I received the following brief essay from one of James's classmates:

Last Monday I unsuspectingly went to class. I did not know what I was about to hear. The disclosures in that room, that day, were more than I ever expected. There is one that particularly got to me. James's essay about his father's suicide touched me. I was warned that it might be difficult to hear. I know that I have a sensitive nature, but I am also very composed. I do not readily show emotion. I was staying for the entire essay no matter what it was about.

James started to read. I was very upset because we had been warned, and two of my classmates were talking amongst themselves. I thought that was very rude. James started reading. They continued talking. I was listening intently, I knew this was going to be more difficult then I suspected. It was. James uttered words that I will never forget. "On August 18, 1997 my father sat in the bathroom of Whispering Pines cemetery, just after visiting his own father's grave, stood a rifle on it's butt end, lowered his mouth to the gun, and pulled the trigger." They stopped talking. The whole room went silent. No one moved until he was done talking. James reading his essay was one of the most courageous things I have ever seen someone do. I respect him more than most people I have ever come in contact with. I want him to know that.

I sit next to James in class. When we were getting up to leave I wanted to hug him: I wanted to say I am sorry. I couldn't. I did not know what to do. No matter what I said or did he still had to live through a horrific tragedy. My actions did not fix it. I left the classroom. I walked through the social science building avoiding everyone's glance. The tears were streaming out of my eyes. It affected me a lot, and I do not regret sitting in that chair and listening to that essay.

I am very lucky to have been in James's presence when he read that article. I learned a lot. Not about school subjects, but about strength of character. I congratulate James. He is a strong person. His has lived through adversity and used it to his advantage. I learned a valuable lesson from him that day. I know he will never know that, but at least I said it. Since that class I have given that essay to my friends so that they can read it. I have not done it in an intrusive way. I am not trying to exploit his tragedy. I want everyone to know what he has gone through and use him as an example. It makes the little things seem to be just that, little. Ironically, it was a little thing like him reading that essay that brought me to this conclusion.

Postscript

Several months after the course ended, I contacted Kevin, Alexandra, Colleen, and James and asked each of them to visit me, separately, in my office. I showed each of them the section of the chapter containing his or her own writings, and after all four gave me their approval, I then showed them the entire chapter so that they could see the larger context. James came to my office a few weeks later to tell me that he had shown the chapter to his mother, who was profoundly affected by the content of her son's essay. Suicide was not a subject James's family talked about—his younger brother still did not know the cause of his father's death. I asked James whether his mother would be willing to share her impressions of his writings with readers of this book. He said he thought she would like to do so and a week later delivered the following letter:

To say I am moved by my son's story is an understatement. Emotions that I have kept at bay rose to the surface. Painful as the experience was, it also enlightened me. Qualities such as honesty, courage, love, and strength, which a parent strives to instill in their child, are suddenly quite evident in his words. What a wonderful revelation! I especially admire James's courage. To reveal his life to his peers, an open book so to speak, is something I wish I could do. Unfortunately, I lack what my son possesses.

Acceptance of the fact that my determination and perseverance to get my husband well failed is something that I am still struggling with. To acknowledge to others the fact that my husband committed suicide, in my mind, is a reflection on me. Intellectually speaking, I know this is wrong. Psychologically speaking, I know this stems from having a mother who uses guilt as often as a writer uses a pen. How intelligent I sound.

All my life, rationalization has helped me deal with or understand a situation. It has been my crutch. Unfortunately, the act of suicide, especially my husband's, cannot be rationalized by me. That is why I have lost my balance. Though, after reading James's story, I think I may have overcompensated in the rationalization department. He depicts his father as a hero and mentor. Their relationship was extremely close. When James was a toddler, if his father left the room, he would cry. Their jaunts to the movies were exactly as he said, a means of escape. I was at work and we lived in a small apartment. Going to the movies was beneficial for both my husband and child. The key word here is both. Children are not aware of the politics a mother must play at times to make fathers what they are. As James grew older, rationalization went into full gear. There were many times I played Devil's Advocate between James and his father. Neither of them aware of what I was doing.

By the time my second son was born, my husband's career was in full swing and unfortunately this child lost the most. He did not have the bond-

ing with his father, as James had. Hence, our bond was closer. My husband attempted to go through the motions with him. There were movies and attending little league games; the love was there, but the zest was not, and my younger son sensed it. Again I used rationalization to smooth things over. Daddy's very busy at work; daddy's tired, etc. As time went on and pressures increased, my husband suffered his second nervous breakdown.

I think it's all about protection with me. Protecting my children from any harm, be it physical or emotional. After reading James's story, I feel confident that from a psychological point of view, he is dealing with this tragedy better than his brother or myself. I am proud of the courage he demonstrated when his father died; and the courage he still demonstrates through his writings.

Although my younger son is doing well, both socially and academically, I'm still concerned. He does not want to discuss his father yet; and that's alright. When he is ready, I'll be there for him, as will James, and as fate would have it, perhaps these writings.

CHAPTER 3

The Dark Side of Diversity

I realize that you were taking a chance by giving us a sensitive topic like diversity to write on. I believe this assignment was as difficult to write on as it was to assign. . . . Rarely do students have the opportunity to write about taboo issues, like racism, in a formal class setting. If an empathic class setting is not established, writing and discussing issues like diversity and racism can become explosive.

It may seem odd to admit that until recently I have been reluctant to give writing assignments on diversity, a topic that has received so much attention both inside and outside the classroom. By contrast, I have long encouraged students to write about wrenching subjects such as suicide, divorce, eating disorders, and sexual abuse. What is so different about diversity? Although it is often challenging for students to write about depression or anorexia, both of which are associated with shame, the writers generally do not worry about offending their classmates. But an essay on diversity, including the nation's volatile history of prejudice, discrimination, and racial violence—what Wendell Berry called in 1970 "the hidden wound"—is inherently risky since the writer knows that classmates are likely to take offense even when none is intended. An essay written by a minority student about racial prejudice in a fraternity is liable to produce anger, defensiveness, or stony silence among classmates who may be in that fraternity. I doubt whether any subject is fraught with as much explosive violence.

Moreover, diversity assignments compromise the safeguards that are essential for risky writing. A white or black student who is writing about depression or sexual abuse can remain safely anonymous in a class of predominantly white students; a person of color who is writing about racial discrimination cannot remain invisible. Even if, for example, an African American allows me to read anonymously an essay about discrimination against blacks on campus, the other African Americans in the class may feel uncomfortable, since they will be identified with the essay. Persons of color may thus fear that they cannot write about white racism without alienating their classmates.

A case in point appears in *The Agony of Education* (1996), a study of the

113

plight of African Americans in higher education. Authors Joe Feagin, Hernan Vera, and Nikitah Imani quote the following story about a black student's unhappy classroom experience. (The brackets appear in the text.)

> It was a creative writing class, and we had to write stories, whatever, and we had to sit in circles. And we had to tell our stories and read them. And mine was on racism, of course, because I'm always bringing that up. And it was just like a tragic mulatto story, and this girl couldn't stand being mixed. . . . So she kills herself, right. So this [white] guy goes, "You guys [have to] make the stories . . . fit reality. You can't make like a fantasy-fiction whatever." And he says, "Why did you do that? Why did you write a story like that?" [I said] "Because the girl also went to this university." And he goes, "There's no racism on this college campus." Freaked everybody out. And I was the only black. But there was a Puerto Rican, and there was a Chinese person in the room, and they just freaked. And I had never heard either of them speak before. This guy said: "Where the hell do you live?" You know, "Where do you live? Do you live in this state?" And the teacher . . . goes, "Hold up, honey, I don't know what utopia you're living in." This is a white teacher; she said, "But honey, you can just, inside of this room, outside of that door, on this campus . . . there is a lot of racism." . . . She's like, "Open your eyes, open your eyes there's a lot of discrimination and racism on this campus." And that freaked me out. (69)

Feagin, Vera, and Imani cite this story to illustrate that white students often deny the reality of white racism on campus. I agree with their observation that "[m]any whites fail to perceive the existence of racism, in part because white privilege is taken for granted and in part because most whites have not experienced being in a subordinate position or have not been educated about the character and impact of racism" (70). I also agree with their conclusion that unless white students hear about minority students' experiences with discrimination, there is little hope that racial tensions in higher education will diminish.

One of the problems with frank and open classroom discussions of racism is that they often result in clashes between students in dominant and minority groups. These arguments frequently reflect larger tensions between conservative and liberal ideologies. Students may feel forced to identify themselves as either victims or victimizers rather than discovering the extent to which they play both roles at various times in their lives. It is easier to blame society for the evils of racism than to accept responsibility for perpetuating social injustice. Students may idealize minority groups that have been victimized and demonize dominant groups associated with social injustice. Classroom discussions of oppression may ironically reproduce the dynamics of domination and marginalization that they seek to overcome. The discussions of race, class, and gender that I've had in my literature courses have occasionally left students feeling angry or defensive, unwilling to participate in further conversations. Anger may be, as Audre Lorde asserts, "an appropriate reaction to racist attitudes, as is fury when the actions arising from those attitudes do not change" (129); nevertheless, anger is usually a disruptive emotion in the classroom, blocking meaningful self-disclosure.

Does prejudice exist in all people or only in those who have cultural and institutional power? This remains one of the most contentious diversity questions. The authors of *The Agony of Education* define racism in the following way: "What we call racism encompasses subtle and overt discriminatory practices, their institutional contexts, and the attitudes and ideologies that shape or rationalize them" (Feagin, Vera, and Imani 7). Given this expanded definition, it is curious that the authors' discussion of prejudice is limited to those in dominant groups, suggesting that the prejudice of those in minority groups should not be acknowledged in print.

If some educators imply that people in minority groups are free of prejudice, other educators assert that people in minority groups are immune from the crises of white middle-class students. In "The Pedagogy of Pleasure 2: The Me-in-Crisis," written in the form of a letter to a white undergraduate student protesting the ideological bent of his professor, the Marxist critic Mas'ud Zavarzadeh makes this astonishing claim: "By the way, why is it that all the letters I receive on the crisis of subjectivity are from white (upper-) middle-class students? I have never encountered a person of color who allowed herself/himself the luxury of being *in-crisis* . . . these luxuries are all part of the class privileges of the white (upper) middle class; something you may wish to think about . . ." (228–29; ellipses in original).

Unlike Zavarzadeh, I believe that all people are susceptible to prejudice and crisis regardless of their institutional power. As Maurianne Adams, Lee Anne Bell, and Pat Griffin observe in *Teaching for Diversity and Social Justice* (1997), "members of both agent [majority] and target [minority] groups are capable of prejudice, abuse, violence, and hatred, although only the agent groups have the institutional and cultural power to back up the prejudices against the target groups" (73). Louise Derman-Sparks and Carol Brunson Phillips make a similar observation in their book *Teaching/ Learning Anti-Racism* (1997). "Although racism in America is historically and structurally a White problem, people of color do play a role in perpetuating the system: beliefs among the White dominating population have a kind of counterpoint in the behavior and beliefs of populations victimized by racism" (25).

I suspect that the white student's defensive response in the example cited in *The Agony of Education* may have arisen because he felt others held him responsible for all the evils and injustices of American society. Shame or guilt over ancestors' actions may sometimes have positive consequences, as when children of Nazis devote their lives to fighting prejudice, but shame or guilt often does not lead to enlightened behavior. The white student may have also felt angered by his teacher's patronizing response: "Hold up, honey, I don't know what utopia you're living in." Students of all color are bound to "freak out" whenever they feel that their points of view are invalidated, misunderstood, or belittled. Nor is anything gained when students are intimidated into acknowledging racism, as one radical composition teacher has proposed. "I believe that it is necessary to *force* White people into the position where they *have* to try to put together an argument in support of their continuing unfairly to receive the privileges they unfairly do as a result of racism" (Nowlan 249; emphasis in original).

Diversity assignments can prove especially threatening to students whose teachers embrace a "pedagogy of conflict" while encouraging autobiographical disclosures. Wendy Hesford argues in her book *Framing Identities* (1999) that it is the writing teacher's responsibility to critique his or her students' attitudes toward race and ethnicity. Developing Gerald Graf's idea of "teaching the conflicts" and Mary Louise Pratt's view that the classroom is a "contact zone" in which ideological positions should be contested, Hesford advocates a model of teaching based on conflict. In her view, the classroom cannot be a safe space because it ignores the differences among teachers and students. Hesford does not challenge the appropriateness of a pedagogy of conflict even after acknowledging that the white students in her writing course became angry and defensive during a diversity assignment when they were critiqued by students from other cultural backgrounds. She singles out one student who told her that he felt he was a victim of reverse racism. "It was not my intention to invalidate Stan's feeling of alienation, but it was my pedagogical responsibility to encourage him to situate his claim of victimization within a historical framework" (92). I agree with Hesford that self-disclosure can help individuals "negotiate conflicting identities and contradictory discourses" (105–6), but I believe that students are immediately placed on the defensive when their autobiographical disclosures are critiqued by a teacher or classmates, no matter how accurate or well-intentioned these critiques may be.

Even when teachers strive to create safe classrooms, they may find that the symptoms of oppression and inequality they wish to uncover have infected their own discourse. This was indeed what happened to Elizabeth Ellsworth, who describes a graduate course she taught in 1988 at the University of Wisconsin–Madison. Ellsworth designed "Media and Anti-Racist Pedagogies" to investigate the racist violence that had erupted in communities and on college campuses, including her own. She discovered, to her dismay, that "when participants in our class attempted to put into practice prescriptions offered in the literature concerning empowerment, student voice, and dialogue, we produced results that were not only unhelpful, but actually exacerbated the very conditions we were trying to work against" (298). Part of the problem was that although everyone was opposed to oppression in theory, the students' and professor's "asymmetrical positions of difference and privilege" thwarted genuine dialogue. Ellsworth could not find a way to make the classroom a safe place for students to discuss oppression. She offers many reasons for this failure, including the students' fear of being misunderstood, their fear of vulnerability, their memories of bad experiences in other contexts of speaking out, and their resentment that some forms of oppression (such as sexism, classism, and anti-Semitism) were being marginalized in the name of addressing racism. Ellsworth's conclusion is that unconscious forces can quickly subvert the rationalist assumptions behind "liberatory" pedagogy.

More recently, Sarah Hinlicky, a student at Princeton Theological Seminary, begins her article in the monthly journal *First Things* with a jarring sentence: "The cardinal rule of writing about race is: don't" (9). She lists several reasons, including the following: "it is impossible to avoid offense; or, in laboring to avoid offense, whatever humble point that may have been trying to assert itself will be buried under piles of apologies, qualifications, and assurance of the good-will of the author" (9). Hinlicky relates her undergraduate experiences at a small, private, liberal arts college in the South where, despite the fact that everyone was trying to be "color-blind," whites and blacks were segregated. "Not legally, but voluntarily, and enforced by social strictures more binding than anything government could impose" (9). She recalls her uneasy "white conscience" as she tried futilely to establish a dialogue with black students and to bridge the color divide. She concludes her essay by raising a vexed question: "Is it possible to become culture-blind? Maybe there's an answer to be found, but I think I'd better quit now, since I'm not supposed to be writing about race in the first place" (11).

Writing Honestly about Diversity

Can students write honestly, then, about a subject that is so destabilizing? Should they be encouraged to do so? These are two different questions. Few would disagree that one should write as honestly as possible about every subject regardless of its controversiality. Many college and university English departments offer courses on race, class, and gender, the "triumvirate" of diversity, though a fourth category, religion, rarely receives equal attention. These courses expose the blatant and subtle racism, classism, sexism, and homophobia that are part of American society. Despite the fierce debates that have raged over multiculturalism, most people affirm — or at least pay lip service to — the need for toleration and respect. Yet what people say in public often differs from what they say in private. Only by speaking in safe generalities and platitudes can one avoid provoking heated disagreements over diversity. To speak about the troubled history of race relations or religious intolerance in this country is to risk literal or metaphorical assassination.

Those who claim that the university has become a captive to "political correctness" believe candid discussions of diversity are impossible. The term is often used by conservatives such as Allan Bloom and Dinesh D'Souza to charge that adherence to a progressive "party line" erodes the expression of free speech on campus. Political correctness may exist in certain courses, but the desire for equality should not prevent people representing all shades of the political spectrum to speak truthfully about the existence of racism on both a personal and cultural level. Everyone can cite a litany of depressing examples of being discriminated against: "blame psychology" dominates the media. Yet most people are unwilling to cite the ways in which they have contributed to and participated in the victimization of others. Only if we acknowledge our own stereotypes can we begin to overcome them. As Paulo Freire observes in *Pedagogy of the Oppressed (1993)*: "The central problem is this: How can the oppressed, as divided, unauthentic beings, participate in developing the pedagogy of their liberation? Only as they discover themselves to be the 'hosts' of the oppressor can they contribute to the midwifery of their liberating pedagogy" (33).

To respond empathically and honestly at times may seem contradictory, for it is often difficult to convey feelings that one knows will disturb or perhaps offend others. How does a writer acknowledge prejudice toward a group when a member of that group is present? How does a reader respond to a classmate's essay that is "brutally" frank? How does a teacher affirm tolerance while discussing an essay that reveals intolerance? These problematic situations often arise in the classroom, but they are particularly troublesome in the self-disclosing classroom.

To return to my first question: can students learn to write honestly about diversity? Can they look deep within themselves in order to examine fears and conflicts over their cultural identities? Will they admit to feeling prejudice toward racial or religious groups that are represented by their own classmates? Should these self-disclosures be encouraged and, if so, can they lead to greater understanding and respect? Can self-disclosure lead to more complex writing?

Assignment 1: Exploring Your Heritage

I chose a writing class that was unusually diverse in order to pursue these questions. The twenty-three students came from families originating in a dozen different European, African, and Asian countries. Six students were born in other countries or United States territories—including Haiti, Puerto Rico, Jamaica, and Poland. I waited until the middle of the semester, after the students had become familiar with each other, before giving the following open-ended assignment:

> The biographical assignments have revealed a rich diversity among us: different ethnic, cultural, racial, and religious backgrounds. Many of you are an interesting mix of several backgrounds. I would like you to explore your own heritage in the following essay. After describing your ancestry, please discuss the following questions:
>
> 1. What aspects of your background are you proud of? Why?
> 2. What aspects of your background are you ashamed of? Why?
> 3. Are you ambivalent about your background—that is, do you feel both proud and ashamed of it? If so, please explain why you feel this ambivalence.
> 4. How important is your ethnic, cultural, racial, and religious background in the formation of your identity?
> 5. What stereotypes or preconceptions, both positive and negative, do other people have of your background?
> 6. What stereotypes or preconceptions, both positive and negative, do you have of other backgrounds?
> 7. Have you ever been discriminated against because of your background?
> 8. Have you ever discriminated against another person because of his or her background?
> 9. What would you like to convey about your own background to others from a different background?
> 10. What would you like others from a different background to convey to you?

I knew it would be impossible for students to answer all these questions in a brief essay. Nevertheless, I was curious to see which questions would be discussed. I asked several people to bring multiple copies of their essay for class discussion. I told them they could remain anonymous if they wished, an option that provided greater safety for the white students than for the Caribbean Americans. I also told them they could write on another topic if they found this one disagreeable or threatening.

Pride without Prejudice

Nearly all the students focused on the positive aspects of their heritage. They spoke proudly about their backgrounds, revealing little if any ambivalence toward their racial, ethnic, or religious identity. They acknowledged the extent to which they have been discriminated against for being different, but they did not see themselves as victims. The six students who immigrated to the United States revealed keen appreciation of their multicultural identities. They were aware of the negative stereotypes associated with their cultures, and they reacted in different ways, ranging from gentle or caustic irony to righteous indignation. All six students who were born outside the United States gave me permission to use their writings, but since I was unable to locate four students after the semester ended, to show them how I intended to use their essays, I cannot quote from them. The following selection, however, is representative:

There is nothing that makes me ashamed about my background. I come from a family that are important people in the history of my country. There are two things that I know are hot topics in Jamaica, politics and sports. My grandfather was a member of Jamaican Parliament, which is the equivalent of Congress here in the United States. He was influential in developing policy for the people when my country was just beginning. My grandfather's brother was also a prominent figure in Jamaican history. He won Olympic medals in track and field for Jamaica. Not only proud of my homeland, but also my family's role in making it a better place.

My idea of Jamaica is not the American idea of Jamaica. Most Americans think that it is just one big beach. Every time I say I'm from Jamaica three things happen. Number one, I am asked if I lived by the beach. I tell them, "No, I lived in Kingston (the capital). That's no where near the beach." Number two, I'm told about some sort of honeymoon or spring break a friend or loved one has taken in Jamaica and then asked if I've been to that beach resort. I say, "No, I haven't been to that beach resort. I don't live near the beach." Number three, I'm told that I don't have an accent. Which is gener-

ally followed by this statement, "I guess you've been there (the United States) along time." To which I reply, "I've never had an accent," and, "no, I didn't live near the beach." I don't know why there is an American preconception that if I say I'm Jamaican I should be greeting them with, "Hey, Mon." Actually I do know why. Americans believe anything they see on television, which I think is scary. That's the only place that I can think of where they're getting their information. It annoys me beyond belief when people have preconceived ideas about what I as a Jamaican should be like. It angers me when they voice their opinions, as if I should be wrong for being me. It terrifies me that the images and portrayals of Jamaicans are taken to heart. We aren't all pot smoking, beach going, rastafarians, nor do all of us speak patois. I've gotten so many different stereotypes of what I should be, before someone stopped to ask me who I was.

Those students whose families have lived in the United States for several generations also valued diversity, though many did not feel strong kinship with their ancestors. They referred briefly to the prejudice to which they have been exposed but did not dwell on this aspect of their heritage. The white students were generally less aware of their race and ethnicity than were the nonwhite students, supporting Harlon Dalton's observation that whites "tend to take race for granted or to view it as somehow irrelevant" (107). Some of the white students were defensive about the history of colonialism associated with their ancestors, but they did not believe this affected them directly. Nor did most of the white students disclose ambivalence toward their ethnic, racial, or religious backgrounds. Rather, they affirmed multiculturalism and found metaphors to convey the many differences that constitute American society. Many of the essays could have been submitted to college admissions officers: despite the uneven quality of the prose, they are interesting, informative, often lively, though generally not self-exploratory.

Caroline: "I Assume That My Family Were Nazis"

There were exceptions, however—three women who used the diversity assignment to investigate troubling aspects of their cultural identity. Caroline spent most of her essay discussing pride in her family's Germanic roots, but she reveals in the last paragraph an aspect of her heritage that she has long found unsettling:

I cannot truly say that I am ashamed of any part of my family background. But there was one incident that shaped my youth which almost did. When I was younger I learned about World War II and the Holocaust. I was mortified by the destruction of so many Jews at the hands of the Nazis. I learned that the Nazis began in Germany. I could not believe it. What little I knew about my family history played into this ignorance. I assume that my family were Nazis because we were of German descent. I was totally neglecting the fact that my family had been in America for a hundred years. I also dismissed the fact that many in my family served the American armed forces during the war. I just assumed that my family was guilty somehow. When I finally learned more about the events of the times, I realized that I had overreacted. But part of that still haunts me. I never like hearing about the Nazi party, either in Germany or the United States. I always assume that there would be people in this world that aligned my German heritage with the atrocities of that war. I have learned that I must take each individual person separate from anyone else and get to know what they think.

Roseanna: "The Question That Still Eludes Me Is What It Feels Like to Be an American"

Roseanna probed in her essay the nature of being American. She focused on the search for her Italian roots, her devotion to her beloved nonna (grandmother), the family tensions arising over an interracial relationship, and her feelings of cultural alienation while living in New York City:

After I moved back home [from the Southwest], I continued to meet interesting people through work and school. One of them was a Caribbean who became my boyfriend and best friend. We had to endure a long distance relationship since he was living in New York City. About a month after we met, while he was visiting Albany, I brought him home and he briefly met my parents. My mother was happy to meet him, but my father later told me that he did not want me to see my new friend any more. I suffered the burden of many arguments on behalf of our relationship. My father claims that he is not prejudice, but simply feels it is wrong for me to be part of an interracial relationship. I believe that he is contradicting himself. His feelings are so strong, however, that he has threatened the stability of his marriage should my mother take my side. Even my inheritance and the acceptance of my relatives became a fragile and uncertain issue. It seemed as if I would end up a martyr for the devil's cause. All of this led me to question the unconditional love that I thought always surrounded me.

I then became tuned in to the uncomfortable vibes of racism. Before I left my first college to move to New York City, my grandfather offered me some advice which I swiftly yet silently disregarded. He told me that I should stay away from "all those Blacks and Chinese." This way, I wouldn't destroy my chances of meeting a nice white man. I responded that any man who had a problem with my friends wasn't worth meeting anyway, but I doubt that he understood.

In New York City I felt like a minority for the first time in my life. At first I enjoyed the situation. I felt it was a good learning experience for me. But I began to wonder whether I belonged to any culture at all. At this point I was studying Italian and Spanish. It frustrated me that so many people already spoke a second language. I was extremely jealous of everyone, especially the beautiful Hispanic girls who would walk by me in lively groups, shifting their conversations easily between two languages. I was then struggling to learn languages, which seemed an uphill battle for me. It was during this period that I especially wished my mother had also been Italian and that I, like some of my cousins, grew up speaking the language.

I often visited my boyfriend and his mother in a neighborhood inhabited mostly by Hispanics. Whenever I would enter this neighborhood, I felt as if I had entered another country. The sounds of merengue, salsa and the Spanish language would spice up the air, as I blandly walked down the sidewalk, my face paling and my grasp of language suddenly insufficient. I think that part of the alliance with my boyfriend lies in the fact that we both feel as if we remain outside of our cultures. Although he physically blends into the neighborhood, he doesn't feel comfortable there. However, I ingest a dose of their culture every time I visit him, whether it be eating his mother's delicious comida or listening to them argue in Spanish.

As I became accustomed to life in the city, I also became more aware of the looks of hatred that were thrown at me. I always knew that prejudice could be inflicted on me, but it had never affected me on that level before. It upsets me to realize how many people hate me. I sometimes notice the hurt behind the anger and wish that I could show the person that I am not every white woman. One night, an old black man on the crowded subway train directed all of his anger towards white people and women to me. Obviously mentally disturbed, he unloaded all of his hatred by glaring at me and yelling out cruel names. His anger was so thick that I remained hurt and frightened for some time. It is these occasions which inhibit my own progress in chipping away the prejudice that I unfortunately have learned.

My prejudice usually surfaces when I am jealous. Unfortunately, it has always been easier for me to make friends with men, so my cultural experiences have usually been lopsided. One particular group with whom I've regrettably never been close to are African-American women. I admit that sometimes their strength of spirit takes me aback, but what I've never been able to accept without a cringe is when I hear the term "sister" used. This is not to *say that I don't approve of its usage. But it makes me feel isolated and I can't understand why I fall well outside of the "sister" range. That kind of camaraderie is missing among European-Americans. I'm not sure who to blame for my loss: the black women for not embracing me with their sisterhood, or the women of my own background for not strengthening our ties. . . .*

The question that still eludes me is what it feels like to be an American. Maybe for some people, the answer is obvious, but I find myself lost between the divisions of ethnic separation. After visiting my relatives in Sicily, I long to live in a country where traditions are shared among all, or at least most of the people. I dreaded returning home, where overcrowded cultures bump into one another and remain ignorant of the words for conveying an apology to the other. Some days I wish I wasn't born into this country; most days I wish it was never "discovered." However, I always want to remain close to my family. I often dream of my children playing with their cousins and feeling as if they belong to something special. And what's more, there are sides to myself which I have yet to explore. I hope that in time, my mother and I learn more about the cultures and characters she has passed down along the lines of her ancestry.

Angela: "I Think His Racism Snuck Up on Me"

Angela was the third student who wrote about a confusing aspect of diversity—her involvement with a white supremacist when she was living in another state. The relationship ended when she moved, but she continued to feel guilt, shame, and horror. She had never written about the experience and feared incurring the reader's disapproval.

One experience has probably taught me more than anything I have learned through academia. This experience still has me confused to the day but has reconfirmed my dedication to diversity and curiosity about multiculturalism. Although I have reflected on this experience exhaustingly over the past four years, I have yet to understand it or surpass the embarrassment and shame I have as a result of it. I have talked about this in the past but I have never before written about it and imagine that I will have difficulty doing so. I do not know how to even begin such a complicated tale.

My father is in the military, and we have moved several times. When we were living in the South I became involved with a white supremacist group. For those who have had little exposure to these groups, I imagine that sounds outrageous. I remember them being around during my adolescent years and became rather accustomed to their presence. Most of the ones in my area did more harm to themselves than anyone else. Although I associated with some of them, I figured it was a whole world of trouble I just did not want to get involved in. A few friends of mine had dated white supremacists, gotten into a mess of problems and I vowed that I would never date one. I was young and fickle and my desire to date guys won out over my vow to avoid white supremacists like the plague. I started dating one named Judd in high school. This is where my shame is involved. As a teenager, I was not discriminatory in the type of people I spent my time with. I did not believe the philosophy "birds of a feather flock together" that my mother had stressed throughout my life. I thought I was being open-minded by having such a variety of friends. My family often jokes about the invisible "tatoo" I must have on my forehead inviting all lunatics and losers to seek me out. At first I did not know about Judd's involvement with white supremacists. Now that I have a glimpse into his world, I realize that I never knew him as well as I had thought. My shame lies with the fact, that when I found out, I did not turn face and go running like I should have. It took me a solid six months before I got really scared and left him. Being with him, allowing myself to be associated with that, is probably the most racially discriminatory act I will ever commit in my life and it sickens me. I look back and I wretch and I wish I had more discretion as a teenager. I feel that any other person would have known not to get involved with someone like him. I think his racism snuck up on me because I certainly did not see it coming. As weeks passed, he revealed more of his beliefs to me and I learned more about what he was involved in. Somehow I managed to look past those beliefs and associations for a while; although in retrospect, I can not even imagine how. Writing this, I can not imagine what the reader must think of me but I know that this experience is a reality I will have to continue to face. Nothing was ever said straight out and it took me a while to figure a few things out. One weekend I went camping with some of Judd's friends. I tried to be as hospitable as possible without showing my fear. They slept with guns under their pillows and talked about violence in a way that blew my mind. Raised in a household where guns were for hunting deer only, this talk disturbed me. When I started to put the pieces together, I realized not only that I did not want to be involved with this but that these were people I did not want as enemies. Fortunately, in my junior year of high school my father was transferred to the Northeast. I did not tell Judd my new address, and I parted ways with him much easier than I thought I would be able to.

What I have been left with is a tremendous amount to process. It has scared me knowing there are people out there with so much hatred for themselves and others that they are able to exclude all but one group of people from their lives. It scares me that I allowed it to come so close before I recog-

nized it. It has left me ashamed and full of questions about myself. I can not understand what it is about me that allowed myself to be around people like that, especially with the perspective my parents have. I used to wonder why my parents did not forbid me to date Judd or hang out with his friends. Now I realize it was because they knew if they forbid me it was almost a guarantee that I would do precisely what they forbid me to. I only recall my mother remarking once about white supremacists. Judd and a group of his friends were at my house. One of the guys had "white supremacist" on his sweatshirt. My mother asked me if the words were a reminder in case he forgot. I thought that was pretty funny but in retrospect, I think she viewed them as misguided and stupid kids. At a time, I thought they would always be to drunk or too dumb to do any harm to our society. I learned some pretty unbelievable lessons from that experience and am grateful that it did not take up my whole life. One of the lessons I learned was that just having people out there that have racist beliefs and stereotypes harms all of us. I know that I have not processed my experiences to fullest but I imagine I have taken a step in having written them down. At the time, I only looked at the experience as another loser guy I dated and have since only started to analyze it for further meaning. I started to become truly embarrassed and ashamed the more I analyzed the experience and realized how incredibly naive I was. I do know that the experience has awoken a new understanding of how important diversity is in this world. Although it was the lesson my mother tried to teach me when I was a child, I have always been stubborn and learned most lessons the hard way, and on my own. What I learned goes beyond anything I could have ever learned listening to my mother talk about diversity or sitting in a classroom.

Caroline, Roseanna, and Angela took a chance in writing about cultural and religious conflicts, describing aspects of diversity that are seldom discussed in the classroom. Shame and secrecy characterize their writings. The essays are not easily shared with parents, teachers, or friends. How would Caroline's parents react if they knew about their daughter's guilt over being German? How would Roseanna's father respond to the disclosure that he could not accept his daughter's relationship with a nonwhite? Would Angela feel safe if the white supremacist whom she dated learned of her whereabouts?

These essays are risky, however, not simply because they may anger readers or even provoke some of them to violence. They are risky because the authors acknowledge responsibility for beliefs or acts they now regret. Caroline admits she overreacted in assuming that every German was a

Nazi; Roseanna concedes that her own prejudice surfaces whenever she is jealous; Angela cannot forgive herself for remaining with a man whose views were so repugnant to her. These admissions are important because they locate problematic thoughts or actions not within abstract society but within the writers themselves. The students are not content with demonizing society; rather, they know that they must change themselves before they can change others.

Caroline, Roseanna, and Angela wrote compelling personal essays. Each writer confronts shameful feelings and investigates the subtle implications of racism. The essays are emotionally intense and thoughtful. There is nothing narcissistic or solipsistic about their self-disclosures, which are embedded in a social, cultural, and political context. In depicting the ambiguity and ambivalence surrounding diversity issues, the writers move beyond surface truths. They write with uncompromising honesty—one can feel unresolved tension in their essays. Thus Caroline remains haunted by her German ancestry despite the fact that she knows her family is not guilty of Nazi atrocities; Roseanna seeks to define what it means to be an American; and Angela struggles to come to terms with her past involvement with a hate group.

Assignment 2: Changing an Element of Your Identity for One Day

Roseanna read her essay aloud, without experiencing visible discomfort. Caroline and Angela allowed me to read their essays anonymously. Since we did not discuss their anonymous essays, I can't be certain how Angela's classmates felt about it, but I suspect they found the paper as disturbing as I did.

The diversity assignment produced several interesting essays—and no class explosions. The empathic classroom encouraged people to listen without judging or criticizing others. People wrote about their own experiences and did not contradict their classmates' stories. They began to discover multiple perspectives and to use personal experiences to understand larger social and cultural issues. Emboldened by the results, I decided to give a second diversity assignment:

> Imagine waking up one morning to discover that an important element of your identity has suddenly changed—your race, class, gender, sexual preference, or religion. Describe in a short story what it would be like to live for one day with this difference. Try to describe how your relatives and friends would respond differently to you. Tell us at the end of the story whether you are happy or sad to return to your "old" identity.

Most students chose to change their gender, describing their physical and psychological metamorphoses. The men imagined what it would be like to be a woman and experience sexual harassment; the women imagined what it would be like to be a man and enjoy greater freedom and opportunity. The gender transformation essays were generally humorous and light-hearted in tone, ending with the authors rejoicing in their return to their former genders. "In my dream, I thought that being a guy would be good," one woman wrote. "If I had the opportunity to decide if I want to be a guy I would say no. I think women have a beauty inside them that makes it different from men in this world. Even though the women go through many injustices and discrimination, they have many things to offer to the world."

Other essays included a woman turning into a Homer Simpson cartoon character, sleeping and eating all day without a care in the world; a woman becoming her own revered grandmother; and a Catholic woman turning into the Pope. A student who disclosed in the autobiographical assignment that she had had an abortion imagined herself becoming a mother. "I awake to find that having a baby was a dream. I am relieved, yet slightly saddened. I feel as if a part of me is missing. I enjoy having my freedom returned, yet I long for the day when I am ready to have a child of my own." Three people wrote about waking up with serious disabilities: one person imagined being blind, another deaf, and a third transformed into her schizophrenic boyfriend.

None of the black students wrote about being white, but several white students imagined themselves black. These essays were among the most serious in tone and revealed the authors' concern for social justice. A man described in specific detail the social and economic disadvantages of being a black male: earning less than whites; having little or no health insurance; often being raised in a broken family, without a father; and facing the likelihood of being locked up in a penitentiary. A woman wrote about the discrimination she experienced while shopping in an upscale dress shop. "The clerks were anything but subtle, whispering nervously while eying me suspiciously. It wasn't long before one of them began to follow me around the store. Surely, she did not think that my intentions were anything but honorable. The white patrons were free in the shop to browse about without suspicion, what was it she saw in me?"

This second diversity assignment encouraged students to imagine being the "other" for a day. They projected themselves into characters who were generally disadvantaged because of racial, cultural, or physical reasons. Though the tone of these stories was generally relaxed and playful, the assignment allowed students to glimpse the dark side of diversity.

Assignment 3: The Dark Side of Diversity

I now hoped the students would be willing to write a third essay in which they disclosed the fears, contradictions, and tensions associated with diversity. I thought it would be helpful for them to hear about my own struggle, so I distributed the following assignment, revealing a central ambivalence in my life:

> From my point of view, and, I hope, from yours, the two assignments on race, class, gender, and religion produced interesting and valuable essays. Most of you wrote on this subject for the first time and began exploring issues that are of great importance in your life. Your essays were unfailingly sensitive to controversial issues and respectful of cultural differences. Each of the essays affirmed, without exception, the need for tolerance, understanding, and compassion for all people. The most powerful essays explored aspects of race, class, gender, and religion that are highly conflicted, involving feelings of embarrassment, guilt, shame, and confusion. These writers disclosed, if only momentarily, the darker emotions surrounding diversity and acknowledged the existence of prejudice, anger, and fear within themselves.
>
> Some of you may disagree with me, but I believe that prejudice and bigotry are germs that dwell within everyone. The germs may be innocuous at times, but they can suddenly erupt into a full-blown disease, one that is highly contagious and virulent.
>
> How do we prevent this disease from occurring? The best way, in my opinion, is to acknowledge it within ourselves, though to do so is neither easy nor risk-free. Let me give you some personal examples of the insidiousness of prejudice both within others and myself.
>
> I am Jewish, and while I don't think I have been discriminated against because of my religion, I am very conscious—and self-conscious—of my Jewish identity. Several years ago my wife and I were having a picnic with a neighbor, with whom we were (and are) friendly. Our neighbor's mother, a warm, elderly woman of whom we were quite fond, mentioned that she had gone to a garage sale where she found a table that she wished to purchase. She told us that while the price was too high, she eventually "Jewed" the price down. My wife and I couldn't believe our ears. Had we misheard her? A few minutes later she used the same expression. She knew we are Jewish and that we would therefore be offended by the word. Her daughter—our neighbor—was standing next to us and surely heard her mother use the offensive expression; nevertheless, our neighbor did not say anything to indicate her regret. My wife and I decided not to say anything: we felt that a comment would be embarrassing for our neighbor and for us. We were mortified, however, and never forgot the incident. In retrospect, I was sorry that I had remained silent.
>
> Several years later I was speaking to another neighbor, who had just had his driveway repaved. I was interested in having my own driveway repaved

and asked him how much he paid. "He wanted $1,400 but I Jewed the price down to $1,100." I immediately thought of the incident with my other neighbor and resolved not to remain silent this time. "I wish you would not use that word," I said; "it's very offensive." My neighbor immediately realized that he was speaking to a Jew, but instead of apologizing—or perhaps as a way of apologizing—he claimed that he was using "Jewed" positively. "I have the utmost respect for Jews and regard them as very shrewd and thrifty." This only reinforced the stereotype of the cunning, avaricious Jew. We talked for a few more minutes, each of us speaking in a civil if strained tone, but I felt when I left that I had failed to convey to him why the word is so hateful to Jews. I suspect that from his point of view I was defensive and overreactive, whereas from my point of view he was prejudiced and insensitive. Our relationship has never been the same.

I often think about these two incidents. They were minor, and I do not want to attach too much significance to them. Nevertheless, they were upsetting at the time. Did I make too much of a single word? Did I see prejudice where none was intended? Do I wish to see myself as a victim, forgetting the many times I have been insensitive to other groups? Were these incidents and others responsible for my peculiar habit of silently calling myself a Jew whenever I stoop to pick up a penny on the road—a habit that both confirms and denies the image of the stereotypical Jew? In the presence of perceived anti-Semites I feel very "Jewish"; yet in the presence of certain Jews, I feel anti-Semitic. In the shower I recite the Hebrew songs I learned when I was bar mitzvahed at the age of thirteen, but in temple I sit tight-lipped, unwilling to participate in any of the rituals and traditions of my religion. You can imagine my religious schizophrenia.

Two nights ago, while watching a performance of Shakespeare's play *The Merchant of Venice* on campus, I felt acutely the pain of religious stereotyping. The play contains the most notorious anti-Semitic stereotype in English literature—Shylock, the greedy and vindictive money-lender who would exact, in a horrifyingly literal way, a pound of a man's flesh in order to revenge himself on Christian society. The other characters refer to him as "the villain Jew," "the dog Jew," "the devil." They despise him not because he is a detestable person but because he incarnates the qualities of a loathsome race. It is true that Shylock has one sympathetic moment in the play, when he argues that "I am a Jew. Hath not a Jew eyes? hath not a Jew hands, organs, dimensions, senses, affections, passions? Fed with the same food, hurt with the same weapons, subject to the same diseases, healed by the same means, warmed and cooled by the same winter and summer, as a Christian is?" (3.1). Nevertheless, he is portrayed elsewhere as a monster, and at the end of the play he loses all his money as well as his daughter, who marries a gentile and converts to Christianity.

I doubt that *The Merchant of Venice* would have offended me in high school or college, when my need to assimilate into Christian society was stronger than it is today. My professors would not have looked kindly upon the idea that a canonical text might be deeply prejudiced. For example, when reading F. Scott Fitzgerald's *The Great Gatsby* and Ernest Hemingway's *The Sun Also Rises* in graduate school, I did not believe that the two authorial narrators, Nick Carraway and Jake Barnes, respectively, were anti-Semitic, as I now believe them to be. As a student, I was far less aware of race, class, gender, and religion than I am as a teacher. Moreover, I suspect that, when I was much younger, I was unconsciously embarrassed that I was Jewish and therefore denied the many unfavorable references to Jewish characters.

Nor did I have any Jewish teachers to encourage me to analyze a text's anti-Semitic implications. Even if I did, I'm not sure I would want to "read like a Jew," that is, to admit how my background influences my interpretation of literature. Ironically, many of the non-Jewish students in my Fitzgerald/ Hemingway course believe that I now spend too much time discussing this subject. They might be right: sometimes I fear that the real anti-Semitism that I need to confront lies in myself.

This brings me to your next assignment: the opportunity to explore in more depth the complexities and contradictions of diversity. I suspect that, like me, most of you feel ambivalent about an aspect of your identity, whether it be race, class, gender, or religion. If so, I hope you are willing to write one more essay on diversity's dark side. Please try to be as honest as possible in your essay, particularly when acknowledging aspects of your identity of which you are not proud. Don't be afraid to reveal your vulnerability and anger. While it's easier to write about being a victim than a victimizer, I think that we play both roles. Try to describe at least one incident in which you have been victimized by prejudice or ignorance and another in which you participated, however unwillingly, in an act of discrimination against another person or group. You don't need to reach an unambiguous conclusion at the end of the essay. You can dramatize the problem without necessarily solving it. As Fitzgerald noted in his autobiographical book *The Crack-Up* (1945): "The test of a first-rate intelligence is the ability to hold two opposed ideas in the mind at the same time and still retain the ability to function" (69).

This essay is due in two weeks. You can use your first essay on diversity as an introduction to the new essay, and if you significantly revise the first essay, I will count the revision (as well as the original) toward the forty pages. You need bring only one copy of this assignment. Please make this the best writing of your life! I would like to read some of these essays to the class; please indicate at the end of your essay whether you are willing to read your essay aloud or allow me to read it anonymously. If you do not like this topic, you can write on another.

There are benefits and risks of this assignment. The benefits include learning more about yourself, educating others about your identity, feeling better

about yourself, and strengthening your bond with classmates; the risks include feeling embarrassment or shame, being rejected or misunderstood by
classmates, and being betrayed by a self-disclosure. I will ask you in a future
assignment to decide whether the benefits of this essay outweighed the risks.

Teachers who encourage their students to reveal the uncertainties and
contradictions surrounding their identity should be prepared to disclose
their own conflicts. I could have cited additional examples of ambivalence,
but I thought these were enough. (I am reminded of Franz Kafka's wry
observation: "What have I in common with the Jews? I scarcely have anything in common with myself" [qtd. in Shechner 24].) Although I didn't
find my self-disclosure painful—it has been generally easier for Jews to
assimilate into American society than African Americans, Hispanics, or
Asians—I believe, with bell hooks, that teachers should be prepared to
take the same risks they ask of their students.

To acknowledge prejudice within oneself or others is not to imply that
all prejudice is the same. Nor do I wish to suggest that one can understand
prejudice without examining its complex historical, cultural, psychological, and economic implications. Elisabeth Young-Breuhl's book *The
Anatomy of Prejudices* (1996) provides an elaborate taxonomy of the different manifestations of intolerance. Yet even she acknowledges that all oppressed groups have one goal in common regardless of the differences that
separate them: "all want and need education about prejudices to be part of
each new generation's heritage" (542).

The third essays on diversity proved to be more introspective and candid
than the first and second. Without explicitly repudiating their first essays,
students now acknowledged the many problematic aspects of diversity that
they were reluctant to disclose in their earlier writings. The confident image of cultural diversity projected in their first essays gave way to a more
conflicted portrait in which they struggled to maintain their cultural heritage while at the same time trying to assimilate into American society.
They recorded darker emotions—guilt, shame, anger, and fear—and in
many cases disclosed feelings or experiences they had never previously
admitted. They moved away from the image of America as a melting pot,
the loss of which Arthur Schlesinger has lamented in his influential book
The Disuniting of America (1998), and toward a more complex if precarious definition of diversity affirming unity-in-difference. The assignment
proved to be, for some students, the riskiest writing of their lives.

Maria: "I Actively Avoid Filipinos"

Maria began her first essay with a memorable paragraph. "My mother once told me 'Never trust a Filipino. They'll stab you in the back.' Although I was young when she warned me, I silently questioned if that meant I shouldn't trust my own family or myself. Did that mean that I was destined to betray other people simply because of where my parents came from?" Maria never returned to these questions in that essay, focusing instead on her smooth assimilation into American culture. I asked her during a conference whether she shared her mother's attitude toward Filipinos; she said she was uncertain but would think about it. She returned to this question in the third essay, intimating that she has followed her mother's advice—with a vengeance.

I suppose I hold a slight discrimination even though I so proudly say that I try to be fair to everyone. My hypocrisy begins with my dishonesty and is completed with my odd tendency to literally run away from people who are quite possibly the most similar to me. I actively avoid Filipinos. I don't understand why although I have many reasons for my actions.

I have mentioned in an earlier essay how I do not classify myself as Filipina but as an American. This division in my identity is surely the starting point of my discrimination. I think the reason I classify myself as American is my aversion to Filipinos. Although after writing that statement I instantly question whether the situation is the reverse, sort of like the whole chicken or egg predicament, I believe my aversion to Filipinos came first. Yes, my parents raised me with looser ties to homeland customs but that does not destroy my mental identification with being Filipino.

My journey toward complete Americanism began when I began to observe how other Filipinos, and even Asians, act socially. In high school as well as in college, Asians tend to flock together. Other common tendencies lead me to revert to stereotyping, but I swear they are true. The Asians I have observed, which are quite numerous since perhaps I hold a fascination with them, nearly always posses extreme materialistic values and compete with one another as to who drives the coolest car or who wears the most expensive name brand clothing or who is the trendiest/fashionable. This is not who I am. I do not posses values that in any way resemble their values nor do I wish to associate with people who do.

I need my freedom, perhaps one could say my American freedom, to do what I want to do. I don't want to speak tagolog, the Filipino dialect, or limit myself to friends who specifically look like me (although one could say I am doing the absolute opposite), or only date men who are Filipino. It may sound funny, but I am scared of them. I feel that whenever I am around them, the greatest potential of our conversations would be about something to do with being a group of Filipinos. I have tried to talk to other Filipinos on campus and without fail the discussion is ethno-centric, about which island our parents are from or which Filipino customs our household has retained from the homeland.

As a result of my difference in values from other Filipinos, I do my best to avoid them. I believe Filipinos have this great mission to either seek out other Filipinos or try their best to detect others of their kind with the people they come into contact with. I too do this but unlike my counterparts who use their powers for the benefit of friendships and relations, I use my power to avoid them at any cost. If I am caught in a spontaneous conversation with another Filipino who has detected my heritage, I'll lie to him/her and say I am in a hurry somewhere and cannot stay. When on campus I see the Liga Filipina, the Filipino cultural group of SUNY, table or even a poster of the organization I silently scoff at them or walk away so I'll be out of their Filipino-radar range.

I don't intend to sound violent or vicious because the root of all my actions toward or against others of my ethnicity is purely out of fear. What specifically that fear comes from, I am not sure. Perhaps it is fear that spending time with them I too may become materialistic and participate in the silent competitions. Maybe there is something about myself of which I am afraid but I do not think this is it.

I am not proud of the fact that I consciously discriminate against other people, but my fear of other Filipinos outweighs my desire to be open and free with everyone. Maybe what my mother said to me many years ago had a greater impact than I realized. I wish I could not be immature and shed these generalizations about people I don't know and am not willing to familiarize myself with. I have tried but I just feel uncomfortable around them and expect them to be shallow and materialistic. Sometimes I'm wrong, but oftentimes I'm correct which leads me to severe all ties with the person and I revert back to my discriminating self.

Steve: "I Was Afraid to Reveal Racial Issues That Have Followed Me for Years"

Steve discussed in his first essay his parents' diverse cultural backgrounds. After declaring that there is nothing in his past behavior of which he is embarrassed or ashamed, he recalled an incident in which he had expressed a derogatory comment about Spanish people to a friend who was herself Spanish. "I should not have said what I did." Steve imagined in his second essay changing into an African American and being victimized by the racial hatred that the narrator had encountered in members of his white family. The essay includes a revealing exchange between the narrator and his sister and ends with a jarring epiphany. "I started to think back to what my dad said to me about black people and 'niggers.' He said, 'Niggers are those who will steal from you and black people are those who won't.' This was instilled in my mind for years. Now it was turned against me. I wanted to see what others would say about the change. I visited my sister to see her reaction. She knew that it was me right away. My sister has been with blacks, Hispanics, and white people. She said, 'How did this happen?' I said, 'Maybe it was because I have used racial words like dad.'" Since Steve's second essay was a creative writing assignment, the reader cannot assume that author and narrator are identical. Steve records in his third essay additional examples of negative stereotyping, dispelling any doubt that he is writing about himself:

You have asked us to be as honest as possible in our essay's about diversity. Well, I guess since I am writing about this topic again I must have some more diversity to reveal. I revealed in my first essay that I am from many different backgrounds. I also said that only one stereotype had popped into my head. At the time I wrote this essay I was afraid to reveal racial issues that have followed me for years.

When I was in elementary school a considerable change took place. A black family moved into the school district. I was surprised at the fact that there were black kids in our school. Really, I was terrified. While growing up I was exposed to movies that portrayed black people as being bad. They killed people with guns, and fought in groups. What was our school turning into? When I told my dad that there were black kids in our school all he could say was, "There goes the neighborhood."

I never thought about why he said that, until I took this class. My dad as a child probably heard this discrimination through his parent's interpretations of black people. I can't blame him for what they taught him; Why was he teaching his own kids discrimination? May be that is all he knew. My dad had never gone to college. I believe that college has changed my thought's about other races and religions.

I mentioned before about the black kids that had entered the school I was in. My dad's words had followed me all those years; my friend's words had also followed me for years. I am not proud to say that I learned the word "Nigger" when I was in grade school. It seams to be a part of my vocabulary today when I talk with my friend's. Since taking this class I have seen a reduction in my use of this word. I keep thinking that I would not want people to make fun of my race or use nasty words like "Nigger."

When I ran track in High School there were many black kids on the team. We used to joke around with one another while on the bus or at practice. They used to call me a white honkey, and I used to call them cotton pickers. It was a joke between us; we knew that we were all joking around. One day while entering the bus, I sat in the back where one of my black friend's would sit. He said, "You are in my seat." I came back with a remark that was meant to be funny, but one of the black kids took it the wrong way. I said to my friend, "We gave you the right to sit at the front of the bus a long time ago." I could not believe what I had just said. Two of the black kids laughed; the other kid gave me the dirtiest look ever. I never told him I was sorry; from that day on nothing was ever said about someone else's race. A stereotype that developed over the years, was that all black people get money for school. Meaning they received federal money and not loans. I was told this while I was applying to colleges. As I tried to get into college it haunted me. I asked track coaches how much school was, and they would tell me that I would be able to receive federal loans for school. I would tell my parent's this, and they would say, "You will probably have to pay for your own education, because the government uses school money for the black families." I believed this for years while I was in college. I believed this until last year. I finally was awarded Federal Pell Grants and the Tuition Assistants Program money given by New York State. It was not that all black families were receiving the money for college; it was because my parent's made too much money for me to receive the extra assistants for school. Since it was my parent's fault, I should have been mad at them for not paying for my school. I have begun to despise my parent's for not making a college fund, so that I could go to college. I will not make the same mistakes with my kid's.

Other stereotypes that I have made about black people in the past is that they are all on welfare and they can't hold a job. The welfare part of my stereotype has changed over the years. It changed because I have not seen many black people who are on welfare. I have seen white people that have been on welfare. My sister was the first person that I have seen on welfare. She is a single parent of a beautiful young girl. Without welfare she would not have been able to survive on her own. She has since found a job and is off welfare. The part about black people not holding jobs has changed. It's not that they can't hold a job, but they are still discriminated against when looking for jobs. On one hand, I have seen black people that do not have jobs; On the other hand, I have also seen black people that have succeeded in finding good paying jobs.

Enough about black stereotypes. I have also had stereotypes about Jewish people. I was afraid to put this in my paper for fear that I would hurt my teacher. This stereotype was started when I was in High School. I am ashamed to say this now, but I used to make fun of a Jewish boy that was in my school. On the bus rides home all the other students and I used to gather all our pennies together. When the Jewish boy was dropped of at his bus stop, we would throw the pennies out the window and watch to see if he picked them up. It was a game we played almost everyday. This stereotype of Jewish people changed one day in High School. I told a joke to a friend that went like this: "Have you seen the new Jewish tire. It not only stops on a dime it picks it up." When I said this to him I thought he was going to kick my butt. He said, "What in the hell is your problem?" I said, "I'm sorry, are you Jewish." He said, "No, but my mother married a Jewish man; I wish that you would not say jokes like that again." I was devastated and have never said any jokes about Jewish people since that incident. I have tried to find out more about the religion, and the holidays they celebrate. I did ask a Jewish lady about Hanukkah. She explained the entire process with the candles and the gifts.

I have other stereotypes that have changed. I believe that I have learned many aspects of different races from being in college. I have learned about other religious problems from watching television. I watched "Shindler's List" about three years ago. I was devastated by what took place. It makes me sick to see what one religion would do to get rid of another religion.

Racism in the world will never change. People are so driven by their beliefs; they are blind to their faith; faith that says people are all created equal. Why can't people go with their beliefs, and not with what some psychotic freak says is right? If people were not afraid to turn against their leaders, when they knew he/she was wrong, then the world would probably be a better place. I am afraid to bring a child into this world. What will they learn from this bigotry? Racism, religious bigotry and other problems can scar a person for life. We must teach the next generation to respect others for who they are as people, and not by their background or the color of their skin.

Taylor: "Who Am I to Tell Him That He Cannot Express His Religion"

Taylor began her first essay by admitting that although Judaism does not play an overwhelming role in her daily life, it has shaped her identity. After describing her grandparents' opposition to her non-Jewish boyfriend, whom she has been seeing for several years, Taylor wrote: "I plan on becoming engaged to Robert even though it is met with opposition." Only in the third essay does she reveal that some of the opposition to her boyfriend's religion comes from herself.

My boyfriend is of German descent. He has short blond hair and beautiful blue eyes. He works for Bavarian Motor Works (BMW) as an auto technician. This description differs from whom I dreamed I would marry when I was twelve. It does not help that after five years of being with Robert, my grandparents still make snide comments. They wonder how serious I am with him and whether there are any Jewish boys up at school whom I could date. I think my grandparents see him as a threat because he is German, Catholic and works for BMW even though his family has been in America for over a hundred years. It also annoys me that some Hasidic Jews drive around in their $70,000 Mercedes Benz but when I discussed getting a BMW to my grandparents they were disappointed at me. They did not express the disappointment orally but I could tell by their body language and how quickly they then changed the topic.

Until recently, the differences between our relationship lapsed from consciousness. I have attended religious events at his house and never felt uncomfortable. Why should I? But that would soon change. In September, Robert's great uncle passed away and for the third time in my life, I step foot inside a church. The first two times happened when I attended my friend's Communion and Confirmation. I was young and really did not think what I was doing would affect me years later. But, the last time was different. I went with my boyfriend's family to church for his uncle's memorial service. I remember walking in and thinking to myself "I can not remember the last time I went to Temple." I was inside a church but had not been to Temple in probably two years. I felt so guilty. During the service, it was the first time I had ever seen my boyfriend pray. I could not help but stare. I was overwhelmed with fear. Our relationship had always been religion neutral. Being inside some one else's house of worship became a frightening experience for me. I did not know their customs or practices. I felt as if I was being rude just sitting there on the pew and not participating in any events. I began to think only about myself and not the fact that I was there to support his family. I began to feel more and more uncomfortable as the day progressed. I took my sadness and projected it on his family. I ignored them the whole ride out to cemetery and could not wait until the day was over.

This past Christmas, I bought Robert a gold necklace. He had recently lost one and I had a little extra cash. I bought him the necklace and as I was driving home a thought crossed me mind. What if he wanted to put a cross on it. There was no way he could to that. Everyone in his family wears crosses so what if he wanted too? We are very open with each other so I told him that there was no way he could put a cross on the necklace I bought him. He looked at me and said "that thought never entered my mind, so I have noth-

ing to worry about." After our conversation, I felt that my comment was quite harsh. Who am I to tell him that he cannot express his religion. If he told me that I could not put a Star of David on a necklace he bought me a fight would have occurred.

I believe the reason that I brought up the cross issue to him was because I wanted our relationship to come back to religion neutral. I feel that by attending the church service with him a line was crossed. I began to feel that both our lives would be easier if we did not have to deal with all these differences. It's very easy to feel that you are open-minded, but I found that when I was thrown into an uncomfortable situation, I reverted to what I knew. My own background that day I used as a coping mechanism. My own background caused me to be judgmental and close-minded. After all that has taken place, I'm burden with one important question. If I have these conflicting thoughts about my boyfriend, will I treat my children the same way. I can not understand why I act this way. I have always thought that it does not matter if you pray using the Torah, Koran or Bible because god is still the same. It should not matter if you go to a Temple, Mosque, or Church because to me there is only one god. I know that problems we have now will only persist into the future. I hope that Robert and I can bring these differences aside when we decide to bring children into this culturally diversed world.

Mindy: "Why Do They Keep on Embarrassing Us?!"

Mindy's first and third essays illustrate strikingly different portraits of her Chinese American heritage. She asserted in her first essay that "there are absolutely no aspects of my background that I am ashamed of. I am proud of whom I am and I expect the same respect that I give to each individual that I meet. I am, however, ashamed of those who are embarrassed to be either Chinese or Asian." Mindy qualifies this conclusion in her third essay, admitting that her feelings about her heritage are more conflicted than she had implied earlier.

I have a tendency to become defensive when asked my opinion on diversity and racism. My initial response is that I am an open-minded individual who demands the same respect that I bestow on each person I encounter. I judge people by who they are; not by the stereotypes they are associated with. This is the person I strive to be; not the person I have already become. In my previous essay, I focused on educating my peers about my culture and my family, how they struggled to create a better life in America and how I have been confronted with racism. It's easy to discuss one's own positive opinions regarding controversial topics, like racism, and discussing being a victim. What's difficult is dipping below the surface and facing one's own prejudices, whether they are justified or illogical. Initially, I felt that my previous essay regarding diversity was thoroughly written. I realized, though, that there were a few issues that I failed to address and purposely omitted.

As a child, there were a few occasions in which I was embarrassed by my family and culture. I remember going out to eat with my entire family, which included my paternal grandparents who have now passed on. They could hardly speak English, so my father had to order for them. The waiter asked questions pertaining to how they wanted the meat cooked and what type of salad dressing they wanted. My father then translated these questions to Cantonese so that my grandparents would understand. I was embarrassed that they were talking in Cantonese and I was also embarrassed that they were speaking it so loudly. I actually believed that the waiter and customers who were in earshot would think that we were weird because they were speaking in a different language. This is the language which I now wish I possessed the ability to speak. When our meals were served, another incident occurred. Instead of using a fork to scoop out the baked potato, my grandmother held the potato and took bites from it. I thought, "Great! Now everyone must think Chinese people are stupid. Who eats a potato with their hands?" At the end of our meal, my grandfather began wrapping up his leftovers with a napkin so that he could bring it home. He did not realize that the waiter could have wrapped up the leftovers for him. I burst out, "Why do they keep on embarrassing us?!" My father scolded me and I remained silent until we arrived home. Recalling incidents like this evokes feelings of sadness and regret. I regret my disrespectful behavior towards my grandparents on that particular evening. I can't blame myself for being so immature. I was only ten. I had an aversion to being different, like many children do. Still, it hurts me to think that my grandparents may have possibly known that I was ashamed of them, even if it was only for a moment.

I attended and graduated from the Bronx High School of Science. It was located half a mile away from the train station. Half a block from Bronx Science stood another high school, Clinton. The majority of the students that attended Clinton were black and most of them were local residents. Throughout my four years at Bronx Science, numerous students were victims of crimes perpetrated by Black males. Some of these perpetrators were students at Clinton. It was usually muggings or beatings that occurred; on some occasions, verbal taunting. There was one wide, long block that all students took to get to the train station. This is where most of the offenses took place. I remember walking to the train station after school had let out and observing a group of Black males approach two white males. I had that gut feeling that something was about to happen. I overheard one of the black males say to one of the white males, "Hey, you have a dollar I can borrow? No?! What if I check your wallet? If I find some money, we're going to fuck you and your friend up!" Once I heard this, I began to speed up my pace and thought to myself, "Don't stare and get the hell away from here." They continued to physically and verbally antagonize the two males until one of them yelled, "Get the fuck out of my face." Although my back was turned from this scene, I could still hear the sounds of bodies hitting the floor, bodies being kicked, moans of pain and screaming. "Oh God! What if they're headed to the same train station I'm going to? What am I going to do if they start harassing me?!" I was scared. My heart was pounding and I was too afraid to look back to see whether or not they were headed in the same direction as me. I ran up to the platform and caught the train that had just pulled in. I was only fourteen at the time. Several similar incidents occurred over the four years I attended Bronx Science. I witnessed some of the incidents; other times, I saw the victim(s) after the incident. I saw the ripped clothes, the bruises and the blood. Females were hardly victims. When incidents did occur, they were usually mugged by either Black or Hispanic females.

Prior to entering college, I held a great deal of animosity towards certain Blacks and Hispanics. It slowly diminished throughout the past four years. It happened as a result of meeting and interacting with a variety of people. Some were my suitemates; others were classmates. During my junior year, I met my friend's suitemate and we immediately became friends. Ironically, she attended Clinton High School. She told us (her suitemates and I) how she used to get into fights in high school and how she mugged a few girls from Bronx Science. She wasn't proud of these incidents. She explained that in the part of the Bronx where she grew up, she was faced with violence on a daily basis. Violence became a normal part of life for her. She was arrested during her senior year in high school. It was after this incident that she realized she wanted more in life. She wanted to attend college and make a better life for herself. She decided to leave the Bronx and head upstate to SUNY Albany. She was intelligent, kind and open to meeting different people. She even admitted that she never had Asian friends before and she was not fond of them until she met her suitemates and myself. My friendship with her is just one of the experiences I've had in college that had made me a more open-minded person. It has also helped me to stop impulsively judging people by their surface appearance.

I mentioned in the beginning of my essay that I tend to become defensive when discussing issues such as diversity and racism. I become defensive because I'm afraid to admit that I have opinions that conflict regarding these issues. I like to believe that I am open-minded, but on occasion, I may give in to one of the many stereotypes that have been embedded in my mind. I hate the sound of derogatory, racist words, yet they cross my mind when I am provoked by a particular group of people. I sit here, exhausted from digging up memories and feelings of confusion and anger that I have kept hidden deep within. Throughout the past four years, I believe that I have become a more understanding and accepting person. I know that for the rest of my life, I will face and struggle with issues of diversity and racism. During this process, I hope that I continue to grow as a person.

Salma: "I Do Not Like People Knowing That I Am Italian"

Salma's first essay described her paternal grandparents' colorful Italian customs and her love for foreign languages, traditions, and cultures. Noting that she is "not proud or ashamed of her background," she expressed respect for all nationalities. Nothing in the essay suggests that she would endorse any cultural stereotypes, her own or others. That's why Salma's third essay is so surprising.

After reading your proposal for our next assignment, I needed to think. I know that I wrote a nice fluffy essay on how I feel all people are the same. I am not going to negate my original statements but I feel the need to clarify. I meant everything that I had wrote in that essay. This must be made clear before I proceed. When dealing with people that are not in my family, I feel that they are the same. I also stated in my essay that "if it pleases you, I am an Italian-American." Being an Italian-American does not please me. Actually I am ambiguous about being an Italian American.

I love my heritage and the fact that I am a leaf on a branch that stems from a deep rooted culture. I love my heritage. I love mia nonna and all of the little Italian quirks that she passed down to later generations.

I hate my Italian-American family. It is not that I hate my family, but rather I hate that they embody all of the stereo types. My neighbors dislike my family. At least three times a week a screaming match will take place in my house. This would not be so bad, but they always proceed to leave the house causing a disruption among my neighbors and inevitably causing the neighborhood dogs to join in. By the end of the fight, someone is crying, my neighbors have all turned their lights on and there is always a chorus of dogs howling in the background. I just know that my neighbors sit in their homes and curse the god damn guineas that live down the street.

I love when I bring a friend home to my house for the first time. I have decided that the reaction they normally have on first contact is culture shock. They enter through my front door and it is only a matter of time before my father enters the vicinity. Nine out of ten times my friends' first impressions of my father are usually: a six foot four, two hundred and eighty pound man. A very large man. A very large man who has no shirt on. A very large man who has no shirt on with thick curly chest hair and three gold chains with an ornate crucifix laying in the center of his fury-ness. He usually says something endearing like, "Hi who the hell are you?" This kills me. I don't understand. My father is an orthodontist—he has a phenomenal education, I don't understand when the regression takes place, but by the time he enters our home he turns into a pig headed stubborn ass hole.

My father embodies the stereo type of the dominate Italian male. Since I was a wee age my father told me that he owns me. Charming isn't it? Even now, I am almost twenty years old and he still tells me that he owns me. He is the king of doing wrong and never taking responsibility for his actions. He expects my mother to have dinner ready every night when he comes home from work. He will take his shirt off when he enters through the door and before he even says hello he asks where his dinner is. If my mother hasn't had time to prepare it, because she works as a receptionist in his office and takes care of four children, he curses at her.

I hate my father's blatantly bad habits, they make me sick. I recently had a fight with him. My father had hurt my feelings, before I came home for the weekend quite badly. He had forgotten about me and then would not say he was sorry for treating me like shit. When I came home I did not particularly want to talk to him. He noticed my lack of communication with him and he approached me while I was working in the sewing room. He approached me from behind and I turned around. I asked him to leave me alone. I did not want to spend time with him. I know that sounds cold, but he had hurt my feelings badly and I needed time to calm down. He asked me if I was still mad at him, I said that I was not angry anymore, just hurt. He asked me if he could kiss me on the cheek and if we could make up. I said no. That I was not ready to that just yet and that he needed to leave me alone for a little while.

He did not like my answer. He actually became very angry by my response. Let me kiss you he said. And I said no. Normally my father does not physically scare me, or at least he hadn't for a long time. He grabbed my for arms and pushed me against the sewing table. He told me that he could kiss me if he wanted to. I said no again and then I got scared. I did not think that this was appropriate. I tried to loosen my arms and set them free. I did not want to be there. When I tried to loosen my arms he backhanded me across the face. He said "just remember I still own you." He left the room after that; I was stunned.

I did not talk to my father much during that weekend. I remained quite silent to his ears even during Sunday dinner. When I was packing my bags after dinner and getting ready to be picked up, my mom came into my room. She had a present in her hands and she told me to open it. I did. I unwrapped the most beautiful strand of pearls I had ever seen in my life. I looked at her confused. She told me that they were from my father. She then proceeded to say "don't you think that you should apologize to him now?" I said no and packed up the rest of my bags while she sat there. I then threw my bags over my shoulders and headed for the car that was honking for me outside. I just looked at my mother for a while. I don't know how she deals with it. I can't. I told her to tell him thank you, that they are beautiful and then I told her to put them in the safe. She gave me a very strange look for my response and I left.

I know that the pearls were my fathers way of saying that he is sorry, but for me that is unacceptable. I dislike him for his Italianness. I have seen him working on his patients and these stereo types are never incorperated into his demeanor so I don't understand why they are in my home. I know that his father had acted the same way. I will never apologize to him for the incident in the sewing room. He was wrong. I am almost twenty years old and I don't allow anyone to treat me that way including my father. He has a lot to learn.

I do not like having people know that I am Italian; most think that I am Greek and most of the time I do not correct them.

With the exception of Taylor, none of the above students wished to read his or her essays aloud. They felt that they could not be truthful about revealing prejudice without embarrassing themselves or their classmates. Nor did they indicate willingness to allow me to read their essays anonymously. Consequently, there were fewer essays read that week in class than usual. Indeed, the third diversity assignment produced more "for your eyes only" essays than any other topic I have assigned in five different writing courses. Although I regretted the students' decision not to share their writings with classmates (and made, as I shall describe soon, one unsuccessful attempt to have a student reconsider), I was pleased with the third essays, for they demonstrated a willingness to confront one of the most problematic issues in life.

Maria, Steve, Taylor, Mindy, and Salma were not content with superficial observations. They used their third essays to describe the troubling side of diversity, conceding that they were less open-minded than they had implied in their first essays. Their third essays are richer, deeper, and more truthful than their previous ones. They qualify earlier observations, acknowledge negative stereotypes, probe ambivalent feelings, cite abundant personal examples, and imagine other points of view. They analyze their defensiveness and reach important conclusions about the kind of person they wish to be.

Assignment 4: Evaluation of the Diversity Assignments

How did the students feel about the three diversity assignments? To answer this question, I asked them to write one more essay in which they offered their own evaluation. Caroline believed that writing the first essay "allowed the floodgates of shame to open." She had never spoken to anyone about her shame over the Holocaust. "For some reason, my disclosures are necessary for me. I do not know why it is easier to share them with the class rather than with my family. It just is." Roseanna found it challenging to write about her prejudices and compared the process to grieving. "It is hazardous to deal only with one side of our role in the issue of diversity. When people judge themselves as 'victim,' understanding doesn't usually reach the victimizers. We are rarely asked to look at ourselves as victimizers; but I think it would be a blind-sighted effort to deal with a topic only from one side. Everyone must be allowed to see and grieve their shameful attitudes and actions." Angela observed that although she had written in other courses about diversity, she had never disclosed her experience with white supremacists. "I found it agonizing to write about a world that feels so foreign to me after only a few years. I felt that words simply would not be able to convey the horror of my experiences. However, in not telling my story, I felt as though I was keeping Judd's secret and I don't want to bear that anymore. . . . My diversity essay has allowed me to purge myself of pain that I have harbored for years."

Those who did not begin to explore the dark side of diversity until the second or third essays also valued the assignments. Maria commented on how the third assignment allowed her to discover a troubling insight into her Filipino heritage. "Shame, depression, and relief revolved around my heart the entire time I wrote the third essay. I became fully aware of the prejudice I had hidden from even myself for so long that was focused toward other Filipinos. Of course, I was not proud of this realization but I wanted to continue the essay and try to sort through all of my inner confusion." Steve believed that my self-disclosure made it easier for him to acknowledge feelings about which he had never before written. Additionally, he suggested that the assignments were a safety valve, one that might have defused the murderous violence that occurred at Columbine High School. "I am not proud of my feelings, but I have had them in the past and in the present. I need to stop these bad feelings, because what good am I to the children I want to work with if I have these feelings." Taylor believed that my self-disclosure was appropriate but nevertheless made her feel defensive since she was the only Jewish woman in the class and was afraid that she might have offended her classmates by disclosing her fear of a cross. Mindy reported that she never would have confronted her uneasiness over being Asian American were it not for the third assignment. "As I reread my first essay, I realized that it would have been a stronger essay if I had touched upon my own prejudices. I was ecstatic to have another opportunity to write an essay about diversity. I had the courage to reveal my anger, shame, and guilt that were associated with experiences regarding my own culture and the cultures of others."

Salma expressed the strongest reservations about the diversity assignments, which evoked negative emotions in her. "It hurt me to put those words down on paper because I had never done so before." She believed she could hide her unexpressed feelings about another person but felt exposed and vulnerable once they were written down. Unlike her fellow classmates, who felt closer to each other as a result of exposing their fears and prejudices, Salma felt isolated during this assignment. She told me during our second conference that she did not feel it was appropriate for a student to acknowledge being prejudiced, even if the motive behind the self-disclosure was the desire to overcome that prejudice. She valued honest writing but not when it heightened her vulnerability and shame. She felt anxious when I asked her for permission to read her third essay anonymously, anxiety for which I must accept responsibility. She had not intended to share the essay with her classmates, but when I called her a few days before class, asking for permission to read the essay anonymously, she agreed despite misgivings. I told her that she could change her mind and withdraw permission anytime before class began. As I was walking toward class, Salma passed me in the hall, traveling in the opposite direction. "I've changed my mind—don't read my essay aloud." She never showed up in class that evening, and only when I read her evaluation did I realize that she was too upset to attend class. One of her fears, she later admitted, was that her anonymity would be compromised because there was only one other Italian woman in the class.

It is often difficult to know whether to ask a student to read an essay aloud that was not intended to be shared with the class. Since only about eight students can read and discuss their essays in a three-hour class, the other sixteen students do not need to bring in multiple copies; they know their essays will not be read aloud. Sometimes I receive an essay, written for me alone, that is especially noteworthy; when that occurs, I phone the writer and ask for permission to read it aloud. This happened with Caroline's and Angela's first essays and Salma's third essay. Most students readily agree to read their essays aloud or allow me to do so anonymously, but occasionally they change their mind and withdraw permission, as Salma did. The author may then feel resentment or anger.

Salma asked me during our last conference why I wanted to read her essay aloud, the one essay about which she was the most embarrassed. She could not help thinking that I was taking advantage of her vulnerability and trying to make her feel foolish. "On the contrary," I replied; "I think your classmates will be able to identify with your situation and understand your conflicting emotions. If I didn't feel you wrote a powerful essay, I wouldn't have asked you to read it aloud." I identified with many of her feelings, including embarrassment over a parent's ethnicity. Salma's third essay captures the love-hate feelings that children of all ages often feel toward their parents and ancestry.

"Controlled Vulnerability"

All the students stated in their evaluations of the diversity assignments that my self-disclosure made possible their own. They identified not necessarily with being Jewish but with feeling ambivalent, conflicted, and vulnerable. They saw me both as an authority figure, maintaining control over the class, and as a person who was still troubled about an important part of his identity. As Roseanna remarked, "When a teacher reveals on the same level as the students, it helps the class to open up more, to feel more comfortable. It subdues the negativity surrounding the powers of authority. The students are empowered by the controlled vulnerability shown by the teacher." They probably would have been uncomfortable if I had been excessively vulnerable (and thus out of control) or insufficiently vulnerable (and thus not fully human); as it was, my self-disclosure demonstrated to them that conflicts need not be disabling.

The Pedagogy of Identification

Implicit in my approach to diversity—indeed, in my approach to all the subjects that I teach—is a commitment to the pedagogy of identification. Without ignoring the crucial differences that make each person unique, I emphasize the commonalities of human experience. Roseanna put it best when she observed, "Self-disclosure not only frees the person of their own tangled distresses but also sheds light on the fact that we all come from the same source; we are not as different from one another as we so often are led to believe." These commonalities are especially important when writing about diversity issues, since an emphasis on identity politics can lead to increased cultural fragmentation and alienation. As Martha Minow remarks, identity politics is likely to reinforce people's worst stereotypes of others rather than emphasizing mutual dependence and relationships (56).

Teachers who encourage their students to write about the dark side of diversity must not expect that everyone will be willing to do so. Nor will all students self-disclose to the same extent. Many factors contribute to the degree of self-disclosure, including the racial, ethnic, and religious mix of the class. As I suggested earlier, self-disclosure is riskier for people of color than for whites at a predominantly white university; they generally constitute a small minority, and their anonymity is compromised. This helps to explain why the Caribbean American students were reluctant to explore their racial ambivalence toward themselves or others. In addition, they may have feared that any disclosure of racial antagonism would contribute to racial tension.

Throughout the semester I was concerned with the "boomerang" effect: the possibility that those who disclosed fear, anger, or prejudice toward another group might find themselves harmed by the process. The students were more on edge during the diversity assignments than during the other assignments, and they were relieved afterward when they realized that the class had made it through without incident. I was also relieved. Everyone demonstrated exemplary civility, but it is possible that a different group of students might have achieved a less positive outcome. The results of our experiment support the conclusion reached by the authors of a major study of self-disclosure: "As researchers we are cautious in weighing the pros and cons of self-disclosure. Nevertheless, although disclosure involves possible risks of rejection, misunderstanding, embarrassment, and betrayal, it offers the possibility to get to know another person and to be known by another person. Although self-disclosure by itself is not a sufficient condition for intimacy or closeness in a relationship, it provides a context for these qualities and, hence, is important in understanding a unique feature of human interaction" (Derlega et al. 118).

Unified or Divided Identity?

I asked the students to consider two additional questions in their evaluation of the diversity assignments: "Do you view your identity as unified and stable, on the one hand, or divided and unstable, on the other? Did the diversity assignments change your notion of identity?" Their responses imply that cultural conflicts are rarely separable from identity conflicts. We have already seen that Salma believed that the diversity assignments "tried to rock" the foundation of her identity. None of her classmates ascribed this motivation to the diversity assignments, but several believed that ambivalence over their cultural heritage reflected fundamental identity conflicts.

Caroline felt that her identity was neither stable nor unstable but rather "a work in progress." She viewed her identity as "incomplete" because she still had so much to learn about herself. Roseanna regarded her identity as divided and unstable. She was confused about her identity before the diversity essays but was better able to understand her conflicts as a result of writing. Angela also recognized a split in her identity, "a division between the person I was four years ago and the person I am today." Maria considered that her identity was divided and unstable; she deemed this a strength because she could understand others who are similarly confused about their own heritage. Steve believed that his identity was now stable and unified as a result of making certain positive changes in his life a few years earlier. The diversity assignments gave him greater insight into his classmates' backgrounds. By contrast, Taylor felt that until recently her identity was stable and unified; she now felt that her identity has become more confused because of the realization that she is less open-minded about her boyfriend's religion than she had once thought. Mindy wrote that she could not answer any questions about her identity because it was still in a state of flux.

Writing Wrongs

The diversity assignments allowed students to look deeply into their hearts and acknowledge fears and prejudices. They were initially frightened by these disruptive emotions but were determined to understand them. The writers came away feeling heightened respect for the power of words both to injure and to heal. In revealing vulnerability, they demonstrated strength. They also affirmed human agency, the authority to change their language and, hence, their behavior. Witness Steve's concluding paragraph in the diversity evaluation:

This class has made me realize that peoples lives can change because of a remark that they hear. Words hurt; if a hurtful word is used, then the person saying should know that it hurts. Open up to those people, so may be in the future he/she may look back and see the trouble the word cause some else. Be true to your feelings, and never hold back. If one expresses his/herself to others, then may be he/she will change what he/she believes in. My feelings have changed over the past 13 weeks. I mentioned in an earlier essay that I used the word "Nigger"; I have found myself lately, telling other friends that it is not right to use those words. They may laugh now, but at least I gave them my point of view.

Despite the obvious grammatical errors and lack of proofreading, we see an emerging articulateness as well as a desire to avoid racist and sexist language. We also sense the sincerity of Steve's conclusion. Whereas he had asserted in his third diversity essay that "[r]acism in the world will never change," he now takes a more hopeful outlook. He does not claim more than we can believe: he may not be able to change his friends' behavior, but he has changed his own.

Contrary to my initial fears, the diversity assignments produced no explosions or angry outbursts. I was never aware of any hostility, nor was the classroom polarized into racial or ethnic groups. No one engaged in name-calling or demonstrated incivility to a classmate. No one student or group dominated class discussions. Though always difficult to interpret, the silence following several essays did not appear to be angry or confrontational. Minority groups were not romanticized nor were dominant groups demonized. No one "freaked out."

The diversity assignments produced few outward displays of emotion, at least during our classroom discussions, but the essays themselves were insightful and often riveting. I believe that the compassionate, nonjudgmental atmosphere of the classroom made possible the students' revelations. The emphasis on self-disclosure allowed students to tell their own stories and reach their own conclusions. Hearing these stories affirmed multiple perspectives, enabling contradictions, uncertainties, and ambiguities to emerge. Students wrote about their *lived* experiences. They told stories, offered their own interpretations, and expanded and revised earlier accounts. They took responsibility for these stories and realized that they could change their lives by changing their perspectives. The diversity assignments encouraged them to explore crucial identity issues. Jerome Bruner's observation in "Life as Narrative" is pertinent here. "I cannot imagine a more important psychological research project than one that addresses itself to the 'development of autobiography'—how our way of telling about ourselves changes, and how these accounts come to take control of our ways of life" (15).

Some readers may believe that the absence of rigorous intellectual critique during our class discussions deprived students of the opportunity to analyze the ubiquitous racism surrounding us. I disagree. Such critique would have made many students defensive, preventing them from analyzing the prejudice within themselves. I doubt that Caroline would have been able to acknowledge guilt over her German heritage if she had been forced to read her essay aloud. Nor would Roseanna have been able to articulate her search for cultural fulfillment if she felt that her feelings would be invalidated. Nor would Angela have been able to process her involvement with a white supremacist. Nor would Maria, Steve, Mindy, Taylor, or Salma have been able to reach comparable insights. Sometimes less is more: in this case, less external class critique led to more internal self-critique.

In reflecting back on the course, I am reminded of a comment Maria made at the end of the semester: "Professor Berman's overall rule of empathy between students is like going back to the warm feeling of Kindergarten, where it is best to be yourself and accept others as they truly are." The observation recalls Diane's remark that I quote in chapter 1: "In a way, this course was a flash back to the early grades of elementary school where the teacher was very interested in developing our thoughts." Early in my teaching career I might have resisted such a comparison, fearing that I was not being "intellectually rigorous" enough, but now I find the comparison welcome. I believe it is time to go back to the future and create those classroom conditions in which students can engage in a dialogic show-and-tell without the fear of criticism. The approach I advocate will not replace more traditional multicultural courses, which focus on the institutional changes necessary for the elimination of racism, but it will embolden students to write about the personal changes that often precede institutional reforms. A personal writing approach can be used in diversity courses in which students explore their own identity and engage class readings, as Juanita Rodgers Comfort does in her course on African American feminist writers. Personal writing will motivate students to get the most out of their education—in the words of James Moffett, to "come out right": "If education is supposed to help people get better, that's not only in the sense of 'get better *at* something,' like writing, but in a second sense of 'get well' and in a third sense of 'becoming a better person.' People want to *get better* in all senses at once. We don't just want our *writing* to come out right, *we* want to come out right" (29; emphasis in original). The self-disclosing classroom will enable students to discover, as mine did, the commonalities that illuminate the dark side of diversity.

CHAPTER 4

Sexual Disclosures Revisited

Imagine a university professor asking a student to reveal in class the most intimate details of a childhood trauma like sexual or physical abuse. We would all agree that such behavior would be shockingly unprofessional. And yet, every day in college classrooms and faculty offices across the country, students receive writing assignments requiring inappropriate self-revelation.

SUSAN SWARTZLANDER, DIANA PACE, AND
VIRGINIA LEE STAMLER

The above passage, appearing in a 1993 issue of the *Chronicle of Higher Education*, reflects one of the most persistent criticisms of self-disclosing writing. The two-page article, entitled "The Ethics of Requiring Students to Write about Their Personal Lives," warns of the potential psychological dangers of compelling students to write on intimate subjects and then grading the essays. Many of the article's concerns about personal writing are legitimate, but the authors present a distorted picture by focusing only on the risks and ignoring the many benefits of autobiographical writing. For example, they make no distinction between requiring and encouraging personal writing: neither is acceptable to them. They correctly realize that students are ambivalent about writing on painful or shameful topics but incorrectly assume that this ambivalence cannot be minimized or overcome. They do not trust students to write about traumatic experiences because of the fear that students will be retraumatized; the authors maintain that even if students choose to write about past victimization, they will not know how to observe appropriate boundaries and will later regret their self-disclosures.

Some of the authors' arguments suggest reverse sexism. They envision the male professor as a wolf in pursuit of Little Red Riding Hood or as a Humbert Humbert obsessed with his nymphet Lolita. Their desire to protect female students from exploitation is commendable; yet in arguing that "required personal writing may particularly perpetuate the 'chilly classroom climate' for women, in which a complex of explicit as well as subtle behaviors creates an uncomfortable atmosphere," Swartzlander, Pace, and Stamler seem to be unaware that women's studies courses have long emphasized the value of exploring personal aspects of education (B1). As Cheris Kramarae and Paula Treichler noted (with the same meteorological metaphor) three years earlier, one of the reasons "women experience a 'chilly climate' in academic settings" is because of "curricula which largely exclude the experiences of women" (41). Swartzlander, Pace, and Stamler offer only anecdotal evidence for these and other claims. They conclude with several recommendations to avoid injuring students, including writing assignments that are oriented more to the future than to the past, a recommendation that silences students about their own history.

How pervasive is sexual abuse? As late as 1975 the author of a prominent psychiatry textbook claimed that the incidence of incest is only one per million (cited by Goodwin 160), but a more accurate picture began to emerge with the rise of feminist scholarship in the 1970s and 1980s. One of the most shocking findings reported by sociologist Diana Russell in her book *The Secret Trauma* (1986) is that 16 percent of the 930 women in her sample had been sexually abused by a relative before the age of eighteen; 4.5 percent had been sexually abused by their fathers before this age (10). Thirty-one percent reported at least one experience of sexual abuse by a nonrelative before reaching the age of eighteen (61). Russell's statistics have been confirmed by later researchers. "When defined as sexual contact, ranging from fondling to intercourse, between a child in mid-adolescence or younger and a person at least five years older, the sexual victimization rate is generally considered to be around 20%–30% for females . . . and around 10–15% for males (Briere 4). Russell reported a strong relationship between experiences of sexual abuse in childhood and adolescence and later experiences of victimization (12). Kalí Tal observes in *Worlds of Hurt* (1996): "Trauma has played a formative role in the lives of many, if not most American women. The relative number of women who have been traumatized far exceeds the number of men who have survived combat, or even the number of men who wore military uniforms during the Vietnam era" (136). Tal quotes a 1988 study, administered on college campuses, indicating that one in four female respondents had been victims of rape or attempted rape. In *Diaries to an English Professor* I reported that about 30 percent of the students in my literature-and-psychoanalysis courses disclosed problematic sexual experiences such as sexual abuse.

Stories about sexual conflicts serve many purposes for writers and readers alike. They are stories of suffering and survival, exposing sexual violence and healing hidden wounds. They are transformative in nature, a protest against silence and a call for personal and political change: "They are stories which tell of a need for action—something must be done, a pain must be transcended. There is a move from suffering, secrecy, and an often felt sense of victimisation towards a major change: therapy, survival, recovery or politics. Often haboured [sic] within is an epiphany, a crucial turning point marked by a radical consciousness raising. The narrative plot is driven by an acute suffering, the need to break a silence, a 'coming out' and a 'coming to terms.' These are always stories of significant trans- formations" (Plummer 50). Given, then, the pervasiveness of sexual abuse and the value of bearing testimony, the injunction against writing about this aspect of a student's life is particularly ominous. Noting the growing number of parents' groups and conservative religious organizations op- posed to students writing about sexual abuse, alcoholism, and domestic violence, Cinthia Gannett observes: "Child abuse, and incest, and other forms of violence against women will not disappear just because they can't be written about, nor will these experiences stop having profound effects on students and learners. Indeed, writing about the events that silence and fragment children (female or male, minority or white) can help them heal sufficiently to see ourselves as knowers once again" (126). Or as Louise Armstrong observes, it is not incest but talking about incest that is taboo. It is painful to write about sexual abuse, but potentially more painful *not* to write about it.

Rather than eliminating writing about sexual abuse, as opponents rec- ommend, can we find ways to reduce the potential risks of such writing, so that students do not open a Pandora's box? Can students write about one of the most private topics without winding up in the departmental chair's office, demanding to drop the course, or, worse still, in the university coun- seling center, traumatized by their teacher?

Writing about any traumatic subject is always perilous, as Primo Levi suggests in *The Drowned and the Saved* (1989): "the memory of a trauma suffered or inflicted is itself traumatic because recalling it is painful or at least disturbing. A person who has been wounded tends to block out the memory so as not to renew the pain; the person who has inflicted the wound pushes the memory deep down, to be rid of it, to alleviate the feeling of guilt" (24). Writing about sexuality is especially risky, with an uncertain outcome. One can never predict the classroom dynamics of writing, reading, and hearing essays on sexuality. Every essay that is read aloud involves three different persons or groups: the writer, his or her class- mates, and the teacher. How will each respond during the course of the semester? Can writers disclose the shameful details of sexual abuse with- out sacrificing discretion? Must writing about sexual trauma result in a retraumatization? Can a student write about sexual abuse and tolerate grammatical corrections? Will classmates respond to these essays with empathic understanding? How does an assignment on sexual disclosures affect the student-teacher relationship? How do students feel about their teacher after disclosing a sexual experience? Must the teacher feel like a therapist, confessor, or predator?

Three Assignments

To pursue these questions, I gave three related assignments over a three-week period to my expository writing class. I gave the assignments one at a time, so that knowledge about a later assignment would not influence the students while writing an earlier one. The first assignment asked the students to read "Sexual Disclosures," a chapter in *Diaries to an English Professor*, and discuss those entries that they found most interesting or relevant to their own lives. Students could write about their own problematic sexual experiences but were not required to do so. Although the students were reading "Sexual Disclosures" for the first time, I was revisiting the chapter, seeking to determine whether self- disclosure on this subject was possible in an expository writing course, as it had been in my literature-and-psychoanalysis course. The second assignment, which I call the "response essay," asked the students to evaluate the first assignment: what they liked and disliked about it, whether they had ever written before on this topic, and what they learned from their classmates' essays. The third assignment, which was given shortly before the end of the semester, asked the students to write a letter to the *Chronicle of Higher Education* discussing whether they believed their writing class had experienced or avoided the problems associated with personal writing outlined in the Swartzlander, Pace, and Stamler article.

Before looking at individual essays, I present my criteria for selection. Space does not permit me to quote in their entirety or discuss the essays of all twenty-four students in the course, twenty-three of whom gave me permission to use their writings. Rather, I focus on the risky writings: those that are the most self-revealing, involving the greatest potential for increased (self-)understanding, on the one hand, and vulnerability, on the other. These essays raise crucial pedagogical, psychological, and ethical questions about the benefits and dangers of personal writing.

Rick: "The Threat of Misrepresentation Is My Only Ongoing Conflict concerning My Sexuality"

Writing about being gay or lesbian is generally one of the riskiest topics. Lillian Bridwell-Bowles admits that although her gay and lesbian students sometimes write about their sexual orientation, they do not allow her to publish samples of their writing (56). This was not a problem for Rick, who identified himself as gay and had no problem allowing me to use his writing. He read the following essay to the class in which he criticized an editorial decision I made in *Diaries to an English Professor* to include entries on homosexuality and sexual victimization in the same chapter.

I have identified myself as gay for a very long time. I knew early on that I would have to be very careful as to how I presented myself, that in order to be strong enough to withstand petty scrutiny and judgment, I would have to maintain character and self respect. I never felt abnormal, sick, and I never believed what I felt was wrong. I felt insecure, as anyone is, about many things, but I have been sure of my sexuality for a long time. I learned at an early age that I had to know who I was better than anyone else because I would always be questioned by other people. When you are that sure about something, it is impossible that anything said or done to you can take it away.

I am also very lucky. I have yet to experience any direct anger or ambivalence directed at me because I am gay. My friends and family have been supportive and understanding. My mother going so far as to buy me a ticket so I can go to Europe with my boyfriend this Christmas. I started telling people I was gay when I was fifteen, and to be honest, since then it hasn't really been difficult. Yes, I am aware that the potential for a problem is always there, but if you live your life in fear, you aren't going to have that much fun.

The only problem I have reoccurred to me as I was reading this chapter. My feelings are not represented by anybody who speaks publicly about being gay. The only gay diarist, Craig, writes about years of personal conflict and how he fantasized about sleeping with his father, two completely foreign concepts to me. It disturbs me to think that by saying I am gay, people who don't know me will automatically associate me with the ideas presented by Craig. They will do this because they have no other reference point to associate with. The threat of misrepresentation is my only ongoing conflict concerning my sexuality.

That issue goes way beyond this diary, it goes into media and politics as well. I think the biggest problem lies within the gay community itself. That term in itself "gay community" is an oxymoron. I personally have never seen it, and frankly I don't want to, and as far as I can tell, there is no such thing as "gay culture." In their insistent quest for inclusion and respect, people concerned with identity politics only succeed in alienating themselves more.

If you only have your sexuality to offer to someone, they aren't going to be able to see beyond it anyway. I have learned that if I don't make an issue out of my sexuality, most others won't either.

I guess it may seem to some that I am hiding from the truth or trying to repress my identity to "fit in." On the contrary, I think that my self assurance has been my greatest asset in maintaining my sense of humor and character, and those are the qualities that matter to most people. I feel like I have a million more things to explain about myself, but ultimately I think my being gay is about as interesting as your being straight.

That considered, I would like to say that I wholeheartedly disagree with the inclusion of your discussion of being gay or straight in the same context as rape and molestation. It fails in two ways. Rape and molestation are about power, and are crimes against victims. By including a discussion of sexual orientation here, you downgrade the suffering of those victimized, and you place homosexuality in the context of crime and deviancy, perpetuating myth and prejudice. I empathize with others who have struggled with their sexuality, but they do not represent me and my experiences.

Despite a few awkward sentences, Rick's essay is generally well written and carefully constructed, its form demonstrating the self-confidence of its content. One sentence is particularly revealing, though I did not comment on its significance during our discussion: "I knew early on that I would always have to be very careful as to how I presented myself, that in order to be strong enough to withstand petty scrutiny and judgment, I would have to maintain character and respect." Reading the sentence, I wondered whether Rick placed me in the position of a "petty" scrutinizer— one who was making a narrow judgment of his writings. I admire Rick's candor: he was not afraid to suggest that my discussion of homosexuality misrepresented his own situation. His essay prompted me to question whether I was unconsciously homophobic while writing *Diaries to an English Professor*. I would have denied so at the time, but Rick's essay enabled me to realize that I may have made an assumption about homosexuality that I did not make about heterosexuality. I don't wish to imply that my decision to include Rick's essay in a chapter on sexual victimization is another example of heterosexism; rather, I wish to pay tribute to an articulate student who has enabled me to correct a misrepresentation.

Rick's classmates were moved by his self-disclosure. "Rick's essay had the most impact on me," one student wrote in a response essay. "He is completely comfortable with who he is and he lets you know that. I think we can learn from this. It doesn't relate if you are just gay, I mean if you are anything against the 'norm.' I know I am not the 'norm' on this campus; this essay made me feel better about myself for being different." Another student admired Rick's forthrightness but feared that he might be exposing too much of himself to his classmates. "I was a little hesitant for a moment when I saw the direction the essay was taking. I was hesitant for Rick. I know that's what he wanted to do with the assignment; and that's healthy. However, I always feel a tinge of nervousness whenever someone makes themself vulnerable like that. I'm afraid of how people will react. Luckily our class is so understanding and sensitive. It's almost ridiculous how empathic they are and it's very helpful in self-disclosures."

Tensions in the Classroom

Tensions occur in the most compassionate classes, and a problem arose when a student praised Rick for refusing to remain anonymous. The comment elicited the following angry response from a classmate in her anonymous response essay the following week. "I was extremely upset at a comment made in class. After Rick read his essay, one of the students made a comment that he was courageous not to have written his essay anonymously. I was offended because we have the option to put our names on our essays; that comment made the people who decided to make their essays anonymous feel as though they were weak. Anonymity is an option, not the difference between a courageous person and a cowardly one." I agree with this observation. The capacity for self-disclosure varies widely, and value judgments intended to encourage honesty and openness sometimes have the opposite effect. I believe that honesty in writing requires courage and strength, and it matters little whether an essay is signed or anonymous.

Teachers who encourage personal writing and self-disclosure must be attuned to their students' feelings and aware of the problems that may occur at any moment. Any statement that makes students feel defensive may cause them to withdraw from the class. Apart from the comment about the "courage" of signed essays, there was only one remark that threatened to break the empathic bond among the students in Rick's class, and it came unexpectedly in the second paragraph of Rick's response essay. "I was very pleased with the reactions the class had to my essay. My classmates have always been generous with their comments, and I respect their sensitivity. I am sorry though that some people were absent last week. There is a contingent of males in the class that represent all that I am not. I am not sure of their names but they are big, straight, fraternity-type college men, and are what I perceive as the grown-up version of the assholes I feared in grade school. I hate to admit it, but part of me still feels I have to stand up to these people and assert my dignity."

I'm not sure what would have happened if the entire class had read Rick's response essay—more than one student probably would have been offended by his dismissive remark about "fraternity-type college men." It's ironic that Rick engages here in the stereotyping that he forcefully protests in his preceding essay. He might have retracted his comment had he read the following paragraph written by one of the "big" students who missed class. "I didn't get a chance to hear the class essays, but I did receive some highlights from a friend. I was not surprised to learn that this assignment had more anonymous authors than any other. For those who did reveal their sexual experiences or preferences, I give the utmost respect. To understand yourself and to be able to reveal what you believe says worlds about a person. It says that they have overcome the fears and problems often associated with certain sexual issues."

Fortunately, there were few empathic lapses in Rick's class. He and his classmates conducted themselves with exemplary consideration for each other throughout the semester. Their essays were sometimes poorly written but rarely deficient in sympathy and tolerance. I did not notice a difference in empathy between essays written for the class and those written only for me. There is an explicit agreement in all my writing courses not to criticize another student in an essay written for the class; otherwise, group cohesiveness will dissolve, resulting in the end of self-disclosure.

Bee: "I Lost My Virginity at the Age of Thirteen, but I Lost My Innocence When I Was Twenty"

The anonymous essay Bee wrote for the class could not have been more different from Rick's signed essay.

The readings in Diaries to an English Professor *discuss stories from child abuse to the feelings of homosexuality. Reading these stories made me feel uncomfortable and I don't know why. I am very open when it comes to sex. I often talk to my friends, both male and female, about sex. In todays society it is hard to avoid the subject, especially on a college campus. Sex is a part of life for many and a couple of months ago it was part of my everyday life. Then my life changed. I lost my virginity at the age of thirteen, but I lost my innocence when I was twenty.*

I, like Gina and Heather [students whose writings appear in Diaries to an English Professor*], am a victim of rape. As much as I try to hide from it and bury it, the hold it has is too powerful. May 28th, 1997 was suppose to be like any other day for me; but that date is one I probably will never forget, even though I try to every day.*

Every Wednesday my friends and I would go out. We all had great fake

I.D.'s and had no problem getting into the bars. We usually went to the same spots, just because we could. Wednesday was our night; a girls night out away from our boyfriends. We always had a great time.

Fran picked me up after she got out of work and we met Grace in front of the doors to the bar. The crowd was OK and finding a seat was not to difficult. We proceeded to the bar to get our usual drinks. As the music got louder so did the crowd. We were all having a great time talking and laughing with all of our friends. Then I looked across the room to see the man I use to date, Ned. He was the last person I wanted to see, but in my drunk state I really could care less at the moment. He walked over, gave me a kiss on the cheek, and asked me if we could talk outside. I told my friends I would be only a few minutes and asked them not to leave without me. When I got outside I noticed that Ned's housemate, Luke, was sitting in his car and he waved me over. I thought I was only going over to say hi and as I stumbled over he opened the door for me. I must admit it was very stupid of me to get in, but I knew these guys; I once was in love with one of them. The next hour was, as much as you do not like cliches, hell on earth.

Ned brought me to his mother's house and up to this point I felt comfortable. I slowly made it to the bathroom and as soon as I began to get sick I heard the door open. As I looked up I saw Ned standing over me, screaming for me to finish up. I just wanted to pass out; I did not want to deal with him at the moment. He thought different. He grabbed me by the hair and bashed my head into the toilet. The blood began to gush out of my nose, but he did not care. He cradled my body and carried me to the couch. He unzipped my pants, despite my cries for him to stop. Then Luke came over and helped him. Sometimes I wish I was the drunk who could forget and have blackouts, but I am not. I remember every little detail of that night and what the two of them did. I had to endure what seemed like hours of two guys taking turns with me; to them I was just a whore they picked up on the street corner. I can remember looking up, teary eyed, to Ned and begging for him to stop. I think this made them want more. They like the fact they were dominant to me.

Luke brought me back to my friends; who were at this point mad at me for leaving. As I stepped out of the car I remember Fran screaming at me. I was standing before them with my clothes inside out, bloody, and bruised. They really did not seem to care or notice. I crawled into the back seat of my friends car and passed out.

I crawled into bed with my sister and cried myself to sleep. She slowly woke up and helped me to the shower. I was able to clean off the blood, cover up the bruises and scratches, but I still felt dirty.

Perhaps I should of done something; maybe I could of called the police, but I did not. The damage was done and maybe if I was not as drunk as I was

I could of prevented what happened. No one knows what happened that night, except my sister. My friends believe I went and had a night of rough sex. My mom believes I slipped down the stairs at Fran's house. I can hide it from all of them, but I can't hide it from myself.

I believe I could of written about many different aspects of my sex life, but I needed to tell my story. Rape is not just a guy jumping out of the bushes. Rape can happen to people you know; I am sitting among you right now.

Bee's wrenching essay is highly detailed yet never lurid or sensationalistic. Her grammar is not always correct—"I should of," "I could of"—but her imagery is vivid, and her tone never falters. One can imagine the difficulty of writing about rape, but there is no moment in the essay when her linguistic control breaks down. Nor does she reveal more than she wishes. She questions some of the judgments she made preceding and following the rape but not the decision to relate the experience to her writing class. Her closing sentence—"Rape can happen to people you know; I am sitting among you right now"—reveals the desire to maintain her anonymity while situating herself alongside her classmates.

If it is disturbing for students to read diary entries on molestation or rape written by past students of the same university, what word should we use to describe reading or hearing about these experiences from a person in one's own class? Shocking? Horrifying? How do a writer's classmates respond to an essay like this? Might the essay be too disturbing to hear? Rick's comments in his response essay provide an answer to these questions. "There is an anonymous essay in particular that stands out about a girl who was raped by her ex-boyfriend and his friend. If this were fiction I would be disturbed, that I know this happened to someone in my class puts me beside myself. That this could have happened left me shocked, angry, sad, but most of all I felt helpless. This essay, above all, affected me the most. I give the author a lot of credit for having the courage to write about this, and admire their bravery and strength. This essay reinforced how everyone carries with them a past, and we cannot know the bounds of the human spirit, nor can we know what anyone has had to endure, just by sitting in a room with them every Monday for a few hours."

How does a teacher respond to an essay like Bee's? Opponents observe that it is difficult to critique personal writing and that therefore teachers should not encourage self-disclosure. I agree with the observation but not with the conclusion. Writers like Bee have much more invested in an essay on personal trauma than in a paper on a disaster taking place in another part of the world. That is why there is no class discussion of an anonymous essay without the author's permission. Confronted with the choice of commenting in class or remaining silent on a risky topic, I would choose the latter rather than the former. Yet if this silence strikes some teachers as encouraging self-indulgence or discouraging intellectual rigor, I would argue that in certain situations the audience's silence facilitates the writer's expression of feelings and thoughts that would otherwise remain unverbalized.

Much of the opposition to personal writing lies in its often confessional nature. The term "confessional writing" is pejorative for many scholars, who view it as a form of narcissistic venting. As I note in chapter 1, one of the strongest criticisms comes from Lucia Perillo, who protests the conflation of aesthetic and therapeutic concerns in student writings on sexual abuse. My experience suggests the opposite. Personal writing enables students to focus on aesthetic values: finding the right words to describe complex emotions and thoughts, dramatizing tensions and conflicts, locating proper narrative distance so that they can see themselves clearly, and constructing a coherent explanation for experiences that appear to defy rational understanding. Writing about painful or shameful experiences helps students to overcome the identity of being a victim, enabling them to take charge of their lives. Writing promotes clarity and control, both of which have aesthetic and therapeutic implications.

I believe the "black cloud" descending in Perillo's classroom following her response to a student's poem on sexual molestation would have dissipated had she established clear ground rules regarding discussion. If a writer chooses to read her poem aloud in a creative writing class, an analysis of the poem's form and language is entirely appropriate. If the poem is on a risky subject, the conversation might begin with a statement praising the writer's willingness to address a difficult subject and then move toward the question of which lines work and which need to be strengthened. The teacher should aim for a constructive classroom conversation rather than a pronouncement. If the writer chooses to remain anonymous, the teacher reads the poem aloud. Even if the author has not granted permission to have his or her poem discussed in class, the teacher still has the opportunity to comment in writing on its structure, shape, and imagery before returning it to the student.

Students learn to listen carefully to anonymous essays read in class. No one offers an instant analysis or a glib remark. The silence following an anonymous essay allows everyone to meditate on the words that have been spoken. This silence is, paradoxically, seldom heard in the classroom. Anyone who has taught for several years knows that there are different types of classroom silence. The silence of boredom is probably the most typical, when students fidget in their seats and look at their watches. The silence of anxiety occurs when exams are given out or graded papers returned. The silence of hostility may follow a teacher's scolding of the class. But the silence following an essay like Bee's is different, conveying shock, dismay, anguish, helplessness. Occasionally classmates may leave the room after hearing such an essay, though more typically, they remain motionless, absorbing what they have heard. Students who read an emotionally charged essay may sometimes hug their classmates as they leave class, but authors of anonymous essays cannot do this. They can only remain speechless while they hear me read their essays aloud. Their classmates also remain hushed, mute witnesses to pain. The classroom functions during these moments as a container of volatile emotions, helping writer and listener express and bear witness to potentially overwhelming experiences that are rendered less terrifying.

The silence that sometimes occurs in the self-disclosing classroom resembles that which George Eliot writes about so movingly in her nineteenth-century novel *Middlemarch*: "If we had a keen vision and feeling of all ordinary human life, it would be like hearing the grass grow and the squirrel's heart beat, and we should die of that roar which lies on the other side of silence. As it is, the quickest of us walks about well wadded with stupidity" (189). Both reading and writing sensitize us to the roar which lies on the other side of silence; and while we do not dispense entirely with the protective wadding in our ears, we apprehend voices that would otherwise remain soundless.

Bee's response essay indicated that she neither regretted writing about her lost innocence nor found herself at increased risk.

Last week I wrote my story on how I lost my innocence to two men. I believe this painful event has made me a stronger yet weaker individual. I am stronger because I survived, both the physical abuse I went through and the mental anguish it left. However, it left me feeling "exposed" to the true nature of some people. Because of them I have lost trust in the human spirit and heart. . . .

The biggest problem this experience left me with was the willingness to open my heart to another man. At the time I was involved with a man with whom I loved very much, but I had to leave because the thought of a man next to me made me uneasy. Several months have gone by and I am slowly trying to start up a new relationship. He is a great person and is trying to understand me the best he can. But what he can't understand is why every time he comes close I back up. I want to be with him, but I don't trust him. Or it is I choose not to trust him. He has never harmed me in any way, so why don't I trust him? I just don't want to be hurt again by anyone. I some how put a "shield" up around my heart which allows no one in. I want to destroy this "shield," but I can't. Maybe I need time, I just don't know.

I regard myself as more vulnerable than others. I believe I am a very strong individual often, but some times my weakness is overbearing. I wrote my previous story, partially because of my lack of trust. Over the past month I have learned that I need to be more open and trusting of others, mainly because of the trust they see in me. Writing this essay, I believe, is a step towards me trusting others.

It is not surprising that Bee acknowledges her loss of faith in people. Nor is it surprising that she regards herself as more vulnerable than others. What *is* surprising is that even as she admits mistrusting people, she lowers her "shield" as she narrates her story to a class of strangers. Most astonishing of all, Bee signed her response essay and then distributed copies to her classmates. Her willingness to claim authorship of her preceding essay was based on her growing trust in the class.

Lara: "I Will Never Forget the Feelings of Disgust and Humiliation that Plagued Me"

Bee was not the only student in her class to write about a traumatic sexual experience. Four other women, out of a total of seventeen, wrote about personal experiences of child sexual abuse, incest, or stranger or date rape. The percentage is consistent with the 26 percent cited by Swartzlander, Pace, and Stamler of female college students who experience sexual assault at some point in their lives. All but one of the women who wrote about this experience chose to remain anonymous. They used the first assignment to identify with students in *Diaries to an English Professor* and the second assignment to describe what it felt like to write about a painful or shameful sexual experience. Lara's anonymous essay is similar to Bee's in many ways:

I have just finished reading "Sexual Disclosures," a chapter in Professor Berman's book. It was thought provoking to say the least. In this chapter there were diaries written by past students about a wide variety of sexual experiences. Some were comical in nature, while others were horrifying. It was interesting to see how different sexes wrote on this topic. A topic that some feel is too taboo to even write about. It was also equally fascinating to see how the individual subjects handled writing about their specific experiences.

It was common to find women writing about traumatic sexual experiences. This could have been due to a number of circumstances. Perhaps it was because statistically women are more likely to be sexually abused or raped than men. It also could be due to the fact that most men who have been violated usually do not come forward and admit to it. Such an admission would demasculinize them and make them appear weak. The majority of males in the chapter wrote on funny subjects or nonimplicating anecdotes. What I mean by that is if they did relay a story they did not make themselves look bad in it. Whereas the women who told of past experiences often dealt with feelings of guilt and repression of emotion. That was alarming.

It is often that women blame themselves for incidents where they are either abused or taken advantage of. If they don't blame themselves than they are dealing with the thought of "Did it really happen?" "What if I tell somebody? Will they believe me?" These feelings were expressed in Leslie's diary about being molested. She said, "To tell the truth, I'm not even sure at this point if it actually did happen." She was so torn between feelings of guilt and humiliation by the event she had forced herself to believe it never happened.

Far too often the victim is made to feel like the "perpetrator" and vice versa. Why is that? Why, as a society do we find it so hard to sympathize with the victim? This lack of compassion is most prevalent when the topic turns to rape or date rape. You hear the accused say, "She asked for it. Look at the way she was dressed. She was drunk and all over me. What did she expect?" I'll tell you what she didn't expect. She didn't expect to be forced to have intercourse with someone. She didn't expect to endure a humiliating medical exam after the fact and face a series of embarrassing personal questions about her sexual history. She didn't expect to receive such taunts as "slut" simply because she was brave enough to come forward. She didn't expect to be raped.

At times I get a bit emotional when the subject is rape. I do so because it is the most disturbing. It is the most disturbing because it almost happened to me. Let me clarify "almost." What happened to me can't be defined by any textbook meaning of rape. It can't be defined because it wasn't actually rape. I was not forced to have sex with him; I'll give him that much. But I was violated. I was violated in a way that I will never forget. I will never forget the feelings of disgust and humiliation that plagued me for a time after the incident. The absolute repulsion I felt for my violator is indescribable. I wished he would die. I loathed him. I hated him. I hated him for putting me in a compromising situation. Most of all I hated him for making me doubt myself. No one had ever had that effect on me. Now a random guy who I didn't care lived or died did. That was the worst part.

I was fifteen at the time of the incident. I was young, vulnerable and inexperienced in the field of sexual activity. I was somewhere I shouldn't have been, a club that was for people eighteen and over. The fact that I had an older cousin who I was the spitting image of helped. It also helped that I looked a few years older than I was so it was no problem using her I.D. It was supposed to be a night of fun and inhibition. Instead it turned out to be one of innocence lost and wounds that would take years to heal.

He was a bartender at the club, tall, dark and handsome just like I like them. He was so smooth with his words. Saying just the right things at just the right times, he thought he could have me if he wanted. I was convinced to follow him to the back of the club. "Let's go somewhere where we can be alone and talk," he said. To put it lightly he didn't want to talk.

His idea of a place to talk was the employee bathroom. Real romantic. "What are we doing here?", I asked in my naivete.

"You know exactly what we're doing here," he replied. The sad thing is I didn't. I really believed he wanted to get to know me better. He did. But it was in the biblical sense. Before I knew it the door was locked and so were his lips, right over mine. I gagged.

"What are you doing?"

"Don't act all coy and innocent with me. I know what girls like you are all about." Girls like me? What did he mean? Girls who sneak out and use their cousins ID? I wasn't a slut, but now I felt like one. The next sound I heard would be one that would haunt me for nights afterward. It was his zipper, followed by his hand to the back of my head forcing it down. He had me by my hair so all I could do to get out of the situation was to scream. This he told me would only lead to complete and utter humiliation. He was right. If I screamed who would come to save me? The bouncers? They were probably his friends and all they would see is their buddy in the bathroom with his pants around his knees and some girl who was stupid enough to follow him there. I didn't scream. I saved myself from that humiliation, which now seems like the more favorable option.

To spare the reader details I will just say I proceeded with the act for which he had expected. Afterwards, I stood up and looked in the mirror. My face was streaked with my mascara and remains of his pleasure were on my mouth. "Why don't you stay behind and clean yourself up. You look like a pig." I spit in his face. "Well that's appreciation for you," he said.

I cleaned up and ran out of the club. My friend followed and we took a cab home. I said nothing the whole way home. When we got back to the safety of her bedroom I started to shake and cry. I told her everything and she swore if she ever saw him again he would lose his favorite extremity. She promised never to repeat the story and it was left at that. I never told another soul. I don't know if that was the right thing to do, but it seemed like it at the time. I just wanted to forget the whole disgusting mess ever happened.

I have never performed that act with anyone else. I also had never done it before the bathroom incident. The act is surrounded by feelings of disgust that I never want to have again. When my ex-boyfriend of a year asked me why I would have sex with him but not perform the other act, I broke down in tears. I never came out and told him but for some reason I think he understood and never brought it up again.

A jerk whose last name I don't even know has made me hate something that can be very beautiful. Someone I thought I could like has traumatized my life forever. Gina was right when she said, "No one is as innocent as they look. Not even me."

Shame dominates Lara's and Bee's sexual disclosures. Their sexual violation involves not only the loss of innocence but also an assault on their identity and self-worth. Their experiences were so devastating that each told only one other person prior to writing about it. The two writers invest their stories with secrecy, dread, and self-disgust. Lara and Bee have been successful in concealing the experience from everyone except themselves. Unable to forget or repress the details of what happened, they are ambivalent about sharing the experience with their classmates but are willing to do so because of the safety and trust existing in the classroom. Their resistance to self-disclosure is exceeded only by their resistance to self-concealment.

Significantly, they did not ask their classmates or teacher for help or advice: they simply wanted their words to be heard and believed. Nor did their risky self-disclosures result in revictimization of the writers or traumatization of their classmates. The class recognized the risk that both writers were taking and responded with empathy. Any other response would have been inappropriate.

Lara's essay was one of the most gripping of the semester. She doesn't simply tell us about the ordeal; she shows it to us, evoking every aspect of the experience. Though we never discussed the techniques of fiction writing—plot, dialogue, characterization, setting, imagery—she instinctively conjures up the image of the menacing bartender. She contrasts her older and younger selves and uses foreshadowing to hold the reader's attention. Her bitter ironic humor sets the tone of the story, but she gives her antagonist a line befitting his character—"Well that's appreciation for you." The sentence describing her reflection in the mirror is striking. The reader feels her horror and degradation long after finishing the essay.

Lara's response essay explains why she was willing to risk writing on the most humiliating experience of her life.

I feel that last week's assignment was helpful, for me at least. It allowed me to explore an incident in my life that I was all to happy to forget. It let painful memories resurface. That was the toughest part. Writing down an extremely personal and embarrassing story is tough. Even though it was anonymous it scares me to think that people will realize it was me. I know that sounds paranoid but there is always that chance. Maybe you don't realize it, but when you read an anonymous essay people always look around the classroom and try to figure out who the author is.

You may be asking yourself, "Why, if she wanted no one to know what happened to her, would she volunteer to write about it?" I kept asking myself the same question. I think there is a part of me that wants people to know. For what reason I never will know. Maybe it is because I have kept it bottled up inside of me for so long that it was time for it to come out.

There were so many times, while I was writing my essay, that I wanted to stop and just tell you it was too painful and embarrassing and I would make copies of something else. I must of rewrote it a hundred times. One draft had explicit detail of what had happened and I decided that the class could be spared of that. Another draft was too vague, and I wanted everyone to know exactly what happened so they wouldn't feel cheated and have to guess. I ended up with what I handed in last week and hoped it was sufficient. But how do you determine if an essay of that sort is okay? I guess you don't. I tried to imagine your reaction to it. Would you be surprised or disgusted? I know myself. I know that I will look at you differently now that I have revealed something to you that only one other person in this world knows. Will you look at me differently? I suppose as a professor you have to be totally objective, if that is possible, and treat it like it were any other essay. I know you won't be able to though. These types of things are hard to handle. I don't care how sympathetic or well-trained you are on the subject.

It is weird that I have put so much trust in you. When it comes down to it I barely know you. For all I know the way you are with us in class could be some big show you put on. And when you go home at night, you let your wife and daughters read all of the essays. And you sit around with them and joke about the essays and you describe the author to add in some humor. But for some reason I know you don't do that. I know my secret is safe with you. You are not transparent like some other teachers I have had in the past. A perfect example of that would be my second grade reading teacher. We will call her Mrs. Big-Butt. All year long I had been her prized pupil, reading way above my grade level. She bragged about me to other teachers. Then my best friend passed away and I was a complete mess. I cried for days on end. Not normal tears, but complete hysterics. One day, when she couldn't stand my wailing anymore, she yelled at me in front of the whole class. She said, "Lara, will you get a hold of yourself and stop crying like a baby!" I never understood how a teacher of all people could be so insensitive.

I don't know how I completely veered off the subject, but I had to illustrate my point. You provide all the safeguards necessary when dealing with a subject like sex. No one felt pressured to write about anything they did not want to. At least I didn't. It was an excellent way to open up peoples eyes to subjects they normally do not want to see.

Lara's response essay confirms many of the insights of trauma theory. It was wrenching to describe the traumatic experience but psychologically helpful. As Judith Herman suggests in *Trauma and Recovery* (1992), expressing a painful or shameful experience enables a person to integrate it into his or her life, transforming it into a less traumatic experience. The reconstruction of the traumatic story restories—and restores—a connection between the writers and their community.

Apart from its therapeutic implications, Lara's response essay indicates that she was thinking like a writer as she struggled to find the right words to expose her shame. The desire to communicate with her audience compelled her to organize her experience and construct a coherent interpretation of it. She was both participant and observer, thus expanding her point of view. The need to solve a number of technical questions, including the degree of explicitness in her description, may have enabled her to gain greater objectivity about the event. Writing was an act of defiance against shame. The statement that she didn't want her classmates to "feel cheated and have to guess" about the nature of her ordeal motivated her to produce powerful prose.

Unlike her anonymous essay, which was written for the entire class, Lara's response essay was written only for me, and I want to address her questions about my reaction to her sexual disclosure. What are the "qualifications" necessary to receive a risky self-disclosure? Nathaniel Hawthorne investigates this question in a memorable passage in *The Scarlet Letter*.

A man burdened with a secret should especially avoid the intimacy of his physician. If the latter possess native sagacity, and a nameless something more,—let us call it intuition; if he show no intrusive egotism, nor disagreeably prominent characteristics of his own; if he have the power, which must be born with him, to bring his mind into such affinity with his patient's, that this last shall unawares have spoken what he imagines himself only to have thought; if such revelations be received without tumult, and acknowledged not so often by an uttered sympathy, as by silence, an inarticulate breath, and here and there a word, to indicate that all is understood; if, to these qualifica-

tions of a confidant be joined the advantages afforded by his recognized character as a physician,—then, at some inevitable moment, will the soul of the
sufferer be dissolved, and flow forth in a dark, but transparent stream, bringing all its mysteries into the daylight. (123–24)

Hawthorne tells us that a person who receives dark confessions or self-
disclosures should be sage, intuitive, and attentive to others. In addition,
he or she must be able to identify with others, have a deep understanding
of the human heart, and be unconditionally accepting of any revelation.
Only to such a person should one entrust fearful secrets. The irony, of
course, is that the Reverend Arthur Dimmesdale could not have chosen a
worse person to hear his dangerous confession than Roger Chillingworth,
who is neither benevolent, wise, nor trustworthy. Dimmesdale's betrayed
confidence leads to both men's undoing. Hawthorne's cautionary tale reminds us that we must entrust our secrets to people who will not betray
us—people who will lack perfect understanding because they are human
but who nonetheless will be attentive to our words and faithful guardians
of our secrets.

There is probably no subject about which we are more secretive than
sexuality, and a class in self-disclosing writing is bound to elicit sexual
revelations, many of which evoke shame in the writer and perhaps in the
reader. Will students reveal secrets that they later regret sharing with their
teacher and classmates? I believe that most students are ambivalent about
sexual disclosures, but a teacher's nonjudgmental acceptance can enable
them to tell their stories without being harmed in the process. Students
are discreet about sexual disclosures, avoiding titillating or overly graphic
material and remaining in control of what they reveal and conceal. Most
students know that they must self-disclose carefully and wisely. To reveal
too much about themselves can lead to heightened vulnerability; to reveal
too little about themselves may result in isolation. Students must determine for themselves the degree of secrecy or openness with which they
feel comfortable. As Sissela Bok remarks, there is power both in maintaining and glimpsing a secret. "To have no capacity for secrecy is to be out of
control over how others see one; it leaves one open to coercion. To have
no insight into what others conceal is to lack power as well. Those who are
unable or unwilling ever to look beneath the surface, to question motives,
to doubt what is spoken, are condemned to live their lives in ignorance,
just as those who are unable to keep secrets of their own must live theirs
defenseless" (19–20).

Contrary to Lara's fears, I was neither surprised nor disgusted by her
revelation. Nor did I become judgmental after reading it. I have received

so many distressing diaries and essays over the years that I'm rarely shocked by my students' disclosures. But I was moved deeply and saddened by Lara's writings. She was only a few years younger than my daughters, and I could imagine the grief and rage I would feel if they experienced her sexual degradation.

I served as a witness to Lara's experience, validating her point of view and strengthening her words. I viewed her not as a victim but as a survivor, one who had the courage and determination to write about an experience that would have been daunting for most people her age or older. Lara and I have never spoken directly about this experience, and I hope that my sensitivity to her secret distinguishes me from her second grade reading teacher. I was grateful for the trust Lara placed in me, a trust that affirmed my teaching and, in turn, made possible her self-disclosures.

Lynn: "I Was Never Threatened, I Just Didn't Say Anything"

Lara singles out a student I called "Leslie" in *Diaries to an English Professor* who had written about being molested as a child. Two of Lara's classmates, Lynn and Ashley, also identified with Leslie's diary and wrote essays about similar experiences. Both essays are written with verbal control and emotional restraint despite the feelings of disgust evoked by the experience. Lynn wrote her essay anonymously for the class.

Reading Leslie's diary brought up memories that I would rather forget. Leslie wrote about being molested by her babysitter when she was in elementary school. She can not vividly recall the incident; she questions whether or not it even took place. She thinks she remembers him touching her and then she touched him. Leslie feels embarrassed and has only told her closest friends. She does not remember being bothered by it at the time; she did not know it was wrong.

When I was in the second grade I was molested by my mothers friend. My parents had just separated and she was working a few jobs to provide for us. Her friend offered to babysit us while she was at work. My mother trusted him; she had known him since high school. I don't remember the first time it happened but I do remember he was in my mothers room and called me inside from her window; I was outside playing with my brothers and sisters. When I walked in the room he was laying on her bed and he was drinking a huge glass of red, cherry flavored Kool Aid. He kissed me. Unlike Leslie, I felt that something was not right. I knew that grownups kissed eachother like that. I kissed my father but he never kissed me like that. I thought I did something wrong. At first I did not tell anyone. I remember watching afterschool specials and the little girls (they were always little girls) were told not to tell anyone or somebody in their family would be hurt. Another threat was that if they told, no one would believe them. I was never threatened, I just didn't say anything.

I was always quiet but afterwards I became extremely quiet. I never talked to my classmates and I just sat by myself. He did not care where we were; he touched me in the car, on the way to school, even on the way to pick my mother up from work. At home I acted as if nothing was going on. My eating and sleeping habits stayed the same; I played dolls with my sisters and climbed trees with my brothers. I stopped drinking Kool Aid.

I never once thought the incident was a dream. I knew it happened. When I was a little older I remember having a conversation with my sisters. When his name came up we were all silent. We were all molested by him at one time or another. One day we were watching the news and found out he had been arrested for molesting his niece. We told my mother what had happened to us. I don't think she believed us at first. When she found out about him being arrested she told us not to worry and that he could never hurt us again.

At the time I didn't think it affected me. I thought I was normal. However, when I was fourteen I had my first "real" boyfriend. After a few days he asked me for a kiss. The thought of kissing him disgusted me. The thought of kissing anyone disgusted me. I broke up with him later. I used to become nauseus if I smelled, saw, or drank Cherry flavored Kool Aid.

I always had a hard time being intimate with a guy. I developed a fear of rejection. I had a crush on a boy for seven years and never said anything. Not until I came to college and told my friends what happened did I come to terms with my real feelings. They told me that it wasn't my fault and that I was not to be blamed.

I am still wary when I am alone with a guy. I had to learn to speak up when in uncomfortable situations, but I know now that there is nothing wrong with me.

Lynn's response essay indicates her ambivalence over writing about a problematic sexual experience. "Last week's essay was one of the most difficult assignments I have had to write all semester. Since freshman year I have not talked about the experience. Though I know I was in no way responsible for what he did to me, it remains an uncomfortable topic. Before starting the essay I was frustrated because I did not know what I was going to say. I was nervous; I wanted to tell my story, but I did not want it to seem as if I was looking for sympathy." She felt that since she was writing on such an important topic, she had to be as honest as possible. Honesty, however, was not incompatible with restraint, and she singled out for praise the sentence, "He kissed me," which she liked for its simplicity and understatement. "I purposely did not elaborate. I felt it was unnecessary."

Ashley: "I Felt Like Crying When I Read Those Diaries"

Ashley was the other student who wrote about an extended experience of sexual molestation. Her essay was brief and not read to the class.

I envy the students who write in "Sexual Disclosures." These students seem to write without any reservations, they are very honest. Many of them were relieved after writing their journals. It takes courage to reminisce about personal encounters with sexual abuse and homosexuality. I don't know if I could be as honest or courageous as they were, but I will try.

When I was around four years old I remember sleeping in the bed of my grandparents room. This seems like so long ago, because my grandfather is dead now. Anyway, I remember my grandfather putting my hands where they did not belong. I was only four years old but for some reason I knew that this was wrong. It felt wrong. I have never told anyone this before because I feel embarrassed. After my grandfathers death, this happened with my uncle. However, the acts that my uncle performed extended to my cousin, who is the same age as I am. These acts continued for several years. I remember he would buy us things from the store.

I can relate to Leslie now, I am contemplating if these things really happened to me. I hope they didn't. Maybe it's my imagination. I felt like crying when I read those diaries because they have touched a place that I have kept shut for many years. I have never spoken with my cousin about those years. I remember how one of our male cousins would make fun of us. It was not funny.

Throughout my adolescent years I had no problem having sex. I felt that my sexuality was no longer sacred. Sometimes, I felt dirty. I had problems trusting men and I can not help but think about the effect that this is having on my present relationship. My boyfriend is the only male that I have fully been able to trust, including my father. I have told him about what has happened to me, but not in full detail. I am afraid that he will hate my uncle. This same uncle gives me money everytime that I go home. I feel like a hooker who is being paid off to keep her mouth shut. The price I had to pay was my pure innocence.

I feel that I am possessive of my boyfriend because he is all I have. He knows everything. I hold on tight because if I can not trust family, who can

I trust? Leslie was correct, the offender is usually someone you know and trust.

The opening paragraph of Ashley's essay raises disturbing questions of which she herself might not have been entirely aware. Can a student be subtly coerced into self-disclosure by the desire to write as honestly and openly as the diarists in a book? Might a student's desire to please her professor, even while writing an ungraded essay, also lead to coerced self-disclosure? These possibilities cannot be ruled out. Ashley does not pursue these questions in her long response essay, but she does provide information that lends support to both opponents and proponents of personal writing.

Before last week's assignment, I had never spoken about my childhood experience with sex. I was always afraid and ashamed. Last week was no real exception, I guess that being in such an open class made it a lot easier on me. I didn't come to class to face my classmates courage. I feel like I was a coward. I sent my essay with a fellow classmate. I read those sexual essays and they made me feel much safer. I am no longer embarrassed, I was not in class but I know that some were read. I commend my strong classmates on their decision to write and read on such a difficult issue.

I feel bad because I feel relieved that I am not the only one in the class who has been molested. I should not be happy that others had to endure the shame and confusement that I experienced. While reading about rape and molestation I began to cry. It is so sad to hear any accounts of sexual abuse, because of what I've been through. I sit amongst these beautiful faces every Monday, not knowing that they have been through the most degrading experiences. How could I be so ignorant? So selfish to only think of what I was going through?

While reading the diaries in the professor's book, I immediately questioned if I really wanted to expose myself to you. I was very uncertain. I wondered if you would look at me dirty, or if you would laugh and think that I was crazy for thinking that a family member could treat me so badly. Yes, it was very difficult to write my experiences on paper and let you read about one of the darkest secrets that I hold. I sat and sat, thinking if I wanted to let you in on my horrible secret. I cried and got several lumps in my throat while reading. I did not know if I wanted to go through a complete breakdown, that would surely happen if I decided to write about my secret. So, I told you my story. Now, it seems like I am afraid for you to see my face. I feel like you can hold this over me, but I know you will not do that. You may be the only person who can help me, the only person who will sympathize with my situation. You can be all of those things because you are the only one that I've told.

After I finished writing, I felt a little relieved. But, this relief did not come from telling you about the molestation, it came from knowing that the assignment was done. I don't think that I will get any closure until I have spoken with someone. I have to do this on my own grounds, when I think I am ready to talk. My biggest fear is having someone talk about me or not believe me.

I know that it was not easy for anyone to read about their personal problems, sexual or not. Sex and sexual abuse is a very touchy subject. I was not present to hear any of the intimate essays, but by writing my own, I was there in mournful spirit. I realize now that I share this degrading pain with others. The students who wanted to talk about sex in general are also courageous, like I said, this is a very personal subject.

When we write about subjects like this I think that it is very important for us as a class to have such an intimate relationship. The class is considerate and very sincere. I remember reading my essay on divorce, I cried, but two classmates were there to console me. One of them even cried. The next day a classmate told me that he enjoyed the essay, that made me feel good. This class is like a Alcoholics Anonymous meeting. We are able to vent our feelings and we can be assured there is confidentiality. I don't know how many classmates see each other after class is over, but I think that it helps for us to see each other once a week. Monday's tend to be very hectic for me, but the class seems like a workshop, so I am very relaxed. I think that the only risks presented with essays like last week's are the fear of people telling or laughing at you. Our class has managed to laugh at humor only. I can say that we are very considerate of everyone's feelings, even when we critique each other's writing. More assignments like this need to be given. They help you to get a lot off of your mind and they allow you to discuss your feelings. If I take anything away from this class, it will not be the grammatical aspect, it will be the emotional.

My writing is usually three pages long, but last week it was two. I really want to make my forty page deadline, but the subject seemed to rush me. I did not know how to pour all of my emotions on the paper. Right now, I am trying to make up for that. However, even though my writing was only two pages, it was the most touching thing I've ever written. I think that intimate essays allow us to release all of our pinned up writing skills. For me, personally, these essays allow me to open up my vocabulary and use some phrases and words that I would not usually use. If I were being graded alphabetically I think that I would get A's on every intimate essay that we've had to do. I can not really explain what they contain, but the content and style can not be found in a book report.

I want to thank you for assigning this writing. It has proved to be very helpful. Maybe it is my imaginative mind, but I have felt much better after handing my paper over to you. I did not feel this way after writing it. It is only when my feelings are in someone else's possession that I am relieved. It's like telling a big secret that has been wearing you down for years, finally getting it off your chest is a beautiful thing.

Ashley's response essay demonstrates many of the risks of personal writing. Like her classmates who disclosed sexual trauma, she was ambivalent about disclosing this subject. Her dread was so intense that she decided to cut the next class despite the fact that her essay was not being read aloud. She feared, as Lara did, that the student-teacher relationship would change as a result of her disclosure. One of Ashley's sentences contains a telling grammatical ambiguity: "I wondered if you would look at me dirty." Did she fear that I would lower my opinion of her as a result of her self-disclosure? Or did she believe that I would become sexually aggressive, as her molesters were? Either reading suggests her self-consciousness toward me. Ashley informs us that she not only cried while reading accounts of sexual abuse in *Diaries to an English Professor* but also feared having a "complete breakdown" if she wrote about her own experience. Given the emotional toll of this assignment, it would seem necessary to conclude that certain subjects are simply too risky to be approached in the classroom. And yet, surprisingly, Ashley reaches the opposite conclusion. Why?

I suggested earlier in my comments on Bee's response essay that the classroom functions as a container of volatile emotions, but this simile is too impersonal. Ashley comes closer to the truth when she compares her course to an Alcoholics Anonymous meeting. I know little about twelve-step programs, but perhaps what she means is that her classmates listened respectfully to signed and anonymous essays and offered no criticism or judgment. Nor did the class express doubt over the truthfulness of her writings. Such skepticism might have heightened her own uncertainty over what actually happened in her past. Additionally, a reader's doubt would have disconfirmed her, as it would have disconfirmed her classmates, many of whom were also trying to understand confusing events.

Ashley notes that if she "take[s] anything away from this class, it will not be the grammatical aspect, it will be the emotional." She's right about the need to improve her grammar, as her comma splice confirms, and she's also right when she says that the writing assignments allowed her to "open up" her vocabulary and to "use some phrases and words that [she] . . . would not usually use." I especially like the sentence, "I was not present to hear any of the intimate essays, but by writing my own, I was there in mournful spirit." I'm not sure whether she would "get A's on every intimate essay" if they were letter graded, but they were moving. Just as the entries she read in *Diaries to an English Professor* "touched a place" that she has "kept shut for many years," so do her own writings affect readers.

One other student wrote about a traumatic sexual experience, attempted date rape, but she wrote about it in a later assignment on vulnerability. She describes in the essay how, after trying repeatedly to prevent a male acquaintance from touching her, she became so enraged that she began punching him. "He grabbed my arm and tried to pull me back to the tent but I pushed him away. My fear was replaced by anger. There were only a few people awake and they didn't seem to notice the trouble I was having. The next time he touched me I did it. I beat the shit out of him. I know you hate colloquialisms but it's the only way to describe what happened. I had never been a violent person before this incident nor do I wish to be, I had no other choice."

Absence of Male Narratives of Sexual Abuse

None of the seven men in the class wrote about being sexually victim-ized—a conspicuous omission suggesting the gendered nature of sexual abuse narratives. Only one male entry on sexual abuse appears in *Diaries to an English Professor,* a case of attempted molestation, but this entry is written in a lighter tone than the female entries. Researchers have sug-gested that it is culturally more difficult for males to report sexual abuse because they are expected to be strong enough to resist their abusers. The absence of male narratives of sexual abuse does not imply that the men failed to take the writing assignments seriously. Several commented on the entry in *Diaries to an English Professor* entitled "Thinking with My Penis" in which a male student discusses how his friends' sexual obses-sions seem to be ruining their lives. The male writers did not go into detail over their sexual misadventures, but they did identify with the diarist's ad-mission of not always using good judgment. "I understand this diary in so many ways," one man wrote. "Many times my friends and I will mention the idea of thinking with the wrong head. I'll leave this statement to your imagination." The prevalence of female sexual abuse stunned the men, but they believed it was worthwhile to read diaries and essays about these experience.

Race and Ethnicity

I have not discussed race and ethnicity issues in these writings because to do so would be to call attention to the small number of African American and Asian American students in the predominantly white class. Some minority students' writings appear in this chapter, but their essays are indistinguishable from those of their white classmates. The students made appropriate comments about their racial and ethnic backgrounds when working on the biography assignments, but there was never any discussion of these issues in class. To judge from the writings themselves, racial or ethnic tensions were remarkably absent from the classroom. Our emphasis was not on identity politics but on identification—the commonalities of experience.

Evaluating the Self-Disclosing Classroom

Nearly all the students argued, in their letters to the *Chronicle of Higher Education* evaluating "The Ethics of Requiring Students to Write about Their Personal Lives," that the class had avoided the risks of self-disclosure and reaped its many benefits. In retrospect, I should have requested my students to send their letters to the *Chronicle* for publication: their positive classroom experience would have provided evidence of the value of self-disclosure. Far from believing that personal writing perpetuates a chilly classroom climate for either men or women, the students believed that the safety and openness of the classroom allowed them to write about an urgent subject. No one regretted a self-disclosure, a finding that supports Michelle Payne's observation that those who have been sexually abused will not speak or write about it until they feel psychologically ready to do so (155n. 9). My students' self-disclosures also confirmed research indicating that sexually abused children are more inclined to reveal their experiences when they hear about others' similar experiences (Petronio). Moreover, self-disclosure is a reciprocal phenomenon, as Sidney Jourand remarks: "participants disclose their thoughts, feelings, and actions to others and receive disclosure in return" (66). In short, disclosure begets disclosure.

Lisa: "The Classroom Should Not Promote Intimacy"

There was one student, however, who agreed with the criticisms expressed in the *Chronicle* article, and I want to quote her response.

One issue that the authors expressed and I agree with, was that the amount of emotional energy put into the essay seems to take the focus away from writing and put it on content. Supporters argue that writing on personal topics encourages better writing. I contend that requiring students to write about sensitive, borderline disturbing topics, deters us from focusing on grammar, style and form. I found that every week, as an assignment drew near, I would spend hours trying to think of something to write about without having to reveal too much. I do not think this is where my focus should have been. I should have been focusing on improving my sentence structure and grammar. While I am not the only student who feels this way about personal disclosure, I am a minority. Most of the students love the class and think that it is a great approach to teaching a writing class.

While there are many problems and issues that arise in a student's life while attending college, I don't think that writing about them proves to be a catharsis. Dealing with or addressing issues that are sensitive, should be kept for professionals and intimates. The classroom should not promote intimacy. Although we are all peers and it may be helpful to talk with our peers about our problems to get perspective, the classroom is not the place for such disclosure. In the article discussing disclosure, the authors state, "when the boundaries between professional and personal are blurred by turning personal revelation into course content, paternalism may thrive in the guise of professional guidance." I feel students are put into a vulnerable position by requiring personal disclosures.

Lisa's response surprised me, for she never suggested in her earlier writings any problems with the course. Nor did she indicate misgivings over the personal writing component when I had a conference with her during the middle of the semester. She refers to other students who disliked the course's emphasis on self-disclosure, but only one other person expressed mild reservations about this in the *Chronicle* assignment. Unlike Lisa, most of her classmates felt that we did spend enough time discussing grammar, style, and form. Lisa was the only student in the class who did not give me permission to use her writings for this book, but she allowed me to quote from her *Chronicle* assignment so that I could report accurately her point of view. She told me, a few months after the semester ended, that she had grown to dislike the course's emphasis on self-disclosure because of problems occurring in her personal life, problems that had nothing to do with the course. She said that she might have felt more positively about the course had she taken it at another time.

Lisa's evaluation of the course was untypical but cannot be ignored. There will always be students who dislike self-disclosing writing, and it is the teacher's challenge to respect their privacy and find ways to make the classroom experience as positive as possible. Were I to give future students an assignment on sexual disclosures, I would make a few changes. I would encourage them to write on playful and humorous sexual experiences as well as problematic ones, thus creating much-needed comic relief. Students in Lisa's class had the option to avoid writing on anything they found too personal, but I did not specify alternative topics. Perhaps Lisa would have found the course less frustrating had I done so.

Risky Writing and Wholeness

The title of Gary Kenyon's and William Randall's 1997 book—*Restorying Our Lives: Personal Growth through Autobiographical Reflection*—suggests the possibility of a "therapoetic" impulse: "storytelling (and storylistening) is not merely a method for solving particular problems that crop up in our lives, but has an importance and integrity all its own, as a means to personal wholeness" (2). Janice Williamson makes a similar point when she observes that "for some, psychic healing is in the telling" (148). So too does Jerome Hamilton Buckley: "In the last analysis the autobiographer's review of his past is essentially an act of deliverance, a chronicle of resolved crisis and itself an affirmation of ordered meaning. . . . [T]he confronting of the isolated self even retrospectively may prove therapeutic" (52). The therapoetic impulse reveals a fusion of therapeutics and aesthetics, producing forceful writing as well as psychological relief. One of the challenges for the future, as both Mark Bracher and Marshall Alcorn suggest in *The Writing Cure* and *Changing the Subject in English Class*, respectively, is to propose pedagogical uses of psychoanalytic technique for writing instruction. The adage of writing about one's own experience may be seen in these narratives of sexual abuse, in which students confront painful issues and find the words to exorcize the past.

The process of change is implicit in the movement from illness to health or division to wholeness. This process of change is especially important in survivor narratives, which, as Wendy Hesford points out, "expose oppressive material conditions, violence, and trauma; give voice to heretofore silent histories; help shape public consciousness about violence against women; and thus alter history's narrative" ("Reading *Rape Stories*" 195). Most theorists believe, with Ronnie Janoff-Bulman, that cognitive change tends to be "gradual and incremental rather than sudden and swift" (42). Dramatic changes often turn out to be less far-reaching and long-lasting than people would like to believe. Occasionally, however, one of my writing students will report a transformative experience that I feel compelled to mention. Such is the case with Lara. A few months after the course ended, I asked her to visit me in my office so that she could read an early draft of this chapter containing her own writing. I left the office while she was reading and noticed tears in her eyes when I returned. She told me that rereading her words was emotionally overwhelming, reminding her of the awful bathroom incident. She gave me permission (a second time) to use her writing, and when I sent her the entire chapter a few weeks later, I told her that I was interested in her responses. A year and a half later she sent me the following letter:

Dear Professor Berman,

First, I would like to sincerely apologize for taking so long to respond to your letter. I was hesitant to read the entire chapter because I was afraid to see how my essays related to the others. Once that fear subsided I was as emotional as I had been in your office when I read my section.

I had told you in your office that I had not read my essay since our class. Now I have read it twice in only a few weeks. The same feelings that arose that day in your office occurred again when I was in the privacy of my room. I am no longer the young naive girl in the employee restroom. She is part of the history that makes up my character. She only exists in my memory. It is you I have to thank for that. You have enabled me to take a part of my life that at one time I felt to shameful to even think about and use it to empower my future. I am now a more confidant adult who can embrace what has happened in the past and never allow myself to be so vulnerable again.

Jean Wyatt offers a valuable commentary on the shifting perspectives in Lara's writings. Wyatt notes, in her discussion of an abridged version of this chapter presented at a professional conference, that Lara's writings reveal "three different subject positions for the narrator of a traumatic sexual event—and therefore three different perspectives on the event." The first shift, Wyatt points out, is from the victim of sexual trauma to the narrator of the event: "As is well known, trauma is defined precisely by the inability of the victim to put the event into narrative form. Because a traumatic experience exceeds all the victim's frames of reference, all her mechanisms for making sense of experience, the event cannot be assimilated into cognition *as it happens*. It is not experienced as having a logic of time and place or beginning and end. And because it lacks the normal parameters of lived experience it also cannot be recorded in memory—at least not in narrative memory. It therefore remains largely unsymbolized, not integrated into thought or language."

Once she is given the opportunity and encouragement to write about her experience, Lara begins to structure the event into a coherent narrative. She realizes that if she is to communicate with her audience, either with her teacher alone or with her classmates, she must organize the experience and construct an internally consistent interpretation of it. "So the first shift in the position of the trauma survivor," remarks Wyatt, "places her as the narrator—rather than the blind sufferer—of trauma." The second shift occurs when Lara hears her teacher read the essay aloud anonymously. "The affirmation, both of the veracity of her experience and of its containment within the narrative parameters of meaning, enables a change in the student's relation to the traumatic event and its psychic residue." Hearing aloud her essay, Lara "is no longer a participant in the traumatic event, no longer even the writer struggling to make sense of it for a potential audience, but placed now in the position of the listener whose task is to listen unobtrusively, to be the silent witness to the narrative of trauma." The third position for the narrator of a traumatic sexual act occurs when the student writes a reflective essay on the presentation of her experience. Wyatt compares this position to that of the "drama critic who comments not only on the text of trauma, but on its performance and on the audience's response." Wyatt adds that "just as important as the various meanings that might emerge from different angles of vision would be the experience of movement itself, the shifting from one position to the other, which moves the subject from a frozen relation to the event—as an undigested and unprocessed lump of existence—into a fluid relation to it."

Lara's letter provides a fourth position, I would add, that of the adult survivor who is able to look back upon a traumatic event with distance and objectivity. The Wordsworthian idea of emotion recollected in tranquility comes to mind here. Lara's epiphanic event seems safely in the past, neither repressed nor forgotten but integrated into her history.

I am grateful for Lara's warm acknowledgment of my role in her act of empowerment. I believe, however, that her writings testify not so much to a particular teacher but to an empathic classroom. She may have merely mistyped the word "confidant" in the last sentence, as she obviously mistyped "to shameful" in the preceding sentence, but it's possible that she was making a psychological connection between "confidant" and "confident." If we view the audience's role in a personal writing class as the recipient and guardian of a narrator's self-disclosures, then we may understand Lara's ability to become a more self-assured adult. The words she entrusted to her confidant allowed her to feel more confident about her future and move on with her life.

CHAPTER 5

Unmasking Shame

I refuse to be labeled a victim, a survivor, or a degenerate. I will be an avenger. NICK

He was a member of a Hemingway course I taught one summer. A few years older than most of his classmates, he was unusually articulate and enjoyed speaking in class. He seemed enamored of Hemingway's code of heroism without being either chauvinistic or misogynistic. He struck me as self-assured but not arrogant; nothing about his appearance or behavior indicated anything unusually troubling. I can't recall his ten-page essay or his final exam: his class was too large for me to remember his work. I was pleased when he showed up in my expository writing class a year later. He gave me permission to tell his story and used the pseudonym "Nick"—the name of the embattled hero of Hemingway's *In Our Time* short stories.

Nick never used the word "shame," but his writings explore a frightening childhood event that produced intense feelings of humiliation, powerlessness, violation, depression, and rage—essential elements of shame. He took a calculated risk in disclosing this experience, waiting until near the end of the semester, when he felt secure enough with his classmates to reveal a secret that he had shared only with his immediate family. It is a secret he has allowed me to share with you.

Nick's writing is important not only for the story he tells but also for the way he tells it and for its impact on his classmates. I cannot capture in a brief chapter the dynamics of Nick's class—the ways in which students, slowly and tentatively at first, then more self-confidently, came to trust and support each other, developing a bond that made possible remarkable self-disclosures. Nevertheless, readers will see how Nick opens up to his classmates and responds to their acceptance of him. This gradual self-revelation stands at the center of Nick's story.

Shame is the most unspeakable of emotions, for unlike guilt, which reflects pain arising from an act or thought, shame involves the violation of the self. Nick's writings dramatize the unmasking of shame—expressing the inexpressible. The process of writing leads to nothing less than the reclaiming of the self. In several of his essays, Nick uses the metaphor of a "barrier" to describe how this childhood event has isolated him from his contemporaries. In the following pages, we see how Nick lowers this barrier, allowing readers a glimpse into his life.

In quoting from Nick's writings, I have not changed a word or a punctuation mark. His technical errors are minor, as when he misspells the name of Robert Louis Stevenson's tormented hero, Dr. Jekyll. (Even though I pointed out the correct spelling on an early essay, Nick persisted with the misspelling on a later essay.) Nick is a good writer striving to become a better one, and in rereading his writings he now wishes to rewrite them. Throughout the semester he was extremely critical of his own writing and insisted that I be "tough" on his prose. He was, in fact, less interested in my praise than in my technical criticisms. He was also one of the most rigorous critics of his classmates' prose, though he was always fair and balanced in his comments.

Getting to Know Each Other

The first assignment of the semester involved drawing up a chronology of ten important autobiographical events. Nick's opening paragraph was both striking and mysterious.

At the age of fifteen, a brother, my twin, was taken from my family and me. He was taken by a series of events that are senseless and to this day not fully understandable, and are all the more painful because of this. He was dead upon his 2:54 P.M. arrival at an upstate New York hospital, on August 17, 1982. He had been in a car accident with a family relative, one who was called Uncle, but who was really our Mother's cousin. He was close to our family, like an "Uncle." He took Stephen and I skiing, and to the movies; he gave us rides to places we'd be embarrassed to be dropped at by our parents; he was our friend. Is it fortunate or unfortunate that during that summer I spent less time with both Stephen and John, in running and training for my fall cross country season? That's a question that will haunt me forever.

The details behind the accident are many and strange. They include Stephen's unannounced trip, a few blocks across town, to my "Uncle's"; their decision to go for a drive in the country in John's MG; the discovery that Stephen was behind the wheel when the accident occurred; his death, and John's (my "Uncle's") survival of the accident; the signs of sexual abuse found on the scene and on Stephen's body; and the general lack of information for the family when they declined to press charges to avoid public disgrace. These last few details are the most upsetting. We will never know the facts behind

*this senseless accident. And it may seem strange to one looking at this from
the outside that charges were not pressed, but you must understand, 1982
held much different reactions to sexual abuse than now. I don't know if my
parents did the best they could have done for the family, but they did the
best they could at the time with the knowledge they had.*

*I'll never fully understand the depth of this accident's effect on me, though
I've spent the last five years trying to. In it's most obvious effects, it has shut
me down emotionally and to some degrees mentally. I spent my high school
years in a daze, separated from those around me by a barrier that I erected.
At twenty eight, I'm just beginning to be able to look over that barrier, but I
have not yet knocked it down entirely. This event hasn't just shaped me and
my life. Unfortunately, it has defined it, by causing me to live in separation
from the world around me. It has eclipsed any and all events that preceded it
in my life and colored any events that followed it.*

Nick begins the second biographical event by noting that he looks back
at his high school years without fondness. "I never knew who knew about
the family scandal, and I tried not to think about it, but at the back of my
head, I felt as though everyone knew." None of the many academic and
athletic awards Nick received in high school meant anything to him, nor
did he allow anyone to come close to him.

College was much better for Nick than high school, and his other eight
biographical events are more positive than the first two. In college he was
initiated into the "wonderfully many and diverse worlds of music, art, film,
photography, creativity, sex, friendship, politics, drugs, and fashion." He
formed close friendships; studied film, photography, and journalism; and
traveled and studied abroad. Upon returning from Europe, he completed
college and moved to the Southeast, where he found employment. For a
time he was happy, but upon feeling lonely and depressed again, he decided to return to upstate New York and soon fell in love with a woman
whom he married. He has learned about himself through her. "In her eyes
I see myself as hero and villain, the two extremes, Dr. Jeckyl and Mr. Hyde.
I now realize that it is only through another that one can see anything of
himself."

Nick closes his biographical sketch by observing that the love and support he now receives from his parents and wife have allowed him to move
forward to a new phase of his life:

*I'm getting on, trying to move past the pain of my past and enjoy the me
that I slowly discover. It's a wondrously slow and challenging process to see
yourself as who you really are, beyond just the image you see in the mirror,*

*and the one that exists in your mind, but the you that walks and talks and
lives with others, and works and walks the dogs and shops for groceries. To
this aim I have returned to school to become an English teacher; the career
I have wanted for the past six years, but was afraid to pursue. As a returning
student, I'm getting to live the cliche, "I wish I had known then, what I know
now." For I do know now, the things I need to know, and the things I still
need to learn. I have realized that it's the process of this learning that is life.
Everyday we all come a little bit closer to catching ourselves peeking into the
mental mirror. One day soon I'll be able to look at myself full-on and like
what I see.*

Nick gave his ten chronological events to his classmate Ellen, who, combining his words with her own, proceeded to write his biography. Though
she does not devote much attention to the psychological damage he suffered following his brother's death, she empathizes with his loss.

*If the pain of losing a brother wasn't bad enough, the strange and upset-
ting details to the incident, and the fact that he would never know the truth
behind the accident were. Nick could only wonder about why Stephen was
driving the car, and why there was evidence of sexual abuse. Charges were
not pressed in order to avoid negative public attention. It's no wonder that
Nick would erect such a barrier that would keep him from getting close to
people. How frightening the idea of letting someone in must have been to
someone who had just lost his best friend.*

In reading Ellen's thoughtful biographical sketch of Nick—I did not have
access to his ten chronological events, which I saw only at the end of
the semester—I was puzzled by the reference to sexual abuse. I wrote the
following comment on her essay: "All of this is very mysterious—too mysterious, I think. I would omit the detail about sexual abuse or develop it
further." I don't know if Nick's classmates were as curious about this enig-
matic event as I was, but in the following weeks I found myself buried
beneath an avalanche of essays and soon forgot about it.

Writing about Depression and Suicide

Nick did not refer to this subject again until the middle of the semester,
when I asked the class to write an essay on the chapter "Suicide Survivors"
in *Diaries to an English Professor*. Focusing more on depression than on
suicide, Nick opens his five-page essay with a haunting personification.

*Depression is a strange dark beast that slowly and quietly invades a mind.
There, it grows, feeding off its host, turning thoughts black and tasty, assur-*

ing its own survival. In the beginning, few thoughts come or go that have not been nibbled on by its sharp and rotting teeth. Its greasy, dirty fingers then begin to touch and violate all. It stirs up the vicious cycle of apathy breeding pessimism, giving rise to melancholy. The animal gets stronger. It stretches and tests its power. Eventually it takes over. It cultivates its own nourishment. Its growing season is short, dark and howling. Before long every thought is a dismal one; joyous memories are mauled and twisted out of shape; what was once optimism is beaten into hopelessness. Eventually a door is slammed shut on the dwindling light at the end of the tunnel and the candles of the past, that had lighted the way and given strength, are turned blood red, the color of lies and hate and betrayal. Nothing that was or is can be seen clearly, but only through the dimness of depression's smoky, foul breath.

Nick reveals later in the essay that in his mid-twenties he once again found himself severely depressed. Nothing in his life—neither reading, biking, talking with friends, nor work—brought him pleasure. Sitting in front of the television screen for hours, he saw only the reflection of his life, years highlighted with loss, betrayal, isolation, and torment. He again alludes to Stevenson's novel of the divided self but without mentioning his reactions upon learning of his twin brother's death.

The more I searched for the worthiness in me and my life, the more I saw the past loss, hate, and betrayal; the more I felt I was weak, lazy, and wrong in every decision presented to me. I brutally dissected my past, invalidating any bit of good that was there as superficial and irrelevant to the situation at hand. I second-guessed every decision I had made, and judged that all were the wrong ones. I indicted myself as the sole cause of all my misery. I began to dislike myself more and more, until I truly hated what was in me as if it were something independent and tangible, a monstrous me within the shell of an innocent and overwhelmed me. I was hating and hurting the Mr. Hyde within my Dr. Jeckyl. I decided it was time to destroy the monster. The only question that remained was: could I still save the man, were the two that separable?

Without disclosing the reasons for his depression, Nick observes that the most powerful deterrent to suicide during this period in his life was his family, who loved him for the positive traits that he did not always see in himself. Slowly he emerged from his depression, realizing that he could learn to live with the monster, a self-integration Stevenson's tormented character never achieves. Nick ends the essay by giving credit to therapy; he is confident about "fight[ing] off the monster I have been working so hard to keep at bay."

"A Lie Covering Up a Much More Painful Truth"

Nick's next essay was a revelation, a turning point for him and the class.

The time has come to confess to a lie; that, and to share something few know about me. I'm not sure why I feel I must share this but I've felt it coming out since I began to write the first essay for this class. It was there that the lie began. Now, it will end. This essay is an experiment for me, an experiment in self-acceptance and emotional control. So in the spirit of introspection, acceptance, empathy, and admission to the truth, here goes . . .

The first entry in my chronicle of ten life shaping events was a lie. Unfortunately, it's a lie covering up a much more painful truth. It's not a good lie, but it's the best I could come up with at the time. There was no twin brother; there was no car accident and there was no death. There was only me and John, a family relative, who was also a child molester. I was the child. The dates are true to the best of my recollection, and the results you read were the true end results. Though, the end has not yet been reached. I couldn't chronicle ten events in my life without this one because it has defined who I am. I also couldn't admit it to a bunch of strangers on our second day of class. Now, I am ready.

I was sexually abused, cunningly and systematically, for what seemed like years. I'm not sure how long the abuse went on. My heart says years; my head says it might not have been that long. I will never know. My feelings and reactions read like a textbook case in abuse. My silence was won through naive trust and bribery. I said nothing to no one. I'm still hesitant to speak of the abuse to others for fear that they will think less of me, the victim.

But I am no longer a victim. I gave up that role a long time ago. I don't handle pity too well, either my own or others'. The acceptance of this event in my life has been difficult. Initially I just ignored it. I didn't block it out as many do; I simply didn't let it affect me. This worked for ten years or more. It worked well enough for me to actually forgive my uncle, enough that I thought about telling him this in person. I never did, however. As I went through the various stages of acceptance, I developed two sides: one sensitive and empathic to everyone's emotional difficulty, and another, devoid of all emotion when it came to self. Unfortunately the inhuman side seems to dominate when problems arise with those closest to me.

Several years ago I began battling with depression. It seemed to come out of nowhere, and I'll probably never know the true cause behind it. I began to wonder. As I sunk deeper and deeper, I looked back on my life for the first time and blamed the abuse from years ago on my present situation. I realized that everyday of my past had been altered just a bit by this sick and selfish man. As I further retraced my path, I wondered what would have been. I became furious. I felt that a monster had been created within the man I should have been. How could someone take another's life and twist it so out of shape, then fade into the distance? My anger rose to new heights. I lay in bed one night and planned how I could get away with killing my abuser. I seriously thought about taking his life. I have since considered blackmail, harassment, and legal battle; I still haven't ruled out physical violence. It seems to me now that sexual abuse was not the reason for my depression, but depression was the catalyst which prompted me to deal with sexual abuse.

The death of a twin, a part of me, was the only suitable disguise I could find for my ugly past. The real death was that of my innocence and child-hood. A huge piece of me was sliced out on the day John first decided that I would be his little sex toy. As the days became years, my mind compensated for what had been killed. I wish I could explain what that kind of abuse does to a young boy and the man that follows, but I haven't yet reached that point of understanding myself. Right now every hard fought answer comes surrounded in question.

I continued to visit my uncle regularly after the abuse started. I didn't understand what was happening. He was an adult and my friend; why would he involve me in something bad, hurtful? At times I even thought that in some strange way he was doing something for me. I just couldn't understand how. I blindly trusted him, as only a child could. Several years of his ma-nipulation and abuse later, my father and brother showed up at his house unannounced. The truth exploded out into the world. What they found, I can never imagine from their perspective. There was their son and brother naked on the bed of their trusted relative. It is only by fate and my father's restraint that John lived.

What followed for me was a summer of conflicting emotion and confu-sion. I gave a statement to the police, then I was cut out of the proceedings. My parents tried to shelter me, to save me from this bomb that had been dropped into our life. I don't think they knew that this had been going on for several years and that anything for me would be easier than continuing the abuse. I never admitted to them its duration for fear of their disappointment that I didn't come to them for protection. They asked me if I thought I needed counseling, but I said no. I was a teenager, all I wanted to do was move on. In the end, my parents dropped all charges against John in order to protect me from the publicity that it would generate in the small town. I immedi-ately put the days of abuse behind me.

Thirteen years later it still amazes me that I was the victim of sexual abuse at the hands of a man who was old enough to be my father. Whenever I think about it, my mind becomes so paralyzed with conflicted emotion that I have to put it aside. Only once in the past was I able to write about it. It was almost two years ago. I wrote a letter with the hopes of releasing some of the emotions that were devastating me at the time. I can't bring myself to edit the original emotion of the letter. It's not eloquent and it's not pretty:

> *You dirty sick bastard . . . Many years ago you took something from me that I can never really get back . . . ever . . . My innocence and youth. Can you imagine how that feels??? To have part of yourself missing . . . I doubt you can. I doubt you even really know what I'm talking about or maybe even who I am. Let me refresh your memory . . .*
>
> *Many years ago you were caught in bed with a little boy!!! That may not even clarify things because I'm sure there was more than one. But who cares who I am . . . you will never know who I am, so I'll appoint myself as spokesman for all the children you may have abused and molested, and all the children that other sick bastards just like you rape and fuck up for the rest of their lives.*
>
> *First of all let me say that I hope you have lived a horrible, tortured, guilt ridden life and that you regret your acts daily. I hope you sincerely want to die. I hope nightly you wake up screaming and sweating thinking of all the evil that's inside you. If you have forgiven yourself, reconsider because what you did is so inexcusable to me or any other normal person. I hope your life has been ruined by your actions (if it hasn't, give me some time and I'll ruin it by mine). I want you to live in HELL every day that you are on this earth, and when you die I'll feel a bit better because I'm sure then you'll truly be where you deserve to be with others like you.*
>
> *You took the youth, innocence, adolescence, and life from a child. A CHILD. What the FUCK were you thinking? . . . And to think for a time I forgave you and felt that you didn't mean to do what you did. That you were sick, that you had good intentions at heart, that you didn't want to hurt me. Where the fuck have I been? I'll tell you where . . . With my head in the sand afraid to hurt the loved ones around me by bringing this horrible incident in my life back up. I did that because I wasn't ready to deal with the anger deep within me, but now that my mind and my life are at a point to be ready, I welcome the anger and I try to bring it out. I'm no longer worried about hurting any of my loved ones, because I know they would want me to be rid of the hurt I feel. I was going to face you in person (and I still may) but I am truly afraid of what I'd do to you. I want to tear you apart and watch you suffer and plead. I want to pound you around that house of yours, so I can drive down that street and not have to hide my eyes when I pass it. I want to hold my head up and get the weight off that's been holding it down for so many years. To do that I want to knock your head off.*
>
> *You victimized a boy because you knew you would have power and control, but now I have the control, and I'm sure you never considered what the boy*

might do to you twenty years later. You never thought of one single thing except your sick, perverted desires. Of yourself. You never gave one second of consideration to the young boy who's dick you had in your hand as often as you could get it there. What in HELL did you think would become of that situation? That it would go on forever, that it would just end without a trace and everyone would be okay? The entire time you were molesting me I feared being caught most of all. In my young mind I thought I was doing something wrong. Well FUCK that!!! I did nothing, except not turn you in. If I had only known ... You didn't think of my family, of my friends, of my life and what this would do to it, of how I'd be affected at twenty-seven years old, of how this would potentially eat at me forever and fuck up my life. You selfish, sick, perverted, piece of shit, worthless bastard!!!!!

You should dread every knock at the door and every phone call, because you never know where I might choose to approach you ... at work (do your friends and co-workers know what you've done in your past??) ... at home (do your neighbors know??) ... in the street ... I haven't decided myself. All I know is that you are no longer off the hook as far as I'm concerned. I don't know what you have suffered on account of your actions, but it's not enough. Nothing is enough! What I do know is that I want your life ruined. I want you to live in tortured hell for the rest of your life. I want to take from you so you know how it feels, and I want you to know that you deserve everything you get. I'm going to release all the anger and hurt that I've suppressed for years. Release it and move on with my life, putting my head back together and putting you as far behind me as is possible, but ... I WILL NEVER FORGIVE YOU!!!!!

Don't misinterpret this as a threat of physical violence, because I don't think I'm like that. I've never struck anyone in anger (but if I do, rest assured that it WILL be you.) I'd love to pound the shit out of you. I'd love to dominate you like you did me. I'd love to be in the control position and hurt you over and over, but that's not in me, at least yet. All I want is to completely ruin your life ... forever ....

Very Sincerely,
Nick

After I wrote this letter, I wrote nothing more for over a year: no journal, no letters, no nothing. Words stopped coming. It is only within the past six months that I have again turned to my computer keyboard for the consoling that only it knows how to give. I find that in my time away, the thinking I have done has moved me to a new level of awareness. I am getting closer to knowing myself as who I am. I can embrace my past and be thankful for the inner strength it has given me. I am finally starting to like the person that looks back at me from the bathroom mirror.

It has taken me over ten years to reopen the inner box that has held all these emotions tight. It feels good. Depression is behind me for now, and I *see a million goals ahead. Everyday I grow and learn. My battle with the past is not won yet, nor will it ever be. I will always continue to fight to regain the unknown but tragically missed piece of me that was taken away so many summers ago. But only recently have I been able to turn and fight head on instead of turning to flee. I have found that the enemy is not so strong when you can actually see it.*

My heart goes out to any and all in this class who may be the victims of similar abuse.

Reading Nick's essay, I felt first shock and horror, then admiration. I have never read a student paper containing more shame, anger, and hurt, yet the writer expresses his feelings with power and eloquence. He tells us in the first paragraph that the essay is an experiment in self-acceptance and emotional control, and after reading the essay, with its righteous fury expressed in nearly flawless language, one can only agree that the experiment is a success. Writing about himself with remarkable objectivity and detachment, he acknowledges a lie designed to conceal a terrible truth; now ready to reveal that truth, he also confesses to his own dark impulses. What makes the essay more authentic is the furious emotion within the unedited letter, written nearly two years earlier. The contrast between Nick's past rage and present composure is striking.

No less striking is the contrast between Nick's letter to his molester and his essay for the class. The letter, which represents Nick's first attempt to write about sexual abuse, is filled with rage. Indeed, if words can kill, the letter is nothing less than the writer's attempt to annihilate his reader. Nick makes little attempt to distance himself from the avenging first-person speaker; the respectful closing, "Very Sincerely, Nick," hardly defuses the threat of violence. Nick does not tell us whether he experienced cathartic release from writing the letter; nor do we discover why he wrote nothing else after the letter for an entire year. Nick's writing for the class is far more introspective than the letter. His purpose is not merely to vent his feelings, important as that impulse is, but to understand and communicate them to the reader. He analyzes in depth his conflicting emotions; acknowledges the antithetical sides of his personality—the sensitive side and the "inhuman" side, devoid of all emotion; recounts in abundant detail the shame he experienced following his family's discovery of his relationship with John; and anticipates his readers' response to his story. He writes lucidly about a confusing time in his life and never loses control of his words. He ends the essay by reaching out to those classmates who may themselves have been victims of sexual abuse and who may thus benefit from reading about his experiment in self-acceptance and emotional control.

Nick recognizes that he will probably never be able to forget or over-come entirely the psychological effects of sexual abuse, but his writings demonstrate the progress he has made. In expressing the shame he has experienced for so many years, Nick is able to confront and, to a large extent, exorcize his inner demon. He now likes the person he sees gazing at him from the mirror; one suspects that he also approves of the words that reflect his renewed self-confidence.

Narcissistic Injuries

Though I did not realize it until after the course was over, when I had the opportunity to study his writings closely, Nick's description of shame re-calls the traumatic injuries experienced by many nineteenth- and twenti-eth-century fictional characters. For example, *Frankenstein* (1818), *Wuthering Heights* (1847), and *Great Expectations* (1860) portray charac-ters who are victimized by crimes committed against them in childhood. As I suggest in *Narcissism and the Novel* (1990), these crimes awaken within the Creature, Heathcliff, and Pip, respectively, feelings of intense shame, a response to the perception that the self is radically defective or deficient. The narcissistic injuries experienced by these characters produce shattered identities, heightened vulnerability, empathic disturbances, and massive rage. The theme of the dark double pervading these and other novels about the divided self may be seen in Nick's metaphor of the "monster" threat-ening to destroy him. The death of his "twin brother" represents the split-off part of the self. The victim's feeling of complicity is perhaps the most insidious aspect of sexual abuse of children. The violence committed against a child's body penetrates the spirit and produces unspeakable suffering.

For thirteen years Nick had concealed his shameful secret from every-one outside his immediate family. During the three months in which he was a member of English 300, he had carefully considered whether to open himself up to his classmates' and teacher's scrutiny. Writing about the experience, he unmasked his shame—and therein gambled that he would not expose himself to further humiliation.

How did Nick feel about his self-disclosure? Here is what he wrote in a later essay:

I couldn't get through the semester without writing about my darkened past. Thoughts and visions welled up with each accumulated assignment. My life, my parents, my thoughts of depression and suicide; they all brought me back to the abuse I experienced as a youth. I couldn't avoid it any longer; the time was right to give my past the recognition it deserved in writing. At

*last, I welcomed the opportunity. The truth is that without me, my paper
began writing itself almost three months ago.*

*As I watched the semester progress, I saw also the pattern of assignments
develop. Read a chapter; write about it. I skimmed through* Diaries to an
English Professor *to see just what was in store for us. The first chapter I read
in the first week of class was "Sexual Disclosures." I realized then that writing about my abuse would be inevitable if I was to remain true to who I am.
After all the searching I have done for answers about sexual abuse and what
it does to an individual, I couldn't cover it up again. I had to own up and
face it. I felt guilty enough presenting the charade I had in the first assignment. I felt I had taken a step back in my hard and long fought march
forward; I had watered down a past that made me uncomfortable. I had to
show the truth of who I am. For who are we, and what is writing without
honesty? The paper grew without me.*

*I had no fear in writing my essay. In fact, the atmosphere of safety gener-
ated by the class made me comfortable with the thoughts I gave credence to.
I knew I had a sympathetic non-judgmental audience for at least three hours,
but probably beyond that. The worst that could happen was that my writing
would be criticized. (That is also the best thing that could happen. God
knows, I need it.) As many others in class have admitted, this is a support
group of sorts. There are few places where you can admit to, even speak, the
absolute truth without fear. One is the psychiatrist's couch, the other is a
stranger's ear. Our classroom has elements of both. And as we have seen and
read, admission is a big step toward healing.*

*As I wrote, I wrote for myself and for the class. This is the first group I
could safely reveal my truth to. I had to take that step and more. I had to
shine a light on a problem that is forever shrouded in haze. As a society, we
are afraid of sexual abuse; not as afraid as we used to be, but afraid all the
same. It is so ugly and brutal that no one wants to run the risk of further
victimization by those around them when they admit their truth.*

*The truth of sexual abuse is that it leaves the victim with ambivalent feel-
ings about themselves both physically and mentally. They share the blame
with their abusers, and are sensitive to how the world sees them. The lines
between abuser and abused can be very skewed in the mind of the victim.
Thus it takes very little in the way of disapproval for them to re-silence the
truth they so want to scream out. Any hint of disapproval or discrimination
is a continuation of an abuse that will not end. After years of silence, fear
and pain, I no longer worry about appearance and disapproval. I know who
I am and accept that. The world's stare no longer keeps me silent. My opinion is if my words disturb you, you can dismiss them with your denial, pity,
or blame; it makes no difference to me. The strong and open minded will*

embrace what I say and ask how it could be so. It is the latter that solve the problems of this world and change the future.

I refuse to be labeled a victim, a survivor, or a degenerate. I will be an avenger. I want to avenge the wrong that was done to me and millions of other children. My essay was one of the early steps in that quest, for until we can speak about abuse in concrete, non-judgmental terms, no one will come forward. The truth will remain locked in the minds of the abused, where it spins and turns like a rock in a jeweler's tumbler, losing its rough edges and original shape, only coming out when it's attractive to the eye and smooth to the touch. Abuse will perpetuate itself in millions of lives that could have been saved through empathy and self-understanding. There should be no stigma in being an abused child. Our world has enough illusion; let's face some cold, brutal reality for a change. Believe it or not, it's freeing.

Before I wrote my essay, I reread the letter I had written the year before. I loved it's anger. It was my first and most formal declaration of anger and hurt at the man who so altered my life at his whim. My anger hasn't changed since then, but it has become more refined. I am no longer afraid of it, but welcome it as a healthy emotion. As I understand more about myself, and how I have been shaped by sexual abuse, I feel more comfortable with my emotions. I still have not taken any actions against my abuser, and maybe never will. I now let my mind dictate my actions. I don't force issues and I don't turn away from them. When they come up, or bring me down, I face them and resolve them. Here I oversimplify the process greatly, for it has taken years for me to face some issues, and still more years for me to understand and deal with them.

My essay was one more step in the process of resolution. As abstract thoughts become ink on paper, they enter the world of the writer. For the first time, they can stare into my face, and I into theirs, instead of them staring out from within, while I see nothing. On the page thoughts become real; when spoken, still more real.

I value the opportunity this class has afforded me to examine my reality and share it with a few sympathetic strangers. It has also provided me with the impetus, safety and structure to write such an important essay (important to me, that is) without fear; the fear of loosing control over the subject, and the fear of the judgment of my peers. It took me a long time of searching, not for the right words in the essay but the reason. Now it is out and I am better for that.

Especially intriguing is Nick's observation that both the worst and the best that could happen to his writing is that it would be criticized. Anyone reading his essays must be aware of how important language is to him, how he regards it as essential to his continued recovery. Language is both a defensive and offensive weapon to Nick: it holds in check dangerous emotions that threaten to overwhelm the self, and it is the instrument of choice to avenge past humiliations. Such writing serves many purposes, enabling one to express and purge toxic emotions, master intolerable fears, memorialize loss, avenge wrongs, create a lasting record of experiences, connect with readers, and unify a divided self.

"A Reprieve"

Ironically, the week that Nick turned in his essay on child sexual abuse, prepared to read it aloud, a backlog of undiscussed papers prompted me to inform his classmates that no new writings would be read in class for the next two weeks. Nick felt both relieved and disappointed when he heard me say this—he later told me wryly that I had given him a "reprieve." As soon as I read his essay, however, I realized it would be valuable for the entire class to discuss it, and so I telephoned him and requested enough copies for his classmates the following week. I also asked him if he was willing to write a brief essay describing his feelings during the class discussion, a request with which he was eager to comply.

As I sat before class, I tried not to think about what I was about to do, to reveal about myself. Thoughts kept creeping back. Would everyone, in unison look up at me, horrified by my past? Would they gasp in horror? Would they slide their chairs a little bit further away? Would I break down and have to leave the room? Would I be unable to face them? Or would we be presented with an overwhelming and uncomfortable silence? Would they find my essay and my revelation to them extreme and inappropriate? As fast as my uncertainty piled up, I crushed it to the back of my mind. I had carried these thoughts and these papers too far not to give them their due.

Once in class, I nonchalantly dropped the stack of essays face down on the desk. In my mind the papers fell as if in a movie: an extreme close up as the papers fall in very slow motion, filling the screen and crushing the viewer; they fall as a single stack, landing on the desk, with an overwhelming and deep thump; they compress slightly as they hit, then bounce and settle into place, each slightly askew. The deed had been done, and my truth would be known. I could have turned back anytime, but I never considered it. Now there was no turning back; the class had the paper in their hands. Since the paper was held till last, I spent two hours unable to truly concentrate on the work at hand. I read and responded to what I could, the entire time thinking, "let's just get this over with." At last, that time came.

Everyone began to read. The silence grew thick and heavy like I was underwater. I tried to read along, but could not. I pretended to read; I read certain sentences, and I fidgeted in my seat. The lights hummed louder and louder. I couldn't look up for fear that anyone would look me in the eyes with anything resembling disapproval or, even worse, disgust. The only sound I heard was that of pages flipping louder and louder as the minutes slowly ticked away. What the hell had I done? Was I thinking clearly in deciding to do this? What had made me do it? I had to . . . It seemed they would never stop reading. Finally, they did. All sat in silence, stunned, uncomfortable or both. Finally I looked up and tried to smile feebly as if to apologize for what I had done, what I had put them through. Again I wondered at the appropriateness of my confession to the class.

After an uncertain silence, the discussion began. To my relief, but not to my surprise, no one moved away from me and no one gasped. In fact I felt as if all took a step toward me in support and maybe amazement. The first comment was that the reader felt as if she had just witnessed a horrible accident, a second reader said she was on the verge of tears. As others confessed their horror, sickness, and disgust at my abuser, I felt my lips raised into a sincere and heartfelt smile. I wondered about the appropriateness of my expression. I figured that I should try to look sincere and serious about such an event in my life. I tried to suppress the smile, but it flowed through my body. It came for two reasons.

For the first time in my life a roomful of twenty people all knew who I was, and what I'd been through in my life. I had momentarily dropped the barrier that I have so carefully erected over the years. The class seemed to understand. They expressed understanding for the past I have shown them, and the past I have not. They tried to understand more; they asked questions; they wanted to know. In trying to understand me and empathize with me, the class has helped me take one more step toward understanding and accepting myself. I had to smile at the open acceptance I felt after my admission of such a horrible event.

My smile also came from my sense of accomplishment as a writer. As all know I am my own harshest critic, but for a few minutes I was happy with something I had written. It had affected. It had an effect. My writing had taken on life before my eyes. Today, I would rewrite much of the essay, and I realize its content probably had more effect than its style. But it did have life, independent of me, for a short time. For the first time in my life, I felt a rush of adrenaline from a page of prose. It recommitted me to the life of the writer. Although I still would not label myself as a writer, I felt like one for awhile.

As my smile grew, I felt guilty and overjoyed at the classes responses. I was sorry that I had hurt them so, but glad that they could feel empathy deeply enough to hurt. I had no idea what to expect, but I couldn't have asked for a better response from the class. I knew that all were on my side, and had vividly glimpsed, however fleetingly, a painful piece of my life.

It would be false to say that I feel better as a result of the class. Twenty years of scarring doesn't heal that easily. I do feel that I have taken steps forward. I know now that there are twenty people who can either accept me or not based on the truth of who I am, with no falsity. It's hard to admit to something that I have kept in the dark for so long, but it feels freeing to be able to.

Aesthetics and Therapeutics

Nick's essays reveal, as we have seen elsewhere, that writing about risky topics brings aesthetic pleasure as well as therapeutic satisfaction. He uses the metaphor of "reopen[ing] the inner box that has held all these emotions tight" to describe the process of writing, but this is no Pandora's box: there is no explosion, no unleashing of evil, no chaotic consequences. Though he refers to the essay as "writing itself," he remains fully in control of when and how to drop the barrier of secrecy he erected over the years to conceal the truth of his life. In his autobiographical paragraphs he chooses a fictional disguise to begin the account of his dark past; in his essay he lowers the mask to reveal the truth as he sees it. He views himself not as a Jekyll or Hyde, hero or villain, but as a complex figure who must find the words to create his existence for readers. He sees himself, perhaps for the first time, as an author, writing for both himself *and* his audience. His classmates' acceptance of his story heightens his own self-acceptance. One can sense his delight in writing: he tells us that he "loved" the anger in his letter and that he felt a "rush of adrenaline" from his prose. His paragraphs affirm the craft of writing. He hints at feeling guilty pleasure from the creation of art, suggesting the writer's aesthetic gratification in transmuting a painful or shameful experience into powerful prose.

Responding to Nick's Writing

Nick's 1995 section of Expository Writing was the first time I taught English 300 as a personal writing course, and one of the biggest surprises was that although it seemed odd at first to correct comma splices or faulty subject-verb agreement in an autobiographical essay on a risky subject, students expected and accepted grammatical criticisms. Two students, including Nick, complained during the middle of the semester that I was not being rigorous enough in my class criticisms—a complaint I took seriously and tried to rectify. It is true that in discussing Nick's essay on sexual abuse, we talked almost entirely about how we felt while reading it. But I always made technical corrections on my own copy, which I returned to the students the following week. Different teachers have different styles of responding to student essays; my own style is to circle every grammatical, spelling, and typographical error and sometimes to rewrite a sentence. This "formalist" approach has been criticized by composition scholar Anne Ruggles Gere for representing an "extremely narrow view of writing" (11). I agree that good writing involves far more than technical proficiency and that making technical criticisms may become counterproductive, especially if a teacher's tone becomes angry or impatient. Nevertheless, I believe that most students need these technical criticisms in order to improve their writing and that they will accept these criticisms if they are expressed constructively. Students will take their work seriously when they realize that others do too.

More important than my technical comments on student essays are the affirming, validating ones. Effective teaching is affective learning; intellectual and emotional development are complementary. I praise my students' writing in order to be what Heinz Kohut calls a "mirroring selfobject," that is, an extension of themselves, thus helping them to realize their potential. It is seldom hard to find something to praise in their personal essays, whether it is their willingness to confront a challenging subject, their emotional openness, or a felicitous phrase. I always thank students for sharing personal information with me. Corny as it may seem, sometimes I pen a happy face at the bottom of an essay to indicate how touched I am by it. Whenever I come across an essay that I think others outside of class might like to read, I encourage the writer to share the contents with them.

At the bottom of Nick's essay on his close relationship to his father and mother, for example, I urged him to send a copy to them. Sometimes I suggest, as tactfully as possible, that the writer has not yet fully succeeded in conveying an idea or feeling to the reader. When Nick mentioned in his essay on depression that he had been in therapy and that he had reached insights about himself, I wrote in the margin: "Do you want to share any of these self-revelations with the reader? I think it would be helpful. Otherwise, the reader remains at a distance from you."

There were several questions that I deliberately did *not* raise on Nick's essays for fear that they would be intrusive. For example, I did not ask him why his parents decided to drop all charges against John and whether he now believes that they made the right decision. I did not ask Nick to elaborate on how his father and brother must have felt when they caught him in bed with John. I inferred from the following sentences that Nick would have told us had he been willing or able to do so: "What they found, I can never imagine from their perspective. There was their son and brother naked on the bed of their trusted relative." Nor did I ask Nick how his experience with John has affected his relationships with men and women. These questions are important for understanding Nick's story, but I feared that they would be invasive and threatening. I did consider asking Nick a question about the reliability of his narration; since he deceived his readers once, fabricating the story about a dead twin, how do readers know that he is not being deceptive elsewhere? A close reading of his writings reveals a few chronological inconsistencies. I decided, however, not to raise any of these questions. I don't wish to read Nick as an unreliable narrator or attempt to psychoanalyze or deconstruct his story, as I would if he were a fictional character. As Cathy Caruth has pointed out, the "story of trauma" is the "narrative of a belated experience" (7), and it may take a lifetime for survivors to construct a coherent interpretation of a traumatic event. In general, the more personal an essay, the more reluctant I am to raise a question that the writer might not be ready to confront. As Nick noted, "it has taken years for me to face some issues, and still more years for me to understand and deal with them."

"The Stranger's Ear"

Nick refers to the two places where one can "admit to, even speak, the absolute truth without fear": one is on the "psychiatrist's couch" and the other is to the "stranger's ear." A colleague to whom I showed an early version of this chapter made the intriguing observation that Nick's class resembled the Catholic tradition of the confessional but without absolution or confidentiality. I was surprised by how many of Nick's classmates declined confidentiality when their highly personal essays were discussed in class. Some students who chose to remain anonymous noted that although classmates would probably guess their identity, they were still willing to disclose aspects of their lives. I suspect that it was not only trust that enabled students to self-disclose but also the realization that they would never see each other again after the semester ended.

The Impact of Nick's Essay on His Classmates

Nick's essay on sexual abuse turned out to be liberating for several students, inspiring them to write about painful or shameful experiences they had never revealed before. Nick's self-disclosure emboldened a male student to write about the sexual abuse he also encountered as a child, and he paid textual tribute to Nick.

When the paper on sexual disclosure Nick wrote was given to the class, I would have bet money I was the first person to read it. If I can remember correctly I was the only one who did not comment on it. I could not. I was so moved and so upset that any words I would have said would have never come out the way I wanted them to. I feel now I can say those words. The paper Nick wrote dredged up feelings from my past that I was not ready to deal with. It brought to light memories that have been eating me up for years. For the first time in my life I was able to transfer those memories from my mind to paper. Dealing with this issue was, for me, taking a step in reclaiming who I am. It is probably one of the biggest I will ever take. What Nick did I will never forget. I believe in my heart that I was not the only one Nick helped through helping himself. For me, however, it is the most I have ever learned from someone I have never really known. Thank you.

Others shared agonizing experiences. One person wrote about her boyfriend's suicide. Another wrote about the terror she experienced when she was date raped at a party: the worst part of the experience, she said, was the fear that she would be disowned by her strict parents. A Latino man wrote about the shame he experienced when his parents moved into an all-white community and received a petition from neighbors who demanded that they leave. A woman wrote a letter to her father expressing indignation over his constant belittling of her when she was younger. An alarming number of students wrote about their anguish growing up with alcoholic parents. The students discovered the truth of Shoshana Felman's and Dori Laub's observation in their book *Testimony* (1992) that one must have a witness in order to recover from a traumatic experience. Students bonded to form a close classroom community. In the words of one woman, "I am still completely astounded by the revelations that you, my fellow class members, have shared. I can honestly state that I know more about the lives of students in this course than I do about many of my 'closest friends.' We are no longer acquaintances; we have become an extended family that can be considered both diverse and unified."

The students in Nick's class were strangers to each other when the semester began, but the bond that developed among them did come to resemble that of an extended family. Most of the students were nineteen or twenty years old, but two women were older, one in her fifties, the other in her sixties. These two women wrote poignant essays about their families, including the death of a husband and a child, and their presence in class created an intergenerational connection. I always encourage students to view life experiences from as many perspectives as possible, including both a child's and parent's. The students came to feel not only that the family was an appropriate subject for an essay but also that the class itself was a close-knit group in which each person was part of a larger whole.

The Teacher's Self-Disclosures

Research on self-disclosure indicates that the ability to reveal one's feelings to another person promotes close relationships (Mikulincer and Nachshon). Research also demonstrates that self-disclosure encourages reciprocity: "as one individual discloses more intimate information, his or her partner (often a confederate) also discloses more information" (L. Miller and Kenny 713). I believe that self-disclosure in the classroom fosters the exchange of points of view. During class discussions I talk about my experiences as a son, husband, and father, especially those experiences that have proven to be cautionary tales. When discussing shame, for example, I share with my students the mortification I experienced when I came up for tenure in the late 1970s and was told that my scholarship was "deficient"—a criticism that called into question not only my worth as a scholar but also my identity and self-esteem.

Teachers who encourage self-disclosure must be able to acknowledge their own shame experiences without guilt or defensiveness. Andrew Morrison's clinical observation has important pedagogical implications: "[T]he shame of patients is contagious, often resonating with the clinician's own shame experiences—the therapist's own sense of failure, self-deficiency, and life disappointments. Painful countertransference feelings may thus be generated in the analyst/therapist, feelings that he or she, like the patient, would just as soon avoid, feelings that not infrequently lead to a collusion, preventing investigation of the shame experience" (*Shame* 6). I have never taught a course on shame in literature, but were I to do so, I would encourage my students to write personal essays relating fictional characters' lives to their own. I would also invite them to explore shame from a variety of theoretical perspectives: psychoanalytic, feminist, historical, reader response. The aim of such a study would be to examine the various masks of shame and to come to terms with the painful past. Unmasking shame evokes intense resistance, and it is the students themselves, not the teacher, who must decide whether to disclose their fears to others. If they wished, students who have been abused or shamed might describe the experience from the abuser's or shamer's point of view, thus gaining another perspective. Judging from my students' experiences, I believe that the writing or literature classroom is an appropriate setting to unmask shame and initiate the process of self-understanding and healing.

I want to let Nick have the last word in this chapter, for it is his story, after all, I have presented to you. Evaluating the course at the end of the semester, he writes:

I have thoroughly enjoyed every session of this class. It's not very often that one can sit around with a group of intelligent peers and discuss such sensitive and important topics. I only wish there had been more time: time to discuss the issues in depth, time to discuss the writing in depth, time to learn about each other in depth. But you can't accomplish everything in three hours a week.

As for me, I'm not a person that joins well with others. I feel more comfortable at the fringes watching everyone like a hawk, and avoiding their gazes as quickly and deftly as possible. I won't fool you and tell you that now I'm different and you're all my new best friends and role models. You're not . . . but you can be proud that you have entertained me, perplexed me, taught me, helped me, supported me and constantly surprised me. That's impressive for such a small group that I had such small hopes for. More importantly you have taught me to reserve judgment on people until I have at least some of the facts. That discovery of the unknown value and respectability of people has cracked open a door on a new world where I just may see myself a bit clearer.

CHAPTER 6

Writing under the Influence

To be honest, I am having some difficulty writing an essay on binge drinking. I am in distress because I drank too much on Saturday night.

Until the fall semester of 1996, I had not asked students to write on a subject with which nearly all of them are all too familiar: binge drinking. To be sure, alcohol appears in the background of many of the diaries I receive from students in my courses on literature and psychoanalysis. Men and women write about getting "smashed," but alcohol is never the central focus of their diaries, not even when they describe their feelings about a friend's death in a traffic accident caused by drunk driving or about a case of date rape where alcohol has been a factor. Alcohol is frequently mentioned in many of the essays appearing throughout this book, but getting drunk seems to be such a part of the college scene that students rarely question this aspect of their lives. Why write on alcohol when there are so many more important subjects to pursue in a diary or essay?

My lack of interest in drinking may also have prevented me from wondering about this side of my students' lives. I am not opposed to drinking, but my body has little tolerance for alcohol. One glass of wine or beer gives me a buzz; two glasses put me to sleep. I have been drunk only once in my life—at a Christmas sherry party when I was a first-year graduate student. Unable to walk a straight line on the way home, I judged myself inebriated and promptly lost interest in altered consciousness. On another occasion several years later, I drank a few ounces of wine during a reception for English majors and then went to teach a class. I began to giggle while taking attendance, and my students looked at me as if I had just stumbled out of a bar. I've never aspired toward Hemingwayesque machismo; in fact, I identify with Robert Cohn, the Hemingway antihero in *The Sun Also Rises*, who cannot drink without embarrassing himself. I am not naive about the role of alcohol in real or fictional characters' lives, but it never dawned on me that this might be a timely subject for a student essay.

Widespread ignorance persists despite the media's frequent reports of the seriousness of binge drinking. In a study called "Millennium Hangover: Keeping Score on Alcohol," a nonprofit Washington, D.C., research institute found that "only 3 percent of parents believe their high-school-aged children have slugged as many as five alcoholic drinks in a row over the past month," despite the fact that "federal statistics have shown that a third of 9th- through 12th-graders have done so" (*Albany Times-Union*, 17 December 1999). The National Institute on Alcohol Abuse and Alcoholism, a federal agency, reports that one in four U.S. children under eighteen live in households with an adult who has a serious drinking problem (*Albany Times-Union*, 31 December 1999). Nor is this a recent problem: alcoholism rates have not changed significantly in the last decade. Henry Wechsler, director of College Alcohol Studies at the Harvard School of Public Health, reported in 1998 that "[a]mong more than 14,500 students surveyed at 116 institutions, 43 per cent reported that they had binged at least once in the preceding two weeks, compared with 44 per cent in the earlier [1994] study" (*Chronicle of Higher Education*, 20 November 1998). According to Hank Nuwer, the author of a book on the subject, "all current studies of alcohol use among men and women attending institutions of higher education point to binge drinking as *the* major campus social problem, particularly among fraternity and sorority members" (57). The problem is not limited to American college students. An article in the January 2000 issue of the *American Journal of Public Health* concludes that alcohol abuse and alcohol dependence are the two "most prevalent and deleterious psychiatric disorders not only in the United States but in the world" (Grant 112).

Midway through the semester of an expository writing class I taught in the fall of 1996, I began to wonder how students would respond to an essay on binge drinking. Earlier in the semester, two students had written movingly about the impact of alcoholism on their families. Both students read their essays aloud, and neither attempted to minimize the dangers of alcohol addiction. No one denied the role of alcohol in physical or sexual victimization or in traffic fatalities. Weeks later, the students revealed a different attitude when the subject of campus drinking arose. They now seemed to believe that while drinking among "older" people was sad and sometimes tragic, drinking among college students was no cause for alarm. "Everyone gets drunk in college," one student exclaimed. "We'll be able to cut down on drinking after graduation." They looked at me with condescending amusement when I pointed out that drinking is a serious problem among college students. It was one of the few times when I found myself openly critical of my students' attitudes and behavior.

Binge Drinking

Around this time, an article appeared in the *New York Times* about a study by the Harvard School of Public Health indicating that 86 percent of fraternity residents and 80 percent of sorority women are binge drinkers. The principal investigator of the study observed that "[f]our or five drinks doesn't mean they're drunk or alcoholic . . . but it puts them in a group that has problems related to drink, such as missing classes, getting hurt or having trouble with the police" ("Study Ties Binge Drinking to Fraternity House Life," *New York Times*, 6 October 1996). The article reminded me of a 1992 study of University at Albany students documenting widespread alcohol consumption, particularly among underage drinkers: "While only 28 percent of the students surveyed were of legal drinking age, over 90 percent reported using alcohol, frequently in abusive quantities. Of the men, 44 percent reported consuming alcohol about three times a week or more; 23 percent of the women reported that frequency of consumption. On a typical occasion, 42 percent of the men reported consuming seven or more drinks; 14 percent of the women reported that frequency of consumption" (*University Update*, 18 November 1992) . As disturbing as these figures are, I was not entirely surprised, for I remembered my daughters' experiences. Neither drank in high school, but they discovered the bar scene as soon as they arrived in college. One of them, who had never broken a law in her life before entering college, proudly told me over the telephone that she had acquired a fake ID card the first week of her freshman year. She did not believe she was doing anything wrong— her behavior, she insisted, was no different from her friends'. "Dad, you've been teaching for a long time, but you have no clue what college students are like!"

I found myself in the same bind as most parents of college-age children. My daughters knew that I disapproved of their underage drinking, yet I was reluctant to scold them lest they stop confiding in me. College is a time for experimentation, and I believe that children will drink with or without their parents' permission. My daughters assured me that they would not do anything really dangerous, such as drinking and driving. They survived their experiences with little more than a few wretched hangovers. Nevertheless, whenever my children are driving late at night, I fear for their safety because of all the drunks on the road. I have heard too many horror stories of lives lost or destroyed by alcohol.

Universities have established alcohol-free residence halls and alcohol prevention programs to deal with the growing problem. Most universities have counselors who are trained to help students suffering from alcohol drug addiction. Research indicates that the most effective programs to combat alcohol addiction involve peer education: students talking to other students. If so, might another effective educational strategy involve students writing about binge drinking and sharing their writings with classmates?

I have never believed that a single writing assignment can change a person's drinking habits. Nor have I believed that my role in the classroom is to exhort my students to reduce their binge drinking—though their academic performance and general well-being would certainly improve if they drank less. (Recall Shakespeare's observation in *Macbeth*—drinking "provokes the desire, but it takes away the performance" [2.3].) What I did (and still do) believe, or at least hope, is that writing about alcohol may encourage students to identify problems not otherwise acknowledged and take appropriate steps to solve them.

And so I distributed copies of the *New York Times* article on binge drinking and asked each student to write on the following assignment:

> Studies indicate that as many as half of today's college students engage in binge drinking—having five or more drinks in one setting at least once every two weeks. As many as 80 percent of college students living in fraternities or sororities engage in binge drinking. The author of a major study on the subject has said that "the frequency of binge drinking by fraternity men and sorority women leads to an 'Animal House' style of living."
>
> For your next assignment, write an essay discussing your perception of the problem. Are many of your friends binge drinkers? Do you or your relatives have problems with alcohol? How do these problems manifest themselves? How do you explain the prevalence of binge drinking? What can be done to reduce the amount of drinking on and off college campuses?

Because I planned to spend only one week on this assignment, I asked about one-third of the students to make copies for the entire class; the remaining two-thirds were to make a single copy for me. We agreed that if I came across essays written for me alone that I thought might be valuable for the entire class to hear, I would ask the authors if they were willing to read them aloud or allow me to do so anonymously. They could decline if they wished.

Female Disclosures of Alcoholic Relatives

Prior to this assignment, I had asked each student to write ten autobiographical paragraphs, share them with a partner, whom he or she would interview, and then write the other's biography. The two students who referred to alcohol in their opening autobiographical paragraphs were both women, and they revealed chilling portraits of alcoholic fathers abusing their wives and children.

Alice: "A Raving Alcoholic . . . Could Not Be Cured with Love"

Alice observed that the most painful experience in her life occurred when she was twelve years old and watched her alcoholic stepfather assault her mother.

> *He was extremely drunk. Being in that state made him cruel, angry, mean, and abusive. We were walking in the door and he was holding the door as my sister and I walked inside. My mother was the last to walk in. She did not make it inside though. As she started to enter the doorway he pulled her by her hair and dragged her back outside and said, "You are staying outside with me!!" She cried out in pain and shock and said, "Please, please not in front of my girls." I did not just stand there and watch him do this to my mother. I immediately ran to him and beat my tiny fists on his strong chest. I cried out as he let go of my mother. I continued to beat on his chest with all my strength. I repeatedly said, "I hate you, I hate you, I hate you!! Don't you ever touch my mother ever again. How could you hurt her like that?" I was hysterical. I remember how it felt as my heart pounded in my small chest and my tears burned as they dropped down on my chest.*

In a later essay on divorce, Alice returned to her stepfather's drinking:

> *The years that followed were like a long roller-coaster ride with many twists and turns, and nauseous stomachs. My mother learned of Bill's drinking problem after she had fallen in love with him. My mother wanted to cure him and help him in any way that she could. Little did she know that a raving alcoholic, such as Bill, could not be cured with love. She sacrificed herself many times for him. I understand why, because she loved him. My mother is far from being uncaring. She wanted to help him in any way that she possibly could.*
>
> *I remember my mother coming home one night and walking into our house before Bill had gotten out of the car. I knew that Bill would be drunk. Out of desperation, she pulled me aside and said, "Alice, Please do something for mommy. Bill is sick and he needs help. I think that if you show him that his drinking upsets you, then he will get help. He will not listen to me. I think this will be the last chance that I am giving him." Because I loved him, and I did not want him to go away forever, as he entered the house, I broke down in tears. He rushed to me and asked me what was wrong. I told him that he*

was hurting me by being drunk and that I wanted him and my Mom to stay together. He said that he was going to get help because he loved us all too much. This was his last chance. My crying worked. I thought to myself, "I would do anything for mommy."

Bill went into rehab for a couple of months, we thought that the disease would go away. His sobriety was only temporary. That is when all the abuse began. Immediately after they married.

Bill was a different man. He was callous, cheap, and a drunk. He verbally and psychologically abused my mother and, at times, he physically abused her. The nightmare had begun. Every day was difficult. My sister, my mom, and I were affected in ways that I could not possibly explain. I felt unstable. We experienced involvement with the police, court, poverty, and most of all, pain.

Kyra: "I Always Knew . . . That It Would Be the Bottle That Killed You"

Kyra also wrote about her experience growing up with an alcoholic father.

My life did not compare to the usual seven year old that is in first grade. My life was one that was plagued by a father who was an alcoholic and made a daily ritual of beating up my mother and myself, when she wasn't around. Although many people would wonder why she wouldn't leave a situation like that, at that time women were not given support from the authorities and there weren't any shelters for battered women. My life was pretty much in complete turmoil, whereas my brother chose not to see any problems. During that time frame my mother was working approximately two jobs, as a nurse to make enough money to survive. My father by this time was extremely abusive to myself and especially to my mother. The alcohol consumption was so out of control he began to get paranoid and in return always thought that my mother was plotting against him. I too took much of the abuse since I was "my mother's daughter" and was in his eyes "out to get him." My father finally lost control one day and attacked my mother in front of me because she hadn't bought him pretzels or something as stupid as that. Being the only person home I had to get help. So I made my first call to the police when I was only seven years old. However, the worst of it wasn't even that, the infuriating moment came when the police officer told my mother that they would not take my father away for psychiatric evaluation because she wasn't being a good wife and buying her husband what he wanted. So again the same scenario happened the next day when he really did make an attempt on my mother's life. I am just grateful that I was there and could get help for my mother and finally get my father taken away. Although this was a difficult time in my life, it also came to represent a new life for myself and my family. We were finally free from my father and I was given the chance to experience some happiness as a child. Up until that point I had never been happy but after that day I felt free and not scared for once.

Alice's and Kyra's vignettes are poignant and sad, evoking a grim portrait of alcohol abuse and domestic violence. Their brief accounts relate the helplessness they felt at the time and the disruption of family life. In a later assignment involving a letter to a parent, the two students describe the anger, confusion, and bitterness arising from their fathers' alcohol addiction. As they read their letters aloud in voices filled with emotion, their classmates were stunned by the self-disclosures. Kyra's letter was especially touching because her father had died years earlier—he staggered home from a bar one winter night, lost his bearings, and froze to death. Nor could Kyra sort through her tangled feelings toward him.

Another situation that has affected me is your death. I still don't understand why you had to die the way that you did. It hurt me to see the circumstances of your death and also humiliating because once again I was forced to answer for your actions. I always knew it was only a matter of time, and that it would be the bottle that would kill you. But why did you have to die alone and so idiotically. I am so furious with you because once again I feel sorry for you. You did this to yourself, however, I feel bad. Why do you always get to be the martyr. Why do you always get to have control.

Male Disclosures of Alcoholic Relatives

Two men wrote about alcoholic relatives, not in the autobiographical essays but in the assignment on binge drinking. Their writings do not contain the same terror and violence that appear in Alice's and Kyra's, nor do they express feminist indignation over male oppression. They do reveal, however, the painful consequences of drinking and the difficulty of knowing when recreational drinking becomes problematic. Both acknowledged in their essays a family history of alcohol abuse in which they found themselves implicated.

Stuart: "I Too Am Guilty of Being a College Binge Drinker"

Stuart's fear was that sooner or later binge drinking would come back to haunt him.

Unfortunately, the abuse of alcohol is a subject with which I am familiar. Thus, I have mixed feelings about binge drinking in college. I have wit-

nessed members of my family destroy their lives with alcohol. Two of my mother's brothers and her father literally drank themselves to an early grave. My father's sister as well as my mother's are also alcoholics who are currently tearing my family apart.

The first to die from the bottle was my grandfather. I know very little about this man because he died before I was born. All that I know about him are simple facts told to me by my mother. He was a good soldier and a good father; and he was too young to die. The next victim was my Uncle Joseph. He has given me many fond memories, as he was a major part of my early childhood. Alcohol was this man's best friend as well as his family. Unmarried with few friends, he turned to the bottle for company. I remember the conversations he and my mother had about his drinking problem. He refused any help because he felt there was no problem. His non-existent drinking problem caused him to develop cirrhosis of the liver. I think it was when he was lying in the hospital bed dying that he admitted that maybe he drank too much.

Uncle Owen was next in line shortly after his brother died at age forty. What can I say about my Uncle Owen, other than that I loved him. His drinking took him by the hand straight into a heroine addiction. He spent many years in jail for his drug and alcohol problems. Nevertheless, he was still my favorite. His heart was bigger than most men's. Unfortunately his addictions were bigger. I remember watching him struggle to get sober for my sister, my brother, and me. He tried so hard, and I think that is what lead to his death. My grandfather was in his mid-fifties and my uncles their early forties when alcohol claimed their lives.

This leads to my two aunts, one of them my father's older sister and the other my mother's oldest sister. These women are friendly because of marriage but they could be the same person. Both of them are a disgrace to the rest of us. Unlike my uncles, who kept their problems to themselves when they were unable to admit it, my aunts remind the family of their alcoholism every chance they get. They phone my house all of the time drunk off their ass and mad at the world for all of their hardships. It has gotten to the point that when birthday cards come in the mail, they are returned to the sender. I am not allowed to talk to them when they call drunk, and I have to keep my eleven year old sister away from them as much as possible. It doesn't matter to me that I am forbidden to listen to them, because my brother and I usually hang up on them anyway. We usually hang up the phone on them because they tell us how rotten their lives are. Sometimes they tell us how our parents are bad people and we should move out. Once, I came home and my brother was on the phone with my aunt trying to explain to her why *we don't call her anymore. He was being polite, but I could hear her yelling at him through the phone. They make up stories telling us how they were abused as children, just so we would feel bad for them. We have reached the point where it is easier just to hang up the phone and not deal with them.*

Despite these family alcoholics, I can't understand why I drink as much as do. My brother has never touched alcohol in his life and I don't think he ever will. Maybe he is stronger than I am, or maybe he is smarter. I know my drinking upsets my mother greatly, but I drink anyway. Yes, I too am guilty of being a college binge drinker. Sometimes, I feel as if I am more than a college binge drinker. I can honestly say that I am following in my uncle's footsteps as I drink some form of an alcoholic beverage every day of my life. It is more than one drink per day. Most of the time I feel myself trapped in this fog, that is caused by days of drinking catching up to me. At home it is acceptable for me to drink alone. My father's rule for me is, as long as I am not driving I am allowed to drink as much as I want. My parents are constantly arguing over my drinking. My mother gets terribly upset and my father views the drinking as acceptable.

Blowing off steam from a stressful academic week is a popular excuse for this college behavior. Our lives are so tough that we need to go out to bars and drink until we are laughing at every comment and lose the power to see straight. Or maybe it is that we are young and are just looking to have a good time. Whatever the reasoning behind drinking, college kids take for granted how dangerous alcohol really could be. I know I take it for granted and I have first hand experiences.

I try so hard to lead a stress free life because my whole childhood has been nothing but stressful. Drinking makes everything go away for the moment and believe it or not helps me deal with these problems. Problems going away for the moment is superficial because they are still there when you wake up. I can't help but to want these problems to disappear. It isn't so bad to want to be at peace with yourself, but I know I am doing it the wrong way. I can understand how people become alcoholics, I just hope that I don't.

Stuart knew that he was taking a chance by reading his essay aloud. Self-disclosures such as his require the ability to accept the possibility of criticism, rejection, and even embarrassment. Stuart's classmates sensed his vulnerability and responded empathically, praising his courage and honesty. I was gratified that he took the assignment so seriously, and while I was concerned for his well-being, I did not feel that it was my responsibility to tell him what he already knew, namely, that heavy drinking is dangerous to his health. Nor did I voice my disagreement with his statement that college students' lives are "so tough" that they must drink. Instead, I limited my comments to grammatical suggestions, circling syntactical errors and recommending punctuation and vocabulary changes. I also praised many of the sentences, including "His non-existent drinking problem caused him to develop cirrhosis of the liver." The assignment on binge drinking inspired Stuart to write his best essay of the semester. I wrote only one substantive comment, in the form of a question: "Do you see any solution to the problem you are describing?"

Matt: "I Realized That I Was Drinking Too Much"

Unlike Stuart, Matt wrote his essay not for the entire class but for me alone.

Alcohol is a major part of my life. My family has been seriously effected by the abuse of alcohol. My grandfather is a recovering alcoholic. He has been dry for over ten years.

My grandfather began drinking when he was only fifteen years old. As the years went on he would see nothing wrong with going after work and having more than a few drinks. The problem was the way alcohol effected my grandfather's personality. Drinking often resulted in violence with my grandfather. Whether it was one of his buddies or him, it seemed as though there was always trouble after a day of drinking. I don't know if my grandfather always thought it was coincidence, but he never realized he had a problem. He was hurting everyone around him, but never thought about anyone but himself. Eventually, my grandmother could not take it anymore and took my mom and uncle and left my grandfather. This produced an ugly divorce that was painful to all involved.

My grandfather's drinking strained his relationships with my entire family. For years he and my mother had an off and on relationship because of the many factors that came into play when someone is abusing alcohol. To this day my grandparents can't stand to be near each other, and my uncle refuses to speak to my grandfather.

Lucky for everyone involved my grandfather realized he had a problem and sought help. Since my grandfathers commitment to himself he has rebuilt his life. He got married, had a beautiful daughter and now lives the life of a retired carpenter. My grandfather's life has been greatly improved and under control since he decided to address his major problem of alcohol abuse.

My family obviously doesn't learn from other's mistakes, as is evident from this next account. This past Thursday, I talked to my dad on the phone. He told me about some trouble that my uncle has gotten into. Last Saturday my uncle was driving his car home and crashed into the guardrail on the Saw Mill River Parkway. The police came and arrested my uncle for driving while intoxicated. My uncle also has a problem with alcohol and becomes quite violent when he has had some drinks. Anyway, he got a little wise and feisty with the cops and they beat the shit out of him. He spent some time in the hospital before being returned to jail. It turns out that my uncle does not have a driver's license because of another DWI incident in February. He kept this secret from everyone in my family except my other uncle, who bailed him out of jail.

My uncle has a good job and is supposed to be married next year. Right now he faces time in jail, the prospect of losing his job, and the serious realization that his fiancee might leave him. Even with all these terrible situations, my uncle refuses to admit he has a problem. It has been recommended to him that he check into a hospital to help begin his fight against alcohol, but he doesn't see this as necessary.

I am a binge drinker. Almost everyone of my friends is a binge drinker. I was shocked by the low percentage of binge drinkers that do not live in fraternity or sorority houses. I only know a handful of people that live in fraternity houses and still know many people that are binge drinkers.

I go out and binge drink about four times a week. This is a definite increase from my first two years at college. This is also an increase from when I am home and when I lived on campus. My parents know that I drink, but not at the frequency that I do and they are still very much opposed to it because of the effects that alcohol has had on my family. I enjoy going out and having drinks, listening to music and meeting people. Just recently I began to wonder about my habits with alcohol. I became worried about what I was doing to my body and my mind. I thought about the problems that alcohol has caused in my family, and the effects that my problem could have on me and my family.

After a night of heavy drinking a few weeks ago I came home and sat in my living room. I suddenly felt very upset. I realized that I was drinking too much. I needed to and couldn't stop drinking. I woke up the next day and asked my housemates to help me in solving my dilemma. Although I asked for their help, I realize that only I can correct my problem.

Since that night I have tried to cut back on my binge drinking. I don't go out and binge drink as much, but I have not stopped drinking. This was before I heard my uncle's story. That event has made me think even more about my situation. I don't plan on drinking this week, but like I tell my friends, tomorrow is a new day and I don't know what will happen. I hope this essay and my promise to myself will help me work through this week.

It's interesting because I don't feel these urges at home, and this weekend I'm going home. I know that if I can make it through this week I can go at least two weeks without drinking. I don't really think I have a drinking problem, but I do think that my habits could easily become a drinking problem if I let it get out of hand. That is why I want to limit myself now before my life takes a turn for the worse.

I'm not sure how a person becomes a binge drinker. In my case I think it was hanging out with binge drinkers and being able to do so without running into many problems. I have never been in trouble with the law, and have never had any problems resulting from the use of alcohol. However, these are certainly possibilities, and that is why I would like to limit my consumption of alcohol.

I also don't know why so many people are binge drinkers. I thought it had something to do with college, but I know many people that are binge drinkers that never attended college. I just think that drinking has been changed from a social atmosphere as a whole to an abusive attitude that people use to feel an altered state. I believe that fewer people than ever just go out and have one or two beers with some co-workers and then go home. Instead people go out and have eight to ten beers then drive home. I know very few people that come out of bars and are sober.

As for reducing the amount of binge drinking on and off college campuses, I don't think it's possible. If a school increase penalties for drinking on campus, then students will go off campus to drink. A student off campus is much more dangerous. He/she might drive somewhere and drive home drunk, they also have to walk the streets of the city and they often cause trouble as drunk college students among area neighborhoods. As a school I think you would rather have students just sitting in their room and getting drunk than entering into all the risks of being drunk in the middle of a city.

The University at Albany has tried to limit off campus drinking by contacting the Albany police about bars serving minors. This was a result of Albany's party ranking from the Princeton Review. Even with these attempts, drinking continues to be a problem that seems to have no end. This problem has been unable to be solved including America's attempt at prohibition. This was a major example of no matter what people try, alcohol will always be a problem in our society.

What most impressed me about Matt's essay was his willingness to acknowledge a drinking problem and take personal responsibility for it. Like Stuart, he knew the risks of drinking and wanted to reduce his alcohol consumption, yet he knew there were no easy solutions to the problem. He neither expected nor, I suspect, would have welcomed any advice from me. My only recommendations were technical: I suggested several changes in grammar and diction: like many of his classmates, he confused "effected" with "affected." In addition, I asked him if he was willing to read the essay to the class or allow me to do so anonymously. He did not feel comfortable with the former but agreed to the latter. Matt was absent on the day I intended to read the essay to the class, and I didn't know whether he had misgivings over hearing me read it aloud. I decided to wait until he reappeared in class before reading his essay—I thought it was important for him to be present. He came to the next class and listened attentively as I read his essay aloud.

Students' Pessimism over Solving the Drinking Problem

Most of the students concluded in their essays that although excessive drinking is a serious and sometimes life-threatening problem, there is little if anything that can be done about it. They seemed to believe that the college "culture of alcohol" could not be changed. This pessimism extended to both heavy and light drinkers. In the words of one student, "alcohol definitely affects people in and out of college. People worry about students drinking so much, but hopefully when the students graduate, the binge drinking stops. Unfortunately, not everyone will stop, but at least a good portion will. I really don't think there is much we can do to stop this problem. Whether the drinking age is raised or the age to get a license is raised, kids still will drink. There's always ways around it. Maybe if we have a required course about alcohol or have speakers come to our school, the numbers will decrease, but most kids will stick with the attitude that 'it won't happen to me.'"

Other Student Essays

Not all students were so pessimistic. Two wrote about bad experiences with alcohol in high school that were not repeated in college: both had managed either to stop drinking entirely or reduce their alcohol consumption. One wrote about drinking so much during high school that he would "down bottle after bottle, sometimes mixing in hard liquor." He would then start yelling, annoying his friends, and frequently blacking out. "My attempts to be liked through drinking backfired on me; it didn't slow down my consumption, though. Alcohol became my crutch. I'd be up at three or four in the morning, drunk to an extreme, screaming or crying for no particular reason. I look back at these times realizing how pitiful I was." The other wrote a short story called "Drowning Thoughts" in which she describes an experience when she was sixteen years old. After "poisoning" her body with alcohol, she accepts a ride home from a party despite the fact that the driver is also drunk. "The swerving of the car creates a sleepy feeling, and my mind and body slowly fade away. I hear the screeching of tires and feel the pain in my jaw as my face violently collides with the front seat. With my eyes still closed, I drift away completely. I awoke to the sound of pounding on a door but realized it was my head. Upon my eyes regaining focus, I was in my room, and my mother was sitting by my bed. She started to cry when she noticed that I was awake. When the haze cleared from my mind and my thoughts, I was free to evaluate what happened the previous night. We were in an accident that destroyed my friend's car and nearly destroyed my friend herself."

Sean: "Four Lives Cut Short at Eighteen Years Old"

Of all the essays I received, Sean's was the most memorable and haunting. He wrote about every parent's nightmare.

It was a typical cold winter March night for upstate New York. The bitterness of the wind didn't stop the students from going out on this Thursday night, though. After finishing off a few beers in their dorm room, Chuck, Ben, Jim, and Alan decided it was time to meet up with the rest of their friends out at the bars. So they sprinted out to the Freshman lot where Jim's 1989 Dodge Shadow was parked. After arguing over who was going out to get "shotgun" in the front seat, they piled in and with music jamming, were off.

The bars were only a few miles away, but it required going on a highway and then some dark side roads. After driving around the block a few times, Jim finally found a spot not too far from the first bar, where they were to meet up with the rest of the group. The four got on line outside and got their fake ID's ready for inspection. Actually, it was more like a quick once-over by the bouncers, for it was more of a formality than a real check of age. Once inside, the bar was crowded with laughter, loud music, smoke, and the lovely smell of beer. It was a typical college dive that during the day wouldn't be recognized, but somehow at night transformed into the hotspot for the (mostly) under-age college crowd.

The four met up with their friends and were greeted with a pitcher and four empty plastic cups. Without hesitation, they all filled up, and the mara-

thon began. Pitcher after pitcher was emptied and then filled up by whoever's turn it was to pay. The talking and laughter continued, as the night went on. People became more and more familiar with one another. The music and the rest of the noise merges into one continuous drone. The walls too begin to disappear, and all that is seen is a mass of bodies. The process of getting over to the bar to buy a pitcher becomes a battle with elbows being jabbed, shoulders being thrust, and beer being spilt all over people's shirts. So now the buyer is so relieved just to get to the bar, that he or she decides to buy a round of shots along with the pitcher.

Now it's three in the morning and everyone decides to go back to the dorms and hang out in somebody's room, and drink some more. So once again Chuck, Ben, Jim, and Alan burst outside into the cold, biting wind, coming from inside the hot, humid bar, and head for the car. Of course, no one really gave thought as to who was going to drive back, but the decision was made with very little argument. Ben demanded the keys because, he felt, that Jim was "too drunk." Of course Jim being too drunk, was unable to pass judgment on how much more sober Ben in fact really was. But, the keys were handed to Ben and in they all clamored. Off they went, with music blaring and everyone singing and laughing.

So they sped down the dark highway and came to the exit for their school. Now, no one knows if he forgot there was a light at the end of that exit ramp or if he just didn't see that it turned red, but Ben didn't slow the car down. Not until he was almost under the light, did he slam on the brakes. It all took but a few seconds. The black Mercury Sable that had a green light just couldn't stop in time. It broadsided the little Dodge Shadow and reduced it to little more than the width of a motorcycle. Needless to say, they all died either instantly or before the ambulances got to them.

I waited at the Rensselaer train station for my train to arrive. My bags were sitting at my feet and my suit on a hanger with laundromat plastic covering it, lay across my lap. I sat there in complete silence with so many thoughts racing through my mind and I couldn't sort them out. That was the worst train ride in my whole life. I sat with my head resting against the window, staring blankly out at the snow covered trees and fields as they blurred by. There was a song that I listened to on my walkman that cloudy, grey afternoon that brought back floods of memories from when Chuck and I were kids. I sat there with my head against that cold window with tears streaming down my cheeks, fighting back the sobs. All I could think about were his combined birthday and Halloween parties every year when we were kids; him sitting behind me in Spanish class in tenth grade making noises and lewd comments about our young female teacher; him telling me about his first sexual experience a few nights before, while we walked home from school; all of us during our senior trip to Florida, and Chuck sitting on a lounge chair with a straw hat and sunglasses on, and a Pina Colada in his hand. Now, there will be no more memories. Four lives cut short at eighteen years old.

Chuck and Ben were both classmates of mine, and Chuck had lived down the road from me the whole time I lived in New York City. They were both on the football team, both very popular, and both decent students. I was friendly with Ben too, but Chuck and I were from the same neighborhood. We were always on the same sports teams and in many of the same classes. Although we became parts of different groups of friends, we always thought to call one another whenever something was going on. There were so many things that went through my mind at the funeral. Everybody and their grandmother had gone to the wakes the night before; there were lines down the block from the funeral home. But the funeral was on a cold, rainy day and not nearly as many people showed for that. The church portion was the hardest of all. I sat with my old high school friends and listened to other classmates and friends give the eulogy. One of my closest friends gave most of it along with a little bit from Chuck's girlfriend. Neither one could finish their sentences without breaking down. We sat there in the pews, each with our own personal memories swimming around, trying to understand how this all could have happened. At the graveyard we all stood together with our heads down, holding hands, tears rolling down our cheeks. It was the most difficult day to get through in my life.

I wish I could say that Chuck and Ben's death changed me forever. I certainly didn't stop drinking; in fact I believe I drank quite heavily for at least a month after. Marc, my close friend who gave the eulogy at the funeral, goes to school here, so he and I sat at the bars reminiscing about the times we all had together. We still do, occasionally. We swore that we would never drink and drive again, but I wish I could say that I stuck to that promise. When I think about it when I'm sober, I want to kick myself in the ass or slap myself and say, "What the fuck is wrong with you?" But when I'm drunk or buzzed, I think I can navigate my way out of a maze. The worst thing is, is that my friends have come to expect that of me too. Because I have been lucky for so long in getting us home safely, they think I'm the best driver. I could be driving on sidewalks hitting every fire hydrant and they wouldn't even know because they're too drunk! My confidence has gotten so that I am not only confident just driving home from a bar in my neighborhood to my house drunk, but now I drive a half hour from Manhattan, on the dark, narrow *Palisades Parkway to my house—drunk. I'm sitting here typing this and shaking my head, not able to believe just how stupid I really am.*

Here at school, I live within walking distance to the bars. I certainly have done my share of drinking over the years here at school, but I'm hoping that being twenty-one now, the novelty will wear off. But then again, what else is there to do here? It's sad to think that I have to drink in order to have a good time now. It starts off just being a twice a week ordeal, maybe Thursday and Saturday night. Then it expands to Friday night happy hour. Then it goes to Monday night football and wings. Then, hey Wednesday has some good specials too. So now it's up to five nights a week. When does one stop and wonder if there is a problem? I don't know because I don't think I've reached that point yet. Who knows, maybe I just don't want to stop yet. I'm sure it will slow down a lot after I graduate. Anyway, it's almost seven o'clock and the Yankee game will be getting started soon. Gotta get out to the bar before all the good seats are taken.

Sean read his essay in an unemotional voice, almost as if he had written about another person, yet despite the low-key reading, the essay implicates the reader in a wrenching story. The opening two paragraphs re-create a familiar situation to college students. In the third paragraph, the writer switches from past to present tense and evokes the intoxicating rhythms produced by alcohol. The fourth paragraph contains hints of an ominous resolution to the story of the four revelers. The fifth paragraph, written with stark restraint, dramatizes their deaths. The essay then shifts from third to first person as the frozen landscape reflects the speaker's desolation. The writer conveys the survivors' devastation without resorting to melodrama or sentimentality.

Had the essay ended here, it would have been an effective cautionary tale. The author continues, however, for another two paragraphs—and it is this part of the story that is so distressing. He tells us that he too seems to be speeding down the same treacherous road. The third-person omniscient narration used at the beginning of the essay changes to unreliable first-person narration at the end, with the narrator revealing that he is only partly in control of his own life. He knows that it is dangerous to drink and drive but seems unwilling or unable to act upon this knowledge. Honesty requires him to admit that his present drinking is out of control, and he ends the essay by heading toward a nearby bar.

Sean's essay produced conflicting feelings in me. I felt torn between my admiration for his writing and apprehension over his well-being. I try to avoid revealing my feelings about an essay until others have the opportunity to do so, but in this case my discomfort was visible, and I expressed it to the class. I was especially troubled by the essay's fatalistic ending. This was an essay written not by a stranger but by a member of the class, one whose welfare I valued. Moreover, not only did I feel affection and concern for Sean, who could have been my son, but I couldn't help thinking about my own children, whose safety is imperiled by drunk drivers. In short, Sean's essay challenged my ability to remain empathic and nonjudgmental, qualities that are essential for self-disclosure.

"How Did You Feel Writing about Binge Drinking?"

Sean's classmates praised his essay's power and honesty in the brief discussion that followed, but I didn't know whether they found it as unsettling as I did. I began to wonder how the class felt about the assignment on binge drinking. Was it a difficult topic for them to write on? How did they feel when they were reading their essays aloud or hearing others discuss them? Which essays made the strongest impression on them? Did they feel it was an appropriate subject for an essay? Did it change their attitude toward binge drinking—and, if so, how would they judge the assignment's short- and long-term impact? I decided to ask the students to respond to these questions in their next writing assignment. Here is Sean's response:

This was definitely the hardest essay for me to write so far. This was a topic that no one has ever asked me to write about and I never would even think to write about it on my own. Writing this was like reliving the whole experience over again, which was both bad and good. It was so hard going through all those emotions again, but it felt good to get it out. I had to stop typing a few times because I got so wrapped up in my emotions it was hard to think straight. I wanted the essay to come out coherent even though my thoughts weren't. There was so much more I could have said in that essay about how it affected everyone and how many more thoughts and emotions were going through me those first few weeks. But how can it all be put in one essay? Is that even possible? There was so much to say yet no way for me to say it. I hope the essay sounded coherent and that my thoughts were put into words as closely as possible.

After I finished typing I thought, "Shit, I told Berman I'd read this in class. There's no way I'm gonna be able to read this!" I'll never make it through this!" I honestly was scared to read it! Deep down I knew it was something I needed to do, but actually going through with it was another story. So many times I was going to tell you that I just couldn't do it and for you to read it for me. Then I wouldn't have gone to class that day. But I knew I had to do it. It's not something that I talk about very often and never in front of a group of people. The night before I knew I was going to have to read it, I sat down on my bed and just read it aloud. I wasn't reading it to anyone or even standing in front of a mirror—I just wanted to see if I would make it through the whole thing without getting choked up. And I did. The next day when I went to class I was still nervous but confident that I'd make it through it. Once I started reading it, I got so wrapped up in my thoughts that I didn't even hear my own voice anymore. The rest of the class just disappeared and I wasn't even seeing lightness or darkness—just words on a page flowing from my mouth without my brain interfering. I don't really know how to explain it. It was like being in a hypnotic state. When I finished reading and looked up, I was surprised by the light in the classroom and the other students sitting there. Some of them were looking at me while others looked down at their desks or I don't know what. The silence afterwards seemed like an eternity.

I found the other students comments to be helpful and sympathetic. Hearing that they felt the emotion in the paper really made me feel good. It told me that I was able to share with them some of my feelings and they felt it. I knew it came across as being disturbing and depressing but I felt that I needed to be honest. That's why I knew you were going to comment on that. I found your comments to be helpful too, and although you were torn between your feelings as a teacher and as a parent, that too helped me. I was just glad that people understood what I was trying to get across and that after I was done reading it they didn't look at me as if I had two heads. The bottom line for me was that I read it out loud and got those feelings out and off my chest, though they will never leave my soul.

I enjoyed (although I'm not sure "enjoyed" is the right word) hearing the other classmates stories. There wasn't one whole essay that made an impact on me, more like pieces of a few different ones that made lasting impressions. I thought all the students were very honest and did a great job of describing the college drinking scene. I found some of the personal accounts to be touching and disturbing. . . . Overall I'd say I was not surprised by the content of the essays but it was good to hear everyone talking about it—honestly.

I don't think I could speculate on the short or long term effects of this assignment on my life. It certainly has reminded me again of how stupid drinking and driving is and that I'm really going to try and never do it again. I don't think anyone is going to quit drinking as a result of this, but maybe being brought aware will get some people to slow down a little. I'm going to *try to slow down a bit, but I don't know how long that will last. As I said in my essay, what else is there to do socially at night?*

I found this to be the most beneficial assignment so far, and probably the rest of the semester. I think that every writing class should give this assignment because almost every college student drinks, and drinks too much. By writing about it you're being forced to think of how often you drink, and maybe it will worry you a little and cause you to think twice about getting bombed every time you go out. Or maybe it won't. I'll find out soon enough.

Sean's response to his essay on binge drinking has much in common with Nick's response to his essay on child sexual abuse. Both wrote on risky topics and disclosed aspects of their lives that they had previously concealed from others. Both strove for clarity, specificity, and honesty. Sean's challenge was to find the words to order his disordered thinking. "I wanted the essay to come out coherent even though my thoughts weren't." To this extent, he succeeds. His essay conveys his ambivalence over drinking and shows, in controlled language, the state of being out of control. Like Nick, Sean experiences both aesthetic satisfaction and therapeutic relief. He tells us, for instance, that he practiced reading his essay out loud to avoid losing control while reading it in class. It was important for him to perform well so that his essay would make an impact on his readers.

Responses to Sean's Essay

Sean's essay made a strong impression on his classmates. They were affected as much by his disclosure of a drinking problem as by the description of his friends' deaths. They identified with his situation, empathized with his grief, and reflected on its implications. "The brutal reality of such an essay is what makes it so powerful. I think Sean's essay was well written and if read to any class would have a definite effect on its students. This is the type of essay that could be read at D.A.R.E programs or other organizational meetings such as M.A.D.D. and S.A.D.D."

Student Responses to Their Own Writings

The students implied in their response essays that although they had never written before about their own binge drinking and had in fact concealed the problem from relatives and friends, seeing their words first on a computer screen and then on paper gave the situation an undeniable reality. They did not learn anything new intellectually, but in the words of psychologist Hadley Cantril, the essays on drinking challenged the students' "assumptive world": "The only world we know is created in terms of and by means of our assumptions. It is the world which provides what constancy there is in our environment; the world which gives our experience its constancy. And it *is* a world of assumptions—a world which we could not have at all except for our past experience in acting for the purpose of enhancing the quality of life" (87; emphasis in original). The assignment had the greatest impact on those students who had written about their own drinking problems. Some students, like Stuart and Matt, regarded the essay as a wake-up call, and they found the assignment sobering. Others felt that the assignment created a strong bond among their classmates. Kyra noted that the assignment allowed her to reach an important insight about herself, namely, that she could have one or two drinks without becoming like her father. All felt the drinking assignment had the greatest relevance to their lives.

Cathartic Writing

The two assignments on binge drinking allowed students to express their feelings about a subject that hit close to home. Despite campuswide efforts to publicize the dangers of binge drinking, students seldom discuss the subject among themselves—largely because to do so requires acknowledging painful and shameful issues. I doubt that high school and college students are encouraged to be self-disclosing even when they write about the terrible toll of alcohol and drug addiction. It is easy to remain detached and impersonal in a research essay on binge drinking, thus denying its relevance to one's own life; by contrast, a personal essay motivates writers to confront and work through problematic issues in their own lives.

Nowhere is this better illustrated than in Sean's essays. Writing caused him to relive his friends' deaths, and the emotion was so intense that he felt momentarily overwhelmed. He describes writing the essay as a form of mourning, as if he were transported back in time to his friends' funerals, forced to grieve anew their horrifying deaths. Writing was so painful that he had to stop several times in order to compose himself and his sentences. He felt relieved and unburdened after memorializing his deceased friends, as one often does after paying respect to the dead. Additionally, writing helped him to construct a meaning to the experience, one that he wished to convey as coherently as possible to the class. With so much at stake, he felt he had to make his audience understand his feelings and thoughts. Reading the essay aloud posed the greatest challenge to Sean, and he prepared for it like an athlete training for a competition.

Not all the students were as self-revealing as Alice, Kyra, Stuart, Matt, and Sean. There were, as to be expected, varying degrees of self-disclosure among the writers, and some took longer than others to develop trust in their teacher and classmates. Resistance to self-disclosure may be intense, and students often take a wait-and-see approach before deciding to open up about their lives.

Jamie: "I Tried to Make My Essay Impersonal"

Two students felt particularly strong resistance to self-disclosure in their first essays, in which they denied that binge drinking is a serious college problem. They reconsidered their views in the response essays and were more forthcoming about their own drinking habits. Their essays demonstrate how self-disclosure leads to more accurate self-representation. In her first essay, Jamie said that she disagreed with the definition of binge drinking, since she and all her friends would then fall into that category. In her second essay, however, she acknowledged a drinking problem.

While writing the essay on binge drinking, I felt a little sick to my stomach. I tried to make my essay impersonal and not tell any specific story, instead I kept it to my opinion. If I had been more honest I would have told you how my dad drinks all the time, and that my mother asks him to go to AA all the time. I would have told you how I once got so drunk that the next day I had to go to the hospital because I was so sick, and get a shot so I would stop throwing up. I would have told you that at least half the time I go out and get really wasted that I end up hysterical crying about all my problems. I have never written on this topic before, so that may be why I chose to write it the way I did. Writing the essay was not hard for me because I tried to forget about how alcohol has really effected me. I believe that if I had been completely honest that it would have been very hard. I do believe what I wrote that binge drinking is normal in college. I just decided not to write about myself. This assignment seems harder, pretty ironic.

I felt a little nervous when we discussed my essay out loud. I always do. I always wonder what the rest of the class is thinking, the things they want to say but don't. I felt that your comments were normal. You added your opinion, but didn't use it to comment on my essay; it seemed that you had a very open mind.

The short term impact of this assignment was fear. I was afraid by the statistics and the personal stories. I was afraid about thinking about what I've done and got away with. My personal attitude towards binge drinking changed last year, when I had to go to the hospital. I try not to drink that much anymore, but sometimes I do drink too much. I have cut down and plan to cut down even more. Looking long term, I think I will be more aware of the drinking among college students and even younger. My brothers and sisters will be in college before I know it, and I plan to be fully aware of what they're doing. I hope to not only be the big sister, but a friend they can trust.

I think assignments like this and the ones we've done already are appropriate. Personal writing is interesting and students enjoy doing it more. If our assignments were not as personal as they are, I don't think everybody would love this class as much as they do. Assignments like this are what I believe really teach students. It teaches them about real life, issues that can change them forever.

Josh: "Do We Think We're Invulnerable?"

Josh was also more self-revealing in his response essay than in his initial essay, in which he objected to the facts presented in the New York Times article. "I feel this whole topic has been blown wildly out of proportion, this study is a farce, and the real problem lay with those people who don't understand the uses, effects, and social implications of drinking." He admitted in his response essay that drinking was a more serious problem than he had implied earlier, recounting a recent incident in which he had become sick as a result of mixing alcohol and drugs:

This night, one of many, consisted of mixing drugs and alcohol, specifically a Roche, nicknamed the "date rape" drug due to its severe and uninhibiting effects and lack of ability to remember the duration of its influence. I recall only flashes of my masquerade, and friends have informed me of the extent of my irrationality. The events consisted of my experiencing an emotional roller coaster and eventual breakdown, physically scuffling with several of my friends, becoming uncharacteristically violent, and crying out of control.

While sitting here writing about my unfortunate night and listening to my classmates' riveting, powerful essays of "living-it-up and dying" I have reflected upon my own practices. My physical health in high school, when drinking was an occasion rather than a habit, was far superior to what it is now. My dedication to physical prowess and intellectual stimulation has long ago taken a crushing blow. My mind has taken its toll, as frustration of not getting work completed has led to an even more lax disposition, laziness, and lack of motivation or caring. My combining of every level and type of drug with alcohol should not be condoned, but it will. Most of all because I don't care. Being under the influence in a great sea of confusion, forcing reality to sober me up, is one of my many fetishes, my many compulsions. As I stated in my prior essay, college is a time in my life where I feel I can get away with these actions. Or can I? My grades have definitely suffered, as have aspects of my personal life due to drinking. What if I want to attend graduate school in a few years? I don't often plan ahead, and live my life day to day. Living in the moment, which barely means "getting me by," may have consequences for the future I will most certainly regret.

My intentions, unfortunately, do not call for much change. I do intend to resume my long-missed work out routine, to cut back on the alcohol and drugs, and to arrive at some "peace of mind." I have an extremely calm, "chill" personality when sober or under the influence of drugs. My actions this Halloween not only surprised and shocked me, but depressed me. . . . As frequently occurs when I drink heavily, I pass out and vomit in my sleep, an immensely dangerous act that could be life threatening. AM I THAT IG-NORANT AND FUCKING STUPID that when a potentially life threat-ening situation presents itself I simply ignore it? I suppose just as the death of Sean's friends, as he reminisced eloquently of, hasn't ended his drinking and driving, neither will my situation or hazardous actions stop me. This does not justify my acts, and they are inexcusable to the point where this conflict is tearing me apart. I FEEL SO STUPID, AN ABSOLUTE ASSHOLE; HERE I AM WRITING ABOUT AND RECOGNIZING A PROBLEM AND NOT ATTEMPTING TO CHANGE IT, SIGNIFI-CANTLY!!!!! Is this the epitome of immaturity? Are my peers and I really that careless, or do we think we're invulnerable? Do we possess "Superman Syndrome?"

Regretting Self-Disclosure

Only one student expressed regret over self-disclosure, and her comments are worth heeding because I was the cause of her discomfort.

Dora: "I Felt I Have Given a Horrible Impression of Myself"

Dora revealed in her essay on binge drinking that she and her friends would buy the cheapest beer available in high school and then roam the streets "like juvenile delinquents" until the police chased them home. The incident did not strike her as disturbing, and she ended the essay on a hopeful note.

As I look back on my high school and college days thus far, I would not change anything that I have experienced. I treasure all these memories. I know that once I graduate college that life for me is going to change. I will not be that "party girl" any longer. At least not to the extent that I have been. I will have responsibilities that I cannot conceive of right now. I will be a career woman dedicating myself to teaching little kids and enveloping their innocence by giving them their first chance at learning.

I wrote at the bottom of Dora's essay, "Does the last sentence imply that when you graduate from college, you will stop drinking? Will it be so easy to break such an ingrained habit?" She found my questions unempathic and resolved not to disclose any more information about her life.

As I sat down thinking about this assignment, I asked myself how personal I was willing to be. I was not sure how revealing I wanted to be. I was hesitant to release important details of my life. Exposing your habits to your professor can be a little scary because you have no idea how your professor is going to react, and I did not want you, Professor Berman, to think bad of me in response to how candid I was. I have to admit that I regret being so open and revealing. I just do not feel right about it. I feel like you, my professor, should not know about those details of my life. I am not surprised if reading my paper caused you to think things about me that I do not want anyone to think. I partly came to this conclusion as I read your comment, "Will it be so easy to break such an ingrained habit?" I felt I have given a horrible impression of myself. I have never written so candidly to a professor before.

I did not intend to criticize Dora, but her response indicates that she felt dismayed by my comments. I remember thinking at the time that she responded defensively to my comment, but I now believe, upon further reflection, that she accurately sensed my disapproval. In assigning a pseudonym to her, I unconsciously chose the name of Freud's recalcitrant patient in *Fragment of an Analysis of a Case of Hysteria* (1953). The case study reveals Freud's aggressive pursuit of Dora's secrets and his efforts to impose his interpretations on her. Freud felt spurned when she abruptly left analysis after three months, and her unexpected return to analysis provoked his sarcastic comment at the end of the case study: "I do not know what kind of help she wanted from me, but I promised to forgive her for having deprived me of the satisfaction of affording her a far more radical cure for her troubles" (7:122). Like Freud, with whom I identify in so many ways, I was not only playing the role of therapist to "my" Dora but also judging her, contrary to my stated intentions. She accurately discerned my disapproval of her drinking and declined further self-disclosure. Instead of making a judgmental remark, I should have asked Dora whether she wished me to provide her with a list of resources for further information on reducing alcohol consumption. Even if Dora had declined my offer, I would have felt that I had done all I could to help her.

How do we finally view these narratives of binge drinking? Without exception, students found the two assignments valuable. Many thought the assignments were the most memorable of the semester. Statistics on binge drinking are just that—statistics—and after a while they become numbing, like alcohol itself. But personal essays are different and cannot be dismissed as easily as dry facts. If binge drinking reflects loneliness, alienation, and withdrawal, then writing about binge drinking may help an author to regain control over his or her life. Alcohol blurs self-awareness; writing about alcohol restores clarity. Significantly, most of the students' response essays were less pessimistic than their initial essays on binge drinking. The belief that "nothing can be done to solve the problem" gave way to an acknowledgment of mortality and the necessity for change. Writing was a form of peer education in which students narrated their own drinking experiences and shared them with classmates. There is a greater degree of open-endedness in the response essays along with a greater emphasis on human agency and the possibility of change. The response essays encouraged students to understand the seriousness of their earlier writings on binge drinking and engage in constructive problem solving. Few writers romanticized drinking in the first essay and none in the second essay. The "living-it-up and dying" narratives, as Josh called them, were riveting not because they glorified alcohol but because they revealed the extent of drinking gone awry.

The assignments on binge drinking have intriguing implications for "social-norms theory," which predicts, in the words of Alan Berkowitz, one of its cofounders, that "students overestimate the prevalence of attitudes and behaviors associated with problem drinking, while underestimating attitudes and behaviors associated with health" ("How to Tackle the Problem of Student Drinking," *Chronicle of Higher Education*, 24 November 2000, B20). Although some students may conclude erroneously from their classmates' essays that everyone drinks excessively in college, others will conclude that a great many students would like to reduce their drinking. Students who admit that they have been in denial about a drinking problem are more likely to make an effort to reduce their drinking than those who either do not admit to having a problem or who believe that the problem cannot be overcome.

To what extent did the students' writings improve over the semester? It is difficult to answer this question from the excerpts included here. The two essays on drinking were written one week apart, not long enough to demonstrate any dramatic change in writing. The students themselves indicated in the anonymous questionnaires at the end of the semester that they believed their writing improved significantly over fourteen weeks. I would agree. Most felt that their writing improved more than it would have in a traditional writing class, largely because they wrote about subjects that were important to them and because they wanted to express themselves as articulately and honestly as possible.

The writers were involved in a dialogic process in which they played multiple roles—authors, critics, participants, observers, speakers, listeners. They were alternately visible and invisible. They found the words to describe their experiences, constructed their own writing voices, and used language to tell and show. Their writings are powerful, engaging, unsettling. The writers were as surprised by their self-disclosures as were their readers, and these unexpected revelations dramatize the process of self-discovery. They described what it feels like to be drunk and out of control despite the fact that writing required them to remain in control. They reevaluated their own behavior and reached potentially life-saving insights. The assignments on binge drinking created a powerful bond among the students that continued throughout the semester. Of all the topics on which they wrote, binge drinking provoked the most lively discussions inside and outside the classroom. A number of students observed, with perhaps more irony than they intended, that they talked about their essays with classmates over beers. I must confess that I find this detail disturbing. Does it affirm or undercut the efficacy of writing as a strategy to combat alcohol addiction? I hope the assignments did not encourage anyone to get drunk in order to write, literally, under the influence. Only time will tell whether the assignments have a lasting impact on students' lives.

CHAPTER 7

Pedagogy of Risk

Throughout this book I have used a case study approach to discuss self-disclosing classroom writing. As noted in the introduction, from 1995 to 1999 I taught English 300 five times, each class forming a separate chapter in this book. It is time to summarize the results of my experience, and to do so I present the results of an anonymous questionnaire I asked each student to complete at the end of the semester.

Before doing so, however, I acknowledge the limitations of the questionnaire, which the students filled out on the last day of the semester, preceding an in-class party to celebrate the end of the term. They had submitted the required forty pages of writing to receive a "pass" in the course, and so they didn't have to worry about a letter grade. They were in a relaxed, festive mood, which might have affected their attitude toward the questions. They had no particular reason to withhold their feelings about the course, but I cannot be sure that their responses would have been the same if an impartial investigator had conducted the evaluation at a different time and in a different setting.

The questionnaire is not as precise as it could have been. Many of the questions gave students only three choices: "yes," "no," and "not sure." When I later showed the form to clinical psychologists and statisticians, whose quantitative sampling tools are far more sophisticated than my own, they pointed out that it would have been preferable to give students more choices, such as "strongly yes," "moderately yes," "strongly no," "moderately no," and so on. Since I could not change the questions for the later classes without invalidating those used for the earlier classes, the students' answers are not as precise and detailed as they might have been.

The questionnaires evaluated students' short-term responses to the course. How they might have responded several years after taking the course remains unknown. The relative shortness of the academic semester—fifteen weeks—makes it difficult to know the long-term consequences of the personal writing course. Several students, including Diane, Roberta, Lara, and Nick, have remained in touch with me since taking English 300, but this does not constitute long-term results. As a colleague noted after reading a draft of this book, "What you end up having to do—to offer an analogy—is to make sense of a short film clip (or, maybe better, a series of stills), without having access to the 'movie,' the fuller narrative of what came before and will come after." This is a valid criticism. Until the long-term consequences of the course are evaluated, we cannot determine the extent to which the students' classroom self-disclosures actually changed their self-representations.

Grading the Course

All 105 students who completed the questionnaire judged the course to be valuable, 79 percent grading it "A," 20 percent "B," and 1 percent "C." (I have rounded off percentages to the nearest whole number.) When asked what they liked most about the course, they cited the opportunity to improve their writing (41 percent), learn more about themselves (38 percent), learn more about their classmates (11 percent), and share their feelings with classmates (10 percent). No one indicated that he or she "did not like anything about the course." When asked what they most disliked about the course, they indicated the need to share their feelings with classmates (22 percent), the lack of time spent on writing skills (14 percent), the discussion of painful subjects (9 percent), and the emphasis upon personal writing (2 percent). Fifty-three percent "did not dislike anything about the course."

Ninety-one percent of the students believed that the quality of their writing improved during the semester, while the remainder were not sure. Fifty-four percent felt that their writing improved "a great deal," 41 percent an "average amount," and 5 percent "not very much." Seventy-four percent believed that their writing improved more than it would have in another writing course; 4 percent believed that it improved less than it would have in another writing course; 21 percent believed that it improved about as much as it would have in another writing course. Seventy-one percent believed that enough time was spent in class discussing the technical aspects of writing.

Eighty-two percent of the students believed that class discussions of their own essays were helpful and constructive, and 91 percent believed that my comments on their essays were helpful and constructive. To the question, "Would it have been problematic for you to write on personal subjects if the course were letter graded instead of pass/fail?" 38 percent indicated "yes," 45 percent "no," and 17 percent "not sure." To the question, "If the course were letter graded, do you think I would be objective in grading you?" 52 percent indicated "yes," 17 percent "no," and 31 percent "not sure." When asked to letter grade their own work, 51 percent felt that they deserved an "A," 43 percent a "B," and 6 percent a "C." When asked to predict how I would have evaluated their work, 45 percent indicated I would have given them an "A," 49 percent a "B," and 5 percent a "C." Fifty-nine percent felt that they would not have worked harder in the course if it were letter graded. Forty-nine percent felt that the course required more work than their other courses; 9 percent felt that the course required less work than their other courses; 41 percent felt that the course required about the same work as their other courses.

How representative were the students? Although I did not define what I meant by the question, 69 percent felt that the students in the class were representative of those who study at the same university; 6 percent felt that the students were unrepresentative; 25 percent were not sure. Seventy-six percent did not know in advance that the course would focus on personal writing. (The university schedule of classes simply listed the course as "expository writing" although the English Department brochure, which apparently few students read, listed my section as personal writing.) Sixty-four percent indicated that they would have signed up in advance for a course on personal writing. Ninety-six percent said that they would recommend the course to a friend, and 91 percent believed that there should be other courses in the university like this one.

A number of questions asked students how they felt about being "research subjects." To the question, "In the beginning of the course did you feel coerced or manipulated into personal self-disclosure?" 12 percent indicated "yes," 77 percent "no," and 12 percent "not sure." To the question, "Now that the course has ended, do you feel that you were coerced or manipulated into personal self-disclosure?" the figures were slightly lower: 6 percent indicated "yes," 88 percent "no," and 6 percent "not sure." To a related question—"Do you feel that I am manipulating or pressuring you into giving me permission to use your writings for my research?"—1 percent indicated "yes," 92 percent "no," and 7 percent "not sure."

Some of the most important questions I asked involved the honesty of students' writings. "How often were you honest in your writing? That is, how often did you tell the truth as you saw it?" Eighty-one percent indicated "all of the time," 18 percent "most of the time," and 1 percent "some of the time." Interestingly, when asked "How often do you think your classmates were honest in their writing?" the figures were much lower: 40 percent indicated "all of the time," 56 percent "most of the time," and 5 percent "some of the time." I reported the same phenomenon in *Diaries to an English Professor*, where close to 100 percent of the polled students reported that they were honest in their *own* diaries, whereas only between 60 to 70 percent of the polled students believed that their classmates were honest in *their* diaries.

Rating the Degree of Self-Disclosure

The questionnaires revealed that students were much more self-disclosing in their writings than they would have predicted at the beginning of the course. Twenty-eight percent indicated that in general they were high self-disclosers, 56 percent average self-disclosers, and 16 percent low self-disclosers. Yet 50 percent rated the degree of self-disclosure in their writings as high, 42 percent as average, and 7 percent as low. When asked to rate their classmates' written self-disclosures, the figures were even higher: 69 percent believed that their classmates were high self-disclosers; 31 percent believed that their classmates were average self-disclosers; and—most surprising of all—not a single person believed that his or her classmates were low self-disclosers. Ninety percent were surprised by the degree of self-disclosure in their classmates' writings. Seventy-two percent believed that their classmates' self-disclosures encouraged their own, confirming the reciprocal nature of self-disclosure.

Exactly 50 percent of the students believed that I was a high self-discloser, 40 percent an average self-discloser, and 10 percent a low self-discloser. These figures varied considerably, however, in the five different courses. In the course in which I gave the diversity assignments and revealed my ambivalence over being Jewish (chapter 3), 71 percent believed that I was a high self-discloser. By contrast, only 14 percent of the students in the class that wrote on sexual disclosures (chapter 4) regarded me as a high self-discloser. When asked what kind of teacher they preferred, 34 percent indicated a high self-discloser, 34 percent an average self-discloser, 6 percent a low self-discloser, and 26 percent indicated no preference. Only 19 percent stated that they had been encouraged to be self-disclosing in their other classes.

Painful Writing

Seventy-six percent of the students found it painful to write one or more essays. Seventeen percent of these students found one essay painful; 32 percent found two essays painful; another 32 percent found three essays painful; 11 percent found four essays painful; and 9 percent found five essays painful. Eighty-six percent of these students indicated that they were glad that they wrote on painful topics. They felt the experience was valuable because writing (in order of decreasing importance) made them feel better, brought them new insights, helped them to identify problems, helped them to master fears, and made them feel less isolated. Less than a quarter of the students had ever written before on the topics assigned in class, including divorce, eating disorders, sexual conflicts, suicide, and binge drinking. The only exception was the subject of diversity, on which half the students had written for other courses. When asked how many of their essays were anonymous, 52 percent indicated none; 34 percent indicated 1; 9 percent indicated 2; and 5 percent indicated 3 to 5. Eighty-seven percent stated that they did not regret any of their self-disclosures; 5 percent stated that they did regret a self-disclosure; and 8 percent stated that they were not sure.

Self-Disclosure and "Emotional Intelligence"

One of the most noteworthy findings is that the overwhelming majority of the students—86 percent—believed that the ability to disclose personal information about oneself contributes to health and well-being. (Only 1 person among the 105 polled disagreed with this statement; the rest were not sure.) Nearly the same percentage believed that the course heightened their "emotional intelligence," which Daniel Goleman defines in his best-selling book as self-awareness, impulse control, persistence, zeal, self-motivation, empathy, and social deftness. The responses to related questions confirmed important changes in students' attitudes toward themselves, their classmates, and their teacher. Forty-seven percent believed that they became more self-disclosing as a result of the course. Sixty-four percent believed that the course helped them to cope with personal problems. Fifty-nine percent believed that the course heightened their self-understanding, and 70 percent believed that the course heightened their understanding of classmates. Sixty-three percent indicated that the course heightened their empathy. This empathy was reflected in their responses to related questions. To the question, "Did you feel like a voyeur or a 'rubberneck' when reading your classmates' essays (a 'rubberneck' is a person who takes pleasure in gazing at others' suffering)?" 81 percent indicated "no." Nor did they believe that their classmates felt like voyeurs when reading their own essays. Fifty-three percent believed that the course heightened their connection with their classmates, and 68 percent believed that the course heightened their connection with me.

The students also indicated that they experienced therapeutic relief as a result of writing. I defined "therapeutic relief" as "feeling better about yourself, more in control of your problems." Eighty-six percent indicated that they experienced therapeutic relief as a result of writing. Ten percent of these people felt the relief would be temporary, 49 percent permanent, and 40 percent were not sure whether it would be temporary or permanent. Sixty-one percent experienced therapeutic relief as a result of reading their classmates' essays, and 51 percent experienced therapeutic relief as a result of reading about fellow students' lives in *Diaries to an English Professor*.

Becoming at Risk

I have reserved the most disturbing statistics for the end—responses to the questions whether students found themselves becoming at risk as a result of class writings, readings, or discussions. I defined "at risk" as "feeling anxious, panicky, depressed, or suicidal—feelings that were serious enough to warrant clinical attention." Fourteen percent—a total of fifteen students—indicated that they became at risk as a result of writing; 82 percent indicated that they did not become at risk; and 5 percent were not sure. When asked to identify all the writing topics that placed them at risk, they indicated suicide (identified by four people), sexual conflicts (four), the biographical assignments (four), divorce (three), diversity (two), and eating disorders (one). (Some students identified more than one topic.) Eighty percent indicated that the heightened risk was temporary, and the remaining 20 percent indicated that they were not sure whether the risk was temporary or permanent.

Nor was writing the only activity that placed students at risk. Three percent indicated that they became at risk as a result of reading their classmates' essays. Another 3 percent became at risk while reading *Diaries to an English Professor*. Five percent became at risk as a result of our class discussions. About two-thirds of the students who felt at risk as a result of class readings or discussions believed that the risk would be temporary; the rest were not sure.

I was surprised by the number of students who indicated that they had become at risk. Seven of the fifteen were in the course that wrote on the diversity assignments, though it was not that topic alone that proved risky to several students. By contrast, none of the students in Nick's class (chapter 5) indicated becoming at risk. None of the fifteen students believed that the risk would be permanent, but this did not change the fact that, however briefly, they felt anxious, panicky, depressed, or suicidal. When I looked more closely at the fifteen questionnaires, I was startled to see that ten had answered the following question in the affirmative: "Were there adequate safeguards in the course to protect you from becoming at risk?" Only two of the fifteen felt that there were not adequate safeguards to prevent them from becoming at risk, while the remaining three were not sure.

How do we explain the fact that two-thirds of the students who indicated they became at risk as a result of writing also maintained there were adequate safeguards in the course to prevent them from becoming at risk? If we assume that they took the questionnaires seriously and answered consistently, then we must conclude that writing is so painful for a small group of people that they may inevitably become at risk no matter how many safeguards are in place. The fifteen students' questionnaires indicated that they felt positively about almost every aspect of the course. Indeed, in their responses to most of the questions, there was little difference between the fifteen students who became at risk as a result of their writings and the ninety students who did not become at risk. Ninety-three percent of the at-risk students experienced therapeutic relief from writing; the same percentage felt that the ability to disclose personal information about oneself contributes to health and well-being. Eighty percent were glad that they wrote on painful topics and did not regret any of their self-disclosures. All fifteen said they would recommend the course to a friend.

There were some differences, however, between the at-risk and non-at-risk students. Those who became at risk while writing were more likely to become at risk during class readings and discussions. More than three-quarters of the at-risk students felt their writings were highly self-disclosing, while only half of the non-at-risk students felt their writings were highly self-disclosing. Similarly, a higher percentage of the at-risk students felt that they had become more self-disclosing as a result of the course. One hundred percent of the at-risk students found writing on certain topics to be painful, compared to 80 percent of the non-at-risk students. Eighty-seven percent of the at-risk students, as opposed to 54 percent of the non-at-risk students, felt that the course heightened their self-understanding a great deal.

Both the at-risk and non-at-risk students believed that the class was representative of those who study at their university, but more than half of the former knew before signing up for the course that it would focus on personal writing, whereas only about one-quarter of the latter knew this. In addition, a higher percentage of the at-risk students indicated that they would have signed up in advance for a personal writing course. Another difference involved being in therapy. Sixty-seven percent of the at-risk students indicated that they have been in therapy, compared to forty-nine percent of the non-at-risk students. Both figures are higher than I would have expected. A third of the at-risk students stated that they might consider entering or reentering therapy as a result of the course, as opposed to 18 percent of the non-at-risk students.

The number of students who have been in therapy should give us pause. Should teachers encourage students to write about personal topics that will place some of them at risk regardless of the safeguards existing in the classroom? As we have seen, the possibility of risk can be reduced but not completely eliminated. Moreover, trouble may occur when least expected. According to Rüdiger Trimpop, a researcher in the area of risk homeostasis theory, "people will voluntarily increase their exposure to danger when the perceived risk is low! This has very important implications for industry, traffic-regulations, health issues, and one's personal life. The findings essentially suggest that when we make the environment safer, people will compensate for this increased safety by taking more risks" (290).

Teachers with a low tolerance to risk may conclude, based on my students' responses and risk homeostasis theory, that even a low degree of risk is unacceptable in a writing course. In a litigious age such as our own, why should teachers engage in pedagogical practices that might expose them to admonitions or lawsuits from college administrators, parent groups, or religious organizations? In an age in which the "personal" is viewed with so much suspicion, why should teachers encourage openness in the classroom? In short, why should teachers look for trouble? Few would argue that the writing classroom should be less safe than the literature classroom, yet *how safe is the literature classroom?* That is, to what extent do students in literature classes become at risk as a result of class readings, without the teacher's awareness that they have become at risk? And if students do become anxious, depressed, or even suicidal during class readings, what precautions should teachers take? We cannot explore risky writing without briefly discussing risky reading, a subject that college teachers seldom consider.

Chrissy: "People Do Not Often Think of the Consequences of Reading Violent Disturbing Material "

Recently, for example, one of my literature students, Chrissy, told me during a conference at the end of the spring semester that reading D. M. Thomas's novel *The White Hotel* produced nightmares and insomnia. *The White Hotel* was one of several texts in English 447, the "Historical/Hysterical Imagination," which focused on the cultural and psychological implications of mental illness. Chrissy was horrified by the novel's graphic description of the heroine's rape and murder at the infamous Babi Yar in Kiev during World War II. She told me that *The White Hotel* was not the first book that triggered this reaction, and she agreed to my request to write a brief essay describing when the problem first occurred. She noted in her essay that although reading has always been one of her greatest pleasures, she learned when she was young that she could not read certain books—not because they were too difficult but because they prevented her from sleeping at night. The first story that evoked this response was *The Diary of Anne Frank*, which she read when she was ten. "As I read the book I noticed that I was more afraid of the dark than normal. I had trouble sleeping, and often had nightmares about being hunted and captured by the Nazis. I would hear sirens in my sleep, and at night, once it was dark outside I would sometimes have the sensation of being stalked like some kind of prey." She never finished the book. In junior high and high school she was able to avoid texts with a disturbing content, but when she went to college and began studying the Holocaust, the nightmares returned. Reading an account of the murder of the Romanovs literally made her sick. "The authors went on to say how the bodies were first dropped down a mine shaft and then later relocated to another grave by train tracks. They went into minute detail of how these bodies must have looked, not leaving out one detail, making sure it was understood that no one could have possibly survived the carnage. For days after this I would be able to picture the bloated bodies with their matted hair turned black from all the blood, and feel like I might just hurl."

The White Hotel was wrenching for Chrissy because she participated in and experienced the heroine's gruesome death. "As Lisa tried desperately to save herself and her son, I was reminded of my nightmares where I was being hunted and I had to try to outwit and escape those who would capture and kill me. Every part of that section from the rape to the description of the layers and layers of murdered corpses in that ravine sickened and frightened me." She finished the novel but was angered that she was forced to read it. "People do not often think of the consequences of reading violent disturbing material when you are older." Nor did she think that her response was unusual. "Anyone who can read a book as though they are seeing a movie in their mind could be similarly affected, and I think for this reason teachers ought to be careful in what they assign. Professors ought not take it for granted that because students are past a certain age that they can handle anything. Why should anyone assume that at a certain age you become jaded enough that you are unaffected by death?"

Chrissy's vivid imagination allowed her to visualize every gruesome detail in *The White Hotel*. Her identification with the doomed characters was so intense that she too felt hunted and trapped. It was as if the boundaries between self and other, and life and art, had vanished. She must have known while reading *The White Hotel* that she could have closed the book at any time, but the story invaded her unconscious mind, evoking a nightmare from which she could not escape. The story literally sickened her, producing intense anxiety, gastrointestinal symptoms, and agoraphobia. She observed elsewhere in her essay that reading novels or seeing films containing gratuitous violence is not nearly as troubling to her as art depicting historical violence, such as *Schindler's List*: "movies like this are so awful, and true. I think that part of the reason these things disturb me is because they happened, and that is the most disturbing thing of all."

History cannot be banished from literature simply because it is disturbing, but should teachers take special precautions when assigning novels like *The White Hotel*? Should teachers warn their students that some of them might find class readings painful, even traumatic? I routinely alert my writing students to the possibility of becoming at risk but had neglected to alert the students in Chrissy's literature class. But how representative is Chrissy's response? Do a significant number of college students find reading so upsetting that they actually become physically and psychologically ill, as several of my writing students have reported? In *Surviving Literary Suicide* I discuss how graduate students respond to "dangerous" literature, but I have never looked at undergraduates' responses. I decided to pursue the question further. A month later, while teaching the same course in summer school, I informed the students that some of the books on the syllabus might place them at risk and urged them to speak to me if this occurred. I also told them that they could write their formal essay on this topic. Within a few weeks two of the twelve undergraduates came to my office, separately, and revealed that they felt anxious and depressed while reading Kate Chopin's *Awakening* and Sylvia Plath's *Bell Jar*, both of which portray suicidal female characters.

Justine: "*The Bell Jar* Made Me Think about Suicide"

Justine was one of these students, and she described in her essay how reading the two novels was almost more than she could endure. She began by noting that she was depressed and lonely the preceding summer. "My grandmother's death, being isolated in the dorm, attempting to write at the time what seemed the most impossible paper to make up an incomplete, most of the summer away from my boyfriend, and fear that I had a sexually transmitted disease drove me to putting an iron in the bath tub in an attempt to electrocute myself (grateful then and now that the cord could not reach an outlet). I turned my incomplete in on time and it turned out I did not have a sexually transmitted disease."

With her mother's help Justine recovered, but this summer she started to feel depressed again, particularly when she identified with Esther Greenwood's symptoms. "*The Bell Jar* made me think about suicide more clearly because of its realness in terms of Esther's suicide attempts. I hate to admit the similarities between us like our age, being English majors, having difficulty writing, knowing what you want to do but no motivation to do it, and paranoia among other things. I laughed when Esther looked up depression and saw her symptoms matched. Looking up illnesses got the better of me last summer when I thought I had a sexually transmitted disease. I was surfing the internet and reading anything I could find out about the disease. Many of the symptoms described what I thought I had. I think I made myself think I had them." Justine also identified with Edna Pontellier's feeling "as if life were passing by, leaving its promise broken and unfulfilled" (Chopin 70). Justine acknowledged later in the essay that she has more resources than either Esther or Edna had, including a supportive family. She concluded that "it is important when a teacher assigns *The Awakening, The Bell Jar,* and similar books to take precautions. He or she should be prepared if a student is feeling depressed or suicidal during and after reading these novels. Talking to their students before and after is therapeutic and essential in assuring that students do not get the wrong message. If a student is showing signs of serious illness they should be directed to the appropriate practitioners."

Justine found herself at risk as a result of identifying with two fictional characters whose feelings of loneliness, anxiety, and sadness paralleled her own. The knowledge that Sylvia Plath committed suicide shortly after writing *The Bell Jar* made the novel more frightening to her. Justine never romanticized suicide, but she described how depression may lead to constricted thinking. Rather than broadening her perspective, as literature often does, reading seemed to narrow her vision, at least temporarily.

Justine allowed me to read her essay anonymously to her classmates, and she later observed that she was glad she wrote on the topic despite the fact that it was painful to hear her words read aloud. "I believe that I am stronger after writing that paper. Writing can be very therapeutic. As I wrote I realized that there were things that I never thought about and some I gave second thoughts about in regards to my depression and near attempt at suicide. Questions come to mind like what if my mother was not there during that crucial time? Or what if the cord in the iron did reach an outlet? I still get upset remembering how low I had been. But I am glad that I am even able to write about that experience. Sharing one's experiences is beneficial to those that have gone through the same thing because it lets them know they are not alone."

Olivia: A Fortnight with Insomnia and The Bell Jar

Olivia was the other student who found herself at risk in my summer school course. One day she walked into my office appearing tired and somber, having missed the previous three-hour class, her first absence. A few days earlier she had sat in class, her usual animated self. An excellent student, she had turned in a thoughtful essay the preceding week on *The Awakening*. Now the student sitting in my office seemed as gloomy and incommunicative as Chopin's protagonist. For a few seconds Olivia remained silent, and I looked at her, anticipating the worst. Was there a death in the family? A serious illness? A breakup in a relationship? When she finally spoke, Olivia told me that she was feeling anxious and depressed, not for any of the reasons that I guessed, but because of the two novels we had just read, both of which, she said, felt like receiving a one-two punch. *The Awakening* and *The Bell Jar* unexpectedly reminded her of the depression she experienced five years earlier, when she was sixteen. The old feelings of melancholy had returned in the last two weeks, engulfing her in sadness.

Alarmed by Olivia's appearance, I suggested that she visit the counseling center, but she replied, "My parents would kill me if they knew I was seeing a therapist. I don't stigmatize mental illness in others, but I do in myself." We spoke for a few minutes, and then I made an unusual offer to her. Instead of taking the final exam, would she prefer to write an essay describing how the two novels placed her at risk? I told her that the reader-response essay would probably require more work than the final exam but that it might enable her to understand the novels' impact on her life. I didn't know whether writing about this topic would help or hurt her, but she readily agreed to my suggestion and a week later submitted a detailed account of her experience reading the two novels.

Olivia's essay described her growing fear that her past depression was returning. Reading *The Awakening*, she found her sleep patterns disturbed and, like Edna, began to lose herself in "mazes of inward contemplation" (Chopin 57). Nor did the mood lift by sunrise. "Surrendering and acknowledging defeat, I rolled out of my bed and sat Indian style on the floor. I stayed there for a while, limp of energy. It was eight a.m. (which is early for a college student). I felt claustrophobic, though I was in the middle of the room, with nothing around me. Sitting there quietly, I felt cornered, cramped, suffocated. Suddenly, I thought of Esther's bell jar, her type of 'indescribable oppression.' I could sense the boundaries of the transparent bell-shaped glass; within it, I was trapped in this feeling, this mood of unsettlement and extreme anxiety. This was the way I felt in high school, not even comfortable in my own skin."

Olivia's mood lasted for the two weeks in which we discussed *The Awakening* and *The Bell Jar.* She viewed the novels not only as "fascinations" but as "entrapments" since Edna and Esther conjure up a world from which she tried so hard to escape. "Edna's societal oppression, insomnia, feelings of depression, her struggles with womanhood and individuality, and finally her love of music branded the deepest impressions in my mind." Olivia found herself becoming like a "zombie, walking along, mechanically," and she could see no difference between herself and Edna. Olivia described living in what she calls a "muted state" in which she became the "observer and the analyzer, watching the people around me, in the alien world." She knew that she must separate herself from Edna's story in order to preserve her health.

Upon finishing *The Awakening,* Olivia began *The Bell Jar,* which proved to be far more disturbing. "Knowing that Plath committed suicide after the completion of this novel casts a very dark cloud around depression and recovery from it. With Plath's suicide, Esther's character lays void. The trace of hope developed at the end of the story, with Esther being reviewed by the committee, is pushed aside, when in real life the bell jar could not be lifted from Plath." Olivia believed that everything she felt during her reading—insomnia, confusion, loneliness, hopelessness, nothingness—was condensed by Plath into two words—bell jar. Though still wary, Olivia felt the bell jar lift as the course ended. "I am in my soul's summer day, thankfully. I find myself fortunate that I am in such a positive stage in my life and that this was only a short summer session. I am also thankful that the precautions the professor took were well-suited, and very congenial with a sympathetic approach. He left the door wide open and gave a fair warning of what may happen. His availability comforted me while I was trapped in this spell. Though I experienced such haunting things, I am glad to have read the material. I know that I am not alone. Nor does this hinder me from putting *The Awakening* on my shelf as one of my favorite novels."

Like Justine, Olivia identified so closely with the suicidal characters in *The Awakening* and *The Bell Jar* that she experienced nearly all their symptoms of depression. A clinical psychologist might infer from her symptoms that reading the two novels produced an anxiety or panic attack. Olivia's description of "feel[ing] myself drifting away to the background, merely an observer" recalls William Styron's depiction in *Darkness Visible* (1990) of his suicidal depression: the "sense of being accompanied by a second self—a wraithlike observer who, not sharing the dementia of his double, is able to watch with dispassionate curiosity as his companion struggles against the oncoming disaster, or decides to embrace it" (64). Olivia never mentioned feeling suicidal, but her description of a wraithlike observer suggests a form of psychological splitting in which one part of the self gazes impersonally at another part of the self that is immobilized by anxiety or fear. She thus reexperienced the anxiety of a younger, vulnerable self whom she thought she had safely outgrown.

Olivia acknowledged that writing was one of the "tools" that allowed her to emerge from the bell jar when it first descended at age sixteen. She told me in a conference after the semester ended that writing also helped her escape from the depression induced by reading *The Awakening* and *The Bell Jar*. When I asked her what would have happened if she hadn't had the opportunity to write about becoming at risk, she replied that her anxiety and confusion might have lasted longer. She felt that writing the essay was therapeutic because it enabled her to discover not only the similarities but also the differences between her own situation and those of the fictional characters.

I have cited Chrissy's, Justine's, and Olivia's essays to demonstrate that readers, no less than writers, may find themselves becoming at risk in a college course. This does not mean that teachers should avoid asking their students to read emotionally charged texts or to write on challenging topics. But it does mean that risks cannot be eliminated from the reading or writing classroom. We generally assume that reading and writing are parallel activities leading to empowerment, but in some cases the former may induce a crisis that the latter may help to resolve.

PSYART Responses to Risky Reading

Do college teachers inform their students that they might become at risk when taking a reading or writing course? If so, what precautions do teachers take to minimize these risks? Have students in other college courses experienced reactions described by Chrissy, Justine, and Olivia? To pursue these questions, I decided to send a posting to the literature-and-psychology electronic listserv PSYART, moderated by Norman Holland at the University of Florida. I asked subscribers if they had encountered the phenomenon of "risky reading" in their own classrooms, as I had in mine, and whether they had ever themselves become at risk while reading fiction or nonfiction. I invited them to email me either through PSYART, which has more than 850 subscribers, or through a private email. My query produced a lively and prolonged discussion, with more than twenty people participating. Respondents were generally divided into two positions, those who objected to the specter of censorship they inferred from my question, and those who believed that literature could indeed pose a threat to certain readers.

Eight people feared the censorship implications of my query and questioned whether teachers "[can] place ideas in people's heads." They implied that only a severely disturbed student might become at risk from reading. Interestingly, all eight respondents "went public" by posting their responses to everyone on the listserv. Allison White Ohlinger referred to the highly publicized lawsuits in the past twenty years that alleged a causal relationship between song lyrics and violent behavior in teenagers. "Anyone genuinely at risk of suicide might 'go over the edge' after reading a book or listening to a song that glamorized death, but such a person might also be influenced by seeing a vase of dead flowers, passing a funeral cortege, or hearing of the death of a celebrity. No one could reasonably blame the victim's suicide on the object or occurrence, but on their condition of being suicidal—just as assigned course reading can't be the sole cause of students' reported feelings of paranoia and depression, just because the reading is 'risky.'" Norman Holland cited being contacted years earlier by a woman who wanted *Romeo and Juliet* banned from the high school reading list because she was convinced that reading the play caused her son's suicide. Another person brought up a more timely example of censorship, the attempt to ban the Harry Potter books in England because of the belief that they are violent and therefore not fitting for children. All these respondents objected to the idea that teachers should avoid challenging their students' thinking. As Randy Fromm observed, "I find the idea that we should somehow coddle students who appear unequipped to meet life's challenges antithetical to the aims of education, at least so far as I see them. Where else are they to get or develop the principles by which they will live in their chosen future if not through tough challenges of their fundamental beliefs?"

Two respondents in this group implied that some of my students might have become at risk through the power of suggestion: that is, because I had alerted them in advance to this possibility. "Maybe women are more responsive to suggestion," Patricia Sloane wrote. "When I was the age of your students, I went into therapy with a Jungian analyst who spent the first session telling me how important dreams are. I sure did dream up a blue streak after that, maybe because I wanted to do what I thought was expected of me." John Buksbazen agreed that the power of suggestion might explain this phenomenon:

> While there are certainly books which can affect some readers traumatically, we should also consider the role of suggestion in Jeff's "alerting" his undergrads to an experience which several appeared to then have. Such a communication, however well-meant as I'm sure Jeff's was, carries with it an embedded and possibly hypnotically-influential message, which, potentiated by the asymmetrical teacher-student relationship, might quite possibly precipitate an adverse reaction, especially where such a predisposition is present in the student-reader. I think Jeff is justified in his concern about the student vulnerability, but would urge all of us in similar circumstances to be specially aware of the unconscious communication phenomena we may create by the ways in which we formulate our metacommunications.

For every respondent troubled by the censorship implications of my query, another acknowledged that reading could pose a serious threat to readers. One of the most interesting responses came from Claire Kahane:

> I have had the experience you describe for the last several years, not surprisingly, since I have been teaching Holocaust narrative and trauma. The first time I presented traumatic material, a girl ran out of my class crying. That hasn't happened again, since I have become more sensitive to the issues of teaching this kind of risky reading. And certainly, as you suggest in your query, I and my colleague who also teaches Holocaust representation have ourselves been deeply disturbed by the material we engage. Actually, to have a distance on traumatic representations is in a sense to declare their failure. Yet a distance must be had in order to talk about these texts in a classroom setting.

Professor Kahane noted in another PSYART posting that Primo Levi admitted becoming at risk while translating Franz Kafka's *The Trial*: "Rightly or wrongly, consciously or not, I have always tried to move from obscurity to clarity in my writings. . . . I take up dirty water, I throw it out purified, transparent, almost sterile. Kafka takes the opposite path. He disappears in the depths. . . . He never filters what presents itself to him. The reader feels polluted. . . . Through reading Kafka, I discovered that I had unconscious defenses. These defenses collapsed when I began to translate. I found myself profoundly bound to the fate of Joseph K. Like Joseph K., I began to accuse myself" (qtd. in Rosenblum 17).

During the same week in which I received responses to my PSYART query, an article appeared in the *Wall Street Journal* about a new and growing phenomenon, "cyberchondria," which apparently had afflicted Justine a year earlier:

> The Internet is making it easier than ever to be a hypochondriac. The anxious used to have to trudge to the library to research symptoms in tomes like the Physicians' Desk Reference or the Merck Manual. Now, the explosion of medical information on the Web—there are an estimated 15,000 health-related Web sites—has provided a powerful new tool for wired worrywarts, including the "worried well," on which they can pore over highly technical medical journals and commiserate electronically from their homes. (Reprinted in the *Albany Times-Union*, 10 October 1999)

Yet one does not have to be a hypochondriac to experience intense anxiety or depression while reading. Five PSYARTers cited examples of their own emotional reactions to literature:

> I don't respond to postings through the PSYART-list, but your letter affected me. I took an advanced degree in post–[World] War [II] literature, knowing I was drawn to the writing of this period, but not really scrutinising why. During the one-year stint of reading volumes for my qualifying exams, mostly works from survivors, I fell into one hellova depression. This phase of revaluation of my aims in persuing an academic career occasioned my recognition that I, as a bastard of the first order ("Mischling ersten Grades," a legal term), would have been exterminated and surely by many of those who were my colleagues. This statement was/is not hyperbolic. I did not at the time or subsequently share this recognition with colleagues. Or with family.
>
> I guess the reason I write is to say that the literature only opened me to realising what I knew very personally. It did not invoke this response solely by being "out there." And, of course, there is the beautiful anonymity of writing someone "out there" who will register this, who appreciates what the experience is.

> I hope you'll forgive the rushed quality of my response—I'm late for class but upon reading your entry felt compelled to write immediately. I'm a doctoral student and in a course on Biography and the Arts we did a lot of in-depth readings of Virginia Woolf. My train rides home after class at night were almost always quite tearful! We were reading *To the Lighthouse* and *Mrs. Dalloway*, and yes—I became pretty depressed and withdrawn during this time (although it yielded a whole bunch of insightful journal entries).

> When I was a freshman in college (several years ago) I had begun to read a lot of Kafka. *The Trial*, especially, had a profound effect on me, and to some extent must have been responsible for grounding me into a deep depression and overall discomfort with the world. I have read *The Trial* since then and do not experience the same states of mind. Some of the contributing factors

must have been that I was reading Kafka on my own, without the guidance or structure of a class, and that I was relatively immature at that time and could not readily distinguish the fiction of the work from the message of a stinging condemnation of existence.

I read *The Bell Jar* when I was probably too young (mid-teens) or too impressionable or both. It affected me a great deal. It was the summer of my "moodiness." Never thought to trace it to the book. Interesting. Will have to reread it.

I agree it [literature] can work as a triggering device. I don't think it was any coincidence that my own mental breakdown—from which I have recovered nicely—was due in part to my reading Nietzsche's "My Sister and I," which was written while he was in a mental hospital.

Significantly, four of the five responses were emailed to me alone rather than to the entire listserv. All five gave me permission to quote their words, but four did not want their identities revealed. Why? I suspect that they felt uncomfortable acknowledging that literature can be a risky art form, even (or especially) to those who later devote their lives to teaching and writing. Readers are reluctant to admit that literature can have powerful consequences that are not always anticipated or desired. They may have also feared that revealing their names publicly would hurt their careers.

Traumatic Art

It should not be surprising that reading, no less than writing, can become painful or traumatic to some students. In *Surviving Literary Suicide* I document the ways in which the self-inflicted deaths of Virginia Woolf, Ernest Hemingway, Sylvia Plath, and Anne Sexton have affected readers. Literature can, in an Aristotelian sense, purge readers of toxic emotions and lead to catharsis (see Berman and Luna, and Berman and Schiff), but it can also, in a Platonic sense, "infect" readers and lead to illness. The most striking example of the "infection" or "contagion" theory of literature is *The Sufferings of Young Werther* (1774), Goethe's confessional novel about a passionate young man who kills himself because of unrequited love.

Goethe based some of the details of Werther's suicide on a friend who took his own life, but the novelist was also writing about his own tormented feelings. He was actively suicidal when writing the story and "even kept a dagger at his bedside and made repeated attempts to plunge it into his breast" (Steinhauer 20). Goethe may not have romanticized suicide to the extent that Werther does, but he identifies so closely with his hero that he blurs the separation between author and character. Werther views himself as a Christlike martyr and, before shooting himself, tells his beloved Lotte, who was modeled closely on Goethe's Charlotte, that she will be better off without him. Werther also offers a long philosophical justification of suicide, claiming that it leads to eternal freedom.

Goethe was later embarrassed by the novel and distressed that it provoked numerous readers to imitate the event. "Sentimental young men sported Werther's costume: blue coat and yellow trousers and vest; some lovelorn creatures followed his example and committed suicide with copies of the novel in their pockets" (Steinhauer, *The Sufferings of Young Werther* 24). Goethe healed himself through the telling of the story and lived a long and productive life, but this consolation came too late for those readers whose identification with his suicidal hero proved fatal. (*Surviving Literary Suicide* 26)

The suicide rate always jumps when a famous actor, actress, or rock singer takes his or her own life. Sociologist David Phillips, who coined the expression "the Werther effect," has estimated that celebrity suicides raise the suicide effect by an average of 1 percent for about a month. "The largest increases in British and American suicides occurred after the deaths of Marilyn Monroe, the actress, and Stephen Ward, the British osteopath involved in the Profumo affairs. In the United States, suicides increased by 12% in the month after Marilyn Monroe's death and by 10% in England and Wales" (Phillips 306). But it is not simply the Werther effect that comes into play here: any work of art can evoke a wrenching emotional response from a reader or viewer. For example, Stephen Spielberg's 1998 film *Saving Private Ryan*, which graphically reenacts the D-Day invasion at Omaha Beach in Normandy, traumatized not only soldiers of World War II but of Korea, Vietnam, and the Persian Gulf, awakening long-repressed memories of combat. "Across the country, veterans' hospitals have been inundated with calls from men seeking help coping with disturbing memories uncovered by the movie's realism. In some cases, the film's stark portrayal of torn flesh and frightened soldiers watching their friends die triggered post-traumatic stress disorder in veterans who had never experienced such difficulties before, counselors said" (*Albany Times-Union*, 31 July 1998).

One does not usually think of *The Awakening* or *The Bell Jar* as producing the violent effects of a war film, but these novels may evoke powerful fantasies of self-martyrdom in young adults who are already depressed or suicidal. Nor are we talking about an insignificant number of college or high school students who may be at risk. As Kay Redfield Jamison observes in her 1999 book *Night Falls Fast: Understanding Suicide*, the "1995 National College Health Risk Behavior Survey, conducted by the Centers for

Disease Control and Prevention, found that one in ten college students had seriously considered suicide during the year prior to the survey; most had gone so far as to draw up a plan" (21). The figures for high school students surveyed in 1997 were even more troubling: one in five students had seriously considered suicide in the preceding year; most had drawn up a suicide plan. Jamison adds that "[o]ther research, conducted in Europe and Africa as well as in the United States, has shown that mild to severe thoughts of suicide are common, occurring in 20 to 65 percent of college students" (36). She cites research done by Cynthia Pfeffer, a Cornell University child psychiatrist, indicating that "more than 10 percent of a sample of 'normal' schoolchildren, that is, children with no history of psychiatric symptoms or illnesses, report suicidal impulses" (38). Jamison, a professor of psychiatry at Johns Hopkins University, has written eloquently about the devastating personal and interpersonal consequences of suicide; her best-selling memoir An Unquiet Mind (1995) chronicles her own lifelong struggle with manic-depressive illness. According to a 1999 New York Times/CBS poll, 46 percent of teenagers knew someone their own age who had attempted or completed suicide. Many more girls knew about suicide attempts than boys: 56 percent compared with 37 percent (New York Times, 20 October 1999).

To acknowledge these figures is not to argue for censorship or for the "coddling" of students but rather to recognize the power of reading and writing for both good and—quite literally—ill. A striking confirmation of this power is hinted at by Andrew Solomon in his review of Night Falls Fast:

> Jamison notes that suicide is catching, and avers that one death often enables many others, as localized suicide epidemics have indicated. If suicide is contagious, is not Jamison's book itself a potential source of infection? Her evocations of the suicidal mind invite too much empathy at times; her eloquence can be dangerous, and I felt a will to self-destruction rise in me as I read on. If the material is somewhat toxic for the reader, however, it must have been more poisonous for the author. It is something to have lived through the writing of this book; it took at least as much courage to write "Night Falls Fast" as it does to live through the woe that has afflicted Jamison's living subjects. (New York Times Book Review, 24 October 1999)

Given literature's power to disrupt, subvert, and even overwhelm the reader's defenses, teachers need to rethink pedagogical strategies designed to "destabilize" students in the name of social and political reform. To cite one example, Gregory Jay invokes Lacanian theory to argue that "the teacher's task is to undo certainty":

A pedagogy of the unconscious must dislocate fixed desires rather than feed us what we think we want to know. Unfortunately, this means that the teacher's task is to make the student ill (which we often do unknowingly anyway). Where the psychoanalyst seeks to stabilize a shattered self, the pedagogue hopes to unsettle the complacency and conceptual identities of the student. Education becomes subjective in the sense that the student experiences his or her existence as a being subjected to various discourses, including that of the teacher. The disturbance that ensues includes the split between the self-as-subject and the subject-of-knowledge, since the latter comes into being in skeptical reflections on the former—even to the point of finally doubting the value of such reflection. Like psychoanalysis, education can only begin with self-doubt, and its disciplinary self-analyses should be interminable. (790)

It is one thing to "unsettle the complacency and conceptual identities of the student" but quite another to destabilize identity to the point where a student becomes clinically at risk. Yet this is precisely the pedagogical strategy advocated by Jay, who casually informs us in a parenthesis that teachers "often" make their students ill. He may be using illness as a metaphor, but the word takes on a much more frightening reality in an age in which, according to one Harvard Medical School researcher, an estimated 37 percent of Americans aged fifteen to twenty-four, many of whom are college students, have a diagnosable mental illness (cited in "Treating Mental Illness in Students: A New Strategy," *Chronicle of Higher Education*, 16 June 2000).

The Teacher's Responsibility

If reading or writing may be dangerous under certain conditions, how can teachers challenge students without shattering their identity? To begin with, they can alert their students to the possibility that some classroom assignments and texts may induce symptoms not unlike those experienced when receiving a flu vaccination. Generally these symptoms are mild to moderate in intensity and disappear in a few days, as students in my writing classes have reported. While it is true, as two respondents to my PSYART query noted, that alerting students to the possibility they might become at risk may induce some symptoms that would otherwise not occur, literature works precisely through the power of suggestion. A novel like *The Bell Jar* may be so real to certain readers that they cannot help imagining themselves suffering from the protagonist's fears and maladies. Just as physicians and pharmacists routinely inform their patients of possible adverse reactions to a drug, so might teachers alert their students to the untoward consequences of a novel or a writing assignment. Even then, it is not always possible to detect when a student is at risk. Reading Olivia's first essay on *The Awakening* in light of her second one, I could not infer that she was at risk. Nor would I have known that Justine was at risk had it not been for my conversation with Chrissy, who sensitized me to risky reading. Yet it is not unusual for students to tell a teacher that they are "having problems" with a reading or writing assignment, and a simple question may help students to reveal when these are "emotional" problems. It doesn't require much time or effort to alert students to the possibility that they might become at risk. The present strategy of "don't ask, don't tell" is no more effective in education than in the military.

The knowledge that others have experienced and survived depression can be comforting, as both Justine and Olivia told me. Memoirs like William Styron's *Darkness Visible* and Kay Redfield Jamison's *An Unquiet Mind* affirm survival. These narratives are especially welcome when reading novels and poems by Virginia Woolf, Ernest Hemingway, Sylvia Plath, and Anne Sexton, all of whom suffered from severe clinical depression or manic depression and lived in an age when effective treatments were not available. Students need to know that major advances in psychopharmacology and psychotherapy have made these illnesses far more treatable than in the past.

Beyond this, teachers can make themselves available to students who become anxious or depressed from a reading or writing assignment. They should be sensitive to the many students who, sitting alertly or perhaps not-so-alertly in their classrooms, struggle with personal problems that seem overwhelming to them. Teachers can play a vital role in suicide prevention, for they are among the first to realize from a diary or personal essay that a student may be depressed. Mark Bracher has recommended that "[e]ducators in all roles—from teachers and advisors to administrators and policy-makers—should receive training that allows them to understand, recognize, anticipate, avoid, and (when necessary) counteract the numerous ways in which the various aspects of education can threaten students' identities and thus disrupt the various ego functions essential to learning" ("Editor's Column" 180).

Teachers are not trained to be psychiatrists, but they should avoid glorifying or stigmatizing mental illness and remain hopeful about the power of knowledge. Teachers' positive or negative attitudes toward education strongly influence their students' attitudes. Hope and hopelessness are both contagious. As Jamison states in *Night Falls Fast*, "hopelessness is strongly related to eventual suicide in both depressed inpatients and outpatients.

. . . People seem to be able to bear or tolerate depression as long as there is the belief that things will improve. If that belief cracks or disappears, suicide becomes the option of choice" (94).

Hope, or the belief in positive expectations, is the force behind the powerful "placebo" effect, a phenomenon that has attracted increasing scientific and medical inquiry. Many studies have shown that placebos, which are pharmacologically inert substances, are associated with a 50 percent reduction of pain in about one-third of patients suffering from a wide range of illnesses (Frank and Frank 136). Favorable expectations often lead to favorable conclusions—hence, the importance of hope. Like the physician, psychotherapist, and minister, the teacher who maintains a hopeful attitude is more likely to achieve positive results than one with a less hopeful attitude. To remain hopeful is not to be naive about the often terrifying reality of mental illness but rather to recognize that most people survive the experience. Those who write about illness can play a crucial role in helping others to overcome it. Teachers can also play a significant role by helping to make reading and writing come alive and by supporting a student whose identity is threatened by a text.

Finally, we need to acknowledge that some risks cannot be avoided and, in many cases, may actually contribute to health and well-being. I have implied throughout this book that risk is bad—hence, the binary "benefits and risks." The word "risk" admittedly has negative connotations, suggesting loss, injury, or even death, but many risks are essential to personal growth and maturation. Any attempt to confront a problem and search for a constructive solution is fraught with risk. Reading and writing can alert us to inner conflicts that may lie dormant for many years only to erupt explosively in later life. As Charles Paine observes, reading and writing can help students to uncover and work through serious conflicts or imbalances. "If our immune systems are to be flexible, they must be clever enough (not just tough enough) to enter risky situations (the world is a risky place of germs and disease), where contagion can never be prevented but only responded to" (17).

Psychological research lends support to this conclusion. In Jerome Frank's words, "heat that melts wax tempers steel. Despite the enormous popular health literature on the importance of avoiding stress, most moderate stresses in fact promote health. To use another analogy, life, like a violin string, is no good unless it is stretched. Some highly successful people may even seek stress to enjoy the triumph of mastering it" (Frank and Frank 22). Ronnie Janoff-Bulman agrees. "There is some evidence that prior stressors may inoculate an individual against extreme trauma following negative life events. Generally, these appear to be stressors of moderate magnitude, sufficient to challenge and even slowly change some assumptions in the direction of decreased naivete" (90). In this context, Mary Ellen Elkins's insightful response to my PSYART query is worth quoting:

> As has been pointed out by others, there are life experiences, some dangerous, that we unconsciously bring to our reading. When these are accidentally brought to consciousness by the act of reading, a student would feel the panic and anxiety that Jeff has described. This confrontation can feel so dangerous to our psychic health that it may seem better to hide from it than to advance, unaided, toward what appears to be certain annihilation. In other words, are there not psychological equivalents to finding oneself accidentally faced with an angry Grizzly Bear? Perhaps a teacher cannot offer a student a gun or its psychological equivalent in such a situation, but he can offer a means of survival: Play dead but only until the Grizzly runs away, i.e., the immediate danger is over, then get to safety and write about the experience—deal with what's happened.
>
> By inviting students to write about their experience, the teacher validates the students' responses and, by example, teaches students to value and embrace their experience, negative or otherwise, and to engage a deeper or more whole awareness of their feelings. The teacher also conveys a message of confidence: "I know there are terrors but I also know that we humans can face and survive them and come out the better for it. *That* is the way towards life." In acknowledging pain that we are presented with and telling the student he can write about it, we validate and open a door to a constructive act, then we can let go, we do not step over any boundaries, we do not coddle nor do we assume the mantle of psychologist. Is this not a valid response for a non-psychologist to make? Perhaps it will be enough; if not, the teacher can recommend professional help.

In short, composition and literature teachers need to discover a responsible pedagogy of risk that will allow their students to confront painful or shameful subjects without becoming unduly vulnerable. "*Risk is essential to growing up,*" Stephen Smith observes emphatically, and it can lead to self-direction and self-confidence in children and adults (181). Risk and fear are "twin themes of life," John Urquhart and Klaus Heilmann suggest: "Fear drives us to shun risk, yet risk accompanies any action, however trivial. To grasp opportunity, one must act, and, in acting, one incurs risk: opportunity and risk cannot be separated, and no goal can be attained without accepting risk" (ix). This pedagogy of risk will encourage students to tap into the transformative powers of writing and reading while minimizing harmful side effects. A pedagogy of risk will also allow students to write about conflicts and identify rhetorical strategies and survival techniques.

Teachers will undoubtedly want to create their own versions of personal writing courses in which they devise different assignments and link writing (either expository, critical, or creative) to other courses in the curriculum. One such course might be, to cite the suggestion of my colleague Stephen North, "The Rhetoric and Poetics of Writing about the Self," in which students use a variety of genres and points of view to explore conflicted subjects, in the process recasting their experiences and aiming for the widest audience. Whatever forms of personal writing appear in the future, a pedagogy of risk will challenge teachers and students to decide for themselves how best to strike a balance between fear and opportunity.

Confronting and Exploiting the "Cringe Factor"

LINDA MARTIN

When you take a deep breath and address the things that scare the hell out of you, that drive you to grief you thought was beyond words, that amaze and confound and baffle you, that keep you up at night and give you nightmares, that cause you joy so keen it begs to be expressed, you can come to terms with the truth of your own experience.
PHILIP GERARD, *CREATIVE NONFICTION*

Creating One's Writing Voice in the Classroom

I didn't decide until time for the third class of Jeff's English 300 course to take on the formidable task of researching my cringe factor theory, and I was late for that class. "So much for maintaining anonymity," I thought to myself as I opened the door to a room full of students packed into a tight circle. Almost instinctively, they moved their desks even closer to make room for me. I relaxed; I was just another student late for class.

The truth is that I was not just another student late for class—at least not a conventional student. I had returned to college in my mid-forties to study writing—an action that was the result of my coming to terms with the truth of my own life experiences.

Pounding Grammar Basics into Their Heads

Jeff was sitting on a teacher's desk at the front of the classroom. He held a paper in one hand and peered over his bifocals at the group. He glanced at me sideways and, without breaking his concentration, handed me a stack of copies of the assigned biographies being workshopped that day. A student was reading the biography of her classmate she had prepared for the assignment. After she finished, Jeff explained that at least a third of every class would be appropriated to the process of developing writing skills, and he turned our attention to one of the paragraphs of her essay. "Is it necessary to begin with 'To be honest with you?' Do you think your reader might think that you are being less than honest?" There was silence in the classroom. I glanced quickly through the biographies in front of me. They were replete with stale clichés, passive verbs, and comma splices. "Uh-oh," I thought to myself. "This is going to be just another remedial grammar course. He will, no doubt, spend the rest of the semester correcting misplaced modifiers and pounding grammar basics into their heads."

I felt frustrated and disappointed; this was a clear setback. I had grappled for three weeks with whether I should expend the effort required to complete a longitudinal study that would examine my "cringe factor" theory, and I was anxious to get started. My task meant weeks of commitment—attending all of Jeff's expository writing classes, interviewing students, observing body language and speech methods, and reading student essays, yet I felt the work would be worthwhile.

Coming to Terms with My Own Cringe Factor

Simply stated, my "cringe factor" theory is that personal writing of any kind must be spirited, graphic, and original to be effective. To develop the ability to portray such events vividly, an effective writer must first face head-on her own "cringe" episodes and describe them in the unique fashion of a person who has "owned" the experience. This is not to say that a writer must experience firsthand every situation that he or she writes about, but by working through the process of writing personal hardship and addressing the very issues that frighten and amaze, a writer is better equipped to get below the obvious and describe old subjects with a new spin. In his book *Creative Nonfiction*, Philip Gerard points out that the hardest obstacle the writing student faces is learning to craft original language (139). If such is the case, the hardest task for the writing teacher must be to help the student develop that skill.

To write well is to be able to confront what we dare not write, what we dare not say—what we cringe even to think. My own breakthrough in the process of writing what made me cringe came a year after I experienced clinical depression. It was painful to write about having considered suicide a natural and beautiful flight even as my daughter screamed into my frozen face, which was deadened by depression. It was no less painful to write about her terror over my state of mind. In describing my inability to feel even the slightest sympathy for her pain, which was rendered insignificant by my own, I came to realize that only through writing the unspeakable could I find a way to express the inexpressible. How else could I educate my reader about not only the psychological and chemical changes in an altered brain but also how these changes can reconstruct the basic nature of one's personality? In my own ignorance, I had once considered depression to be a trendy condition of baby boomers. Following my own clinical depression, a friend's son ended his life, and I wanted to find a way to alleviate her intense guilt and questioning remorse by describing how the mind works in a depressed person. Above all, I wanted my reader to understand that depression belongs to everyone and to know how to react to the signs of depression.

I read the account of my experience to a group of students in a workshop setting. After class, students came forward to tell me about their own experiences with depression. Following his father's suicide, one student had felt close to taking his own life. He expressed his relief hearing about my own sense of entrapment at having to remain alive in a tortured mind because I still had enough sanity to consider the lifetime sentence I would inflict on my family if I had taken my life. Picturing his mother's pain at losing a son as well as a husband had kept him alive.

One of the surprises I discovered in writing about a personal subject in a classroom setting was the reaction of my professor. Shortly after class, I had an email message from her asking me if I could meet her outside class for coffee. During our meeting she told me that most professors in her department were cautious about personal writing in a classroom. She felt, however, that I should make an effort to get the essay published, and she wanted to encourage me to do so. This meeting took place before my cringe theory began to take shape, and I never questioned her remark concerning the English department's discouragement of personal writing in the classroom. Reflecting on this class, I recall my apprehension at presenting my "skeletons" to a room filled with strangers. I realize how important the empathy expressed by the students was to me, and how relieved I felt that I wasn't alone. I wonder now that I was able to muster the courage to write so honestly about the images that were imprinted in my memory in an atmosphere where such writing seemed uninvited. I think of how different I would have felt writing the essay in Jeff's class.

The attempt to make sense of depression marked the beginning of my writing career, enabling me to create my own writing voice. After I gained some emotional distance, describing that personal experience allowed me to write with insight and with an honesty that encouraged attention to specific detail and distinct imagery. I discovered that, as I wrote, my memory became sharper—repressed anxieties, fears, and joy flowed out almost before I could get the words on paper. I knew that to educate my reader about the depressed mind, I must make him recoil at my mental anguish and struggle with me through my dismal transport from hopelessness to prospect. As I wrote about emerging from the clouds of depression, the tension and subsequent release were so intense that the words "Breathe now" actually ran through my mind. At that point, I recognized that my reader must experience the same sensation if I had done my job as a writer.

The important lesson I learned from monitoring Jeff's writing class is this: in a writing class of any type, especially one structured on the interdependence of creation and personal revelation, a good teacher doesn't pound grammar, syntax, or anything else into the students' heads. In "The 'Banking' Concept of Education," Paulo Freire compares the traditional methods of education to a bank in which students are empty vessels who receive "deposits" of knowledge from their teacher. He says, "The teacher presents himself to his students as their necessary opposite; by considering their ignorance absolute, he justifies his own existence" (*Pedagogy of the Oppressed* 58–59). Freire, who fought oppression in impoverished countries in South America, maintained that "the banking concept of education regards men as adaptable, manageable beings" (60). Today, many educators, having found merit in Freire's theories, are striving for a more egalitarian classroom in which his "problem-solving" method of education is applied. Freire explains this method: "Through dialogue, the teacher-of-the-students and the students-of-the-teacher cease to exist and a new term emerges: teacher-student with students-teachers. The teacher is no longer merely the one-who-teaches, but one who is himself taught in dialogue with the students, who in turn while being taught also teach. They become jointly responsible for a process in which all grow. . . . Here, no one teaches another, nor is anyone self-taught. Men teach each other, mediated by the world" (67).

The opening exchange between Jeff and the students didn't help my mood, and I entered presumptuous snippets in my journal. "These students are so young," I wrote, "he's coming across like a paternalistic high-school English teacher; they're going to check out mentally very shortly." After a minute of the uncomfortable silence that followed the "to-be-honest-with-you" sentence, Jeff grabbed an empty desk, slid it into the circle, and sat down. He sat at eye level with the students, and his voice was low. "If you ever feel that anything I say is wrong, raise your hand. Let's talk about it."

And they did.

From that day on, the classroom became an open-discussion arena. There were few absolute student-teacher oppositions. The mechanics of writing—grammar, punctuation, spelling, and syntax—was never pounded into their heads. The process of writing became a neutral and comfortable medium in which students felt free to disagree with Jeff and to argue among themselves. Many times, after debates such as "why-the-use-of-jargon-works-only-in-certain-situations" showed no promise of ending, he acted as a gatekeeper and curtailed the action with the arrangement of "agreeing to disagree." The following exchange was typical:

> Student: "You don't want detail. What if we need all 40 pages to effectively describe something?"
>
> Berman: "How can you have good writing if it is not detailed? Am I arguing against detailed writing? Details are good. Fat is bad. Fat loses the reader. Now, how can we know when writing is overblown?"

On the surface, this exchange might appear argumentative, but students' confidence in posing questions in a forthright way and the flexibility to discuss their immediate concerns allowed them to function within an important realm of trust. Instead of passive observers, they became active, thoughtful, and outspoken participants. Freire's reference to this atmosphere of trust in the context of "the oppressed" might also be applied to any traditionally "unbalanced" relationship—in this case, the relationship between student and teacher. He says, "To achieve this praxis, however, it is necessary to trust in the oppressed and in their ability to reason. Whoever lacks this trust will fail to initiate (or will abandon) dialogue, reflection, and communication, and will fall into using slogans, communiqués, monologues, and instructions" (53).

In his book *The Calculus of Intimacy*, Richard Murphy Jr. addresses the intimate connections formed between student and teacher when teaching is done well. He maintains that the routine tasks of teaching, if done correctly, lead quickly to a personal connection between teacher and students. He observes: "The official subject of Freshman English is 'expository writing.' But its actual subject is reading and writing, and more than those: thinking, and even more than that: living" (4). It should be pointed out here that intimacy and personal connection do not imply sexual connection. That situation would certainly upset any balance of power and prohibit a joint process of learning. Clearly, although much of the class time was spent discussing comma splices and overblown writing, Jeff was preparing an atmosphere of intimacy in which trust could flourish. Murphy goes on to say in *The Calculus of Intimacy* that "at the center of the mundane lies the intimate," an observation that is strikingly relevant to personal writing classes.

Equal Dignity

Once the students passed the ice-breaking biographies and moved into responses to the diarists in *Diaries to an English Professor,* mutual respect between teacher and student and student and student deepened and continued to develop throughout the semester. By the end of the course, these relationships had developed to the point where students embraced each other and wept openly at being parted. One might gather from this open show of emotion that the class was oppressive and morose. Not at all. There was joyful poking at each other, laughter and appreciation of recognizable angst, and open delight when an essay was well written or meaningful.

The opening biographies were fun, and the students expressed delight in getting to know their classmates and hearing their own lives through the view of another person. Time was allowed for each student to read and to hear her own biography read. Jeff used the assignment to familiarize students with the reader-tripping issues of writing style, grammar, punctuation, redundancy, and idiom, but he constantly emphasized the importance of treating fellow students with dignity. After reading aloud a handout that was entitled "Reading Empathically," he explained the importance of empathy not only in a workshop setting but also in the way students listened and responded to their classmates' work. Equal dignity and emotional identification became the workshop tools that set the tone for the course. They were the tools that provided the students with safety, which, in turn, provided freedom to listen, to respond, and to find the most compelling ways to write in their own words the part of themselves they considered shameful or unacceptable.

Subjects That Touch Our Lives

Professors are often reluctant to assign their own publications as a course requirement. They fear— perhaps accurately—that students will perceive such a requirement as a mark of insincerity, egoism, or, even worse, a failure to sell their books to anyone outside academe. In *Creative Nonfiction* Philip Gerard discusses his experience with students and personal writing. He says, "Once they [students] are forced to address subjects closer to home, subjects that touch their own lives . . . , their voices take on a refreshing honesty" (138). During the course of my study, I became convinced that the subject matter of Jeff's book *Diaries to an English Professor* allowed students to write about subjects that were close to them. I discovered that there was no one in the class who couldn't find emotional identification with the subjects addressed by his or her counterparts in

Diaries—the topics of divorce, parental desertion, date rape, eating disorders, and suicide.

One of the advantages of having students read and respond to the diary entries in the book was that they were able to focus quickly on a given subject. While they were allowed flexibility in how they responded, the time- and energy-consuming problem of "what to write about" was avoided, and students were left with the more penetrating issue of "capturing the genuine feeling of the experience" (Gerard 139).

Abandoning "Safe" Writing

By the time students have reached their junior year of college, most have obtained some distance from their parents' view of how the world should work. Many students have experienced a few "cringe" events of their own; yet years of conditioning "to make the grade" compel them to assume a pattern of parent-teacher pleasing language that carries into their writing. As a result of conditioning, they become mediums for what has been called "parent-speak," the canned set of instructional, philosophical idioms that we parents spout forth continuously despite our best intentions, or, worse, they parrot the words of pop culture—perhaps mimicking some melodramatic character in a popular television show such as *Melrose Place*.

In the biography assignments, most students described their subjects' lives with detachment, much like the following account written by a student. In writing the life of her subject, she described a drive-by shooting, which occurred—of all places—at a church fair. "As Lara and her friends were leaving the scene, a dark car rode by and gunshots sprayed everywhere. One of Lara's friends was hit in the leg. Luckily, no one else was hurt. Lara realized in a split second how precious life really is." Instead of capturing the visceral reality of splintered bones and blood, of panic and disbelief, the writer obscures an important event in her subject's past—obviously one Lara felt significant enough to want to include in her biography. Complete with an overused abstraction of life's mystery, the writer echoes the euphemisms that have come to be expected in our society—her friends were "leaving the scene," and "Luckily, no one else was hurt," and "Lara realized in a split second how precious life really is." Philip Gerard addresses similar results he found in his students' early personal essays: "They formalize—and *formulize*—the truth and so keep it at arm's length. Which may be safe—the writer can find reassurance in formulas and platitudes—but does not get him or the reader any closer to understanding the profound experience he is trying to relate. It mummifies the experience, wraps it in euphemism, pushes it away into the rhetorical distance, rather than bringing it to chilling and troubling life right up close" (139; emphasis in original). The writing student who studies in a safe classroom is able to abandon the canned phrases and move toward autonomy in expression. In an atmosphere of nonjudgment, surrounded by empathic listeners, the students in English 300 responding to diarists were free to confront their own troubles with eating disorders, suicide, divorce, and other conflicts that were close to their social reality. Gerard goes on to describe how the process prepares the developing writer: "To understand why a decent young man might end his life, we may have to confront our own temptation to suicide; our own fear of mortality; the guilt we feel at not recognizing how much more friendship he needed than we were willing to give; the profound despair and loneliness he must have felt—that we, too, have felt at times; his not-so-admirable qualities; our unsettling relief that it was him, not us; even our anger at him for acting with such finality" (140).

In the process of critical self-reflection—confronting the frightening and even repulsive qualities of the self—the writer is able to let go of shame and to write unflinchingly the raw details that move and sway the reader. This conditioning permits the writer, such as the student describing the drive-by shooting, to make the reader know the reality of *hearing* the screams and *seeing* the blood, perhaps even *smelling* fear.

Taking on Honesty

During those first weeks, just when I began to wonder if I could sit through another biography, the class was jolted—rather than led—into our first exhibition of passionate exposé. The subject matter of parental divorce was so poignant that Brad's response to the assignment on the chapter entitled "The Sins of the Fathers" shouldn't have surprised anyone, but somehow we were all caught off guard. Brad had volunteered the week before to have his turn at reading his essay aloud. After a drowsy hour spent examining misplaced clauses and comma splices, Jeff called for the designated essayists to make their presentations. Brad made his way to the front of the class. We paid scarce attention to his face or body expression.

"Fuck my Dad. That is all I want to say." That got our attention! Wooden desks creaked against their metal frames as bodies shifted. Brad's face never left his paper, and weighty silence hung in the air as he poured out anger and frustration at his father's abandonment of his biological family for another woman and her children. Brad's bed was where he took his

audience — it was where he lay in tears and frustration in the years following his parents' divorce. It was the place where he took refuge following
his mother's attempted suicide and the place where he coped — always
resolving to break the pattern of selfishness, a trait he saw in his father
and one he feared might surface in himself. He says, "Her [the diarist to
whom he was responding] reference to the biblical admonition, 'The sins
of the fathers are visited on the children, even to the third and fourth
generation,' reminded me of those nights I have spent in bed planning my
future." Yet even as he insisted that, "my father's 'sins' will never reach me
or my children," he revealed his own failure to stick around in any relationship that hinted of intimacy. Anna Freud recognized and labeled the
defense mechanism of identification with the aggressor, which characterizes the self-contradiction in Brad's essay. Frequently, the individual who
has felt menaced by another behaves like that other in dealings with people.
This mechanism is commonly seen in individuals who feel that they have
been abandoned when a parent leaves because of divorce or death. In
writing down his anger, Brad was able to recognize his divided self. He
says, "I can not be alone (and happy)," and "for the smallest reason, I leave
and destroy a relationship."

After reading his essay, Brad glanced upward cautiously. His face was
white, mottled with red splotches. Two of the men sitting nearby nodded
to him as he passed them on the way to his seat. "Yes!" I wrote in my
journal. "It is finally happening." Instead of abstractions and passive verbs,
Brad had given us physical signposts that allowed us to follow him through
his role of the "responsible" child of two parents who were consumed by
their own excesses and crises. Throughout the reading, I had kept my journal in my lap under the cover of the desktop and tried not to be noticed as
I scribbled what I could capture hurriedly as he read the effects of his
father's actions. "But he has made it hard, and he has killed my mother. As
my mother sits on her couch lobotomized from her 'anti-depressant,' my
father strolls around with his [new] wife and his gumball personality, as if
nothing is wrong or has ever been wrong. Seeing my father drive his new
Pathfinder to his Disneyland vacations forced me to say what I started this
essay with. Fuck my Dad."

Jeff thanked him for sharing his essay, and he quickly moved to grammar and structure to defuse the charge of emotion that lingered in the
room. After a few minutes spent discussing the mechanics of the essay, Jeff
asked for "one or two incidents from this essay that are powerful." One by
one, as if awakening from a trance, the students spoke:

"The father belittling the mother."

"I felt liberated when he said, 'That's right, Dad. You're perfect, but at least I'll finish college.'"

"The Mom's attempted suicide."

Still stunned from Brad's reading, students filed out silently. I grabbed my journal and papers and hurried down the hall to catch Brad. He had looked frightened and sheepish as if he had violated some unspoken code, and I felt that someone should tell him how moving his essay was. I found him in the hallway already surrounded by classmates. Theresa, the attractive young woman in the class who impressed me with her spunk, was the first to approach him. "My heart is full for you," she said even as two of the men clapped him on the shoulder. "That took guts, man. Good job." Brad was genuinely surprised at their reaction, and as he looked up to Daniel, the tall athlete of the group, he smiled his relief. I held back and waited until the students had left. I asked him how he felt. He grinned and replied that he was fine.

"Did you know you could write like this before today?" I asked.

"No, I didn't. Once I started writing, it seemed like I had to say it the way I did."

"It was very powerful," I said.

"Thanks. It won't be hard anymore."

The subject was so close to Brad that he felt as if he was laying himself on the line. In his mind, his reception could have gone either way—his classmates could have dodged him for showing weakness or accepted him for his courage. Most writing students can relate one or two horror stories of having their precious labors "ripped to shreds" in a workshop setting, and I have a few of my own. In the three courses I took with Jeff, I can't recall anyone feeling shabby after having shared a revealing experience, nor have I found any incidence of such in my research of personal essay writing courses taught by other teachers. The pains that were taken in each class I was in to promote emotional identification made any destructive response unthinkable. In each of the three courses, the pattern was always the same. Students, having been buoyed by the courage and the positive reactions to the student who is first to "slip through the bars" of constraint, begin to tell openly and unabashedly of their struggles with binge drinking, anorexia, bulimia, date rape, and sexual abuse. These are not transparent issues involving teenage angst or the private concern of the writer—they evoke in the reader recognition of larger social issues. In the process of writing about their own struggles, authors must make their readers cringe. Brad's experience emulates the process Marian MacCurdy describes in her comparison of trauma victims to students in her personal essay classroom: "The impulse to hold the camera up to nature can provide the accuracy of detail which can lead to a kind of epiphany, a revelation of the commonality of experience. Trauma victims, of course, feel isolated by their experiences. They believe that no one can possibly comprehend what has happened to them. And in some ways they are right. They have been irrevocably changed by their experiences. However, as they tell their story they discover that others have been touched by pain as well, perhaps a different pain, but pain nonetheless" ("From Image to Narrative" 86).

Some writing teachers and therapists employ the use of letter writing as a means of working through woundedness. Jeff's assignment entitled "Letter to a Parent" went further than just having the writer get whatever was bothering him off his chest by writing a letter. By having the student compose a return letter from the parent in the language and point of view of that parent, he encouraged a process known by some as "dialoguing." This process allows the writer, through the safety of writing letters to and from another person, to have an imaginary conversation that deals with any unfinished business he or she might have with that person. In this case it allowed the student to step inside the character of the parent and to see, perhaps for the first time, a different perspective. The importance of this exercise to the developing writer is the practice it gives in objectivity. The writer who learns to detach himself enough to write calmly of personal chaos is better suited to write with precision and impartiality the crises of others.

Armed with his newly gained confidence, Brad took the business of precision to new levels in his letter to his father. He writes the following: "It hurts me to think you want to be part of our lives because we grew up to be halfway decent, respectable, successful kids, while the family you decided to take care of, no, we won't get into that. . . ." Later, he asks, "How do I let the person who has abandoned his family without any financial support for fifteen years back into my life?" Brad answered his own question carefully and meticulously; first, he outlined in one paragraph a list of gifts he had received from his father over those fifteen years. In the next paragraph, he placed the value of the relationship in terms he felt his father could understand—money. He explained in a logical, convincing way that his father could become part of his life again for the price of $5,000, which was the amount his father spent on the tax on his new sport utility vehicle and on his last vacation. He explained that he wasn't asking his father to pay for college or a new car—items many of his peers took for granted. In the last paragraph, using the same penetrating voice, he writes: "If I do not get anything out of this letter I want you to at least get this: I would like to thank you for teaching me how not to raise a child. I want to thank you for making (my personal) family a major priority in my life. I would like to thank you for not being there, not raising us, not turning us into you."

Brad's version of his father's reply is the complete opposite of Brad's analytical style. By placing himself in his father's position, he captures the essence of a parent too rushed and self-absorbed to notice the point of his son's letter. The father is so preoccupied with his dysfunctional stepchildren that he can't see the value of his own children. Brad doesn't tell his reader that his father is callous—he makes the letter speak with these lines: "How am I going to get $5000? I can barely make ends meet." And "How come you didn't tell me you were going to Albany?" Brad trusts his reader to understand that his father is referring to his stepchildren in the following lines: "[Steve] got released and he is on probation now. [Christy] is due in three weeks. [Tony] is making problems in school. I have to go down there tomorrow. Kids today." And finally, "It was nice hearing from you. You are too sensitive. You are welcome to come at Thanksgiving."

The two letters reveal much about the difference in character between father and son. Of course, the reader sees the father through Brad's pen, but one gets a strong sense that the depiction is accurate. Brad doesn't ask his reader to take his word for anything; he writes words he believes his father would say. In doing so, he captures the complexity of the conflict between father and son with simplicity and accuracy. In two assignments, Brad accomplished much. He learned several valuable lessons in writing: namely, to be straightforward and honest in presentation; to offer a familiar conflict in a fresh way that the reader wouldn't have thought of; to describe his actions without justifying them; and to present his text in a manner that will allow his readers to reach their own conclusions about him and his characters. Finally, he found the hard-to-define quality of voice that makes his work distinctive.

To imply that Brad may never have learned these qualities in another type of writing class would be presumptuous. Based on what I observed, however, I believe that the act of personal writing was the catalyst in the process. Like the psychoanalyst in training who must experience his own psychotherapy in order to fully understand the process, the writer who undergoes critical self-examination is better prepared to write the humanity of others. What Philip Gerard says of the nonfiction writer is true of any writer: "The things you are, the scars you bear, the experience and insider's knowledge you bring to a subject—are all part of your credentials" (24).

Confronting the Repulsive Self

*You have to take pains in a memoir not to hang on the reader's arm
like a drunk, and say, "And then I did this and it was so interesting."*
ANNIE DILLARD

Like Brad, another student, Lara, whom I cited earlier as the subject of the
drive-by shooting, noticed her own transition from fear to security. In response to the assignment entitled "Acknowledging Vulnerability," she wrote
of the change and the effect it had on her writing: "In the beginning of the
semester I did not think I would be able to handle writing about personal
experiences. . . . Even when I heard that we had the option to remain
anonymous, I was skeptical. . . . In my first essays, I was emotionally detached. I wrote factually. As the semester has worn on, I have become
more open. However, it is an openness with myself that I have developed.
Ideas and issues that I have been holding in my head were released on to
the paper for me to see."

The issues that Lara released on paper were of being forced in her early
teens to perform oral sex on a bartender in the employee bathroom of a
club she had entered using a fake ID. Her disclosure was the result of an
assignment that asked students to respond to the diarists in the chapter
entitled "Sexual Disclosures." At fifteen, Lara naively followed her rapist
to the back of the bar of the club where he suggested that they go to a place
where they could talk. Through the sensory recall that so often occurs as a
result of self-disclosing writing, Lara was able to recount the scene minute-
by-minute. Her reader follows her through each step of transition from an
innocent, flirtatious girl, playing at being grown-up, to that of a grown
woman. In a few brief seconds, she is rendered sexually traumatized for
years by a man of whom she says, "I didn't care lived or died." The reader
is engaged from beginning to end in a primal scene of fear, defense, and
aggression as Lara's rapist yanks her head into the bleak, insulated cell of a
smelly stall. Her fear and panic are palpable as she realizes too late her
entrapment. Her terror turns into calculation of possible ways of saving
herself and, finally, to hopelessness as each of her options expires during
the seconds before the inescapable act. "The next sound I heard would be
the one that would haunt me. . . . It was his zipper, followed by his hand
[going] to the back of my head forcing it down."

These details of her memory provide significant signposts for the reader.
The men's room mirror, to which she rises from her knees to view her face
"streaked with my mascara and the remains of his pleasure on my mouth,"
is metaphorical of the entire text and can be interpreted on many levels.

Not only does the mirror represent the physical evidence of defilement, it also reflects the irrevocable change in her life, the impounding legacy of shame, and the intense humiliation of being victimized. The diatribe of her attacker as he sees her ravaged reflection is as revealing of his misogyny and as defiling to his victim as the physical act. "Why don't you stay behind and clean yourself up. You look like a pig," he tosses at her as he leaves.

Subscribers of Lacanian psychoanalytic theory on the socialization of the subject will recognize the significance of the mirror in Lara's text as being parallel to Lacan's Mirror Stage, the transitional stage from infancy in which there is no awareness of physical boundaries, to subjectivity—knowledge of one's self. Just as the subject can never return to the blissful oneness of infancy, Lara recognizes that she can never completely return to the wholeness of her former self.

The juxtaposition of the rapist's image in the mirror at the moment of her transitional recognition is ironic. He positions himself as the privileged signifier in the flesh and in the mirror image. Not only has he served as the disrupter of her physically and psychologically but his image also appears in the mirror and disrupts the very moment of her understanding. His image is frozen in her mind as a reminder of her loss, and he has affixed in her unconscious mind an image of herself that is based on loss and failure.

Lara never talks about the act of rape as an act of power, but through vivid imagery and the use of actual dialogue, she allows her reader to see and comprehend the attacker's role as oppressor. His modus operandi attests to premeditation. By requiring his victims to perform oral sex instead of intercourse, he forces them to kneel, and he positions himself above them in an unmistakable exhibit of his supremacy. He also guarantees his own immunity because of the difficulty in maintaining the evidence. The honesty of dialogue in this text allows the reader to experience the powerlessness of a rape; moreover, the reader is left to apply the text to issues of loss and oppression that extend beyond this one single event.

Lara's reference to having "released" to paper her experience is significant, because, while she is the author who endured the act, she has released the act to paper for her reader. Through the act of writing, she has not only started the process of her own release from the power that the act still holds on her but also released the act for the interpretation and ownership of her reader. Therefore, personal writing need not result in an I-centered, solipsistic text. As she develops her skills, Lara might just as easily write a third-person, fictional account of rape using the same chain of signifiers. Because she lived the event, she is equipped with the tools of sensation, which allow her to summon her passion and connect it to other forms of oppression. Additionally, the choice of anonymity provided in a safe classroom, which was the manner by which she chose to present her text, concealed the author and demanded that the text be reader-centered. Since the text was read by Jeff (as were all anonymous essays), students were impacted because of the skills used in the telling—not by knowing the identity of the author, which, in this case, might have been any young woman in the class. Even when a student chooses to reveal her identity, she has already confronted and distanced her shame.

Many changes occur in the process of writing about a shameful event, but two are important in expository writing. First, the writer learns to confront and reconcile her own cringe events. In Lara's case, through exposure of her oppressor, she was able to reestablish her sense of self—one that was not based on her loss or failure; she was able to defy her molester's power to position her in the repressed realm of the unconscious and to reestablish her claim to centrality. In the course of reclaiming power, the writer heals. Second, the writer learns through revision to craft the text in such a way that the reader isn't asked to take on the opinions of the writer, but is left to engage with the text in making his own discoveries—perhaps even confronting some repressed anomaly in his own psyche. The candor with which Lara presented her text evoked many types of responses from her classmates—shock, outrage, and, most important, emotional identification. One male in the class noted that he had never given much thought to rape—he had heard guys make jokes about it, but the essay had permitted him to experience what it was like to be raped.

The group spoke softly and reverently following Jeff's reading of Lara's essay. I was so intent on listening that I delayed writing in my journal until I could do so in a quiet place, but I was impressed with the candor of the discussion that followed the reading. I longed for a way to have college freshmen experience what the men and women in this class had experienced. I was also reminded that Lara's story is a norm—not an exception. To label Lara's story as inappropriate and to deny the telling is to deny life as it occurs in high schools and colleges throughout the country. The social problems about which these students wrote are not teenage angst— they reflect real life, and they are the social issues that also surface in the classrooms of bell hooks and other professors of women's studies.

Judith Harris describes the process of crafting a personal essay, one that is consistent with Lara's writing process. In "Using the Psychoanalytic Process in Creative Writing Classes," Harris observes: "After sometimes painful disclosure, the writer restores to consciousness a conflict, if only for a fleeting moment. It is then up to her to discharge the pain encountered through the displacements of language that tell a story that can be communicated to an audience" (104). The need for a safe environment for this process to evolve is particularly relevant to Lara's words, which echo the contradictions that occur when feelings of shame are repressed. She says, "I never told another soul. I just wanted to forget the whole disgusting mess ever happened." Later, however, she shows her inability to forget when she says, "A jerk whose last name I don't even know has made me hate something that can be very beautiful. Someone I thought I could like has traumatized my life forever." Such classrooms are often unique in their ability to develop into an empathic space where the courage and imagination needed to confront unpleasant truths are supported rather than forbidden.

What Matters in a Story

These days most of my writing consists of the work I do as a full-time biotechnology science writer. The only students I see are the graduate school interns in the laboratories of my building. I've seen many come and go, and I've forgotten some of their names and faces. Perhaps it was the emotional closeness I felt to the students in Jeff's expository writing course; it may have been the psychological journey we took together or the insight-facilitating functions we accomplished together that allow me to see their faces and recall their names even after four years. I say "we" did these things together because I felt very much part of the group. I remember exactly how most of them looked as they laughed, argued, and wept together. Most of all, I remember their stories.

I went into this work with the idea of proving my cringe theory, but I came away with much more—an appreciation for the amazing resiliency and stability of the students in the class, some of whom had faced great personal tragedy. I went into the study with the notion that I might see traces of voyeurism or exploitation on the part of the professor, and I looked closely for signs of these characteristics. I saw no signs of either of those, and only one student of the many I interviewed later expressed any negativity, and even he felt that the class was beneficial. I never shared my journal with Jeff, and he never asked to see it. He never knew that I wrote as many notes about his classroom conduct as I did about the students' conduct. If my study was to be objective, I felt that I needed to take a critical approach to his methods. Although he pointed out areas of past criticism of his work, he never once told me how to conduct my study or how to write my afterword. He encouraged me to share my experiences even if they were not flattering to him.

There wasn't time to consider all the students' essays. I found that this job was tougher than I had expected. The job of the attentive writer is always so. Even the scientific writing I do takes as much energy as my essay on depression took; however, the greatest reward I have is being able to return to my work a year later and still be proud of it. There were many insightful essays in Jeff's class, and I saw much improvement in many—not all—of the students' writings. The ones who improved were the ones who met the work head-on. Others seemed unable to throw off the habits of writing in abstractions. To maintain the honesty standard in writing that I addressed earlier, I must admit that my study raised questions in my mind about college courses in which personal writing is encouraged. First and foremost is this: What happens to students when a professor doesn't have the ethical standards and the built-in safety features that Jeff employs? No doubt, most students have enough savvy to perceive insincerity on the part of a professor. The college grapevine may be good at weeding out those professors and alerting students, but it is important that the balance of power be established and maintained. As Jeff has pointed out in his work, students can become at risk when they are graded on the degree of their self-disclosure. Self-disclosure can be encouraged but never required in a writing course. Professors must be constantly attendant to the goal of the course—to teach effective writing. Students may be at risk if they are in the grips of a psychological problem while attending such a course. In *Creativity and Madness* psychiatrist Albert Rothenberg observes that the brain's creative operations—including janusian and homospatial thinking—derive from healthy brain functions. "Although creative people may be psychotic at various times during a day or week, they cannot be psychotic at the time they are engaged in a creative process or it will not be successful" (37). With student-teacher closeness must come the risk of occasionally encountering a student who is under extreme mental strain.

Associated with my cringe theory is the question of how much self-examination and unburdening of oneself in a writing curriculum is necessary to the development of one's writing skills. While I feel that the personal writing course is an important way to create a voice, it is not the only way. A personal writing course should be accompanied by other courses that allow students to experiment with a variety of writing techniques. A personal writing class—if done right—can be very effective in teaching a student to convey an experience to others that evokes further thought and reflection and that is remembered, but to do so, such writing should have application to the world beyond the self.

The letters Jeff later received from his students attest to their own pride in what they accomplished during that one semester of their lives. From hearing and reading their stories, I see the problems of date rape, parental divorce, and binge drinking through new eyes. In that respect, the students accomplished what I had hoped they would—by telling their stories, they informed, they moved, and they prompted reaction. These responses are the substance of our profession.

The following classroom material may be helpful to teachers who encourage self-disclosing writing: (1) a description of my personal writing course, (2) a handout I give to students on the first day of class about "reading empathically," (3) selected writing assignments, including "response essays," which allow students to describe how they felt while writing on risky topics (I use many though not all these writing assignments each semester), and (4) a copy of the "permission to use my writings" form I distribute to students at the end of the semester.

English 300: Expository Writing

This section of English 300 will focus on personal writing. Several of the assignments will be based on my book *Diaries to an English Professor*. As you will discover, the book contains introspective diaries that University at Albany students have written over the years in my literature-and-psychoanalysis courses. These diaries are often highly personal, self-analytic, and self-disclosing. I'm interested in your ability to identify and empathize with the diarists and your willingness to write about your own lives. I believe that personal writing encourages growth and development, particularly when we share our life experiences with other people. There are important differences between ungraded, anonymous diaries and S/U graded, formal essays; consequently, each of you will need to determine how personal you wish to be in your writings. When we discuss your writing in class, typically we will know your name, but if you do not wish to reveal your identity to classmates, you can remain anonymous.

Writing Requirements: The minimum writing requirement for the course is 40 acceptable pages, typed, double spaced. By "acceptable," I mean that in order for a particular piece of writing to count toward the required 40 pages, it must be well written and free from serious grammatical problems. Everything must be typed, preferably on a word processor so that you can easily make revisions. Plan on submitting an essay every week. I will usually give you specific assignments, but there will still be considerable freedom in the way you handle each assignment. You will have advance notice for each assignment.

We will be running the class as a workshop. For each 3-hour class, about 8 students will be asked to bring in sufficient copies of their assignment for everyone. If there are about 24 people in the class, your own work will be discussed every 3 weeks. You'll know in advance when it is your turn to bring in copies. When it is your turn to make 25 copies (including one for me), please photocopy, collate, and staple the pages together—otherwise there will be a blizzard of papers when they are distributed. There are several photocopy machines in the library as well as in nearby stores. To save space and therefore money, single space the material you reproduce for the class. One single-spaced page equals two double-spaced pages. If you are turning in an essay only to me, not to the entire class, then double space it.

You may exercise the "anonymity option" when it is your turn to bring in copies of an essay for the class. If you feel that your essay is too personal to sign with your name, you may bring in a single copy for me, with the word "anonymous" written at the top of the first page. Please indicate whether you will allow me to read the anonymous essay aloud and, if so, whether you wish the class to discuss it. I will tell you in advance when you can exercise the anonymity option. I hope that you will use this option sparingly, since if everyone used it all the time, we would have nothing to talk about in class.

Please keep a folder of all your work. When I return your writings to you, along with my comments, place them in a folder. At the end of the semester, I will ask you to submit your folders to me, so that I can look over your writings again to see how you have progressed as a writer. Please note that I will not be recording how many pages you have written; that's why it is imperative for you to keep all your writings. To complete the course on time, you will need to show me all 40 pages.

Attendance is very important. You are allowed 2 unexcused absences. If you miss more than 2 classes without a good reason (such as a documented medical problem), then you will not pass the course. Please try to come to every class, especially when it is your turn to have an essay discussed. If you can't make a class, please call me.

I am writing a book on self-disclosure in the classroom, and I might ask you for permission to use one or more of your essays. If I do ask you for permission, it will be only after you have completed the course. You will be able to make whatever disguises are necessary to protect your anonymity.

Reading Empathically

Any course that encourages personal writing and self-disclosure runs the risk of heightening students' vulnerability. The more one self-discloses, the more one acknowledges painful and shameful feelings and experiences that generally remain hidden from view. Writing about these feelings requires courage and trust as well as a classroom situation in which all of us strive to read as empathically as possible.

Empathy is a translation of the German word *Einfühlung*, which was used at the end of the nineteenth century to signify a reader's "feeling into" or projection into a text. To empathize means to enter into another person's point of view in order to understand his or her inner life. Empathy is similar to sympathy but implies a more active and intense process. Empathy is a merging with another person without the loss of one's own identity; it thus implies an awareness of both self and other.

Empathy is an important concept in psychotherapy, for it allows a therapist to understand a patient. I believe that empathy is no less important in education, enabling teachers and students to understand and learn from each other. Empathy helps us to intuit each other's *feelings*, which tend to be ignored or dismissed in classroom discussions of literature or writing.

When responding to an essay, let's try to discuss what we like about it and offer constructive suggestions for improvement. There is an art to empathic reading, listening, and speaking, and I hope that we can all develop this ability. Let's not criticize the author's feelings or value judgments. At the same time, we should be able to disagree with an essay's conclusions: we do not all feel or think the same way. If you find an essay to be moving, try to suggest why. If you say that you "like" an essay, I will ask you to tell us specifically what you like about it. The more specific you are in your comments, the more helpful you will be to the writer.

Since even the best essays are seldom written perfectly, I will always ask you to find a word or a sentence that can be improved upon. The mark of the good writer is the willingness to revise.

Selected Writing Assignments

Assignment 1: Writing Ten Autobiographical Events

Draw up a chronology of ten important events in your life, ranging from birth to the present. For each event, write one or two paragraphs on its significance. Such events may include your first day in school, the birth or death of a relative, your first love experience, a particular success or failure, a serious illness, a memorable college experience, an event that shaped your career plans, etc. Provide enough factual material for the details of your life to be known to another person, and enough psychological material to make your autobiography interesting. The autobiographical events should focus on the past but also suggest the kind of person you are now and how you might be in the future.

Assignment 2: Writing a Classmate's Biography

After you have drawn up this autobiographical chronology, exchange it with a classmate. Your classmate will read your chronology, interview you for additional material, and get to know the salient details of your life. You will do the same with your classmate, interviewing him or her for additional information. Your classmate will go home and write a biography of you, using your material as a basis for the biography. Just as your classmate is writing a biography of you, so will you be writing a biography of him or her.

Please start working on your autobiographical chronology immediately. It is due next week; at that time, I will pair you with a classmate whom you will be interviewing. He or she in turn will interview you during the same class. The completed biography of your classmate is due in two weeks. Please bring enough copies for everyone in the class. Your classmate will bring copies of his or her biography of you. All of us will be reading and discussing these biographies for two or three weeks. The biographies should be at least two single-spaced pages long.

Since you will be writing about a classmate's life, it is especially important to be sensitive and accurate. It might be a good idea to telephone your classmate after you have written a first draft of your essay so that you can receive his or her reactions to it.

Assignment 3: Writing Another Classmate's Biography

I will assign you a new partner with whom to work. Choose one biographical event that you find intriguing in your classmate's essay, interview him or her in class about the details of this event, and then develop it into a new essay. Your classmate will do the same with you.

A few suggestions for assignment 3:

- Make sure your classmate is willing to elaborate on the biographical event that you wish to write about. Be sure to handle sensitive material sensitively.
- Don't assume that your reader will be familiar with your classmate's biographical essay. Describe the event in detail: showing is better than telling. Try to capture your classmate's feelings during this moment in his or her life.
- It might be interesting for the two of you to choose a similar event to write about, such as leaving home for the first time, falling in or out of love, losing a relative, going away to college, etc. If you do write about similar events, you might want to discuss (toward the end of your es-

say) the extent to which your classmate's experience of this event resembles your own.

- If you need more time to interview your classmate, try to find another day this week that is convenient for both of you.
- This assignment should be written in the form of an essay rather than an interview. The essay is due in three weeks. You need make only two copies of assignment 3, one for your classmate and the other for me.

Assignment 4: Evaluating the Biography Assignments

For your next essay, I would like you to evaluate the preceding biography assignments. I'm interested in the extent to which writing about other students' lives and reading about your own life, through the eyes of classmates, has enlarged your understanding of other people and yourself. Please discuss the following questions:

Writing about other persons' lives:

1. What aspects of your subjects' lives did you most—and least—identify with?
2. Are there more similarities or differences between your subjects' lives and your own?
3. Did your subjects tell you anything that was surprising or disturbing? If so, how did you treat this material in your essays?

Reading about your own life:

4. How did you feel when your biography was discussed in class? Did it feel odd reading about yourself?
5. Did you learn anything important about yourself as a result of the biographical assignments?
6. Did your biographers do a good job in describing you? Did they omit anything important that you included in your biographical paragraphs?
7. What aspects or experiences of your life would you be willing to explore in more detail in a later essay?

Reading about your classmates' lives:

1. Did your classmates' biographical essays reinforce or contradict stereotypes you may have had of them?
2. Did this assignment teach you anything about race, class, gender, and religion?
3. Did you find yourself becoming at risk as a result of these assignments—that is, feeling anxious, depressed, or vulnerable? If so, please explain.

4. Did you find these assignments useful, and do you think I should use them in future classes? Would you recommend any changes in the assignments?

Assignment 5: A Letter to a Parent and His or Her Letter to You

It's clear from the biographical essays that many of you have parents who are either divorced or estranged from each other. Please write a letter to one or both of your parents in which you describe your feelings about their marriage and the way in which they raised you. Include in the beginning of your letter your reactions to reading the chapter "Sins of the Fathers" in *Diaries to an English Professor*. If your parents are divorced and you no longer see one of them, you might wish to express how you feel about the absent parent. Or you might wish to describe your feelings toward a stepfather or stepmother. If one of your parents has died, you might wish to write a letter explaining your feelings toward him or her. If you are a parent, you might wish to write a letter to your child.

After writing this letter, imagine how your parent would respond in a letter to you. Try to capture your parent's voice and point of view. These two letters should be spontaneous and informal, as letters usually are, but try to make them interesting, articulate, and free from grammatical errors. Remember that you are writing these two letters for a writing class; try to give enough information so that the reader can understand your two letters. This letter is a creative writing assignment and will challenge your imagination.

Assignment 6: Exploring Your Heritage

The biographical assignments have revealed a rich diversity among us: different ethnic, cultural, racial, and religious backgrounds. Many of you are an interesting mix of several backgrounds. I would like you to explore your own heritage in the following essay. After describing your ancestry, please discuss the following questions:

1. What aspects of your background are you proud of? Why?
2. What aspects of your background are you ashamed of? Why?
3. Are you ambivalent about your background—that is, do you feel both proud and ashamed of it? If so, please explain why you feel this ambivalence.
4. How important is your ethnic, cultural, racial, and religious background in the formation of your identity?
5. What stereotypes or preconceptions, both positive and negative, do other people have of your background?

6. What stereotypes or preconceptions, both positive and negative, do you have of other backgrounds?
7. Have you ever been discriminated against because of your background?
8. Have you ever discriminated against another person because of his or her background?
9. What would you like to convey about your own background to others from a different background?
10. What would you like others from a different background to convey to you?

Assignment 7: Changing an Element of Your Identity for One Day

Imagine waking up one morning to discover that an important element of your identity has suddenly changed—your race, class, gender, sexual preference, or religion. Describe in a short story what it would be like to live for one day with this difference. Try to describe how your relatives and friends would respond differently to you. Tell us at the end of the story whether you are happy or sad to return to your "old" identity.

Assignment 8: The Dark Side of Diversity

I suspect that, like me, most of you feel ambivalent about an aspect of your identity, whether it be race, class, gender, or religion. If so, I hope you are willing to write one more essay on diversity's dark side. Please try to be as honest as possible in your essay, particularly when acknowledging aspects of your identity of which you are not proud. Don't be afraid to reveal your vulnerability and anger. While it's easier to write about being a victim than a victimizer, I think that we play both roles. Try to describe at least one incident in which you have been victimized by prejudice or ignorance and another in which you participated, however unwillingly, in an act of discrimination against another person or group.

Assignment 9: Acknowledging Our Vulnerability

I've been impressed with the willingness of so many people in our class to write self-disclosing essays in which they acknowledge their vulnerability. This is not easy to do anywhere, especially in a college classroom. We learn to conceal our fears, conflicts, and weaknesses and, to quote from T. S. Eliot's poem "The Love Song of J. Alfred Prufrock," "to put on a face to meet the faces that we meet." Men, in particular, are taught not to reveal their anxieties and instead to emulate Hemingway's model of macho masculinity.

Although it is risky to acknowledge one's vulnerability, there are good reasons to do so. We become more human when we cease to pretend that we are invulnerable, and we can be more honest in our relationships with others. To acknowledge a limitation or problem is often the first step in overcoming it. In addition, we may become more empathic when we realize that others are burdened with the same fears and worries that preoccupy us so much of the time.

For your next assignment, please write an essay in which you discuss some of your vulnerabilities. You might wish to write about a painful or shameful experience that left you feeling vulnerable and exposed. How have you dealt with this vulnerability? Have you ever spoken or written about it before? Do you regard yourself as more or less vulnerable than other people? Has your vulnerability allowed you to develop new strengths, such as sensitivity to suffering or injustice? It takes strength to write about one's weakness—and perhaps this assignment will help us become more aware of our many inner resources.

Assignment 10: Writing about Sexuality

Please read the chapter in *Diaries to an English Professor* entitled "Sexual Disclosures" and then discuss in your next essay your responses to it. Which student diarists did you identify with and why? Were there any diarists with whom you counteridentified? What were the most interesting issues in the chapter? Were there any surprises? Did you find any diaries particularly disturbing to read? Did this chapter change your attitude toward sex or toward college students? If so, how? If you want, you can write about a personal experience involving sexual abuse.

Assignment 11: Evaluating the Sexuality Assignment

Please evaluate last week's assignment. Specifically, was it helpful or harmful to write last week's essay and to hear several essays read in class? Please address the following questions in your essay:

1. Have you ever written about a sexual conflict or problematic sexual experience prior to last week's assignment?
2. Was it difficult for you to write last week's essay? Please explain. How did you feel before you started the essay? How did you feel after you completed it?
3. What did it feel like to hear these essays read in class? Were you surprised by your classmates' essays? What did you learn from your classmates' essays?

4. What are the potential benefits and risks of assignments like this? Are there enough safeguards in our course to prevent students from becoming at risk as a result of assignments like this?
5. How would you compare the quality of the writing in last week's essay with that of some of your earlier essays?

Assignment 12: Writing about Suicide

Please read the chapter in *Diaries to an English Professor* called "Suicide Survivors" and write an essay on one or more of the following questions:

1. What are your feelings about suicide? Do you think a person has the right to take his or her own life? Do others have the right or obligation to prevent suicide?
2. Do you know anyone who has attempted or committed suicide? How did that attempted or completed suicide affect you?
3. Were you able to identify with any of the diarists in the chapter? If so, which ones? Why?
4. Have you ever seriously thought about suicide? If so, when? Did you ever tell anyone you were feeling suicidal?
5. How did you feel about my discussion of my friend's suicide? Did it change your impression of me? If so, how? In general, how do you feel about a teacher's self-disclosure?
6. Did you find yourself strongly agreeing or disagreeing with anything I wrote in the chapter? Please be specific.
7. Have you ever written about suicide before? Do you like or dislike this writing assignment? Was this a relatively easy or difficult subject to write on? Did this assignment put you at risk?

Assignment 13: Alcohol and the College Student

Studies indicate that as many as half of today's college students engage in binge drinking—having five or more drinks in one setting at least once every two weeks. As many as 80 percent of college students living in fraternities or sororities engage in binge drinking. The author of a major study on the subject has said that "the frequency of binge drinking by fraternity men and sorority women leads to an 'Animal House' style of living."

For your next assignment, write an essay discussing your perception of the problem. Are many of your friends binge drinkers? Do you or your relatives have problems with alcohol? How do these problems manifest themselves? How do you explain the prevalence of binge drinking? What can be done to reduce the amount of drinking on and off college campuses?

Assignment 14: Either "A Letter to the Class" or "Explaining This Class to Someone Who Is Not Part of It"

For your last assignment, please write an essay on either of the following topics: "A Letter to the Class" or "Explaining This Class to Someone Who Is Not Part of It." Please be as specific as possible when discussing your thoughts and feelings about the course. Whichever topic you choose, please discuss as many of the following questions as possible. Is this class similar to or different from the others you have taken in college? What were the most interesting moments of the semester? Do you have any suggestions to improve the course? How will you remember your classmates in the future? How do you wish them to remember you? Did your classmates teach you anything about themselves—or about yourself—that you had not previously known?

This assignment is due on the last class of the semester. You need make only one copy. I would like to read some of these essays to the class during our party. Please indicate at the bottom of your essay whether you are willing to read it aloud or to allow me to read it anonymously.

English 300: Expository Writing

Permission to Use My Writings

I hereby give permission to Jeffrey Berman to use one or more of my writings for a future essay or book on self-disclosure in an expository writing course. I have freely given him permission to use my writings after receiving my final grade in the course. My questions about the purpose of his essay or book have been answered. I understand that my name will not appear. I have disguised my essays to my own satisfaction and do not wish further disguises to be made.

I further understand that before he submits his essay or book for publication, Jeffrey Berman will send me a copy of that section containing my writings. If, after reading that section, I feel uncomfortable with the way in which he has used my writings, I reserve the right to withdraw permission. If I do withdraw permission, I will notify him in writing within three months of receiving the draft copy.

After Jeffrey Berman's essay or book is published, my writings will be destroyed. No reports about my writings will contain my name.

Name _____   Date _____

Signature _____

Please give me two or three pseudonyms (false names) by which I can call you in the book:

_____

Local address   _____

                    _____

Local phone   _____

Permanent address _____

                    _____

Permanent phone   _____

Please indicate whether I may cite your help in the acknowledgments of the book. _____

WORKS CITED

Adams, Maurianne, Lee Anne Bell, and Pat Griffin. *Teaching for Diversity and Social Justice*. New York: Routledge, 1997.

Adamson, Joseph, and Hilary Clark, eds. *Scenes of Shame*. New York: State University of New York Press, 1999.

Alcorn, Marshall. "Changing the Discourse of Postmodernist Theory: Discourse, Ideology, and Therapy in the Classroom." *Rhetoric Review* 13 (1995): 331–49.

———. *Changing the Subject in English Class*. Carbondale: Southern Illinois University Press, forthcoming.

Anderson, Charles, and Marian MacCurdy, eds. *Writing and Healing: Toward an Informed Practice*. Urbana, Ill.: National Council of Teachers of English, 2000.

Anderson, Paul. "Simple Gifts: Ethical Issues in the Conduct of Person-Based Composition Research." *College Composition and Communication* 49 (1998): 63–89.

Armstrong, Louise. *Kiss Daddy Goodnight*. New York: Hawthorn Press, 1978.

Bakhtin, Mikhail. *The Dialogic Imagination*. Ed. Michael Holquist. Trans. Caryl Emerson and Michael Holquist. Austin: University of Texas Press, 1981.

Bartholomae, David. "Writing with Teachers: A Conversation with Peter Elbow." *College Composition and Communication* 46 (1995): 63–71.

Bartky, Sandra Lee. "The Pedagogy of Shame." In *Feminisms and Pedagogies of Everyday Life*, ed. Carmen Luke, 225–41. New York: State University of New York Press, 1996.

Bate, Walter Jackson. *From Classic to Romantic: Premises of Taste in Eighteenth-Century England*. New York: Harper and Row, 1961.

Baumlin, James, George Jensen, and Lance Massey. "Ethos, Ethical Argument, and Ad Hominem in Contemporary Theory." In *Ethical Issues in College Writing*, ed. Frederic Gale, Phillip Sipiora, and James Kinneavy, 183–220. New York: Peter Lang, 1999.

Becket, Samuel. *Waiting for Godot*. New York: Grove Press, 1954.

Benjamin, Jessica. *The Bonds of Love*. London: Virago, 1990.

Berlin, James. "Rhetoric and Ideology in the Writing Class." *College English* 50 (1988): 477–94.

———. *Rhetoric and Reality Writing Instruction in American Colleges, 1900–1985*. Carbondale: Southern Illinois University Press, 1987.

Berman, Jeffrey. *Diaries to an English Professor*. Amherst: University of Massachusetts Press, 1994.

———. *Narcissism and the Novel*. New York: New York University Press, 1990.

———. *Surviving Literary Suicide*. Amherst: University of Massachusetts Press, 1999.

Berman, Jeffrey, and Alina Luna. "Suicide Diaries and the Therapeutics of Anonymous Self-Disclosure." *JPCS: Journal for the Psychoanalysis of Culture and Society* 1 (1996): 63–75.

Berman, Jeffrey, and Jonathan Schiff. "Writing about Suicide." In *Writing and Healing: Toward an Informed Practice,* ed. Charles Anderson and Marian MacCurdy, 291–312. Urbana, Ill.: National Council of Teachers of English, 2000.

Berry, Wendell. *The Hidden Wound.* Boston: Houghton Mifflin, 1970.

Bishop, Wendy. "Writing Is/And Therapy? Raising Questions about Writing Class-rooms and Writing Program Administration." *Journal of Advanced Composition* 13 (1993): 503–16.

Bizzell, Patricia. "Power, Authority, and Critical Pedagogy." *Journal of Basic Writing* 10 (1991): 54–70.

Bleich, David. "Collaboration and the Pedagogy of Disclosure." *College English* 57 (1995): 43–61.

———. *Know and Tell.* Portsmouth, N.H.: Boynton/Cook, 1998.

Boegeman, Margaret Byrd. "Lives and Literacy: Autobiography in Freshman Com-position." *College English* 41 (1979–80): 662–69.

Bok, Sissela. *Secrets: On the Ethics of Concealment and Revelation.* New York: Pan-theon Books, 1982.

Bracher, Mark. "Editor's Column: Psychoanalysis and Education." *JPCS: Journal for the Psychoanalysis of Culture and Society* 4 (1999): 175–92.

———. *The Writing Cure.* Carbondale: Southern Illinois University Press, 1999.

Brand, Alice. *Therapy in Writing.* Lexington, Mass.: Lexington Books, 1980.

Braxton, John, and Alan Bayer. *Faculty Misconduct in Collegiate Teaching.* Balti-more: Johns Hopkins University Press, 1999.

Bridwell-Bowles, Lillian. "Discourse and Diversity: Experimental Writing within the Academy." In *Feminine Principles and Women's Experience in American Composition and Rhetoric,* ed. Louise Wetherbee Phelps and Janet Emig, 43–66. Pittsburgh: University of Pittsburgh Press, 1995.

Briere, John. *Child Sexual Abuse.* Newbury Park, Calif.: Sage Publications, 1992.

Britzman, Deborah. *Lost Subjects, Contested Objects.* New York: State University of New York Press, 1998.

Brooke, Robert. "Lacan, Transference, and Writing Instruction." *College English* 49 (1987): 679–91.

Bruffee, Kenneth. *Collaborative Learning.* Baltimore: Johns Hopkins University Press, 1993.

Bruner, Jerome S. *Acts of Meaning.* Cambridge: Harvard University Press, 1990.

———. "Life as Narrative." *Social Research* 54 (1987): 11–32.

Buber, Martin. *Hasidism.* New York: Philosophical Library, 1948.

Buckler, Patricia, Kay Franklin, and Thomas Young. "Privacy, Peers, and Process: Conflicts in the Composition Classroom." In *Writing Ourselves into the Story,* ed. Sheryl Fontaine and Susan Hunter, 229–45. Carbondale: Southern Illi-nois Press, 1993.

Buckley, Jerome Hamilton. *The Turning Key.* Cambridge: Harvard University Press, 1984.

Bump, Jerome. "Innovative Bibliotherapy Approaches to Substance Abuse." *Arts in Psychotherapy* 17 (1990): 355–62.

———. "Teaching Emotional Literacy." In *Writing and Healing: Toward an Informed Practice*, ed. Charles Anderson and Marian MacCurdy, 313–35. Urbana, Ill.: National Council of Teachers of English, 2000.

Cantril, Hadley. *The "Why" of Man's Experience*. New York: Macmillan, 1950.

Caruth, Cathy. *Unclaimed Experience*. Baltimore: Johns Hopkins University Press, 1996.

Cather, Willa. "Paul's Case." *Great Short Works*. New York: Vintage, 1983.

Chelune, Gordon. "Measuring Openness in Interpersonal Communication." In *Self-Disclosure: Origins, Patterns, and Implications of Openness in Interpersonal Relationships*, ed. Gordon Chelune, 1–27. San Francisco: Jossey-Bass, 1979.

Chodorow, Nancy. *The Power of Feelings*. New Haven: Yale University Press, 1999.

Chopin, Kate. *The Awakening*. Ed. Margo Culley. New York: Norton, 1994.

Cohen, William A. *Sex Scandal: The Private Parts of Victorian Fiction*. Durham, N.C.: Duke University Press, 1996.

Comfort, Juanita Rodgers. "Becoming a Writerly Self: College Writers Engaging Black Feminist Essays." *CCC: Journal of the Conference on College Composition and Communication* 51 (2000): 540–59.

Connors, Robert. "Personal Writing Assignments." *College Composition and Communication* 38 (1987): 166–83.

Conrad, Joseph. *Chance: A Tale in Two Parts*. 1913. Rpt., London: Dent, 1969.

Dalton, Harlon. *Racial Healing*. New York: Doubleday, 1995.

Derlega, Valerian, Sandra Metts, Sandra Petronio, and Stephen Margulis. *Self-Disclosure*. Newbury Park, Calif.: Sage Publications, 1993.

Derman-Sparks, Louise, and Carol Brunson Phillips. *Teaching/Learning Anti-Racism*. New York: Teachers College Press, 1997.

DeSalvo, Louise. *Writing as a Way of Healing*. San Francisco: Harper San Francisco, 1999.

Dillard, Annie. *Living by Fiction*. New York: Harper Colophon, 1983.

Ebert, Teresa. "For a Red Pedagogy: Feminism, Desire, and Need." *College English* 58 (1996): 795–819.

Eisenberg, Nancy, ed. *Empathy and Related Emotional Responses*. San Francisco: Jossey-Bass, 1989.

Eisenberg, Nancy, and Paul Miller. "Empathy, Sympathy, and Altruism: Empirical and Conceptual Links." In *Empathy and Its Development*, ed. Nancy Eisenberg and Janet Strayer, 292–316. Cambridge: Cambridge University Press, 1987.

Elbow, Peter. "Forward: About Personal Expressive Academic Writing." *Pre/Text* 11 (1990): 7–20.

———. *Writing without Teachers*. New York: Oxford University Press, 1973.

Eliot, George. *Middlemarch*. London: Zodiac Press, 1967.

Ellsworth, Elizabeth. "Why Doesn't This Feel Empowering? Working through the Repressive Myths of Critical Pedagogy." *Harvard Educational Review* 59 (1989): 297–324.

Emig, Janet. *The Web of Meaning*. Portsmouth, N.H.: Boynton/Cook, 1983.

Erikson, Erik. *Gandhi's Truth*. New York: Norton, 1969.

Faigley, Lester. *Fragments of Rationality: Postmodernity and the Subject of Composition*. Pittsburgh: University of Pittsburgh Press, 1992.

Farrell, Kirby. *Post-Traumatic Culture*. Baltimore: Johns Hopkins University Press, 1998.

Feagin Joe, Hernan Vera, and Nikitah Imani. *The Agony of Education*. New York: Routledge, 1996.

Felman, Shoshana, and Dori Laub. *Testimony*. New York: Routledge, 1992.

Fitzgerald, F. Scott. *The Crack-Up*. New York: New Directions, 1945.

Fleishman, Avrom. *Figures of Autobiography*. Berkeley: University of California Press, 1983.

France, Alan. "Assigning Places: The Function of Introductory Composition as a Cultural Discourse." *College English* 55 (1993): 593–609.

Frank, Arthur. *The Wounded Storyteller*. Chicago: University of Chicago Press, 1995.

Frank, Jerome, and Julia Frank. *Persuasion and Healing*. 3d ed. Baltimore: Johns Hopkins University Press, 1991.

Freire, Paulo. *Pedagogy of the Oppressed*. Trans. Myra Bergman Ramos. Rev. ed. New York: Continuum, 1993.

Freud, Sigmund. *The Ego and the Id. The Standard Edition of the Complete Psychological Works of Sigmund Freud*. Trans. James Strachey. Vol. 19. London: Hogarth Press, 1961.

———. "Extracts from Freud's Footnotes to His Translation of Charcot's Tuesday Lectures." In *The Standard Edition of the Complete Psychological Works of Sigmund Freud*, trans. James Strachey, 1:137–43. London: Hogarth Press, 1966.

———. *Fragment of an Analysis of a Case of Hysteria. The Standard Edition of the Complete Psychological Works of Sigmund Freud*. Trans. James Strachey. Vol. 7. London: Hogarth Press, 1953.

———. *Group Psychology and the Analysis of the Ego. The Standard Edition of the Complete Psychological Works of Sigmund Freud*. Trans. James Strachey. Vol. 8. London: Hogarth Press, 1955.

Fuss, Diana. *Identification Papers*. New York: Routledge, 1995.

Gale, Frederic. "Legal Rights and Responsibilities in the Writing Classroom." In *Ethical Issues in College Writing*, ed. Frederic Gale, Phillip Sipiora, and James Kinneavy, 21–38. New York: Peter Lang, 1999.

Gallop, Jane. *Feminist Accused of Sexual Harassment*. Durham, N.C.: Duke University Press, 1997.

———. "Resisting Reasonableness." *Critical Inquiry* 25 (1999): 599–609.

Gannett, Cinthia. "The Stories of Our Lives Become Our Lives: Journals, Diaries, and Academic Discourse." In *Feminine Principles and Women's Experience in American Composition and Rhetoric*, ed. Louise Wetherbee Phelps and Janet Emig, 109–36. Pittsburgh: University of Pittsburgh Press, 1995.

Gardiner, Howard. *Frames of Mind: The Theory of Multiple Intelligences*. New York: Basic Books, 1993.

Geertz, Clifford. *Local Knowledge: Further Essays in Interpretive Anthropology*. New York: Basic Books, 1983.

Gerard, Philip. *Creative Nonfiction*. Cincinnati, Ohio: Story Press, 1996.

Gere, Anne Ruggles. "Teaching Writing: The Major Theories." In *The Allyn and Bacon Sourcebook for College Writing Teachers*, ed. James McDonald, 11–25. Boston: Allyn and Bacon, 1996.

Gilmore, Leigh. *Autobiographics*. Ithaca: Cornell University Press, 1994.

Giroux, Henry. *Schooling and the Struggle for Public Life: Critical Pedagogy in the Modern Age*. Minneapolis: University of Minnesota Press, 1988.

Goldstein, Arnold, and Gerald Michaels. *Empathy: Development, Training, and Consequences*. Hillsdale, N.J.: Lawrence Erlbaum, 1985.

Goleman, Daniel. *Emotional Intelligence*. New York: Bantam Books, 1995.

Goodwin, Jean. *Sexual Abuse*. Boston: John Wright, 1982.

Graf, Gerald. *Beyond the Culture Wars: How Teaching the Conflicts Can Revitalize American Education*. New York: Norton, 1992.

Grant, Bridget. "Estimates of U.S. Children Exposed to Alcohol Abuse and Dependence in the Family." *American Journal of Public Health* 90 (2000): 112–15.

Harris, Judith. "Using the Psychoanalytic Process in Creative Writing Classes." *JPCS: Journal for the Psychoanalysis of Culture and Society* 2 (1997): 101–7.

Haswell, Richard. *Gaining Ground in College Writing: Tales of Development and Interpretation*. Dallas: Southern Methodist University Press, 1991.

Hawkins, Anne Hunsaker. *Reconstructing Illness: Studies in Pathography*. West Lafayette, Ind.: Purdue University Press, 1993.

Hawthorne, Nathaniel. *The Scarlet Letter and Other Tales of the Puritans*. Boston: Houghton Mifflin, 1961.

Hemingway, Ernest. *For Whom the Bell Tolls*. New York: Scribner's, 1940.

Herman, Judith Lewis. *Trauma and Recovery*. New York: Basic Books, 1992.

Hesford, Wendy. *Framing Identities*. Minneapolis: University of Minnesota Press, 1999.

———. "Reading *Rape Stories*: Material Rhetoric and the Trauma of Representation." *College English* 62 (1999): 192–221.

Hill, Carolyn Ericksen. *Writing from the Margins*. New York: Oxford University Press, 1990.

Hinlicky, Sarah. "Don't Write about Race." *First Things* 98 (1999): 9–11.

Hoffman, Martin. "The Contribution of Empathy to Justice and Moral Judgment." In *Empathy and Its Development*, ed. Nancy Eisenberg and Janet Strayer, 47–80. Cambridge: Cambridge University Press, 1987.

Hooks, Bell. "Engaged Pedagogy." In *Women/Writing/Teaching*, ed. Jan Zlotnik Schmidt, 231–38. New York: State University of New York Press, 1998.

———. *Remembered Rapture*. New York: Henry Holt, 1999.

Hotchner, A. E. *Papa Hemingway*. New York: Bantam, 1970.

James, Henry. *The Portable Henry James*. Ed. Morton Dauwen Zabel. New York: Viking, 1962.

Jamison, Kay Redfield. *Night Falls Fast: Understanding Suicide*. New York: Knopf, 1999.

———. *An Unquiet Mind*. New York: Knopf, 1995.

Janoff-Bulman, Ronnie. *Shattered Assumptions: Towards a New Psychology of Trauma*. New York: Free Press, 1992.

Jay, Gregory. "The Subject of Pedagogy: Lessons in Psychoanalysis and Politics." *College English* 49 (1987): 785–800.

Jourand, Sidney. *The Transparent Self: Self-Disclosure and Well-Being.* Princeton, N.J.: Van Nostrand, 1941.

Kafka, Franz. *Letters to Friends, Family, and Editors.* Trans. Richard Winston and Clara Winston. New York: Schocken, 1977.

Keats, John. *Selected Poems and Letters.* Cambridge: Riverside Press, 1959.

Kenyon, Gary, and William Randall. *Restorying Our Lives: Personal Growth through Autobiographical Reflection.* Westport, Conn.: Praeger, 1997.

Kirsch, Gesa. *Ethical Dilemmas in Feminist Research.* New York: State University of New York Press, 1999.

Kohut, Heinz. "Forms and Transformation of Narcissism." *Journal of the American Psychoanalytic Association* 14 (1966): 243–72.

———. *How Does Analysis Cure?* Ed. Arnold Goldberg. Chicago: University of Chicago Press, 1984.

Kramarae, Cheris, and Paula Treichler. "Power Relationships in the Classroom." In *Gender in the Classroom,* ed. Susan Gabriel and Isaiah Smithson, 41–59. Urbana: University of Illinois Press, 1990.

Laub, Dori. "Bearing Witness or the Vicissitudes of Listening." In *Testimony: Crises of Witnessing in Literature, Psychoanalysis, and History,* ed. Shoshana Felman and Dori Laub, 57–74. New York: Routledge, 1992.

Lawrence, D. H. *The Letters of D. H. Lawrence.* Vol. 2. Ed. George J. Zytaruk and James T. Boulton. Cambridge: Cambridge University Press, 1981.

Layton, Lynne. "Social Factors in the Case Study." *JPCS: Journal for the Psychoanalysis of Culture and Society* 4 (1999): 325–27.

Levi, Primo. *The Drowned and the Saved.* Trans. Raymond Rosenthal. New York: Vintage, 1989.

Lewis, Michael. *Shame: The Exposed Self.* New York: Free Press, 1995.

Lorde, Audre. *Sister Outsider.* New York: Crossing Press, 1984.

MacCurdy, Marian. "From Image to Narrative: The Politics of the Personal." *Journal of Teaching Writing* 13.1–2 (1995): 75–107.

———. "From Trauma to Writing." In *Writing and Healing: Toward an Informed Practice,* ed. Charles Anderson and Marian MacCurdy, 158–200. Urbana, Ill.: National Council of Teachers of English, 2000.

Macrorie, Ken. *Telling Writing.* 3d. ed. Rochelle Park, N.J.: Hayden Book Co., 1980.

Maltsberger, John, and Dan Buie Jr. "Countertransference Hate in the Treatment of Suicidal Patients." In *Essential Papers on Suicide,* ed. John Maltsberger and Mark Goldblatt, 269–89. New York: New York University Press, 1996.

McGee, Patrick. "Truth and Resistance: Teaching as a Form of Analysis." *College English* 49 (1987): 667–78.

Mead, George. *Mind, Self, and Society.* Ed. Charles Morris. Chicago: University of Chicago Press, 1935.

Mikulincer, Mario, and Orna Nachshon. "Attachment Styles and Patterns of Self-Disclosure." *Journal of Personality and Social Psychology* 61.2 (1991): 321–31.

Miller, Alice. *For Your Own Good*. Trans. Hildegarde Hannum and Hunter Hannum. New York: Farrar, Straus, Giroux, 1990.

Miller, Lynn, and David Kenny. "Reciprocity of Self-Disclosure at the Individual and Dyadic Levels: A Social Relations Analysis." *Journal of Personality and Social Psychology* 50.4 (1986): 713–19.

Miller, Nancy. *Getting Personal: Feminist Occasions and Other Autobiographical Acts*. New York: Routledge, 1991.

Miller, Richard. "Fault Lines in the Contact Zone." *College English* 56 (1994): 389–408.

Minow, Martha. *Not Only for Myself: Identity, Politics, and the Law*. New York: New Press, 1997.

Moffett, James. "Coming Out Right." In *Taking Stock: The Writing Process Movement in the '90s*, ed. Lad Tobin and Thomas Newkirk, 17–30. Portsmouth, N.H.: Boynton/Cook, 1994.

Morgan, Dan. "Ethical Issues Raised by Students' Personal Writing." *College English* 60 (1998): 318–25.

Morrison, Andrew. *The Culture of Shame*. New York: Ballantine, 1996.

———. *Shame: The Underside of Narcissism*. Hillsdale, N.J.: Analytic Press, 1989.

Morrison, Karl. *"I Am You": The Hermeneutics of Empathy in Western Literature, Theology, and Art*. Princeton: Princeton University Press, 1988.

Murphy, Ann. "Transference and Resistance in the Basic Writing Classroom: Problematics and Praxis." *College Composition and Communication* 40 (1989): 175–87.

Murphy, Richard, Jr. *The Calculus of Intimacy*. Columbus: Ohio State University Press, 1993.

Nabokov, Vladimir. *Lolita*. London: Weidenfeld and Nicolson, 1959.

Nathanson, Donald L. "A Timetable for Shame." In *The Many Faces of Shame*, ed. Donald L. Nathanson, 1–63. New York: Guilford Press, 1987.

"New Rules about Sex on Campus." *Harper's Magazine*, September 1993, 33–42.

Newkirk, Thomas. *The Performance of Self in Student Writing*. Portsmouth, N.H.: Boynton/Cook, 1997.

Nowlan, Robert Andrew. "Teaching against Racism in the Radical Composition Classroom: A Reply to a Student." In *Left Margins: Cultural Studies and Composition Pedagogy*, ed. Karen Fitts and Alan France, 245–54. New York: State University of New York Press, 1995.

Nuwer, Hank. *Wrongs of Passage: Fraternities, Sororities, Hazing, and Binge Drinking*. Bloomington: Indiana University Press, 1999.

Odell, Lee. "Strategy and Surprise in the Making of Meaning." In *Theory and Practice in the Teaching of Writing: Rethinking the Discipline*, ed. Lee Odell, 213–43. Carbondale: Southern Illinois University Press, 1993.

Paine, Charles. *The Resistant Reader: Rhetoric as Immunity, 1850 to the Present*. New York: State University of New York Press, 1999.

Parini, Jay. "The Memoir versus the Novel in a Time of Transition." *Chronicle of Higher Education*, 10 July 1998, A40.

Payne, Michelle. "A Strange Unaccountable Something: Historicizing Sexual Abuse Essays." In *Writing and Healing: Toward an Informed Practice*, ed. Charles

Anderson and Marian MacCurdy, 115–57. Urbana, Ill.: National Council of Teachers of English, 2000.

Pellegrini, Ann. "Pedagogy's Turn: Observations on Students, Teachers, and Transference-Love." *Critical Inquiry* 25 (1999): 617–25.

Pennebaker, James. *Opening Up: The Healing Power of Expressing Emotions*. New York: Guilford Press, 1997.

———. "Self-Expressive Writing: Implications for Health, Education, and Welfare." In *Nothing Begins with N*, ed. Pat Belanoff, Peter Elbow, and Sheryl I. Fontaine, 157–70. Carbondale: Southern Illinois University Press, 1991.

Perillo, Lucia. "When the Classroom Becomes a Confessional." *Chronicle of Higher Education*, 28 November 1997.

Petronio, Sandra. *Boundaries of Private Disclosure*. New York: State University of New York Press, 2001.

Phillips, David. "The Influence of Suggestion on Suicide: Substantive and Theoretical Implications of the Werther Effect." In *Essential Papers on Suicide*, ed. John Maltsberger and Mark Goldblatt, 290–313. New York: New York University Press, 1996. First published in *American Sociological Review* 39 (1974): 340–54.

Plath, Sylvia. *The Bell Jar*. New York: Bantam, 1971.

———. *The Journals of Sylvia Plath*. Ed. Francis McCullough. New York: Dial Press, 1982.

Plummer, Ken. *Telling Sexual Stories*. London: Routledge, 1995.

Poland, Scott. *Suicide Intervention in the Schools*. New York: Guilford Press, 1989.

Pratt, Mary Louise. "Arts of the Contact Zone." *Profession* 91 (1991): 33–40.

Progoff, Ira. *At a Journal Workshop*. New York: Dialogue House, 1975.

Rainer, Tristine. *The New Diary*. Los Angeles: J. P. Archer. 1978.

Rancour-Laferriere, Daniel, ed. *Self-Analysis in Literary Study*. New York: New York University Press, 1994.

Rawlins, W. "Openness as Problematic in Ongoing Friendships: Two Conversational Dilemmas." *Communication Monographs* 50 (1983): 1–13.

Rinaldi, Jacqueline. "Rhetorical Healing: Revising Narrative about Disability." *College English* 58 (1996): 820–34.

Rogers, Carl. "Empathic: An Unappreciated Way of Being." *Counseling Psychologist* 2 (1975): 2–10.

Rose, Mike. *Lives on the Boundary*. New York: Penguin, 1990.

Rosenblum, Rachel. "Primo Levi and the Dangers of Testimony." *Congress Monthly* (May–June 1999): 15–18.

Rothenberg, Albert. *Creativity and Madness*. Baltimore: Johns Hopkins University Press, 1990.

Rubin, Donnalee. *Gender Influences: Reading Student Texts*. Carbondale: Southern Illinois University Press, 1993.

Russell, Diana. *The Secret Trauma*. New York: Basic Books, 1986.

Sadker, Myra, and David Sadker. "Confronting Sexism in the College Classroom." In *Gender in the Classroom*, ed. Susan Gabriel and Isaiah Smithson, 176–87. Urbana: University of Illinois Press, 1990.

Salter, Anna. *Transforming Trauma*. Thousand Oaks, Calif.: Sage Publications, 1995.

Schlesinger, Arthur M., Jr. *The Disuniting of America*. New York: Norton, 1998.

Scholes, Robert, and Nancy Comley. *The Practice of Writing*. New York: St. Martin's Press, 1981.

Sexton, Anne. *A Self-Portrait in Letters*. Ed. Linda Gray Sexton and Lois Ames. Boston: Houghton Mifflin, 1977.

Shechner, Mark. *After the Revolution: Studies in the Contemporary Jewish-American Imagination*. Bloomington: Indiana University Press, 1987.

Smith, Stephen. *Risk and Our Pedagogical Relation to Children*. New York: State University of New York Press, 1998.

Smyth, Joshua, Arthur Stone, Adam Hurewitz, and Alan Kaell. "Effects of Writing about Stressful Experiences on Symptom Reduction in Patients with Asthma or Rheumatoid Arthritis." *JAMA* 281 (1999): 1304–9.

Steinhauer, Harry. Introduction to *The Sufferings of Young Werther*, by Johann Wolfgang von Goethe. Ed. and trans. Harry Steinhauer. New York: Bantam Dual-Language Book, 1962.

Sternglass, Marilyn. *Time to Know Them*. Mahwah, N.J.: Lawrence Erlbaum Associates, 1997.

Styron, William. *Darkness Visible*. New York: Random House, 1990.

———. *Sophie's Choice*. New York: Random House, 1979.

Swartzlander, Susan, Diana Pace, and Virginia Lee Stamler. "The Ethics of Requiring Students to Write about Their Personal Lives." *Chronicle of Higher Education* 17 February 1993, B1–2.

Tal, Kalí. *Worlds of Hurt*. Cambridge: Cambridge University Press, 1996.

Tannen, Deborah. *The Argument Culture*. New York: Random House, 1998.

Tanner, Laura. *Intimate Violence*. Bloomington: Indiana University Press, 1994.

Teicholz, Judith Guss. *Kohut, Loewald, and the Postmoderns*. Hillsdale, N.J.: Analytic Press, 1999.

Thomas, D. M. *The White Hotel*. New York: Viking, 1981.

Tobin, Lad. *Writing Relationships*. Portsmouth, N.H.: Boynton/Cook, 1993.

Tobin, Lad, and Thomas Newkirk, eds. *Taking Stock: The Writing Process Movement in the '90s*. Portsmouth, N.H.: Boynton/Cook, 1994.

Tompkins, Jane. *A Life in School*. Reading, Mass.: Addison-Wesley, 1996.

———. "Pedagogy of the Distressed." *College English* 52 (1990): 653–60.

Trimpop, Rüdiger. *The Psychology of Risk-Taking Behavior*. Amsterdam: North-Holland, 1994.

U.S. Center for Disease Control. "Attempted Suicide among High School Students—United States, 1990." *Morbidity and Mortality Weekly Report* 40.37 (1991): 633–35.

Urquhart, John, and Klaus Heilmann. *Risk Watch: The Odds of Life*. New York: Facts on File, 1985.

Valentino, Marilyn. "Responding When a Life Depends on It: What to Write in the Margins When Students Self-Disclose." *Teaching English in the Two-Year College* 23 (1996): 274–83.

Vetlesen, Arne Johan. *Perception, Empathy, and Judgment.* University Park: Pennsylvania State University Press, 1994.

West, Nathaniel. *Miss Lonelyhearts and the Day of the Locust.* New York: New Directions, 1962.

Williamson, Janice. "'I Peel Myself Out of My Skin': Reading *Don't: A Woman's Word.*" In *Essays on Life Writing,* ed. Marlene Kadar, 133–51. Toronto: University of Toronto Press, 1992.

Wind, Edgar. *Art and Anarchy.* London: Faber and Faber, 1963.

Winnicott, D. W. "Transitional Objects and Transitional Phenomena." *International Journal of Psycho-Analysis* 34 (1953): 89–97.

Wispe, Lauren. "History of the Concept of Empathy." In *Empathy and Its Development,* ed. Nancy Eisenberg and Janet Strayer, 17–37. Cambridge: Cambridge University Press, 1987.

Woolf, Virginia. *The Diary of Virginia Woolf.* Ed. Anne Olivier Bell. 5 vols. San Diego, New York, and London: Harcourt Brace Jovanovich, 1977–84.

———. *Moments of Being: Unpublished Autobiographical Writings.* Ed. Jeanne Schulkind. New York and London: Harcourt Brace Jovanovich, 1976.

Wordsworth, William. "The Tables Turned." *Selected Poems and Prefaces.* Ed. Jack Stillinger. Cambridge: Riverside Press, 1965.

Wurmser, Leon. "Shame: The Veiled Companion of Narcissism." In *The Many Faces of Shame,* ed. Donald L. Nathanson, 64–92. New York: Guilford Press, 1987.

Wyatt, Jean. "Discussion of Jeffrey Berman's 'Sexual Disclosures in an Expository Writing Course.'" Sixth Annual Conference of the Association for the Psychoanalysis of Culture and Society, Santa Barbara, California, 4 November 2000.

Young-Breuhl, Elisabeth. *The Anatomy of Prejudices.* Cambridge: Harvard University Press, 1996.

Zavarzadeh, Mas'ud. "The Pedagogy of Pleasure 2: The Me-in-Crisis." In *Left Margins: Cultural Studies and Composition Pedagogy,* ed. Karen Fitts and Alan France, 219–29. New York: State University of New York Press, 1995.

STUDENT WRITERS

INDEX

394191